PROXISTANT VISION

Leonardo

Seán Cubitt, Editor-in-Chief

Social Media Archeology and Poetics, edited by Judy Malloy, 2016

Practicable: From Participation to Interaction in Contemporary Art, edited by Samuel Bianchini and Erik Verhagen, 2016

Machine Art in the Twentieth Century, Andreas Broeckmann, 2016

Here/There: Telepresence, Touch, and Art at the Interface, Kris Paulsen, 2017

Voicetracks: Attuning to Voice in Media and the Arts, Norie Neumark, 2017

Ecstatic Worlds: Media, Utopias, Ecologies, Janine Marchessault, 2017

Interface as Utopia: The Media Art and Activism of Fred Forest, Michael F. Leruth, 2017

Making Sense: Cognition, Computing, Art, and Embodiment, Simon Penny, 2017

Weather as Medium: Toward a Meteorological Art, Janine Randerson, 2018

Laboratory Lifestyles: The Construction of Scientific Fictions, edited by Sandra Kaji-O'Grady, Chris L. Smith, and Russell Hughes, 2018

Invisible Colors: The Arts of the Atomic Age, Gabrielle Decamous, 2018

Virtual Menageries: Animals as Mediators in Network Cultures, Jody Berland, 2019

From Fingers to Digits: An Artificial Aesthetic, Ernest Edmonds and Margaret A. Boden, 2019

MATERIAL WITNESS: Media, Forensics, Evidence, Susan Schuppli, 2020

Tactics of Interfacing: Encoding Affect in Art and Technology, Ksenia Fedorova, 2020

Giving Bodies Back to Data: Image-Makers, Bricolage, and Reinvention in Magnetic Resonance Technology, Silvia Casini, 2021

A Biography of the Pixel, Alvy Ray Smith, 2021

Living Books: Experiments in the Posthumanities, Janneke Adema, 2021

Art in the Age of Learning Machines, Sofian Audry, 2021

Design in Motion: Film Experiments at the Bauhaus, Laura Frahm, 2022

Northern Sparks: Innovation, Technology and the Arts in Canada from Expo '67 to the Internet Age, Michael Century, 2022

The Artwork as a Living System: Christa Sommerer and Laurent Mignonneau 1991–2022, edited by Karin Ohlenschläger, Peter Weibel, and Alfred Weidinger, 2023

Computational Formalism: Art History and Machine Learning, Amanda Wasielewski, 2023

Picture Research: The Work of Intermediation from Pre-Photography to Post-Digitization, Nina Lager Vestberg, 2023

Art + DIY Electronics, Garnet Hertz, 2023

Voidopolis, Kat Mustatea, 2023

After Eating: Metabolizing the Arts, Lindsay Kelly, 2023

Tactical Publishing: Using Senses, Software, and Archives in the 21st Century, Alessandro Ludovico, 2023

The Future is Present: Art, Technology, and the Work of Mobile Image, Philip Glahn and Cary Levine, 2024

Living Surfaces: Images, Plants, and Environments of Media, Jussi Parikka and Abelardo Gil-Fournier, 2024

Heartbeat Art, Claudia Arozqueta, 2025

Ecologies of Artistic Practice: Rethinking Cultural Economies through Art and Technology, Ashley Lee Wong, 2025

Proxistant Vision: Motion, Navigation, Scale, Synne Tollerud Bull and Dragan Miletic, 2025

See http://mitpress.mit.edu for a complete list of titles in this series.

PROXISTANT VISION

MOTION, NAVIGATION, SCALE

SYNNE TOLLERUD BULL AND
DRAGAN MILETIC

THE MIT PRESS
CAMBRIDGE, MASSACHUSETTS
LONDON, ENGLAND

The MIT Press
Massachusetts Institute of Technology
77 Massachusetts Avenue, Cambridge, MA 02139
mitpress.mit.edu

The MIT Press would like to thank the anonymous peer reviewers who provided comments on drafts of this book. The generous work of academic experts is essential for establishing the authority and quality of our publications. We acknowledge with gratitude the contributions of these otherwise uncredited readers.

This book was set in Arnhem Pro and New Frank by New Best-set Typesetters Ltd. Printed and bound in the United States of America.

Library of Congress Cataloging-in-Publication Data

Names: Bull, Synne, author. | Miletic, Dragan, 1970– author.
Title: Proxistant vision : motion, navigation, scale / Synne Tollerud Bull and Dragan Miletic.
Description: Cambridge : The MIT Press, 2025. | Series: Leonardo | Includes bibliographical references and index.
Identifiers: LCCN 2024037285 (print) | LCCN 2024037286 (ebook) | ISBN 9780262552189 (paperback) | ISBN 9780262382816 (pdf) | ISBN 9780262382823 (epub)
Subjects: LCSH: Aerial photography.
Classification: LCC TR810 .B86 2025 (print) | LCC TR810 (ebook) | DDC 778.3/5—dc23/eng/20250219
LC record available at https://lccn.loc.gov/2024037285
LC ebook record available at https://lccn.loc.gov/2024037286

10 9 8 7 6 5 4 3 2 1

EU product safety and compliance information contact is: mitp-eu-gpsr@mit.edu

To Filip and Luna

CONTENTS

SERIES FOREWORD

Leonardo/The International Society for the Arts, Sciences and Technology fosters transformation at the nexus of art, science, and technology because complex problems require creative solutions. The Leonardo Book Series shares these aims of artistic and scientific experimentation, and publishes books to define problems and discover solutions, to critique old knowledge and create the new.

In the early twentieth century, the arts and sciences seemed to interact instinctively. Modern art and modern poetry were automatically associated with relativity and quantum physics, as if the two were expressions of a single Zeitgeist. At the end of the Second World War, once again it seemed perfectly clear that avant-garde artists, architects, and social planners would join cyberneticists and information theorists to address the problems of the new world order and to create new ways of depicting and understanding its complexity through shared experiences of elegance and experiment. Throughout the twentieth century, the modern constantly mixed art and science.

In the twenty-first century, though, we are no longer modern but contemporary, and now the wedge between art and science that C. P. Snow saw emerging in the 1950s has turned into a culture war. Governments prefer science to arts education, yet stand accused of ignoring or manipulating science. The arts struggle to justify themselves in terms of economic or communicative efficiency that devalues their highest aspirations. And yet never before have artists, scientists, and technologists worked together so closely to create individual and collective works of cultural power and intellectual grace. Leonardo looks beyond predicting dangers and challenges, beyond even planning for the unpredictable. The series publishes books that are both timely and of enduring value—books that address the perils of our time, while also exploring new forms of beauty and understanding.

Seán Cubitt, Editor-in-Chief, Leonardo Book Series

ACKNOWLEDGMENTS

This book owes its existence to the unwavering support and intellectual contributions of numerous individuals whose guidance and encouragement have been instrumental throughout its development. While it is not possible to mention everyone, our special thanks go to: Holly L. Aaron, Jørgen Alnæs, Monica Andresen, Charley Bennett, Mark Boswell, Ana Brotas, Andreas Bunte, Øyvind Brandtsegg, Valeria Cafà, Mark Co, Andreas Ervik, Stuart Elden, Thomas Elsaesser, Jon Inge Faldalen, Anne-Karin Furunes, Ed Gilbert, Matt Hauske, Aurora Hoel, Michael Hsueh, Jane Jao, Danielle Jorgens, Jan Kaila, Gertrud Koch, Trine Krigsvoll Haagensen, Mark Lewis, Lasse Marhaug, Massimo Mazzotti, Frank McGrath, Susan Miller, Jorten Mortensen, Maria Moseng, Christopher Myers, Phill Niblock, Vasfi Burak Ozdol, Lisa Parks, Jordan Padams, Lauren Pearson, Cecilie Richardsen, Anneli Røros, Eivind Røssaak, Bruce Andrew Sampson, Gro Skåland, Henk Slager, Alma Suvalic, Eric Theise, Shannon Trimble, Pasi Väliaho, Timotheus Vermeulen, Artemis Willis, Kuan-Ju Wu, Sara R. Yazdani, Susanne Østby Sæther, Espen Ytreberg.

Our deepest gratitude goes to Tom Gunning, Professor Emeritus and a luminary in film studies, whose inspiration and support during this pivotal time were invaluable. Our rigorous and supportive supervisors, Ina Blom, Liv Hausken, and Jeremy Welsh, have provided vital aid in helping us regain focus when we, at times, pursued a blurry target. Mark Dorrian, Trond Lundemo, Scott Rettberg, Ove Solum, and Andrea Sunder-Plassmann provided crucial insights and feedback in their roles as our dissertation committee members. Furthermore, we are deeply grateful to the most supportive curator, Carol Covington, who was instrumental in facilitating the world premiere of our solo exhibition *Proxistant Vision* at the Museum of Craft and Design (MCD), San Francisco. This exhibition would not be possible without diligent support by the Museum's own curator Ariel Zaccheo and lead preparator Jeremiah Barber, who made this exhibition a joyful, if laborious, experience. We extend our heartfelt gratitude to Gallery Anglim/Trimble, formerly Anglim Gilbert Gallery, for its steadfast support over the years, including its instrumental contribution to this research project, which resulted in two solo exhibitions in 2017 and 2022.

An outstanding engineering team has proved invaluable in this project, and we extend our warmest thanks to Jens Brynildsen; Jo Herstad, Department of Informatics, University of Oslo; Torbjørn Helgesen Nordvik; Tønnes Frostad Nygaard, Department of Technology Systems, University of Oslo; Jan C. Schacher, Institute for Computer Music and Sound Technology, Zurich University of the Arts; Magnus Sjursen; and Mikael Valen. In addition, curators Randi Thommessen of the Trondheim Art Museum and Randi Martine Brockmann of the Trøndelag Centre for Contemporary Art supported and encouraged us by showcasing the research project in its early stages.

Throughout the research period, we have received financial and infrastructural support from numerous institutions and assemblies. These include the Archives of American Art, Smithsonian Institution; Arts Research Center, University of California, Berkeley; Berkeley Art Museum and Pacific Film Archive; BITRAF; Center for Science, Technology, Medicine & Society, University of California, Berkeley; Chicago Historical Society; Chicago Public Library; Chicago University Library's Special Collections Research Center; CITRIS Invention Lab, University of California, Berkeley; Douglas County Historical Society, Nevada; FORART Foundation; Jet Propulsion Laboratory, NASA; Lawrence Berkeley National Laboratory; Norwegian Arts Council; Norwegian Artistic Research Programme; Norwegian University of Science and Technology (NTNU); Office for Contemporary Art Norway (OCA); Oslo National Academy of the Arts; Department of Media and Communication (IMK), Faculty of the Humanities, University of Oslo; and the School of Arts, Design, and Media, Kristiania University College. Our editors, Gabriela Bueno Gibbs and Seán Cubitt, the MIT Press production staff, and the anonymous reviewers pushed the work forward in a productive and inspiring manner.

We are deeply grateful to our parents, Anne Elin Tollerud, Stein-Roger Bull, Sofija, and Radoš Miletić, for always supporting our goals and encouraging our adventures. We also thank our amazing children, Filip and Luna, for inspiring and surprising us daily. This book is dedicated to them. Finally, our loyal dog, Evvia, deserves special mention for her steadfast companionship and boundless enthusiasm.

INTRODUCTION

A PARADIGM OF PROXIMITY AND DISTANCE

Cinema isn't I see, it's I fly.
—Paul Virilio[1]

The close-up view of a shiny brass clockwork with steadily operating cogwheels morphs magically into a bird's-eye view of nocturnal Paris. Just as the Arc de Triomphe—with nine dimly lit boulevards radiating in a circle around it—emerges through the clock's central cogwheel, we start our flight sideways towards the French capital's legendary Eiffel Tower. Eventually, after a smooth curve above rooftops, we descend in front of our final flight destination: a 1930s version of the Gare Montparnasse railway station. A cut introduces this film's second aerial establishing shot. With the Eiffel Tower again perched on the horizon, we now fly towards the same train station through the rear entrance. A floating aerial camera movement aligns with the network of train tracks and follows their path from above as they spread into individual platforms under the large station roof. The same forward-moving shot mingles in with the station's interior activity. We swiftly pass arriving and departing passengers as locomotives belch the whirling gusts of white steam. From a low-flying perspective, we observe a multitude of passengers and railroad officials as they board and disembark from the trains. Customers and shopkeepers cross hastily in front as the continuous camera movement proceeds through the station's main hall. Suddenly, a lofty ascent targets the station's interior clock that triumphs high above the throng of people and things. As we fly forwards and upwards, we notice, behind the clock's figure-four, a pair of troubled eyes. The camera finally halts on a close-up of these very eyes, filling the frame with their anxious glance. Connected through a continuous flight between the French capital and the daily routines of its grandiose train station, life is suggestively coordinated by a clockwork operation.

This smooth flight from aerial overview to intimate close-up in Martin Scorsese's 2011 film *Hugo* exemplifies what we call proxistant vision: a visually captivating and dynamic flight that combines proximity and distance in a unified form. This flight in *Hugo*, importantly, is not a real flight in a physical sense. It is composited using live-action animation techniques, in which a visual effects team composes and seamlessly integrates computer-generated visuals with physical actors and buildings on a green screen backdrop.[2] Moreover, 3D-animated flights in cartography and data visualization often involve multiple sensor and mapping techniques, where digital environments are made up of datasets translated into wireframes and composite assemblages. Such smooth flights have steadily multiplied across cinema, data visualization, architectural modeling, cartography, and video games since the early 2000s. A recent surge in aerial imaging technologies, such as shoebox-sized satellites and micro drones, contributes to this trend. First-person view (FPV) piloted drones, for example, enable the capture of physical reality in previously unseen acrobatic combinations of close-ups and vertiginous vistas. In addition, we also see such volumetric configurations in real life, outside the virtual spaces of screens and computer animation. The world's leading cities now compete in building ever-grander urban observation wheels, by which spectators go on circular "flights" between bustling streets and elevated urban vistas.

The advance in aerial surveillance technologies has prompted scholarly discussion on a new centrality of the aerial view in visual culture, observing a turn from central to vertical perspectives. Furthermore, the exponential growth in computer-generated images (CGI) and 3D environments across audiovisual media has been addressed by scholars who point to a new mode of screen spatiality. Here, a new focus on camera movement is crucial, as it has come to side with the previously superior cinematic techniques of editing. These discussions, however, have so far not accounted for the smooth flight that combines close-up and overview through dynamic camera movements. Such research is pressing today as this visual form contagiously extends its feature across real and virtual spaces, information and entertainment industries, and scientific and artistic domains. Most importantly, as aerial perspectives are combined in ever more dynamic ways with close-ups, their historical contingencies and technical operations figure beyond the cinema to the extent that we may call it a visual paradigm of the twenty-first century.

This book identifies, explores, and traces a visual form that currently multiplies across and beyond screens and devices by way of smooth flyover effects in digital maps, computer games, architectural models, data visualizations, drones, observation wheels, and CGI cinema. According to acclaimed human geographer Denis Cosgrove, aerial imaging, or simply, the view from above, can be considered a form of cartographic vision.[3] It enforces great impact aesthetically, ethically, and ideologically upon the understanding of the world and the entities within it. How then does this historically contingent and powerful view from above work in combination with the close-up? In our explorations of this phenomenon, we both connect and meander between discussions concerning the aerial view, the close-up, and camera movement to scrutinize how their combined effects play out in this visually unified form. In the spirit of Cosgrove, we investigate this as a form of cartographic description, exploring how it forms and informs spatial relations from datasets and street corners to the edges of the universe. As both artists and theorists, our methodology is grounded in artistic and media archeological research in which we deep dive into specific cases to explore some of their key features, relations, and connections. As such, the very concept of proxistance can be illustrative of our methodology, as we exploratively combine and move between its micro and macro perspectives. In addition to our artistic and media archeological research, we are informed by a broad range of interdisciplinary scholarships, especially from the fields of cinema and cartography. Our goal is thus to center attention on a visual form that has traveled from peripheral to center stage in the twenty-first-century media sphere. Triggered by this empirical observation, our objective is to reveal some of the recursive operative chains underpinning this specific form of mediation.

THE VIEW FROM ABOVE

One starting point for investigating the paradigm of proxistant vision can be to look at the power of the aerial view in visual culture historically and today. This topic has been a subject of numerous books and articles within the past decade.[4] The aerial view is commonly recognized as modernity's emblematic visual form, a form whose presence in everyday life grew exponentially in recent years due to an unprecedented surge in the development of aerial imaging technologies.[5] When studying the view from above, one quickly enters a dual nature of utopian and dystopian connotations, a duality that film scholar Paula Amad has attempted to diversify.[6] On the utopian side, we have the celebratory emancipative perspective proclaimed by artist Lászlo Moholy-Nagy in his concept of the *New Vision* (1938), and the materialization of previous magnificent imagination as expressed in architect Le Corbusier's *Aircraft* (1935).[7] Constructivist, Cubist, Futurist, and Suprematist avant-gardes exhibit this primarily in painting but also through early cinematic explorations.[8] On the dystopian side, we have the reconnaissance flights of World War I and the harsh criticism of such perspectives in the writings of Walter Benjamin and Siegfried Kracauer, among others.[9] The expansion of aerial views continued to influence what Martin Heidegger famously described as the "world picture," whereby visualizing the whole world is synonymous with a sense of its ownership and control.[10] As artist and critic Alan Sekula claimed, "[w]ith airplane photography, [. . .] two globalizing mediums, one of transportation and the other of communication, were united in the increasingly rationalized practice of warfare."[11] From a closer look at Sekula's text, we understand that he uses the word globalizing here not in an affirmative communal sense, as McLuhan and Fuller do, but as a hegemony.[12] Furthermore, Virilio's much-quoted book *War and Cinema* (1984) famously starts out with a powerful analogy between the eye and the movie camera, based initially on the link between photography and targeting, as shown in Étienne-Jules Marey's chronophotographic rifle camera.[13] The relation between the aerial view and the urban environment has furthermore been the subject of investigation by scholars such as Davide Deriu, Kevin Lynch, Michel de Certeau, and Jeanne Haffner, among many others.[14]

Regarding the utopian accounts of the aerial view, it becomes evident that the dystopian dimension in some sense can be seen as a response to the unprecedented enthusiasm that flight achieved and conceived at the onset of its realization. To this claim can be added Caren Kaplan's recent account of what she calls the "balloon-o-mania" of the late eighteenth and early nineteenth centuries.[15] The aerial view from the hot air balloon worked towards the affirmation of a renewed confidence in vision and this informed scientific knowledge production as well, as film scholar Jacques Aumont has explicated.[16] The moderns of this period in Europe were "feverish for reality" and "delirious for vision, thirsty for visible appearances and pure phenomena," as Beaumont Newhall, author of *Airborne Camera*, expounds about the balloon ride.[17] The aerial view became an important tool in the much-favored encyclopedic knowledge production of this period, ushering in a new sense of objective knowledge based on detachment from the subject observed. This disembodiment that became associated with scientific validity was later subjected to harsh criticism by feminist and science and technology scholars such as Elisabeth Stengers, Bruno Latour, and Donna Haraway. Haraway famously referred to the scientific method as describing "ways of being nowhere while claiming to see comprehensibly."[18]

The power of the aerial view goes further back in history than modernity, however. Vision has by several traditions been associated with both knowledge and elevation. Closely tied to imperial and colonial enterprises, the overview of large areas signals mastery and exploitation. This is argued by human geographer Denis Cosgrove in his large body of work on the aerial view and visual geography.[19] The historical power associated with the elevated view is also exemplified in religious texts, when Satan offers world domination to Jesus at the top of a high mountain in the Judean Desert. Beyond this, we have the consistent link humans make between power, elevation, and authority.[20] An equally Judeo-Christian reference comes from previously mentioned Amad, pointing out how one of our most powerful historical associations of the aerial view was that of God's eye looking down upon the surface of the face of the earth with both creativity and judgement. Importantly, this shows how the aerial view was always already connected to the view from below, where interfacing with God's face from the face of the Earth dictated human's relentless destiny.[21] Through its modern development, therefore, the aerial view was imbued with myths from religion, authority, sovereignty, and the claim of scientific objectivity.

NEW FORMS OF VERTICAL MEDIATION

An ongoing concern with the view from above in our time is the increased operation of surveillance, tracking, and targeting. Remotely Piloted Aircraft Systems (RPAS), along with operations involving satellite sensors, encompass what media scholar Lisa Parks has termed "vertical mediation."[22] The increased drone wars that developed following the 9/11 attack on the World Trade Center mark the central departing point for recent publications by Caren Kaplan.[23] Derek Gregory's article "From a View to a Kill" furthermore offers a strong visual account of the drone war perspective, highlighting the correlation between the distance of the drone and the close proximity with which the drone operator encounters their target.[24] The visual complexity of military drone systems is powerfully analyzed by Parks, as she shows how the drone operator is required to "build a picture" of the ground situation pertaining to the current mission. In this case, Google Earth gives a broader context to the "soda straw view" of the drone camera.[25] In fact, it could be argued that proxistant vision is utilized to the fullest potential with "the combination of intelligence, surveillance and reconnaissance (ISR) and weapons platform" that Gregory lists as the conditional visibilities that currently make up the battlespace and affect target cycles.[26] Here we see how proxistant vision is entangled with the perceptual, infrastructural, and forensic complexity of drone warfare.[27]

Hito Steyerl has argued that the loss of horizon in the vertical perspective equals the loss of stable ground. This turn marks a departure from the linear perspective that has guided imaging since Renaissance realism in painting.[28] The multiple connections between the computer screen and the central perspective is perhaps most thoroughly traced by Anne Friedberg in her book-length study on this theme.[29] Yet, the drones and satellites in our sky today do not simply take vertical photographs but rather collect diverse data through a variety of remote sensing techniques.

Hence, what this book will be focused on is how the data from satellites and drones are turned into smooth visualizations with a proxistant outlook exemplified by interfaces like Google Earth. This is the smooth overview form in which a dynamic "drill down" exposes, locates, and identifies the individual detail that supposedly makes up the whole. Is this smooth proxistance technique perhaps a Trojan horse in data visualization, which seemingly aspires to stabilize the ground and enhance a sense of one's place in the world? A smooth flight between detail and overview seems to make up a majority of the surfaces that we are presented with today on a grand scale. As such, they also make up the grounds by which we are expected to decipher the ever-increasing amount of collected data. Hence, the scholarship of vertical mediation, which includes issues of surveillance, targeting, and tracking, receives a fresh challenge in this book. This field will be explicitly addressed to expand the position from vertical meditation to the combination of proximity and distance.[30] In addition, we bring into our focus the current proliferation of so-called first-person view (FPV) miniature quadcopter drones, which, in contrast to large-scale ISR military systems, have received little scholarly attention and are still not properly defined in their mode and operation. What we find striking here is that the current proliferation of FPV drone videos across online portals such as YouTube and Vimeo provide dynamic close-ups and overviews similar to the aforementioned "drill downs" we see in 3D-animated flythrough visualizations, and beyond this, in the view from ever-larger observation wheels across world's prominent metropolises. Here, we are focused on how these drones, wheels, and 3D-animated flythroughs participate in constructing a visual paradigm of the twenty-first century.

SUPER CINEMA, DRONE CINEMA, AND THE NEW VERTICALITY

The visual form we study in this book takes a variety of shapes and forms, which all have in common a cartographic motion between proximity and distance. From these empirical observations, the neologism *proxistance* emerged, a combination of "proximity" and "distance" to capture this dynamic cartographic movement. Our earlier reference to the virtual flight in the opening sequence of Scorsese's *Hugo* illustrates one way in which this visual form masterfully figures as a location-establishing shot in narrative cinema. Such spatial possibilities on offer through digital 3D animation is similarly explored in films like *Avatar 1* (2009) and *Avatar 2* (2023), directed by James Cameron; *Inception* (2010), directed by Christopher Nolan; *Gravity* (2013), directed by Alfonso Cuarón; and *Interstellar* (2014), directed by Christopher Nolan; to name a few. Often referred to simply as digital cinema, this new plastic spatiality has generated significant scholarly discussion. Philosopher Steven Shaviro's much-referenced *Post-Cinematic Affect*, for example, argues that digital cinema instantiates "new forms of spatiotemporal construction."[31] This point is taken further by Mark B. N. Hansen, who shows how the digital infrastructure now governing cinematic production generates what he calls a "post-perceptual" situation where "we can no longer speak of a relationship *between* images, but rather of an ongoing modulation of the image itself [. . .] at the level of the pixel."[32] Media scholar Steen Ledet Christiansen furthermore argues that digital cinema increasingly leaves the "human model of perception," in favor of "a nonhuman body capable of moving through solid space, speeding across time in a continuous shot or gazing into other spectra of light."[33] This comes close to what media scholar William Brown coins as "Supercinema," a cinema purported of extraordinary powers of impossible camera movements and overtly kinetic maneuvers.[34] The digitally constructed aerial views in these films, as well as the sense of falling and psychological vertigo associated with high altitudes, have also been identified as the aesthetics of a "new verticality" by cinema scholar Kristen Whissel.[35] Although not pointing to the combination of proximity and distance, the sweeping flights and falls that Kristen Whissel refers to as a recurring theme in digital cinema occasionally resonate with our concept of proxistant vision here. However, rather than focusing on the psychological effect of these falls, we focus here on the slow-motion of such falls as spatial descriptions, where the virtual camera perceptually moves from immense panorama to tight close-up within one sweeping shot.

In his study on the return of 3D in digital cinema, film scholar Thomas Elsaesser has remarked how instead of producing a particular type of image, these new screen spaces produce a particular type of spectator. The current shift to 3D in mainstream filmmaking and popular entertainment, he argues, "obliges one to shift attention to the close alliance that has always existed between the entertainment industries and other simulation industries, as well as between media of observation and recording and media of surveillance and control."[36] While some of these developments may generate visual excitement for us, they simultaneously reveal "to machines things that humans can never expect to see."[37] Referring here to remote sensing technologies, vast data analysis, or other computational processes, these images are operative, understood in the words of Harun Farocki as images that "do not represent an object, but rather are part of an operation."[38] Maps, architectural drawings, X-rays, and tele-presence fall into this category, where the objective is to enable action. The logic of 3D in all its applications, therefore, points to a larger reorientation of cultural behavior in which vision is turned into operation.[39] Human geographer Nigel Thrift's article "Lifeworld Inc." is highly instructive here.[40] Thrift shows how we are moving from a military-industrial complex to what he calls, after Bruce Sterling, the "security-entertainment complex," via large global corporations massively entangled in both arenas.[41]

Most importantly for this book is the way the recent development in digital cinema has generated the extended presence of proxistant vision by way of prolonged perceptual camera movements between aerial views and close-ups, and here we emphasize the media archeological interest in cinema of this project. Such camera movements can be said to have pre-existed in urban kinetic architecture, which participated in giving birth to the moving image. Films such as *Panoramic View from the Eiffel Tower, Ascending and Descending*, filmed at the 1900 Paris Exposition Universelle for Thomas A. Edison, Inc, attest to this claim and make up the much-discussed period of early cinema, coined by Tom Gunning as "the cinema of attractions."[42] We will revisit this period in chapter one, where we discuss the materialization of the proxistant visual paradigm in physical space through the urban observation wheel. In 1914, Giovanni Pastrone's *Cabiria* presents dynamic traveling shots that highlight the three-dimensional nature of the cinematic scenery set in ancient Sicily, Carthage, and Cirta during the period of the Second Punic War (218–202 BC). As the camera tracks past the stage props, it displays their three-dimensionality, a stark contrast to the two-dimensional scenography common at the time.[43] Camera movement, however, has received little systematic attention, according to film historian Tom Gunning.[44] In David

Bordwell, Kristin Thompson, and Jeff Smith's key introduction to film art, currently in its eleventh edition, camera movement is categorized as a subtopic of framing, where the "mobile frame" is offered only thirteen pages, primarily consisting of large illustrations taking up most of the page. On the other hand, the same volume thoroughly discusses editing across forty-eight pages.[45] As the digital humanities' study of cinemetrics exemplifies, studies in film style and theory often pay exclusive attention to editing.[46] While editing presents cinema with concrete units of analysis, camera movement is harder to grasp.[47] A study of camera movement in narrative cinema is conducted by Jacob Isak Nielsen, in which he sets out to provide a taxonomy of functions for its communication of the plot.[48] In cinema scholar Daniel Morgan's recent publication on the topic, he questions conventional views on how film audiences interact with and perceive camera movement. Rather than identifying the camera as the character's point of view, spectators fantasize that they move along with the camera in the world of the film.[49] What we find curious, however, is the uncanny perceptual nature of camera movement and the spatial articulations it seems to produce on a two-dimensional screen. The new centrality of the prolonged camera movements in CGI-rich cinematic environments calls for a reevaluation of camera movement beyond associating it with the point of view of a character or a function in a narrative context. This book studyies proxistance as a form of cartographic vision that currently shapes contemporary worldviews through its emergence as a visual paradigm of the twenty-first century.

CARTOGRAPHIC CINEMA

One way to think about camera movement is to notice its unique potential in the description of spatial relations. A camera movement between close-up and aerial view can perhaps be seen as profoundly cartographic in the way it reveals a larger geographical context. A taste of such spatial articulation is already present in the extraordinary experiments of moving image and flight in the Lumière brothers' early actualité *Panorama pris d'un ballon captive* (1898), filmed by their cinématographe from a tethered balloon.[50] A question to which we will return in this book is how proxistant vision in cartography can be seen as having existed for as long as we have been producing spatial renderings. Early forms of proxistant vision are exemplified in many cartographic presentations, such as in the sixteenth-century bird's-eye views of European cities. Here one can see how important elements, such as individual buildings and mountain ranges, are drawn frontally while the rest of the location might be vertically rendered. We will investigate the relevance of these early city views and their inherently dynamic and kinematic (which from now on we refer to as "cinematic") change of viewpoints for the visual modality that has journeyed onto center stage in our time. More media archaeologists than geographers, we allow ourselves with due respect into the territory of cartography to map out early forms of proxistant vision across a longer span of duration beyond what tracing a cinematic apparatus would allow. Our strategy here is to study proxistant vision as a mode of spatial mediation, which in our time of new aerial imaging seems to combine the distinct fields of cinema and cartography in ways that describe and mediate the promise of an everywhere view.

As Cosgrove has noted, the aerial view is closely linked to its cartographic abilities, that is, to providing a contextual overview. Building on Cosgrove's scholarship, we explore how both the aerial image and camera movement can be employed "to create geographies."[51] The visual practice of mapping and surveying is where the aerial view has generated its paramount historical significance from planning and redevelopment to imperialism, geopolitics, and war. This is also the domain in which artists and activists have engaged in counter-mapping projects. Vision, aerial views, and navigation are linked through the practices of landscape and cartography, and the moving image is connected to this historical trajectory in multiple ways. The link between cinema and cartography is not new, and we stand on the shoulders of many prominent thinkers when we study proxistant vision as a form of cine-cartography. Again, however, we find an emphasis on narrative cinema in this scholarship that is different from this book's focus on spatial description. In his book on cartographic cinema, philologist Tom Conley has pointed to how "films *are* maps insofar as each medium can be defined as a form of what cartographers call 'locational imaging.'" Borrowed from Davis Buisseret's book *The Mapmaker's Quest*, location imaging is a pivotal term here, as it designates how the invention of cartography as a scientific practice generated a "new sense of location and a sense of place in the world. It initially takes the shape of topography but is ultimately tied to those agencies—cinema included—that seek to locate their subjects in the places they represent for them."[52] Such perspective opens up various spatial readings of narrative cinema, a theme Timotheus Vermeulen, among others, has investigated as well.[53] Rather than studying narrative cinema's use of maps or spatial narratives, however, our focus is on the cartographic articulation found in a single shot that combines close-up and overview by way of a perceptual camera movement. As such, our approach in this book is more in line with cinema scholar Giuliana Bruno, who in her two books *Street Walking on a Ruined Map* and *Atlas of Emotion*, as well as numerous essays, convincingly interweaves cinematic and cartographic relations, arguing for their mutual co-evolution. In her view, "by way of filmic representation, geography itself is being transformed and (e)mobilized. [. . .] A frame for cultural mappings, film is *modern cartography*."[54]

The relation between cartography and cinema can be traced back to earlier forms of image-making, to the so-called "mapping impulse" of Western visual culture since the Renaissance. As cinema scholar Teresa Castro points out, "the coupling of eye and instrument that distinguishes cartography's representation of space is in many ways very similar to cinema's coding and scaling of the world."[55] This system of power through knowledge combined with cinema's emergence in a time of colonial expansion makes this a relation worth reflecting on. Castro's scholarship is also present in a special issue on cinema and cartography in *The Cartographic Journal* (2009) as well as the more recent anthology *Cinematic Urban Geographies* (2017). The collection of essays in both these volumes is otherwise primarily focused on narrative readings of maps or cartographic readings of films.[56] The relations between cinema and cartography in this emergent field therefore, except for Bruno and Castro, tend to become more of a metaphorical and narrative endeavor. In this book, we seek to widen our critical horizon towards a broader discourse concerning cine-cartographic relations. The cine-cartographic affinities of proxistant vision builds on Bruno's and Castro's accounts of cine-cartographic affinities, as they open the notion of cartography to a broader field of interdisciplinary studies and practices. As will be apparent throughout the following chapters, however, our approach also differs in important ways from previous studies. Rather than a narrative through cultural history, our method is to dig deeper into the practices and technical operations behind this captivating visual form.

DIGITAL GEOGRAPHY

Importantly therefore, while we start our investigation based on a moving image form, we immediately focus on the spatialities produced rather than the story it supports in a cinematic narrative. We relate the visual modality in our focus to a form of cartographic vision and hence to a discussion that involves some of the practices and techniques that participate in forming the field of geography and geopolitics. Entering the scholarly field of political geography, we see that the flat vertical perspective of scientific mapping conventions is meant to define territorial borders that are far from flat. In his essay on "the politics of verticality," architect Eyal Weizman shows how the territorial borders between Israel and Palestine are imbricated and layered from underground tunnels, different strata of roads and highway systems to airborne and orbital machines governing the airspace.[57] Importantly, the vertical does not denote an angle of framing for Weizman, but describes the vertical layering of spatial relations, from below to above. In a similar manner, environmental architect Stephen Graham recently dismissed the "flat perspectives" maintained in urban discourse, especially within geography and the social sciences, relying on flat maps and borders on the ground when faced with geopolitical issues.[58] Similarly, for practices ranging from "deep sea mining and undersea cables to outer, and even arguably interstellar, space," flat maps have come short in their description of the world on primarily a horizontal basis, as geographer and artist Trevor Paglen points out.[59] Acknowledging the three-dimensional work in architecture and philosophy by scholars such as cultural theorist Paul Virilio and philosopher Peter Sloterdijk, Graham and Paglen join geographers such as Stuart Elden, Jeremy Crampton, and Peter Adey in highlighting the question of spatial volumes and volumetric territories as an important issue for geography and geopolitics.[60] Such issues feed into our investigations in this book as well, as they combine and become challenged by a cinematic and media archeological point of view.

Proxistant vision offers a decidedly volumetric alternative to the flat, two-dimensional maps still governing Earth's globalized territories. From the field of geography, it can be sorted under the category known as spatial media. First coined by Jeremy Crampton to denote georeferenced and location-aware networked interfaces, the concept of spatial media particularly addresses the new realm of cartography provided by "the pan and zoom 'slippy maps'" exemplified by Google Earth, which was launched as a desktop application in 2005.[61] Moreover, the current integration of GPS coordinates with IP addresses and smartphones arguably turns all online media into spatial media by being both located and localizable.[62] However, this new life of digital geography highlights how the map was always already "transitory and fleeting, being contingent, relational and context dependent."[63] As Kitchen and Doge have shown, all maps, including paper versions, are "of-the-moment, beckoned into being through practices; they are always mapping."[64] While not focusing here on the online interactivity of maps, nor engaging with the scholarship of spatial media in any substantial way, our analysis of proxistant vision brings in an important dimension to this scholarly field. It accounts for the increased presence of the moving image and camera movement across digital geography, exemplified by the 3D-animated flythrough maps present in everything from city planning to climate change predictions.

What such digital cartographies first and foremost bring to the fore is the ability to effortlessly navigate a rationalized and controlling big picture in combination with a close-up detail of that same space. The cinematic close-up, a subject of extensive film theory, has been analyzed by scholars like Mary Anne Doane, Gilles Deleuze, Sergei Eisenstein, André Bazin, Sigfried Kracauer, and Béla Balázs, to name a few, each contributing unique insights into its relationship with space and scale.[65] While Doane articulates the close-up's power to rupture spatial continuity and intensify emotional engagement, Deleuze perceives it as an expression beyond narrative function, emphasizing the human face's capacity for inhuman affect. Eisenstein considers the close-up a dialectical tool that, through spatial juxtaposition, can evoke complex viewer responses, and Balázs focuses on its humanizing aspect, capturing emotional subtleties and forging connections with the audience. Recent film scholarship builds on these foundations, examining how the close-up's manipulation of scale influences the viewer's perception of space, both on the traditional cinema screen and through diverse modern media platforms, highlighting its evolving role in an era of varied screen sizes and digital immediacy. Particularly relevant for this book are Doane's points concerning the scale of the close-up as not merely a matter of physical proximity but a dynamic element that shapes the viewer's emotional and cognitive engagement with the image. For this book, the close-up is theorized as a detail, emphasizing its spatial connection to the orbital view of the globe suspended in space. As we navigate cartographic and cinematic contingencies of the arguably most paradigmatic shots of our time—the Google Earth zoom from orbital perspective to street view—we emphasize how these scholarly accounts on the cinematic close-up become operational of scalar relations. Recent discussions on scale in the context of media and cultural studies have shown how scale today is central. Authors such as Zachary Horton, Seán Cubitt, and Joshua DiCaglio, to name a few, all line up in arguing for a renewed importance of scale awareness across disciplines as we are faced with environmental challenges on dimensions far beyond the human scale.[66]

From these initial observations, we begin our investigation into the expanding form of proxistant vision. The recent proliferation of this form has made it apparent that the practices and operations of cinema and the moving image might figure as overlooked themes in current discussions on aerial and vertical as well as spatial media. Similarly, scholarship on the recent increase of CGI in cinema does not in substantial ways exend to aerial imaging or spatial media in digital geography. Between these two polarities lies a blank spot where this book takes on a precarious position. While we point to the ongoing cinematification of data by way of slick 3D-animated flythrough effects, we also investigate how digital cinema is plotted across a cartographic grid by way of Cartesian coordinates in ever more present 3D-animated environments. Our main hypothesis is that what brings the two fields of cinema and cartography together so pressingly today is the visual form of an unobstructed view, enabling movement from proximity to vertiginous distance in one continuous sweep.

In this book, we bring the aforementioned research fields together to account for the cine-cartographic contingencies with which this prevalent visual form operates today. We ask the reader to be open-minded and allow certain flexibility in terminology, while we proceed with narrowing in on the concept of proxistant vision. As the previous account shows, the scholarly context that is of most relevance to this research is the work on the aerial view in visual culture and, more specifically, in its relation to cinema, cartography, media archeology, and contemporary art. Further issues voiced in the context of science and technology studies more generally will be addressed within each chapter as we reflect on and take the notion of a worldview seriously, as proposed by Bruno Latour.[67] Our approach entails a borad definition of cinema (for example, observation wheel) and cartographic practices and techniques (for example, first-person-view drone navigation). Hence, this book is inherently expansive and interdisciplinary. Our path here is first and foremost one of connection. Through in-depth analysis of individual cases, we aim to decipher a complex visual form that currently proliferates across the twenty-first-century media sphere.

VISION AND VISUALITY

Proxistance is a concept that brings together the two terms "proximity" and "distance" to define a specific type of spatial mediation rooted in a visual construct. In spatial terms, proximity here denotes closeness, while distance denotes its relational overview, aerial view, or simply its broader context. The need to construct this concept is based on what we have detected as an empirical phenomenon that has long been practiced but which has, to our knowledge, not yet been identified in proper terms.[68] The visual form in focus here is one that combines proximity and distance, close-up and overview, detail and the big picture. This visual form behaves differently from a view in a microscope or telescope unless these instruments are in the action of performing a zoom. A situation where a combination of proximity and distance is in the same visual field is therefore key here, as these viewpoints are present on the same page, zoom or flight. This also excludes tele-presence as discussed earlier.

What seems significant here is how proxistant vision situates vision in multiple positions at once, combining a close-up inspection with a distanced totality, while suggesting a specific relation between them. Proxistant vision takes various forms and shapes. Through our analysis of several cases, we clarify and sharpen the concept as we trace the practices and operations from which it has emerged. We have chosen the term proxistant *vision* rather than *mediation*, to highlight the importance of vision as the main point of reference for proxistant spatial mediation. Mediation is here understood in terms of processes in which vision takes part.[69] In her concept of vertical mediation for example, Lisa Parks notes that "mediation involves demonstrating, putting forward, or bringing to life as much as it involves representing or depicting something that has already occurred."[70] While we do pay attention to this concept of mediation through the various material practices and technical operations that underpin proxistant vision, we also highlight the concept of vision as an important aspect of our investigation.

With proxistant vision, we devise a concept of cartographic visuality that differs from looking. Looking, according to Mirzoeff, is the personal observation from an embodied subject. Proxistant vision, rather, is characterized by offering a technical assemblage of multiple perspectives drawn onto the same visual surface within the same visual field, or on a visually unbroken trajectory.[71] "Visuality is an old word for an old project," Mirzoeff argues, namely, the nineteenth-century concept of the visualization of history. Visuality, then, signals what "is too substantial for any one person to see and is created from information, images, and ideas. This ability to assemble a visualization manifests the authority of the visualizer."[72] Closely related to the aerial view, the concept of visualization emerged with the modern general, as the battle scene became too complex to grasp by one person's physical look. This trajectory of visuality outlined by Mirzoeff lingers with proxistant vision as we define it in this book. Other important thinkers on vision, such as Jonathan Crary, Laura Mulvey, Anne Friedberg, Martin Jay, W. J. T. Mitchell, and many others contribute to this discourse as well.[73]

In this book, vision is therefore understood in its broadest sense as a form of technology or technique. Deriving from the Greek *techne*, technology designates a regular and repeatable practice that increases efficacy in life. Seeing is itself a form of technology, it is an established set of relations that actively selects from the differences and complexities to which it is exposed. As such, seeing is both an extension and a transformation of life, allowing for a practical selection of what is relevant for action, though in this process, perception simplifies the fullness of life's complexity. Whereas the eye-brain sensory operation actively selects and accentuates partial representations from perception, technical apparatuses, such as the moving image, contribute with a vision based on their own logics of operation to create percepts not centered around a human body.[74] Such an understanding of vision is derived from the French philosopher Henri Bergson, who argues that images do not represent a secondary reality but constitute life itself. "Through the hypothesis of the image, Bergson is re-attaching perception to the real."[75] Perception is in the world and our brain, and various media technologies select from this perception to produce an expression, a "slicing up" or a "selection" of this perception.[76] However partial this slice may be, it does not stop the spectator from thinking that the world is constructed according to the way it is expressed.

This insight actualizes the question of what a worldview is today as we are faced with the ecological crisis. Referring to Svetlana Alpers and others, Latour claims that "[a] new visual culture redefines both what it is to see, and what there is to see."[77] Here, Latour is mostly interested in the ways in which Alpers shows how vision and visibility are concretely connected, giving the old metaphor of a "worldview" a material meaning in "[h]ow a culture sees the world, and makes it visible."[78] Throughout this book, we discuss what Latour calls a "four-lane freeway" between the world and its representations as they are inherited from the Renaissance. Such Earth models not only reinstate the power/knowledge regimes of maps but establish objects as finalized entities in a stabilized geometric space. In this book, we discuss how the extensive presence of proxistant vision across screens and viewing devices may affect worldviews in our time of the Anthropocene.

SITUATING THE FIELD

This book traces specific cinematic, cartographic, and artistic techniques across the span of observation rides, drones, and satellites as they combine and intersect with 3D animation and related digitally networked techniques. Rather than a cultural history however, we are tracing the epistemic operators and technical mediations at work within selected technologies and practices. We focus on the contingent evolution of cartographic and cinematic modes that re-surface along the course of new technological development. Such a study is premised on a media archeological approach to history, that is, to thinking the new and the old through a variety of interconnected trajectories. As Jussi Parikka has articulated it, media archeology, although not a unified academic field, can be characterized as plural ways to see "media culture as sedimented and layered, a fold of time and materiality where the past might be suddenly discovered anew, and the new technologies grow obsolete increasingly fast."[79] In this way, it can be understood as a method of doing history on the basis of what Parikka calls a "materialist media diagrammatics."[80] The diagram here is both the electrical circuit that governs technical media devices (hardware) and the mapping of operations of such circuits (software). The figure of the diagram, furthermore, "is a way to understand how society operates through the diagrams of machines."[81] Parikka here refers to the media archeology of Wolfgang Ernst and the attempt to understand the principle and operative logic of the machine. Such archeology of media follows French sociologist and philosopher Michel Foucault's archeology of knowledge, Ernst argues, by "reconstructing the generative matrix created by mediatic *dispositifs*."[82] This notion of the diagram is also productive for understanding French philosopher Gilles Deleuze's reading of Foucault.[83]

Deleuze uses the diagram as a model for thinking the morphogenetic capability of matter to generate form on its own.[84] As such, the diagram is here a figure of emergence, the shaping of form out of matter through intensive differences. The diagram, furthermore, is the abstract machine that structures the space of possibility for a given assemblage. An assemblage, in a Deleuzian sense, can be loosely defined as "a multiplicity which is made up of many heterogeneous terms and which establishes liaisons, relations between them."[85] In other words, an assemblage is a metastable set of relations that act as an entity for a certain amount of time, based on recursive processes. To think with assemblages is to see a whole without losing sight of its heterogeneous elements in a constant state of interaction. Deleuze's theory of diagrams is another way of discussing the actualization of the virtual, the fact that something new arises. A diagram, according to Deleuze, produces something new that could not be seen. It operates by matter and function rather than the commonly mistaken dichotomy of substance and form.[86] Importantly, given as a quality of the virtual, "[t]he diagram is the possibility of fact—it is not the fact itself."[87] Deleuze takes this "divergent actualization" from previously mentioned Bergson, who sought to create an alternative to the inability of the sciences to think past a mechanistic approach to causality, a model that prohibited the ability to think the truly novel.[88] Bergson's model rather emphasizes the future as open-ended, where past and present entail not just possibilities that could turn real, but also a virtual dimension that becomes actual.

Such diagrammatic thinking involves technology in the world as a social agent that can open up for thinking emergence within human-machine relations as exemplified by the work of art historian Ina Blom and media scholar and artist Mathew Fuller, among others.[89] While the diagrammatic reasoning governing the operational workings of machines has one function, it can also be seen as an "operational dispositif" with links to Foucault's way of seeing power structures as diagrammatically distributed.[90] Rather than to historicize a finalized understanding of media, this approach investigates how various media technologies operate as active agents within their associated milieu. As Gilbert Simondon has argued, an entity becomes an individual through a process of individuation. An "individual," organic or inorganic, should never be seen as isolated, but always in the state of an ongoing process of individuation within an associated milieu. The individual is not a pre-given but starts with the pre-individual and it is never final as there are always further potentials for further individuating processes. Simondon refers to this process of individuation as transduction. Exemplified by the growth of a crystal, transduction is the transformation of information through a material medium. The metaphor of the crystal, however, should not be taken as a progressive development. To understand the individual in its ongoing process of individuation, therefore, one has to consider this associated milieu.[91] With this perspective, technicity must be understood in terms of its operation of becoming in a milieu, not as finalized technological objects.[92]

Such evolutionary approach has gained relevance in several studies on the current state of "planetary computation," a concept coined by media scholar and designer Benjamin Bratton and taken further by Jennifer Gabrys, among others. Importantly, such studies point out how aerial imaging and sensor networks not only record the environment but generate new environments and environmental relations.[93] The approach to media archeology exemplified by Ernst is less concerned with the "cultural interface" represented on the screen, and more with the technological performance "behind" the screen. As such, analytic priority is given to the technical operations embedded in the "interplay between non-human and human actors involved in media production and consumption dynamics."[94] This can be seen, moreover, in a productive relation to the field of media aesthetics, in which what happens on the screen, and thus at the representative side of the screen, is in primary focus.[95] The archeological move goes in multiple directions, and, subsequently, through the prism of digital technology, we gain new insights into traditional media.[96] Our focus in this book is therefore not on proxistant vision as a finalized construct, but rather on its various interactions and operations across different practices and fields. Proxistance is thus not linked to a specific author or artistic style but instead to the epistemic orders with which it corresponds. Translated to cartography, this means that the map *is* the territory that is studied as a form of spatial mediation. In other words, this is a study of how proxistant vision operates in the world, not how proxistant vision contains it.[97]

Our version of media archeology also carries significant cinematic references to the extent that it constitutes the primary role cinema carries in this project. With the concept of "the cinema of attraction," introduced in 1986, Tom Gunning took the first steps toward a New Film History that, according to Thomas Elsaesser, was framed within a media archeological spirit.[98] Cinematic development and digital novelty in the start of the twenty-first century can be productively studied through the lens of the previous century's surge of media innovation. We are particularly interested in how the co-presence of early cinema within the plethora of art and entertainment of the period, such as vaudeville, panoramas and dioramas, stereoscopic home entertainment, Hale's tours, and world fairs, attest to the different conceptions of the moving image within its first decade. Here we recognize the discontinuities, continuities, and epistemic breaks that pertain to a Foucault-inspired media archaeology, shunning concepts of linearity and progress.[99] Early cinema scholars such as Wanda Strauven and others have similarly explicated how attention to early cinema's exhibitionist and non-narrative formats opens a new path for understanding cinematic descendants, as formats of revelation and excitement not limited to the narrative drive.[100]

In our analysis of proxistant vision across practices of artistic, cartographic, and architectural operations, the media archeological method can also be seen to have certain affinities with media scholar Bernhard Siegert's concept of cultural techniques, which is founded on a similar approach to history as media archeology outlined previously. A perspective grounded in cultural technique aims to account for the broader field of practices and operations that draw proxistant vision into presence. According to Siegert, cultural techniques are those practices of differentiation that bring about new technologies and new forms of mediation. The cultural techniques approach thus shows how media technologies and visual modalities are not simply invented but drawn into presence by other practices and operations. This is always a complex network of relations between objects and practices, a displacement that emerges within recursive operative chains.[101] In the spirit of Siegert, we here work with the redefinition and expansion of the concept of media into a broader notion of the vast networks of conduits, channels, and intermediaries that participate in shaping culture.[102] Hence, this book traces some of the different ways in which practices and techniques have operated to produce the modality we here call proxistant vision.

METHODS AND CHAPTERS

Why do we need the concept of proxistance? What can we do, critically, with the term? Why is it important to have it now? In the spirit of Deleuze and Guattari, we develop the concept of proxistance to help us navigate and understand what we identified as an emerging visual paradigm across disciplines and practices. The idea of the concept is a matter of cutting and cross-cutting, in the way "each concept carries out a new cutting-out, takes on new contours, and must be reactivated or recut."[103] We see the need for this concept now because this paradigm limits complexity and produces the world as a model. With this concept, therefore, we wish to build critical tools that can analyze its historical contingencies and recursive operative chains. As mentioned earlier, the visual paradigm that combines close-up with overview is prevalent in our culture but does not have a satisfactory term. Several scholars of scale and mediation have turned to the concept of the zoom, a common media concept that is also problematized in recent scale literature.[104] As discussed in section two, the term "zoom" is often imprecise and conflated with camera movement. The concept of proxistance helps emphasize the combination of proximity and distance.

By creating the concept of proxistance, we construct a field of investigation for how a prevalent visual form in our globalized media world operates and from where its historical contingencies can be traced. As such, there are three components to this concept that need to be scrutinized: the close-up; the overview; and the movement between them, be that an actual zoom, a camera movement, an observation wheel ride, or a virtual composition. As Deleuze and Guattari remark, "[c]oncepts are centers of vibrations, each in itself and everyone in relation to all the others."[105] The complexity of this visual construct is what the concept of proxistant vision is invented to help investigate. While this book is focused on proxistance as a visual paradigm, we also recognize the more general idea of proxistance across disciplines. The movement from overview to detail and back again is an ancient and familiar form of storytelling and literature, often associated with the "third-person" form. In a recent lecture, Seán Cubitt, analyzes Thomas Hardy's *The Mayor of Casterbridge*, suggesting that the concept of the zoom existed in literature before becoming a technical reality in film. This technique is used to draw attention to details and to shift between scales of observation, providing a spatial and temporal experience for the reader. The concept of proxistance can also be useful as a thought model for releasing interlocked challenges, such as moving between detail and overview when faced with problem-solving, strategy planning, and leadership. Important for this book is that this prevalent form across disciplines is not merely a move between states but a combination of two perspectives that, in its reduction, also hold power/

knowledge as a privileged position. The challenge we face in our time is to further complicate this constellation.[106]

In this book, we introduce the concept of proxistant vision to identify a specific visual form that has multiplied across the screens and platforms of the twenty-first century. We propose this neologism as an analytical tool that can help identify the historical and operational contingencies of this visual form as it migrates across the fields of fairground rides, drone culture, digital geography, data visualization, and contemporary art. While each chapter addresses case-specific inquiries, the overall concern of the book centers on the following three questions. Firstly, from which historical practices and technical operations can this visual form be traced? Secondly, how is this visual form explored through cinema and cartography in artistic practices? And finally, how might the increased presence of this visual form affect worldviews in the context of the multi-species environmental challenges signaled by the Anthropocene? Our approach to answering these questions here is also threefold. First, we set out to identify and trace the various operations, techniques and practices that interact in the production of proxistant vision, historically and present-day. Second, we actively engage in practical testing and artistic evaluation as well as perform close analyses of artistic works in which alternative configurations of proxistant vision are explored and exhibited. Third, informed by the aforementioned process philosophy and science and technology studies of Bruno Latour, Donna Haraway, and Gilbert Simondon, among others, we analyze and question some of the underlying philosophical worldviews this form conveys. This book therefore has three key objectives: to trace the practices and techniques of the proxistant visual form as it has traveled from periphery to center stage in the twenty-first-century media sphere, to explore its alternative potentialities through our own artistic research as well as in other contemporary artistic practices, and, finally, to reflect on the worldviews that may underpin proxistant vision as a visual paradigm in the twenty-first century.

This investigation pertains to the multiple intersections between cinematic and cartographic practices, and, more specifically, questions how kinetic architecture, drones, and satellites draw on cinematic and cartographic conventions in their production of a prevalent visual form. The book thus adds to a growing scholarship on cartographic cinema and cinematic cartography, as well as related fields within digital geography and spatial media more generally. By plunging into the long-intertwined genealogy of the moving image and cartography, their common roots in the domain of spatial and territorial articulation will be exposed. The foundation for thinking of such a genealogy is the surge in the development of aerial imaging technologies and techniques that combine proximity and distance in a single image or across a dynamic flight or zoom. As we explore the relationships between modern perceptual paradigms and historical spatial technologies, we also invent new cinematographic apparatuses to unearth alternative media archaeological layers in this research. The practical-reflective and knowledge-producing processes involved in these constructions constitute our artistic research approach to the questions posed earlier. We here testify to philosopher Henk Bergdorf's articulation that artistic research happens when the "artistic practice is not only the result of the research, but also its methodological vehicle, when the research unfolds in and through the acts of creating and performing."[107] We furthermore investigate how fellow artists are deploying proxistance as a method for breaking away from stable categories to challenge established hierarchies. Proxistance, therefore, is not simply defined as only good or bad; rather, each chapter highlights its potential in terms of its malevolent and benevolent capacities.

THREE STRATA OF PROXISTANCE

The visual modality that proliferates across screens and platforms today is first and foremost associated with that of an aerial view in motion, but it comes in other forms and formats as well. To systematize the broad field of investigation required for this analysis, we have structured this book into three parts pertaining to the vertical strata within which each machine category exists, as one can see in table 0.1.

In part I, "Grounded Machines," we discuss machines for which grounded and physically attached infrastructure lifts the spectator to an elevated perspective. In part II, "Airborne Machines," we discuss machines in which an engine or construction allows a perceptual flight both physical and digital. Finally, in part III, "Orbital Machines," we discuss

TABLE 0.1.
Structure of the Book

Part	Strata	Machines	Properties	Mode of Proxistant Vision	Trace	Artwork
I	**Grounded**	Observation wheels, cable cars, panoramic elevators, etc.	Movement	Proximity and distance	George W. G. Ferris Jr. *Ferris Wheel* (1893)	Bull.Miletic. *Ferriscope* (1893–2020)
II	**Airborne**	Drones, helicopters, airplanes, CGI, etc.	Navigation	Close-up and overview	Jacopo de' Barbari. *Venetie MD* (1500)	Bull.Miletic. *Venetie 11111100110* (1500–2022)
III	**Orbital**	Satellites, space probes, 3D Earth models (Google Earth), etc.	Scale	Detail and the big picture	NASA/JPL. *Pale Blue Dot* (1990)	Bull.Miletic. *Zoom Blue Dot* (1990–2020)

the machines that orbit or see Earth from outer space, such as satellites and space probes. Furthermore, to grasp and analyze the most prominent cinematic and cartographic contingencies with which proxistant vision operate at these different strata, we have devised three distinct but related cartographic keywords for each section. These are *mobility* for grounded machines, *navigation* for airborne machines, and *scale* for orbital machines. The diagram also shows how the different categories of machines produce different proxistant modalities. Grounded machines, such as observation wheels, operate on a proxistant mode of proximity and distance (to the ground), while airborne machines produce close-ups and overviews, and orbital machines offer a combination of detail and the big picture. While this is not an exact science, and modes will sometimes blur and connect, it nevertheless gives an orientation to the different machine's main operative modes and thus serves well for a media archeological and cartographic analysis. Importantly, our project here is to show the similarities between these modes, and not the other way around.

The underlying logic of the three sections has furthermore been identified through specific events. The first event was the launch of the London

Eye observation wheel in 1999, which generated a surge of ever-grander wheels among the world's leading cities, of which the 2021 Dubai Eye is the most recent edition.[108] Secondly, we respond to the inauguration of the annual New York City Drone Film Festival in 2015, and thirdly, the launch of Google Earth's web version in 2017. The sections furthermore loosely correspond to an imaginary ascent via earthbound, to airborne, to orbital machines, as well as to layers of mediation from physical ride to photographic capture and eventually to remote sensing, big data, and planetary computation. Lastly, we must add that being artist-researchers, we also operate from within an aesthetic practice that is in constant formation through hands-on and material explorations. The questions we pose on a theoretical level in this book have emerged in response to the empirical observations and practice-based investigations we have explored through the construction of three kinetic video installations that loosely correspond to each section of this book. While this structure helps organize and specify the particularities of proxistant vision according to its different cinematic and cartographic modes, we emphasize that its recursive operative chains work across machines and strata and will thus be valid for proxistant vision in general.

The first part, "Grounded Machines," approaches the mobility inherent in the ride from street-level proximity to elevated distance facilitated by the giant urban observation wheel. We take this architectural construction as a starting point to discuss the operational effect of proxistant vision within the context of technology-driven urban development. Within this part, chapter 1, "The Wheel Before the Reel," investigates how the proxistant vision produced by the London Eye, built at the turn of the new millennium, can be traced back to the "original" Ferris wheel crowning the 1893 Chicago World's Fair. Here, we delve into the associated milieu that reinvented a pleasure wheel into a giant celebration of industrial visual mobility. By approaching rides as a form of cinema, we study these architectural structures as optical devices that produce spectacularly proxistant urban environments with specific operational effects. Chapter 2, "London (Eye) Calling," focuses on how the 135-meter-tall London Eye (re)launched the interest in urban observation wheels and was soon followed by an unprecedented boost of urban wheels on a global scale. Building on such contingent practices, how might the introduction of gigantic observation ride, such as the London Eye, into the very core of the urban environment, be seen to suggest an idealized perception of the city? We will see how this simple and seemingly benign maneuver can be understood to play a key role in the processes of gentrification that transforms the city itself into a site for visual consumption. Finally, chapter 3, "Grounded Machines as Cinéma Trouvé," the last chapter in this part, takes a closer look at the relationship between the observation wheel and cinematic technologies through practice-based investigations of cinematic movement rooted in artistic research. Here we discuss how several contemporary artists have studied the transformation of space produced by different types of rides such as cable cars, panoramic elevators, and other kinetic urban structures. These reflections are further developed through the practical exploration of the observation wheel's *cinéma trouvé* that took place in the related artistic research project *Ferriscope* (1893–2020).[109]

The second part, "Airborne Machines," develops along the logic of navigation, by mapping out an acrobatic path between close-up and overview. Beginning this part with chapter 4, "First-Person View (FPV) Dronematography," we focus on the proxistant spatiality drawn up by the daring flights of first-person view (FPV) drone pilots and the aesthetically similar, but operationally different, virtual flights offered by 3D animation. Returning to the 3D-animated live-action flight in *Hugo*, we discuss the issue of lens-based versus 3D-animated virtual camera flights in this part. By navigating physical flight through a virtual image, the FPV drone assemblage can produce and engage new cinematic spaces through rapidly shifting close-ups and overviews. The FPV drone's acrobatic moves can only be matched by a virtual camera, in which equally dynamic spatial dimensions are being shaped by radically different technical means. By adopting a navigational rather than mimetic approach to maps, we show in chapter 5, "A Bird's-Eye View Establishing Shot," how the prism of proxistance can excavate new insight into the operational contingencies of the 500-year-old High Renaissance map *Venetie MD* (*View of Venice 1500*) and its relevance today. Chapter 6, "The Aerial View in Motion," further investigates the similar spatial articulations between physical and virtual camera movements through the work of Italian filmmaker Michelangelo Antonioni and Canadian artist Mark Lewis. Here we again follow the path of the practice-based method of artistic research as we revisit *Venetie MD*, however this time as a Google-like interface at the Venice Project Center website.

The third part, "Orbital Machines," is concerned with the question of scale. Its starting point is the smooth scaling of the world in digital geography through networked interfaces and remote sensing operations. In this last part, we investigate how proxistant vision functions as a cinematic operator across the visual surfaces of digital geography against the backdrop of ubiquitous sensing networks that Jennifer Gabrys has termed "the becoming environmental of computation."[110] This part begins with chapter 7, "Prologue (*Pale Blue Dot*)," a prologue that chronicles a specific image-making process occurring four billion miles away from Earth, rendering our planet as "a mote of dust suspended in a sunbeam."[111] Chapter 8, "Proxistant Earth Models," continues this reflection on scale through the spectacular phenomenon of the Google Earth interface and its ancestor The Eameses' *The Powers of Ten* (1977), along with its prototype, *A Rough Sketch*(1968), in light of recent critiques by scale-concerned scholars regarding the linear nature of this journey through space.[112] Google Earth is perhaps the most hyperbolic version of proxistant vision, where the sphere of the globe is presented through an "all-seeing" swipe, moving effortlessly between globe view and street-level detail. To corroborate the cinematic and cartographic contingencies with which such Earth models operate today, we trace the effort to scale not only the world but the entire universe in the era of the Apollo 11 moon landing and the context of the political, technological, and social changes that occurred after World War II. Chapter 9, "Non-objective Scales," provides an in-depth account of how proxistance figured in significant artistic milieus at the time against the backdrop of the same political, economic, and technological changes that produced the Eameses' famous film. Here we see how post-minimalist artists such as Douglas Huebler and Robert Smithson produce different perceptions of scale within the same backdrop of the Space Race and Cold War. Rather than a function of measurement, these artists saw scale as an emergent property. We furthermore investigate these discussions' relevance today through the artistic research project *Zoom Blue Dot* (1990–2022), in which a revisitation of the Eameses' linear journey is studied through its technological and material support. The conclusion, "Afterthoughts on the Anthropocene," offers a reflection on the relation between the proxistant visual paradigm and our time of the Anthropocene, or what Bruno Latour also has called the new climate regime.[113] Here we broaden our scope through an extended contemplation on the work by Robert Smithson in the context of several scenes from the film *Gravity* (2013), directed by Alfonso Cuarón. These final reflections underscore how the current paradigm of proxistant vision generates worldviews in which Earth is perceived as a geometrical model. Through these three vertical strata of machines—grounded, airborne, and orbital—each corresponding to the cartographic dimensions of motion, navigation, and scale, this study aims to offer a comprehensive insight into the twenty-first-century paradigm of proxistant vision.

I

GROUNDED MACHINES

Ferriscope is a single-channel kinetic video installation in which the video seamlessly alternates between static and dynamic modes in a white cube with a white floor and ceiling.[1] It utilizes a motorized mirror to achieve this effect. In the static mode, the video is cast straight onto the wall. The video image—with a square, 1:1 aspect ratio—is black-and-white with particularly pronounced rounded corners. At a designated moment, the motorized mirror commences a gradual rotation, causing the image to travel vertically across the darkened room. As the rotation gains momentum, the black-and-white video metamorphoses into a continuous strip of pulsating color patterns. The acceleration continues until the mirror, after a minute, attains a peak velocity of 1,000 revolutions per minute, whereupon the rainbow effect achieves its zenith.

Following a brief spell at this maximum speed, the rotation decelerates, leading to a gradual desaturation of colors. Ultimately, the mirror reverts to its initial position, and the monochrome video is once again conventionally projected onto the wall. This cyclical process perpetuates indefinitely.

The video installation comprises aerial footage captured from four iconic observation wheels: the Ferris wheel (1893–1894), Wiener Riesenrad (1897), London Eye (2000), and Las Vegas High Roller (2014). The view from the original Ferris wheel is rendered through a sequence of twenty-four animated photographs and lantern slides, taken during its operation

Ferriscope (1893–2020)

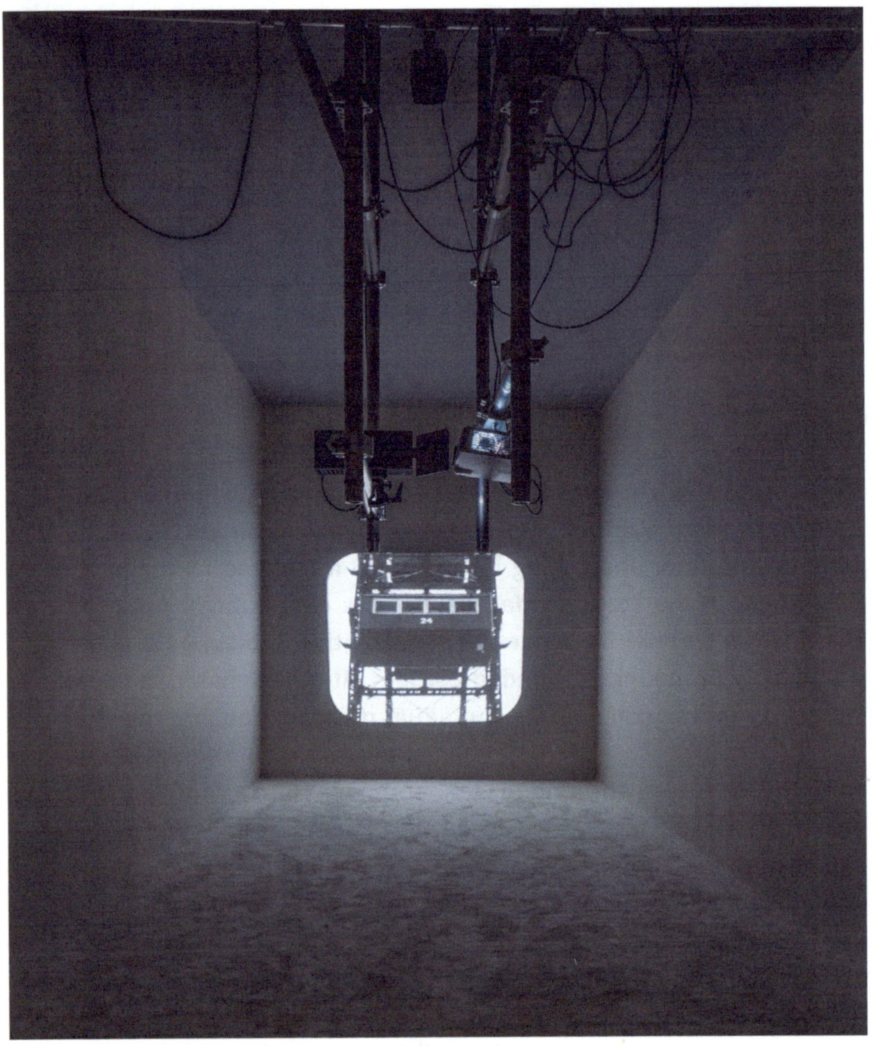

FIGURE I.1

Bull.Miletic. Installation view, *Ferriscope* (1893–2020) at the Museum of Craft and Design, San Francisco. Photo by Henrik Kam. Copyright © the artists.

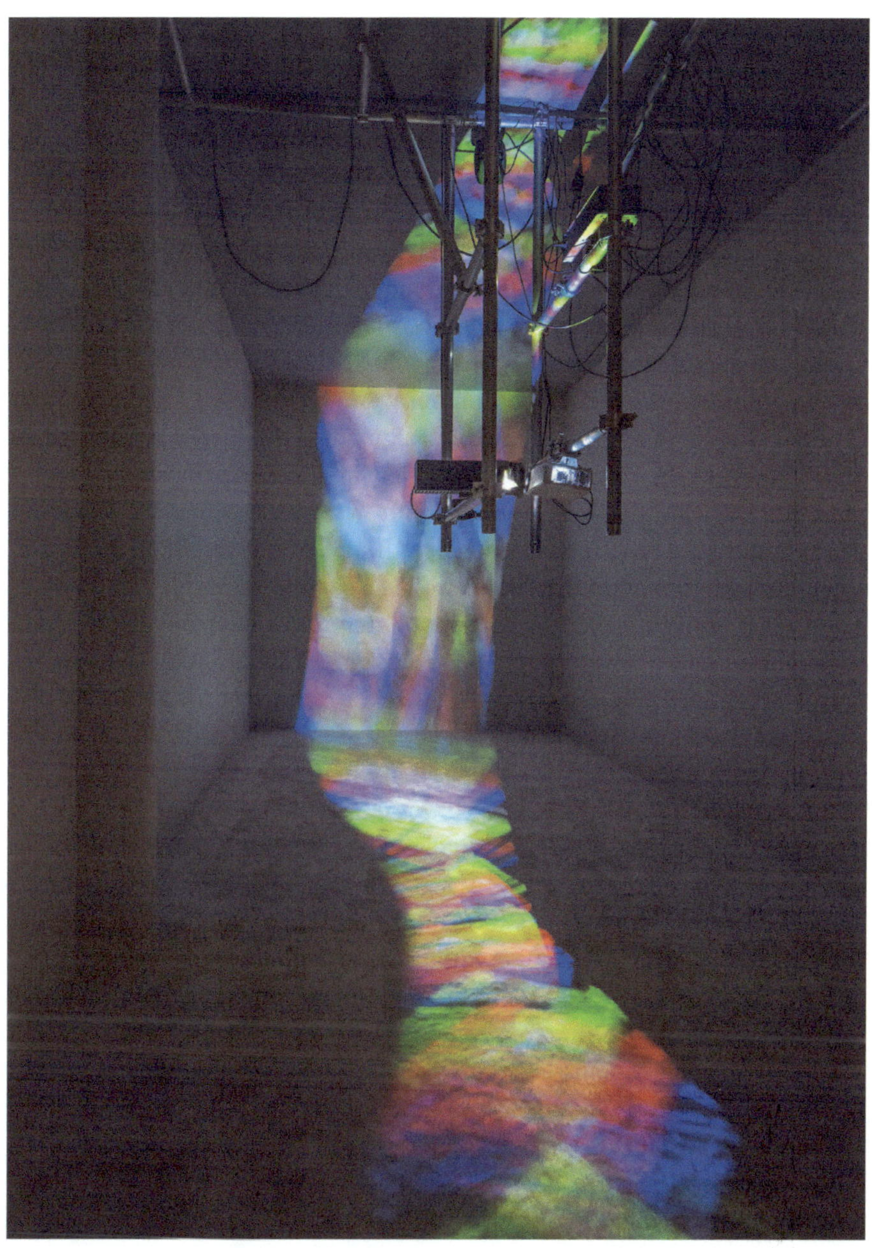

FIGURE I.2

Bull.Miletic. Installation view, *Ferriscope* (1893–2020) at the Museum of Craft and Design, San Francisco. Photo by Henrik Kam. Copyright © the artists.

on the Midway Plaisance between June 21, 1893 and April 29, 1894. These archival images are meticulously aligned to simulate the camera's position on the Wheel when each shot was captured.

The soundtrack is segmented into four distinct phases, each corresponding to the prominent sections of the video. Observed linearly, the initial phase features a two-and-a-half-minute excerpt of "The Ferris Wheel Waltz," commissioned by George W. G. Ferris Jr. and originally sold as sheet music memorabilia. This passionate melody evokes the exhilarating experience of an amorous couple's ride on the Ferris wheel, accompanied by bright piano notes that set an uplifting tone for the subsequent sequences. As the video transitions to contemporary panoramas of Las Vegas and London, the camera's steady ascent highlights the intricate machinery and infrastructure of the modern wheels. The glass capsules attached to the outer rims are particularly prominent, with encapsulated spectators gently entering and exiting the frame. An abrupt cessation of the music coincides with the sudden conclusion of this video section.

After a brief pause, the mechanical hum of a slowly advancing slide projector heralds a new form of image movement. Sequentially, all twenty-four "slides" depicting various views from the original Ferris wheel are projected, accompanied by the narrated libretto of "The Ferris Wheel Waltz," interspersed with extensive pauses between verses. The twenty-fifth "slide" in this sequence transitions into a video still from one of the Wiener Riesenrad sequences, which gradually animates into a moving image. At this juncture, the elusive sounds of a glass harmonica become more prominent, marking the onset of the third and shortest phase of the soundtrack. The lattice structure of the observation wheel, with its riveted steel beams and suspended spokes—an epitome of Victorian engineering—gracefully traverses the screen, fragmenting the image into a kaleidoscopic chiaroscuro of shifting geometric shapes. This sequence transitions back into the "slide" animation, now with a markedly accelerated rate of change. The individual "slides" swap so rapidly that distinguishing one from the other becomes impossible—they optically blend into one another, creating a vibrating field of animated configurations. The abstraction of the image is further heightened by the amalgamation of creaking mechanical sounds and deep droning electronic tones, constituting the final phase of the soundtrack.

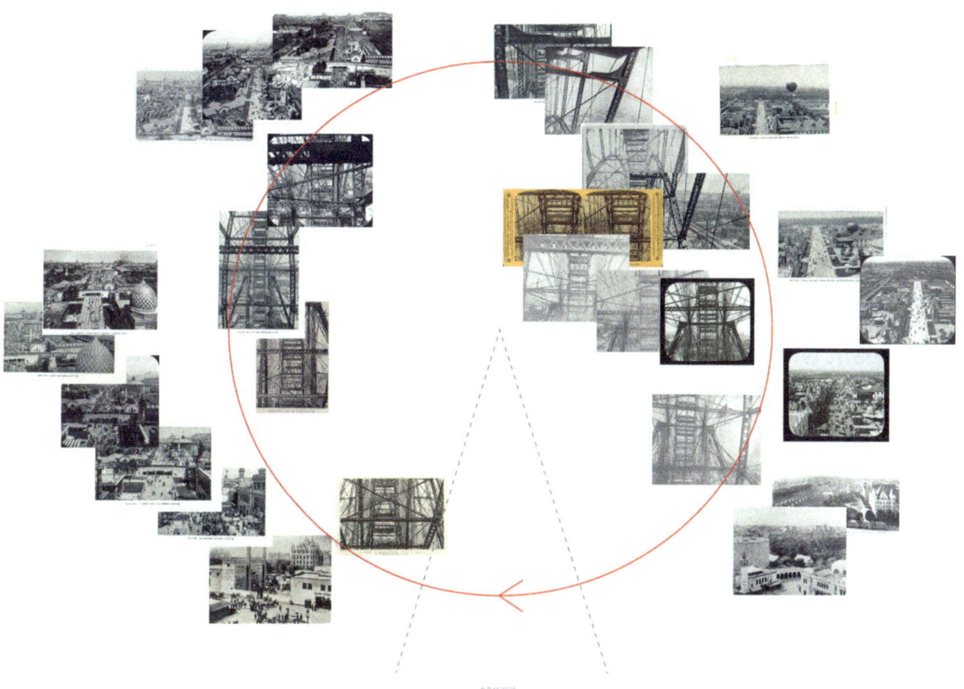

FIGURE I.3

Diagram with photographs taken from the original Ferris wheel at the 1893 Chicago World's Fair. Copyright © Bull.Miletic.

As the camera slowly tracks closer, the pulsating image of rapidly shifting "slides" intensifies. The flicker from the shifting "slides" grows more pronounced with each increment of magnification until the projection begins to traverse vertically around the room. Each revolution amplifies the colors and elongates the image vertically. The resulting rainbow effect evokes the mesmerizing iridescence of a soap bubble. Upon returning to its conventional display, the camera embarks on a spiraling flyover of a sprawling desert city on an atmosphere-less planet, zooming from its outskirts to a colossal wheel at its center. It soon becomes evident that this giant wheel is a 3D-animated model of the Las Vegas High Roller. The camera passes straight through the wheel's axle, and as it emerges from the other side, it is catapulted into outer space, revealing Earth gently spinning at its center. Before the contours of the continents become discernible, the globe morphs into a spinning diagram of Isaac Newton's Color Wheel, which then transitions into the spinning diagram of Tarot's Wheel of Fortune. This circular journey concludes after nine minutes, echoing the duration of an uninterrupted ride on the original Ferris wheel. "The Ferris Wheel Waltz" then recommences, perpetuating the cycle indefinitely. It would be great if these work-descriptions for each section could be in a different font i.e. Courier, or have a design that makes it stand out from the rest of the text. (see Anne Friederg, *The Virtual Window*, for reference).

1

THE WHEEL BEFORE THE REEL

"A ride on [Ferris wheel] still feels like flying to the moon—and oh-oh-oooh, the view!"[1]

The continuous circular motion of the observation wheel takes excited spectators on a smooth ride between the pedestrian street view and the spectacular bird's-eye perspective. The contemporary sizes and functions of this grounded machine have grown exponentially in recent years. Most significantly, they have changed location and thus status, from being a mere fairground attraction to becoming the epitome of the metropolitan skyline at the very center of the urban environment. On December 31, 1999, the 443-foot-high, or 135-meter-high, London Eye (re)launched the interest in large-scale observation wheels and unleashed a rivaling appetite for ever-grander designs worldwide.

In 2002, Sky Dream Fukuoka, at a heigh of 393 feet or 120 meters, opened in Japan, promptly followed by the construction of a number of observation wheels with similar proportions such as the Star of Nanchang at 525 feet or 160 meters (2006), the Singapore Flyer at 541 feet or 165 meters (2008), the Las Vegas High Roller at 550 feet or 168 meters (2014), the Eye of Bohai Sea at 476 feet or 145 meters (2018), and the Dubai Eye at 820 feet or 250 meters (2021), to name but a few.[2]

Furthermore, the New York Wheel, at 630 feet or 192 meters, was under construction until 2018.[3] These giant observation wheels continue to offer

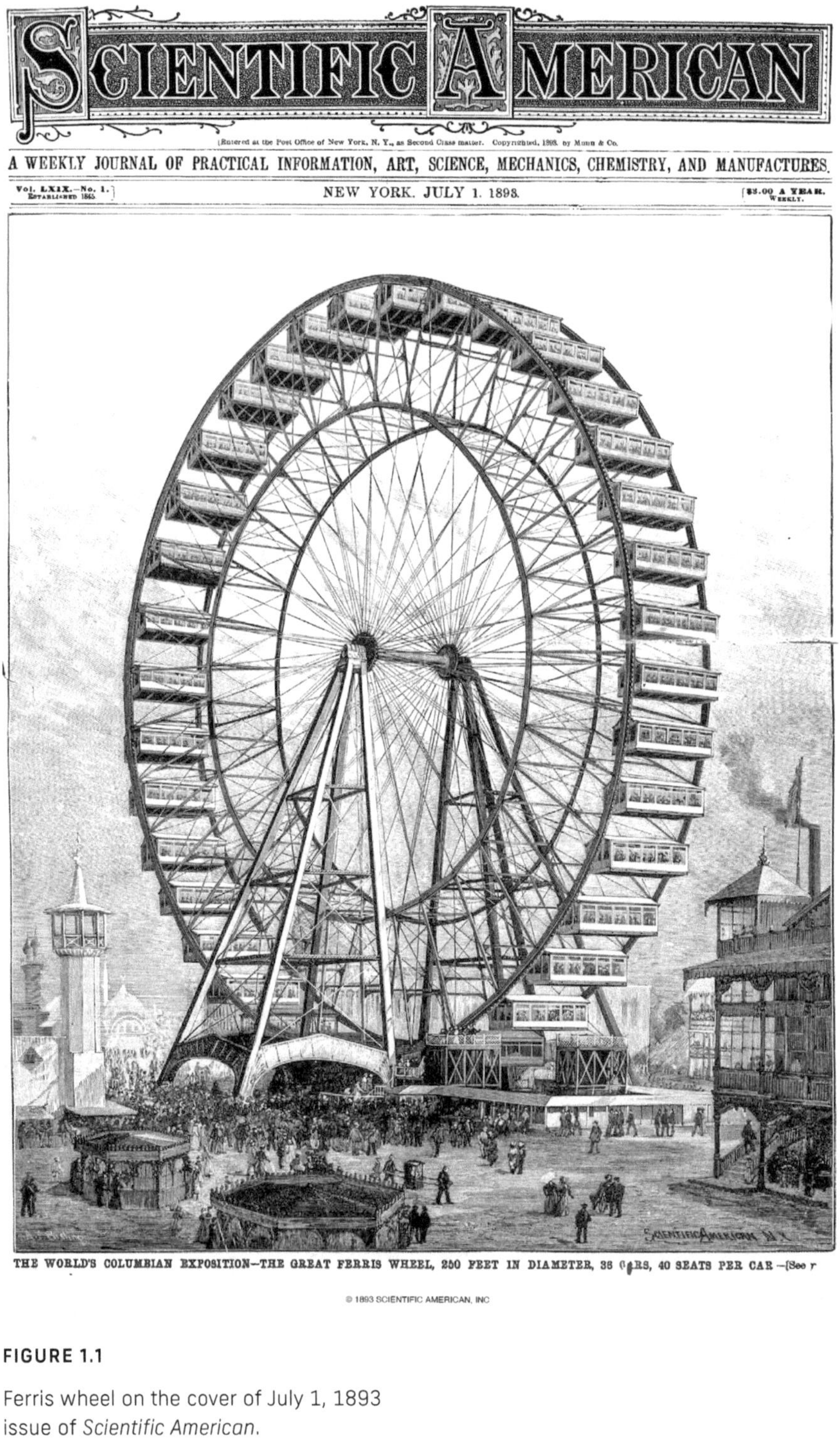

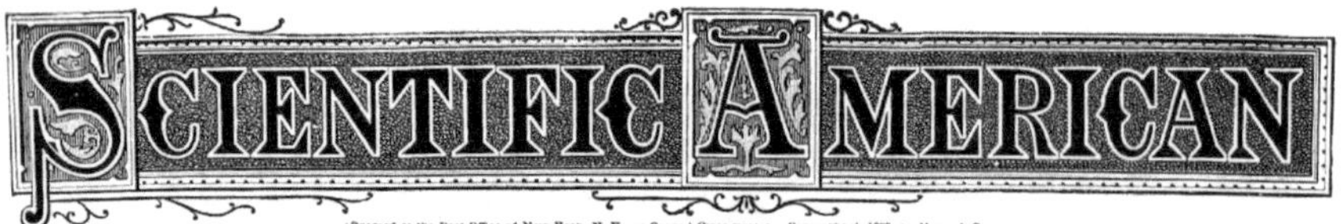
SCIENTIFIC AMERICAN

[Entered at the Post Office of New York, N. Y., as Second Class matter. Copyrighted, 1893, by Munn & Co.

A WEEKLY JOURNAL OF PRACTICAL INFORMATION, ART, SCIENCE, MECHANICS, CHEMISTRY, AND MANUFACTURES.

Vol. LXIX.—No. 1. ESTABLISHED 1845.] NEW YORK, JULY 1, 1893. [$3.00 A YEAR. WEEKLY.

THE WORLD'S COLUMBIAN EXPOSITION—THE GREAT FERRIS WHEEL, 250 FEET IN DIAMETER, 36 CARS, 40 SEATS PER CAR.—[See r

FIGURE 1.1

Ferris wheel on the cover of July 1, 1893 issue of *Scientific American*.

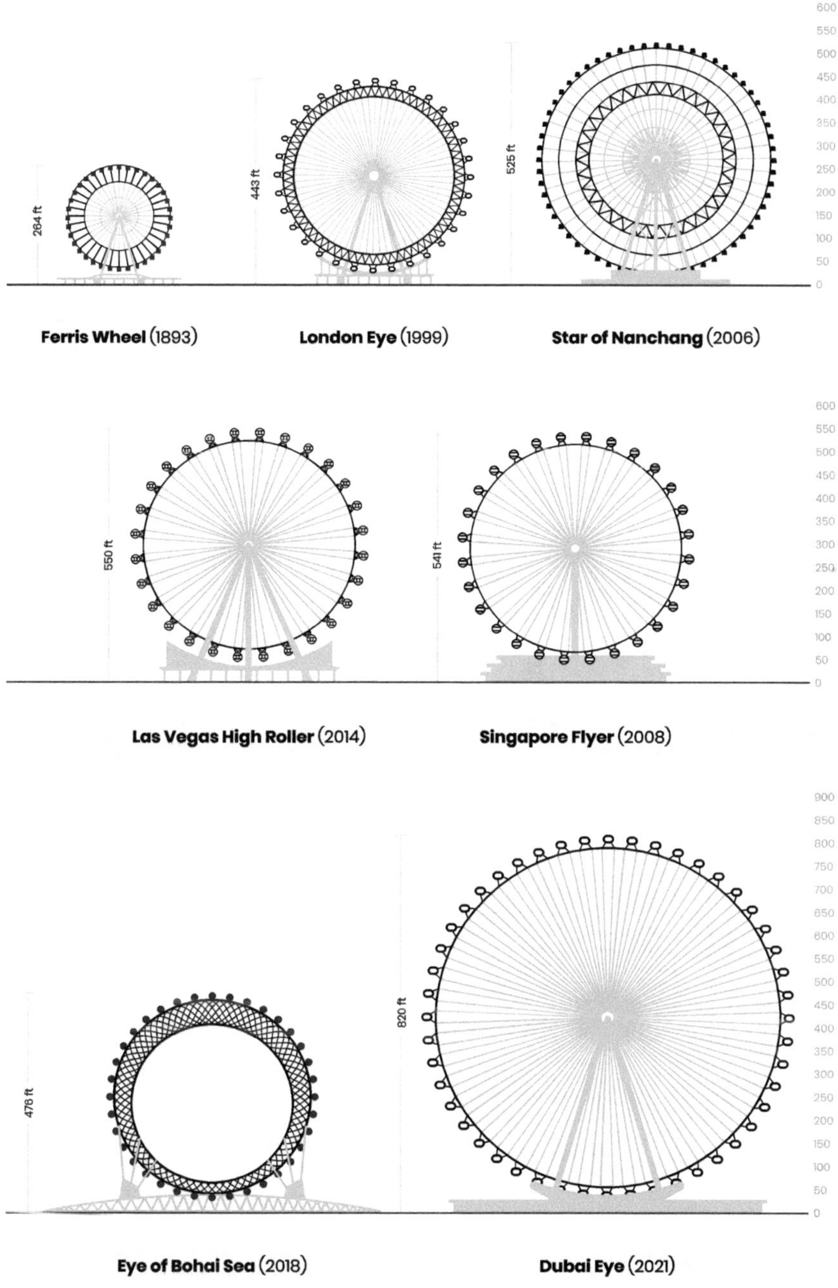

FIGURE 1.2

Diagram of notable Ferris wheels worldwide.

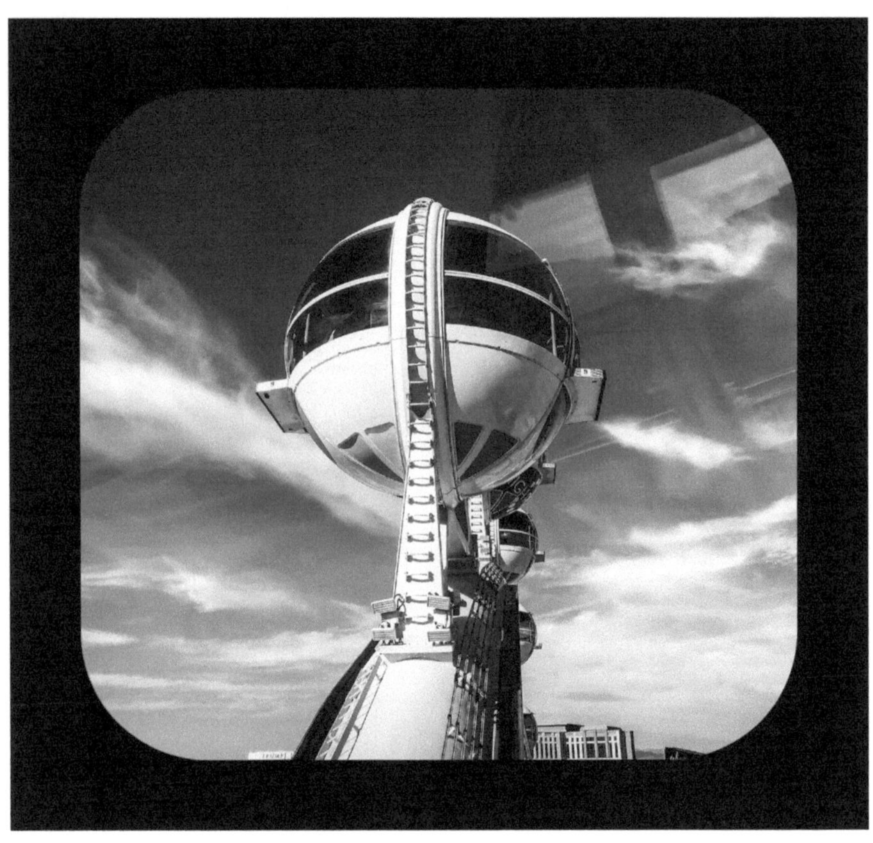

FIGURE 1.3

Bull.Miletic. Video still from *Ferriscope* (1893–2020) showing a capsule on the Las Vegas High Roller. Copyright © the artists.

a mobilized visual experience of the cityscape, suspended between total overview and control on the one hand, and vertigo and instability on the other. The smooth flight from elevated distance to street-level proximity offered by these wheels exemplifies what we call proxistant vision. But how is this apparent wheel-o-mania in the physical world related to the 3D-animated flythrough effect that currently multiplies across the twenty-first-century media sphere?

Our approach to this question started by recognizing that the experience of being on the wheel produces a cinematic experience. This is based on the simple fact that the body remains still while it is being moved mechanically through space. This experience activates some of the same perceptual complexities perceived in front of a moving image that moves the body within the space of the film through the technique of camera movement. Just as traveling on a train or in a car can be experienced as watching moving images on the silver screen, the observation wheel's magnificent panoramic views by way of a concentric journey can inspire ponderings on the mediation of movement and time in film and video.

When one experiences the exterior scenery from an observation wheel, gently rotating at a snail's pace, the bodily involvement can be said to evoke a cinematic experience.

It is a simple comparison, yet also complex and affective. Studying it moves us closer to some of the fundamental questions about how camera movement moves through perceptual uncertainty.

Considering the observation wheel as an optical device imbued with cinematic qualities builds further on our work on the revolving restaurant.[4] Here, we traced the revolving restaurant's cine-dream and panoramic desire through a genealogy of the moving and projected image. We argue that the 360-degree revolving view can be seen as "readymade cinema," or what we call *cinéma trouvé*—a specific cinematic experience outside the conventional cinematic apparatus. We developed this argument based on Wolfgang Schivelbusch's concept of "panoramic perception," a concept he develops based on his reading of Walter Benjamin. In essence, "panoramic perception" describes the visual transformation of spatial experience introduced by the railway journey in the nineteenth century or, in Schivelbusch's words: "Panoramic perception, in contrast to traditional perception, no longer belonged to the same space as the

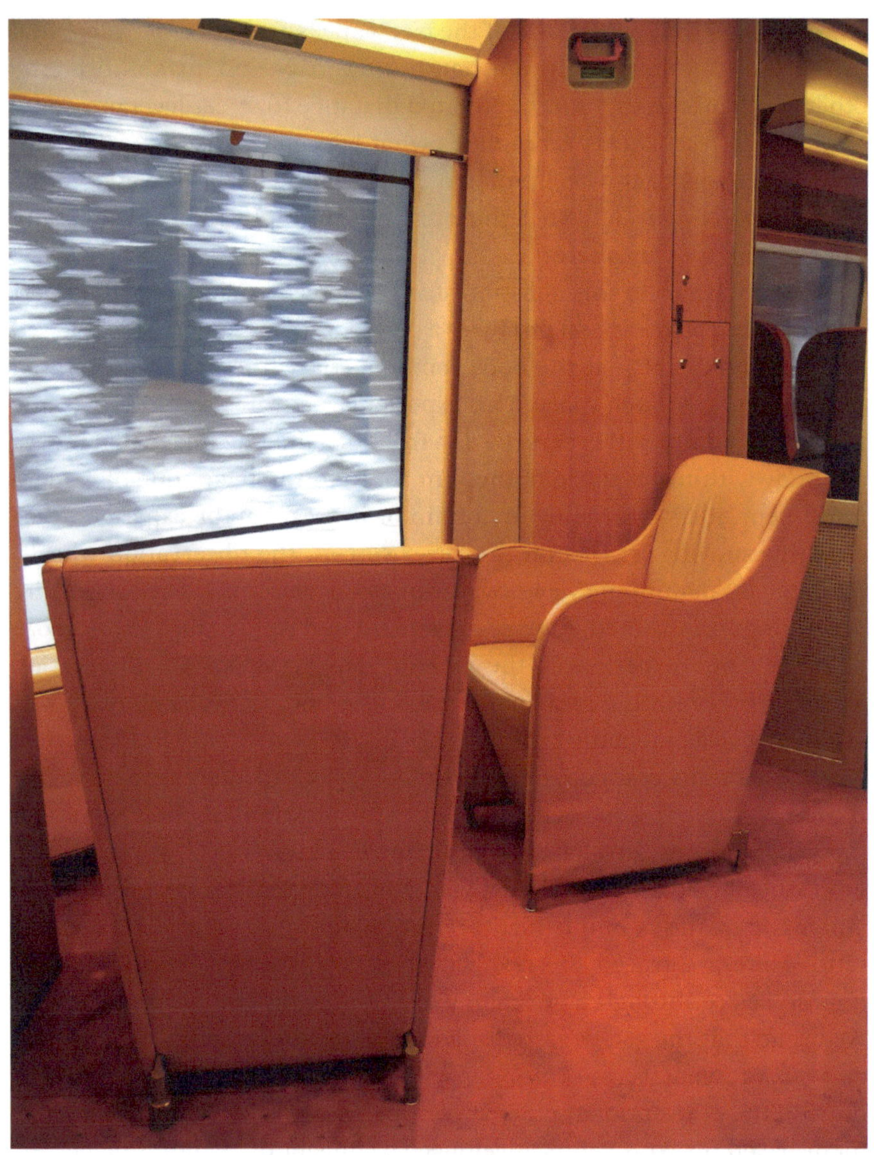

FIGURE 1.4

The seating arrangement for the observation on board the NSB train bound for Trondheim, Norway. Photo by Bull.Miletic. Copyright © Bull.Miletic.

PLATE 98

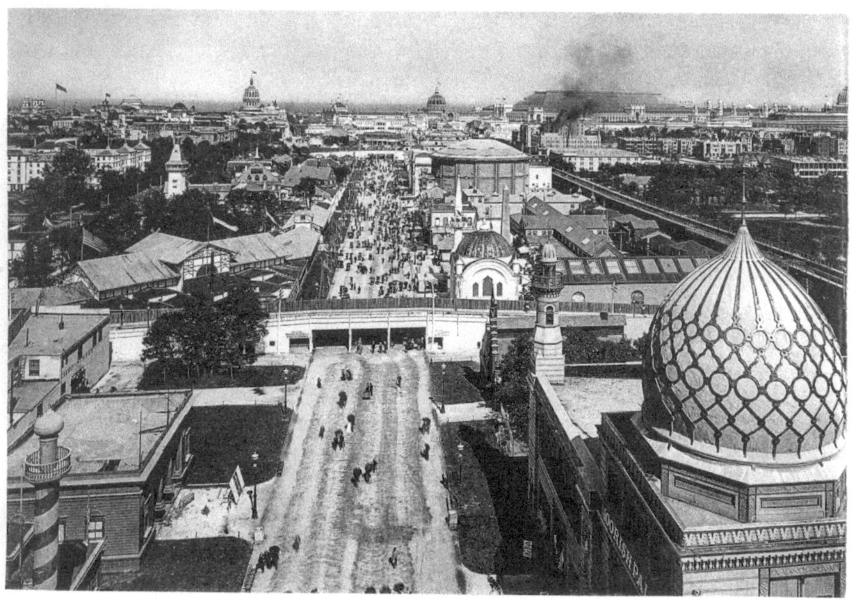

THE MIDWAY, FROM FERRIS WHEEL, LOOKING EAST.

FIGURE 1.5

View of the World's Columbian Exposition in Chicago from the Ferris wheel (1893).

perceived objects: the traveler saw the objects, landscapes, etc. *through* the apparatus which moved him through the world."[5] Similar ideas have been articulated by a number of early cinema scholars, such as Anne Friedberg and Giuliana Bruno. Bruno, for example, describes the city as a site of mobility in which "the new architectures of transit and travel culture prepared the ground for the invention of the moving image, the very epitome of modernity."[6] Friedberg has developed the concept of "the virtual mobile spectator" that emerged in the nineteenth century, when industrial machines started to powerfully influence perception of space and time. Machines of mobility such as "trains, steam ships, bicycles, elevators, escalators, moving walkways, and later, automobiles and airplanes, changed the relation between sight and bodily movement." Exhibition architecture such as "winter gardens, arcades, department stores, [and] museums," encourage mobilized spectatorship on a pedestrian level as well. Such scholarship, furthermore, pays attention to Foucault's argument about the epistemic shift of modernity to "*un regime panoptique*," which is signaled by a reordering of power and knowledge to vision.[7] This can also be understood in the context of the technological sublime, according to David Nye's notion of the term.[8]

The term *cinéma trouvé*, however, works primarily to designate such experiences of cinema by way of other means in contemporary times. Referencing to the French avant-garde artist Marcel Duchamp's concept of the *objet trouvé*, *cinéma trouvé* is an experience powered precisely by the displacement of contexts. This logic of displacement, however, works somewhat differently in *cinéma trouvé*. The cinema-out-of-the-cinema experience that makes up *cinéma trouvé* is interpreted as an inverted kinetic experience, in that the physical reality is experienced as cinema on the basis of previous moving image experiences. In other words, the bodily experience of being mechanically moved through a physical environment is con-fused, as in literally *con* (with)*fused* (blended), with the memory of previous cinematic experiences of, for example, helicopter flight, phantom ride, road movie, simulator, and so on. The trigger for this experience preexists in various architectural and infrastructural constructions, including, for example, observation wheels, revolving restaurants, panoramic elevators, escalators, or any mechanism that physically "displaces" the viewer from one perceptual mode into another. Hence, *cinéma trouvé* occurs when the two experiences (cinematic and physical realities) couple into an indistinguishable perceptual mode. So, in *cinéma trouvé*, instead of cinema (the object) being "displaced," it is the viewer who is "displaced" from one visual mode into another.

Cinéma trouvé can furthermore be seen in relation to Pavle Levi's concept of a "cinema by other means." Here, cinema is understood as a mental state of existence that is remediated through other forms of cultural expressions. Continuing the line of thought previously addressed by filmmakers and critics such as André Bazin, Sergei Eisenstein, and Edgar Morin, Levi is tracing a "'pure' cine-desire," which in his view can be located in "a desire subsequently sustained and perpetuated through the dialectic of film and cinema, of the two non-identical though entirely interdependent phenomena."[9] To fully explain what is at stake "when cinema is presented in the form of a diagrammatic drawing (Picabia, Man Ray), or a theatrical performance (Picabia)," Levi uses the term "retrograde remediation," which he sees as a further development of Jay Bolter and Richard Grusin's category of "remediation," a term used to describe the process when newer media appropriates and surpasses, but also on some level preserves, older forms. Evoking the well-known media theorist Marshall McLuhan and his concept of how "the content of one medium is always another medium," "retrograde remediation" is, according to Levi, articulating "instances of remediation distinguished by some inherent discrepancy, by a pronounced practical/technological *inadequacy* of one ("older") medium to fully assimilate certain aspects of another." This idea complicates the linear progression of new technology by also reinventing and rearticulating its key aspects in other media.[10]

In this way, we can study the observation wheel as a cinematic device through the lens of older cine-cartographic practices and techniques pertaining to concepts of mobility and virtual travel. The most prominent case for such a study is the construction that became known as the paradigmatic "original" Ferris wheel at the Chicago World's Fair in 1893. Our focus here is on the observation wheel as an optical device and on the transformation of vision that occurred in the late nineteenth century, when a popular fairground ride turned into what can be seen as a giant cinematic experience. We start our journey at this grounded level from where an astonished nineteenth-century audience is lifted off

Earth's surface in slow-turning loops between ground proximity and elevated distance.

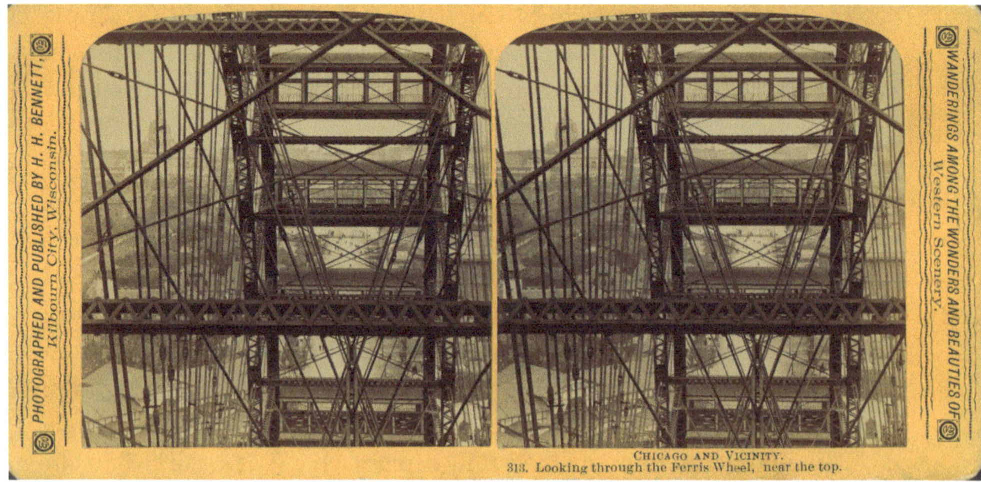

THE GREAT CHICAGO WHEEL

The wheel as a fairground ride constitutes a long evolution of pleasure wheels that met a fertile milieu of industrial-scale amusement park development at the turn of the twentieth century. Presumably, "pleasure wheels" and "ups-and-downs" existed as early as the water wheels and windmills, while the earliest tangible descriptions of these types of constructions date back to the seventeenth century in the Balkans, India, and Siberia.[11] The idea of employing motion solely for accentuating a visual sensation, however, received full attention only in the late nineteenth century. A boom in fairground installations of aerial mobility emerged in this period as a counterpart to the growing popularity and expansion

FIGURE 1.6

Stereoscopic photograph from the Ferris wheel, World's Fair Chicago (1893).

of amusement parks preceding World War I. As historian John F. Kasson has shown, this development coincided with a critical period in American history, in which citizens willingly but strenuously adapted to the new nation's urban industrial becoming.[12] These critical decades around the turn of the nineteenth century negotiated the major social and economic transformations that formed the basis for a new and rapidly growing mass culture.[13] Spearheading this development was the Chicago World's Columbian Exhibition, crowned by the industrial version of the Ferris wheel as a lasting icon.

Perhaps surprisingly in light of its central place and iconic status at the Chicago fair, Ferris' proposal for a wheel was not part of Director of Works Daniel Burnham's original plans. Pressured by the overwhelming success of the Eiffel Tower, the planners of the 1893 Chicago World's Columbian Exposition desperately sought a rivaling design that would outshine the paramount glory of the 1889 Exposition Universelle in Paris. When most of the received proposals figured larger versions of Gustave Eiffel's ingenious design, Burnham resorted to the public announcement that "[m]ere bigness is not what is wanted! Something novel, original, daring and unique must be designed and built if American engineers are to retain their prestige and standing."[14] Ferris Jr.'s enthusiastic proposal to construct a giant observation wheel as the centerpiece of the fair did not find immediate acceptance. Ferris' expertise in large-scale engineering and ample experience in bridge constructions as well as iron and steel testing, however, worked in favor of his case.[15] The convincing detail that eventually secured the deal, was that, unlike Eiffel, who had resorted to iron, Ferris proposed his wheel be constructed in alloy steel—the new material of extraordinary properties that was about to revolutionize city planning.[16]

Ferris is often portrayed as the singular genius in the narrative of the giant wheel but he should rather be seen as a mediator in a fertile milieu. Pleasure wheels in the young nation around this time not only rapidly grew in popularity but also changed their key feature.[17] Supposedly inspired by an old waterwheel where he grew up, Ferris's plans for a large wheel, with partner William Gronau, had already started back in 1891, the same year William Somers installed his "Roundabout" in Atlantic City, New Jersey.[18] The apparent success of the Roundabout motivated Somers to build two more that same year—one in Asbury Park, New Jersey, and another one on Coney Island, New York.[19] Somers's proposal for installing one such Roundabout at the Chicago Fair, however, was refused. The Garden City Company then paid Somers for his patent and ran the Roundabout outside the official fairgrounds.[20]

They also filed an unsuccessful patent infringement lawsuit against Ferris. At least three other applications for building observation wheels at the fairground site were also refused. H. W. Fowler, a Chicago industrialist whose proposal for an observation wheel in the shape of a Dutch Windmill was handed in prior to Ferris's but was rejected, explained that this simply illustrated how most novel, useful, and popular devices come to the mind of several distantly located individuals at the same moment.[21] What Ferris did bring to the fair, however, was expertise, knowledge, and experience from the testing and use of steel.

Another associated milieu for the Ferris wheel at the fair, and thus for the early development of proxistant vision, was the city of Chicago itself. Chicago had been the world's fastest-growing city for several decades and acted as a giant melting pot of immigration, industrialization, and modernization.[22] Chicago's socioeconomic context in the 1890s was a severe incident of a town that had outgrown itself—a merely sixty-year-old city of immigrant population from a variety of cultures and social backgrounds had just undergone an enormous industrial expansion.[23] Within only a few decades, Chicago's population had expanded to reach one million inhabitants, making it the second largest city in the United States, after New York.[24] Designed to commemorate the quatercentenary of Columbus's arrival in America, the 1893 World's Fair was thus seen as a potential to secure Chicago's everlasting status among America's great metropolises. At the city center was the Union Stock Yards, Chicago's meatpacking district, which securely maintained the city's bad reputation. When Chicago ultimately received the well-lobbied yet unlikely honor of hosting the World's Columbian Exposition, defeating both New York and Washington cultural elites, the city's organizers and architects were motivated to make sure it would go down in history as one of the most lavish examples.[25] An additional factor regarding Chicago was the devastating fire of 1871 that had, paradoxically, provided architects and engineers with fresh experience and knowledge from a rapidly rebuilt city through new building

(No Model.)

4 Sheets—Sheet 1.

W. SOMERS.

ROUNDABOUT.

No. 489,238.

Patented Jan. 3, 1893.

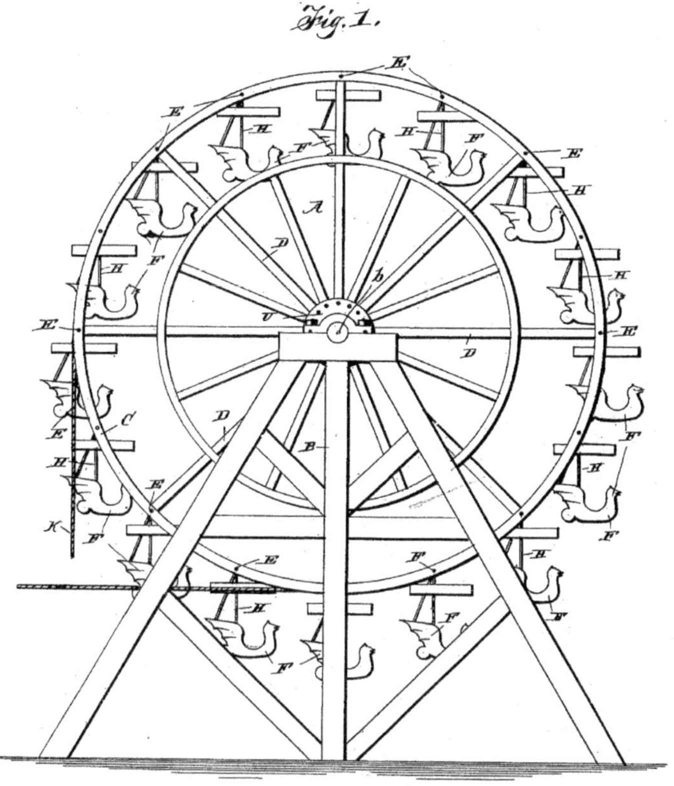

Witnesses

Samuel Kir.

George H. Parmelee

Inventor

William Somers

by E.W. Anderson

his Attorney

THE NORRIS PETERS CO., PHOTO-LITHO., WASHINGTON, D. C.

FIGURE 1.7

William Somers. *Roundabout*. No. 489,238. Patented January 3, 1893. Courtesy of United States Patent Office.

materials and novel skyscraper techniques. Several scholars and authors have argued that the Chicago World's Fair operated as a conscious project of urban recreation on behalf of genteel reformers seeking to control social order and elevate public taste.[26] Such ideals equally influenced the proxistant vision as articulated by the giant Ferris wheel.

This context lets us better grasp the impact of Ferris' proposal. The World's Fair organizers were faced with the aforementioned challenges, and it was eventually decided to divide the fair in two sections: The main section known as the White City, and a side project known as the Midway Plaisance. The former, a compound of streamlined neoclassical architecture emanating high ideals, the latter, a privately financed fairground site balancing on the edge of the morally acceptable.[27] Adjunct to the White City, the Midway Plaisance was one mile long, six hundred feet wide, and it stretched westward to Washington Park. Visitors encountered a creative mixture of different shops, restaurants, theaters, and vulgar dance shows, of which a reputed spectacle included an extensive exhibit of indigenous people from far-off regions of the world, showcasing their animals, tools, and sometimes risqué public performances. Crowds pushed into the "Streets of Cairo" to get a glimpse of "Little Egypt" and the "Hootchy-Kootchy" dancers, while others pursued the latest in visual tricks and wonders, such as Muybridge's Zoöpraxiscope, panorama paintings, or a ride in a tethered balloon.[28]

Ferris' giant wheel figured within this surgical split of disciplinary installments as the Fair's largest attraction, both in size and revenue. Carrying some 38,000 passengers daily on dazzling twenty-minute vertical revolutions, the "original" Ferris wheel offered sweeping views of the fairgrounds, Lake Michigan, and the downtown skyline in the distance.[29] Historians of the fair often point out that this clear distinction between the "high ideals" of industrial progress and "cheap thrills" of all sorts powerfully signaled the attitudes and moral judgments from the fair's organizers and supporters at large. As Kasson has argued, their main agenda was to accentuate a sharp distinction between the arts that elevate and cultivate the spirit, and practices that merely gratify the senses.[30] Mark Dorrian has further pointed out that the Ferris wheel later came to symbolize the very circulation of ambiguities such expositions inhabited, oscillating between the prestige of high engineering achievement and a carnivalesque ride of mere entertainment with the lure of escapism's eternal descent.[31] However, as Jonathan Crary's important study has shown, both arenas can be understood to have held a disciplinary effect. While the authority of the White City relied on cultivated vision, the Midway Plaisance structured a lower-class audience through the attention-grabbing means of spectacular entertainment.[32] This shows how the change from pleasure wheel to observation wheel is more than a simple instance of nomenclature, since mere pleasure—a denigrated lure of entertainment and deceit in the context of the World's Fair—enlists elevation to the status of observation.[33] With a height of 264 feet or 80.4 meters, the "original" Ferris wheel exhibited the epitome of modernist steel engineering capabilities in the service of entertainment, thereby bridging the fair's imagined division by way of a proxistant vision.

As an apparatus of mobilized observation, Ferris' wheel both responded to and participated in shaping a whole new mode of seeing from above. While the giant industrial steel wheel maintained a slower pace than smaller pleasure wheels, it combined such slow motion with an emphasis on observation. Ferris' wheel introduced a smooth ride between the distance of high elevation and the proximity of a street-level view. Ferris's observation wheel thus added cyclical motion to the Eiffel Tower's grand but stationary vista without calling upon the sensation of a pleasure wheel's "cheap ride." A proof of Ferris's emphasis on observation can be found in a quote from Anderson's historical account, upon which a passenger complained after the ride that "he had not felt the whirling sensation he had expected after having ridden small pleasure wheels," and thus he demanded his fifty cents back. As Anderson explains, "Ferris accepted the complaint as a compliment—he wanted people to feel safe and often pointed out that his was an observation wheel, not an amusement wheel."[34] A more welcomed account was that of the passenger Marietta Holley, who recalled that "[M]y feelin's when I wuz a-bein' hoisted up through the air wuz about half and half—Half sublimity and orr as I looked out on the hull glory of the world spread out at my feet, and Lake Michigan, and everything."[35] This was the early formation of a decidedly cinematic smooth proxistant experience. Another insightful remark was offered by Robert Graves' favorable review of the Ferris wheel at the time, which indicates its visual power transcending the fear of elevation:

Slowly, with just enough trembling and oscillating to make the nerves of passengers quiver, the wheel must make one entire revolution. By this time the occupants of the coaches have become somewhat accustomed to the novel situation. They have ceased to think of the possible danger and are occupied with the beauty of the panorama which lies far below them.[36]

Two illustrations were originally published with this article, one was *of* the wheel and another one *from* the wheel, featuring two spectators glued to the car's window. This hints at the technical operation of the grounded machine that departed from a mere carousel ride to produce a powerful view.

The slow motion between overview and close-up that distinguished Ferris' large-scale wheel from the smaller pre-industrial wheels is furthermore clearly communicated in the choice of the photographically captured images presented in the Wheel's official souvenir booklet.[37]

Not being in the possession of a movie camera, the booklet still captures the smooth proxistant ride in a decidedly cinematic fashion as nine out of thirteen photographs in the booklet are taken *from* the wheel.[38] On page one, we find a celebratory text informing the reader about the unprecedented engineering achievements, the strenuous time frame, and every technical detail of the construction. Subsequently, a narrative is laid out across eleven carefully chosen photographs, in which a change in point-of-view is matched by the actual ride experience. The booklet starts with the total image of the wheel as seen from the ground level, flanked on the opposite side with a close-up of the wheel's entrance. The next spread

FIGURE 1.8

Front cover of the *Souvenir of a Ride on the Ferris Wheel at the World's Fair, Chicago*. American Engraving Co. (1893). Courtesy of Douglas County Historical Society, Nevada.

FIGURE 1.9

Lantern slide reproduction of the view through the Ferris wheel (1893).

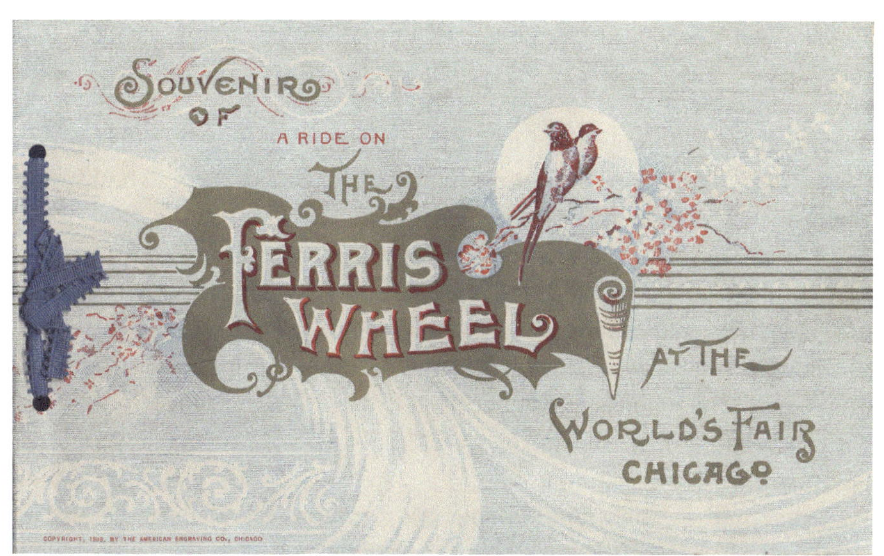
Souvenir of
A Ride on
The Ferris Wheel
at the
World's Fair
Chicago

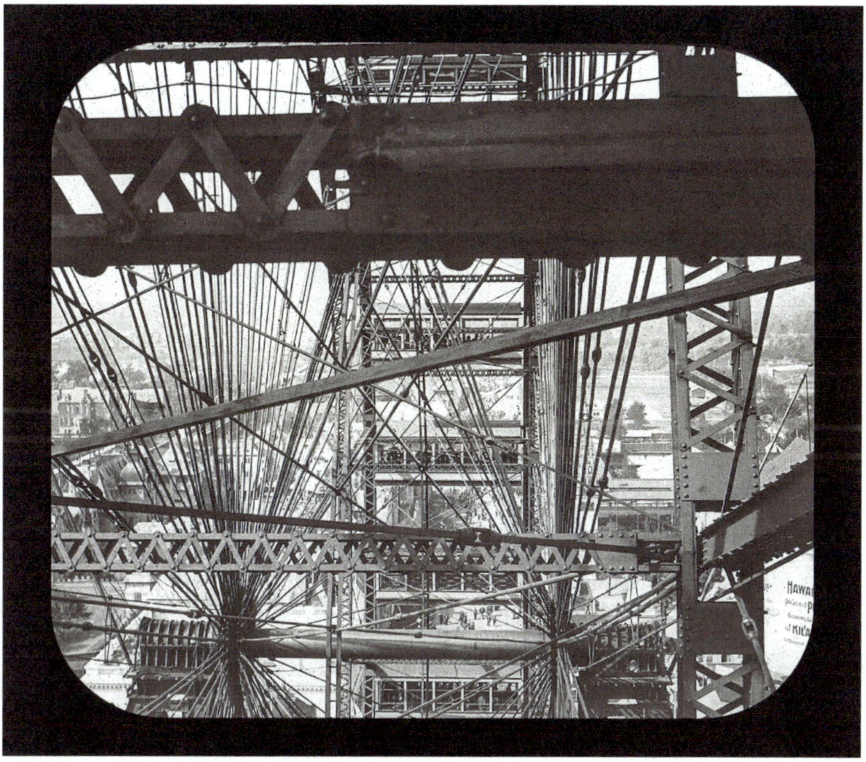

shows the first and second stops with an unobstructed view east towards the White City. The next photograph bears the title: "Third stop—A bird's eye view: south-east," and on the right: "A south-east view part of wheel." The view in this photograph and the subsequent two are seen through the sprockets of the wheel—a newly formed cityscape enmeshed in the wheel's steel-spoked structure.

The last picture from the ride shows the "sixth stop—looking down west, Midway Plaisance and Cottage Grove Avenue entrance," without any of the wheel's structure in view.[39] A subsequent image shows a side view of the wheel before the last picture moves back in historical time to an image from the wheel's construction. Miniaturizing the human workers within it, this image shows the oversized steel axle being prepared for its hoisting.

Presented in such fashion that it articulates the experience of the ride itself, these images show how the aerial views from the Ferris wheel were made to align with the conventions of landscape paintings, panoramas, and prospects of the seventeenth and eighteenth centuries. More importantly, however, they also caught this visual form of an elevated view on its way down into the glee and gloss of emerging mass tourism. Yet, Ferris's enrichment of these image conventions within a newfound mobilizing technology of a cinematic ride re-injects the previous desire for the elevated view to inhabit the flavors of future and progress. Aside from the nine photographs published in the *Souvenir of a Ride on the Ferris Wheel at the World's Fair, Chicago* (1893), our archival research resulted in the discovery of a total of thirty-nine photographs taken *from* the wheel (see figure I.3). These photographs communicate not only the wheel's impressive design but also the pre-cinematic experience of the ride itself, that is, the aerial view in combination with a circular mechanical motion. It is exactly this spatial approximation between proximity and distance, the power of seeing from a high vantage point combined with street-level perspective through technological motion, that forms the historical equivalent of proxistant vision as it proliferates today across the twenty-first-century media sphere. This visual form produces the complex combination of a clear-sighted elevation, with dizziness, bafflement, and sheer spectacular wonder as it repeats the journey between proximity and distance.

The photographs in the Ferris wheel's official souvenir booklet resonate with the sequencing of still frames in a moving image, a technology showcased at the Fair in its embryonic phase. Scientific and artistic experiments to capture motion flourished in the period. A prototype for Thomas A. Edison's kinetoscope was initially shown to a convention of the National Federation of Women's Clubs on May 20, 1891, while Eadweard Muybridge's Zoöpraxiscope had been widely exhibited for over a decade.[40] Considering Edison's business-minded mentality, this situation could only inflame his intentions to exhibit the kinetoscope at the Chicago World's Fair in 1893, which, contrary to some beliefs based on publicity released by Edison, he did not do.[41] Muybridge, on the other hand, did project moving images and lectured about zoöpraxography in his own pavilion, solemnly entitled "Zoöpraxographical Hall," a venue largely considered as the first public cinema in history.[42] In light of our argument in this book, the Hall's physical proximity to the Ferris wheel is interesting to note.[43]

The two wheels, Ferris's giant 250-feet-wheel in diameter and Muybridge's twelve-inch glass-projection disc, might have been turning in the same direction, yet this early form of cinema didn't have the impact one would expect. Zoöpraxographical Hall "closed prematurely through lack of public interest—to be replaced by a painted panorama of Pompeii."[44] The brevity of its operation is evident in the Official Guide to Midway Plaisance, published on August 10, 1893, which "absolutely correctly" identifies attraction No. 11 as Pompeii Panorama instead of Zoöpraxographical Hall.[45] Given that the Fair opened to the public on May 1, 1893, and considering the logistics of repurposing the venue as well as the turnaround time for printing the guide, we may conclude that the operation of Zoöpraxographical Hall could not have exceeded a couple of months. Spectacle-thirsty fairgoers weren't yet ready for the magic of motion pictures. Despite this unfavorable turn of fate, the Hall's operation was well documented and celebrated among film historians.[46] Allegedly, Muybridge gave up experimenting with moving pictures after they failed to ignite the public imagination at the Fair.[47] Although the Ferris wheel became *the* most profitable attraction of the Fair, Muybridge's austere lecturing was displaced in the hubbub of the Midway. It would take decades before these two visual modalities emerged in the same cultural climate and met again in the form of the cinematic location establishing shot.

TURNING THE WHEEL OF WONDER

The transformation of the age-old pleasure wheel into the visionary icon of the Ferris wheel occurred during a period that, aside from Muybridge's Zoöpraxiscope, heralded a plethora of groundbreaking visual experiences in concert with industrial expansion and innovation. The thaumatrope was among the simplest of such optical devices or philosophical toys, consisting of a small circle-shaped piece of cardboard, with images on each side, and two strings attached onto the outer rim, forming a horizontal axis that allows twirling of the assembly.[48]

Common thaumatrope motifs were a bird on one side and a cage on the other or a portrait of a bald-headed person on one side and a wig on the other, for example. When rapidly twirled, the bird magically appeared *in* the cage and the bald character was suddenly no longer hairless. The sheer speed of twirling perceptually fused the two complementary images into a third, semi-transparent, composite. The effect, known as "persistence of vision" at the time, is explained today through a combination of, at least, two phenomena: the so-called "flicker fusion threshold" and the "*phi* phenomenon."[49] Nonetheless, the visual effect's true nature remains to this day only partially rationalized in strictly scientific terms. The general understanding is that the effect is produced within the threshold of visual perception, where a complex retinal activity is combined with the brain's effort in making sense out of the visual stimuli.

In his essay "Hand and Eye: Excavating a New Technology of the Image in the Victorian Era" (2012), film historian Tom Gunning releases the thaumatrope from its common role as a component in a teleological narrative leading to the cinema by showing us something of much greater importance. While similar effects were known, such as the flipping of a coin, Gunning observes that the production of the thaumatrope as both a commercial and a philosophical device in the 1820s signaled the need to control such perceptual effects by making them easily reproducible and integrated into a discourse. In this period, Gunning continues, we can "glimpse the appearance of a modern image culture, at once profoundly technological and perceptual: one whose novelty may lie in how deeply it coordinates the perceptual and the technological."[50] Gunning sees the thaumatrope as being particularly apt for a media archeological

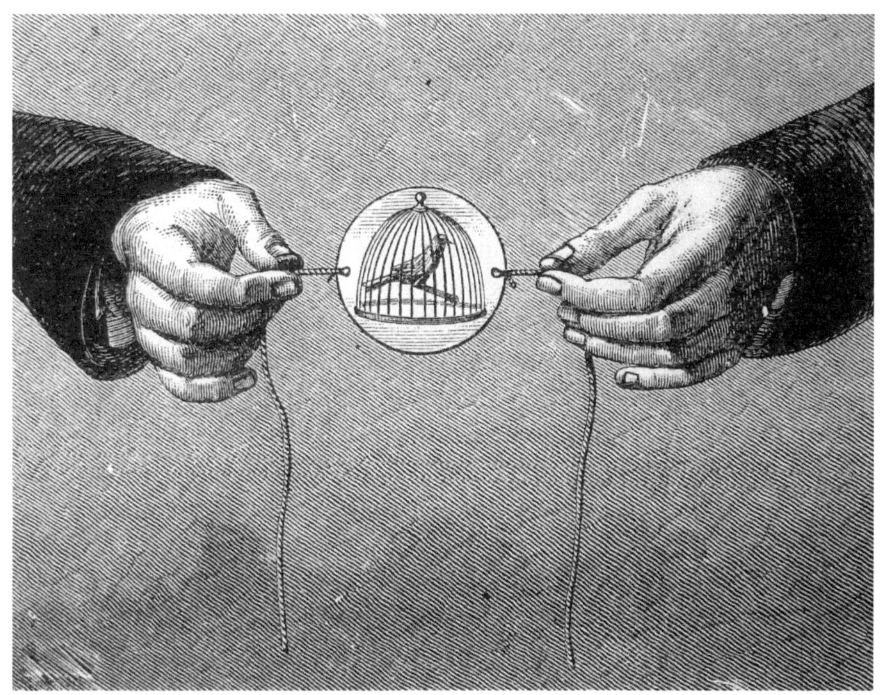

FIGURE 1.10

Illustration of a thaumatrope showing the fusion of two images, a bird and a cage.

investigation of this change since it exemplifies with great clarity how the nature of the image changed fundamentally through its integration with a specific technique.[51] It is exactly this early play of perceptual techniques and their integration with imaging, visualization, and representation that we see as particularly relevant for the proxistant vision that emerges on a grand scale by way of the giant Ferris wheel in 1893.

The thaumatrope was made up of the Greek words for wonder (*thauma*) and turn (*trope*) and translates as "wonderturner, or "a toy which performs wonders by turning around," as Tom Gunning puts it.[52] While "turning around" lingers with the mobilizing path of the Ferris wheel, the "wonder" accompanies the sheer experience of being lifted off the ground only to descend back to security after reaching the wheel's summit. Whereas in the Ferris wheel a stationary audience is moved mechanically through space, the thaumatrope inverts this relationship, using motion to create the perception of a static image. Here, we have a dialogue between stasis and movement, as well as proximity and distance, which develops "a third state." This is a state of perceptual metamorphosis, which in the case of the thaumatrope is achieved when the bird appears to be in the cage and in the case of the observation wheel, when the observer's perceptual mode transitions into a cinematic experience. The metamorphic stage is nowhere permanently inscribed but exists in the temporal morphogenetic capacities expressed in the meeting between visual perception and mechanical motion.

The reflections sourced from the Victorian period on the nature of the thaumatrope have served our investigation of the technological and historical contingencies with which proxistant vision operates today. We have seen how the thaumatrope articulates a new image era characteristic for the time in which the "original" Ferris wheel emerged. This media archaeological investigation of the cultural climate from which the observation wheel and the film reel simultaneously emerged, identifies the network of connections between them. From the study of the World's Columbian Exposition layout and the operation of the commercialized thaumatrope, we see the perceptual culture within which proxistant vision emerged as an observation wheel on an industrial scale, and the visual power with which it became imbricated as it transitioned into our time. We see how the Ferris wheel's smooth proxistant visual modality articulates an ambiguous oscillation between ground and sky, downfall and elevation, emotional muddiness, and rational clarity. These reflections therefore provide the grounding for an analysis of the ongoing individuation between rides, cinema, drones, and data visualization that is currently operating though the proliferation of proxistant vision. Underpinned by the technological operations of the thaumatrope, proxistant vision operates on the tantalizing play of uncertainty and wonder while combining that play with ownership and control.

2

LONDON (EYE) CALLING

"I felt more like I had wings and wus going up, and up and up to the clouds, I looked down an saw that jam o'people, say honest, they looked just like a lot of little ants a crowlin round an ant hill; an them bildins what wus so big inside didn't look no bigger than a pill box."
—Ebenezer Slimmens (A. J. Dockarty)[1]

"This is London as seen from a returning space shuttle; a vision of privilege, limitless budgets, a cure for cancer."
—Iain Sinclair[2]

As a structure confined to a strictly proxistant itinerary, the urban observation wheel presents breathtaking panoramic views combined with the proximity to the city life of the street. As it happens, this proxistant journey is also one of cinema's earliest forms, developing along a cine-cartographic itinerary of panoramic vistas and grounded kinetic structures.[3] Films such as *Panoramic View from the Eiffel Tower, Ascending and Descending* (1900) by Thomas A. Edison, Inc., for example, exhibit a vertical proxistant motion as seen from the Tower's elevator.[4] The elevator car is here a vehicle for camera movement in a similar fashion to how cranes, helicopters, or drones operate in combination with elaborate 3D-animated flights today.[5] The famous shot from *Panoramic View from the Eiffel Tower, Ascending and Descending* belongs to a larger body of early cinema practices characterized by Tom Gunning as the "cinema of attraction."[6] Edison's film catalog entry for *Panoramic View from the Eiffel Tower, Ascending and Descending* assures that the combination of mechanical motion and aerial ascension and descent "produces a most sensational effect. As the camera leaves the ground and rises to the top of the Tower, the enormous white city opens out to the view of the astonished spectator."[7] Filmed on the occasion of the 1900 Exposition Universelle in Paris, the elevator shot combines in its expression the two main novelties at the turn of the nineteenth century: the moving image and flight. This combination, which offers significant proxistant potential, was notably demonstrated in Raoul Grimoin-Sanson's ambitious but unsuccessful Cinéorama at the same Exposition, a ten-projector moving image installation that aimed to simulate a 360-degree hot-air balloon ride over Paris. As Amad and others have pointed out, this effort illustrates the nineteenth-century desire of both film and cartography to visually capture the whole world—a desire mutually underpinned by exploration and control in the motion from ground views to the elevated vistas.[8]

Interestingly, the examples presented of nascent camera movements by way of slow-moving grounded machines have migrated into center stage today across a diverse media landscape. But how does the proxistant vision of such elevators and observation wheels operate within the context of contemporary urban environments? In the spirit of what Cosgrove calls "cartographic vision," which loosely circumscribes everything from "maps, sketches, painting and photographs," we propose that the proxistant vision of the observation wheel could be analyzed within this cartographic concept.[9] Such a concept comes close to what Teresa Castro has called cartographic shapes, in which visual installations such as panorama theatres, as well as the aerial moving image, emerge from the "mapping impulse" of early modernity to visually describe spatial relations.[10] "Studying the map as an image presupposes that it can submit to the same questions as every other visual mechanism," Christian Jacob furthermore points out.[11] While the map shares the cultural codes of its time, it is also a profound site for graphic experimentation. The most important relation between maps and cinema here, however, is what Bruno has articulated as the way both mediums suggest movement through space. Bruno's emphasis on mobility is important here as the itinerant path of the observation wheel takes turns from close-ups and overviews, proximity, and distance. As such, the wheel's proxistant vision is extraordinarily cartographic, in that it attempts to articulate spatial details and the relations between them on a smoothly orchestrated mobile path. As we will see later, earlier cartographic itineraries are firmly imbricated in this effort and show how proxistant vision emerges through the infiltration of cityscapes and media technologies.

THE EMERGENCE OF PROXISTANT CITYSCAPES

In the legendary film *The Third Man* (1949), directed by Carol Reed, the audience is presented with the Wiener Riesenrad, the world's oldest surviving observation wheel, built only four years after Chicago's giant wheel.[12] As such, although considerably smaller, the Wiener Riesenrad replicates in great detail Ferris's marvelous engineering achievement. Returning to the film, we can see that even though the shot from the Wiener Riesenrad is rear projected in the studio, it successfully achieves the dynamic presence of the wheel's mechanical motion. Within the roughly three-minute sequence that features the scenes from the wheel, the film turns the wheel and its proxistant vision into the third character—the third man. As the wheel surrounds the dialogue between Harry Lime (Orson Welles) and Holly Martins (Joseph Cotten), it makes its presence as both mechanical machine and producer of dynamic vantage points of the city. Through the sprockets of the wheel, we glimpse the view from dazzling height descending elegantly to the ground as the agreement between the characters settles.[13]

The circular motion of the Ferris wheel absorbed and articulated an itinerant view that would later be known through the cinema. As Giuliana Bruno articulates it, "[f]ilm emerged out of a visual field of transition. It implanted in a shifting terrain marked by changes in the history of art, visual representation and the design of the city."[14] Bruno's central claim, that motion produces emotion, also works by reversals; hence, emotion produces motion. Such an understanding of motion and emotion is furthermore supported by the Latin root *emovere* of which *movere* means to move and the suffix *e* means out.[15] Yet another etymology on mobility is, of course, cinema, a term derived from the Greek *kinema*, associated with

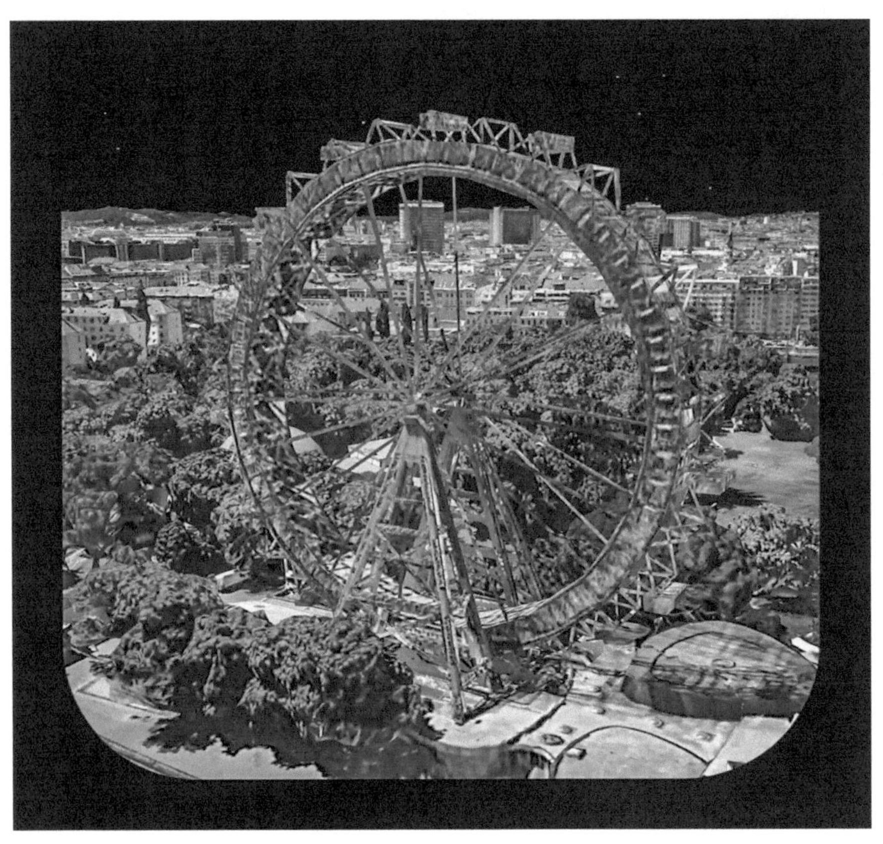

FIGURE 2.1

Bull.Miletic. Video still from *Ferriscope* (1893–2020) showing a digital 3-D model of Wiener Riesenrad (1897). Copyright © the artists.

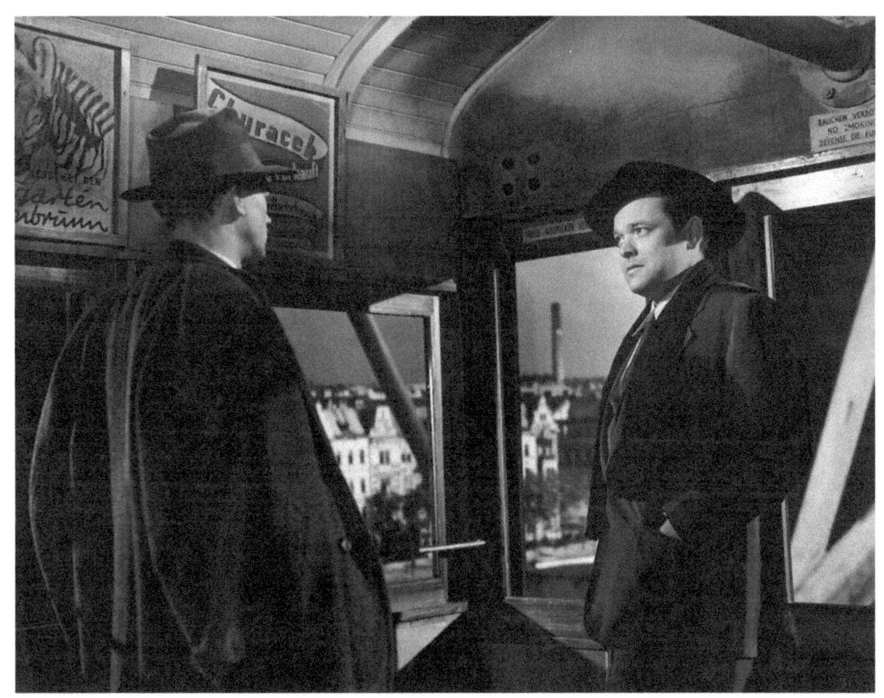

FIGURE 2.2

American actors Joseph Cotten (1905–1994, left) as Holly Martins and Orson Welles (1915–1985) as Harry Lime in the Ferris wheel scene from *The Third Man*, directed by Carol Reed, 1949. Courtesy of Moviepix at Getty Images.

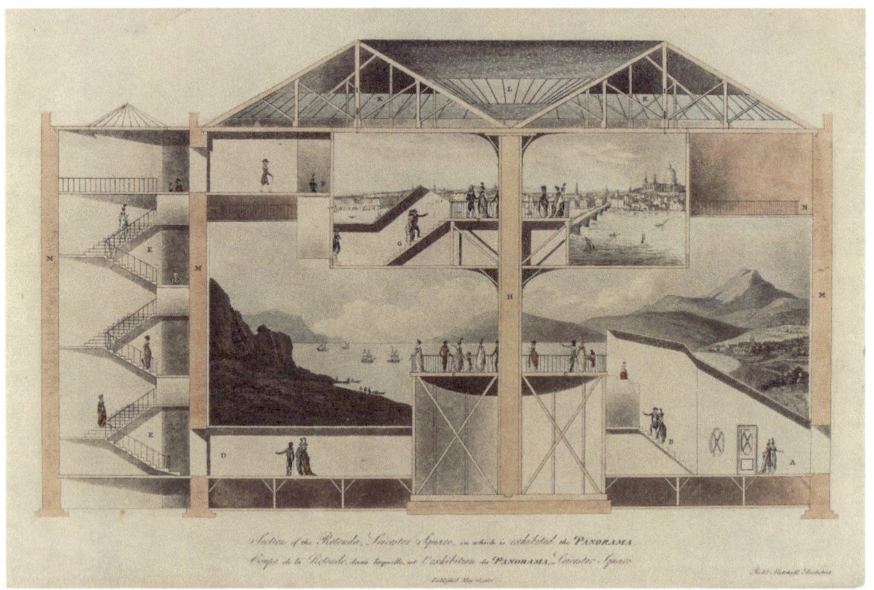

both motion and emotion, Bruno explains. The aerial view and cinema are furthermore intimately connected, exactly, by motion. Cinema's "inner transport," Bruno argues, can best be understood through the lens of early modernity where topographic city maps and urban view paintings flourished. Here we see the double itinerant activity of seeking out such views in physical reality, such as the climbing of church towers, mountain tops, and buildings, combined with the experience of being moved by such views emotionally.[16]

The growing popularity of cityscapes from which both wheel and reel emerged is perhaps best expressed with the 1787 invention of Robert Barker's panorama painting, a word he coined from Greek *pan* (all) *horama* (view) and perfected in 1792 with a designated rotunda theatre at Leicester Square.[17]

FIGURE 2.3

Robert Mitchel. *Cross section of Robert Barker's two-level panorama at Leicester Square* (ca. 1793).

This two-level rotunda tellingly exhibited both a 360-degree view of *London from the Roof of the Albion Mills* in the upper level and a seemingly pastoral landscape with unambiguous propagandist connotations: *The Grand Fleet at Spithead* in the lower, much larger room.[18] Barker's cityscape technology may have responded in particular to the invention of the hot air balloon by the Montgolfier brothers, a proxistant flight demonstrated publicly on November 21, 1783, in Paris, France.[19]

Seeing the 360-degree, unobstructed view of the city fostered modernity's public taste and demand for experiencing the city as a glossy surface. As Walter Benjamin articulated it, "[t]he interest of the panorama is in seeing the true city—the city indoors."[20] While the audience members were confined to a central viewing space, the view itself suggested a virtual mobility promised by the view of the horizon.[21] The subsequent developments of elaborate moving panoramas, luminously studied and documented by Erkki Huhtamo, further underpin the evolving cine-cartographic vision we are tracing here.[22] Importantly, these vision machines provided the combined effect of virtual travel within the structures of stabilizing repetition that would later be adopted by both wheel and reel. As we see in the moving panorama, and eventually the Ferris wheel and the moving image, these various mediated experiences of vertiginous heights later combined with the invention of mechanical motion to produce a spectacular smooth combination of proximity and distance.

As Dorrian and others have shown, however, these celebratory and utopian unobstructed views simultaneously inhabit the problematic notions of power from above. As early as 1858–1868, the somewhat blurry yet powerful vistas photographed from the hot-air balloon by Gaspard-Félix Tournachon (1820–1910), also known as Nadar, additionally contributed to shaping the cityscape as an image.

On this relationship, Nadar commented, in a similar spirit to Diderot: "There is nothing like distance to remove us from all ugliness."[23] The balloon ride was as popular as the images taken from its vantage point, but true public access to the altitudes of such a magnificent spectacle was initially epitomized with the construction of the Eiffel Tower—at the time, the tallest standing structure in the world—as part of Paris' 1889 Exposition Universelle. Within the first year of operation, it reached nearly two million visitors whose experience of the view of Paris from the

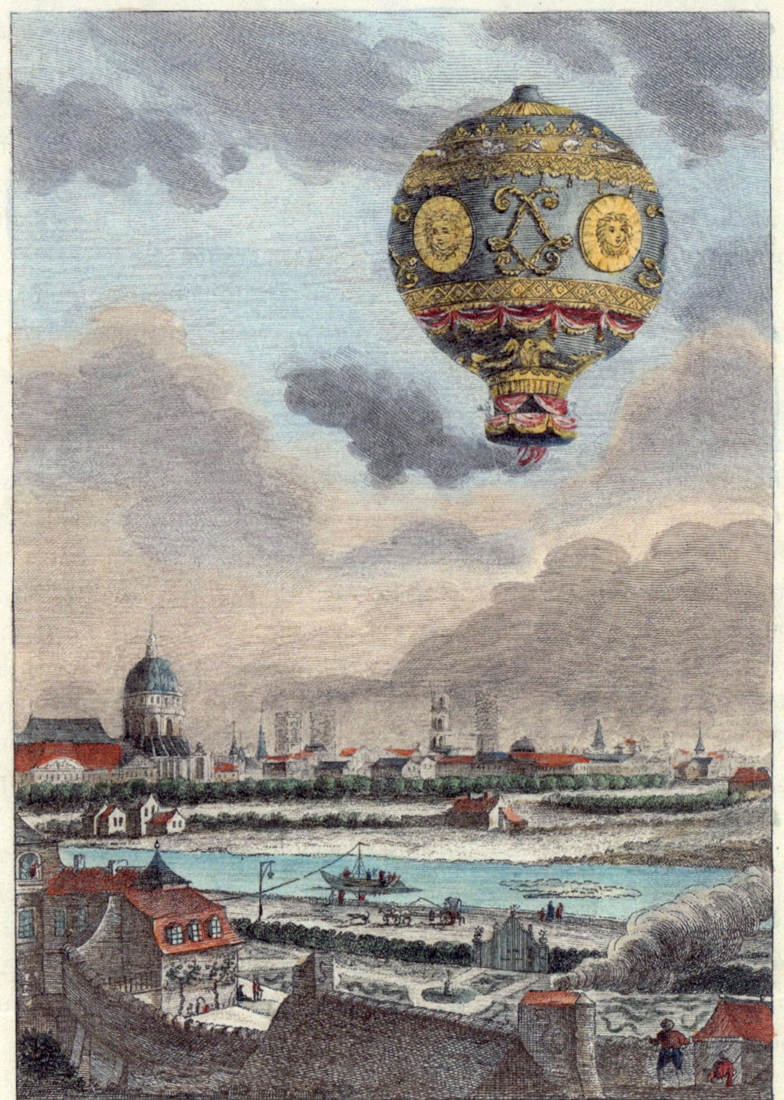

FIGURE 2.4

The first untethered manned flight of a Montgolfier hot air balloon on November 21, 1783 by Jean-François Pilâtre de Rozier and the Marquis d'Arlandes, taking off from the garden of the Château de la Muette in the presence of King Louis XVI. Hand colored engraving (1783). Courtesy of incamerastock / Alamy Stock Photo.

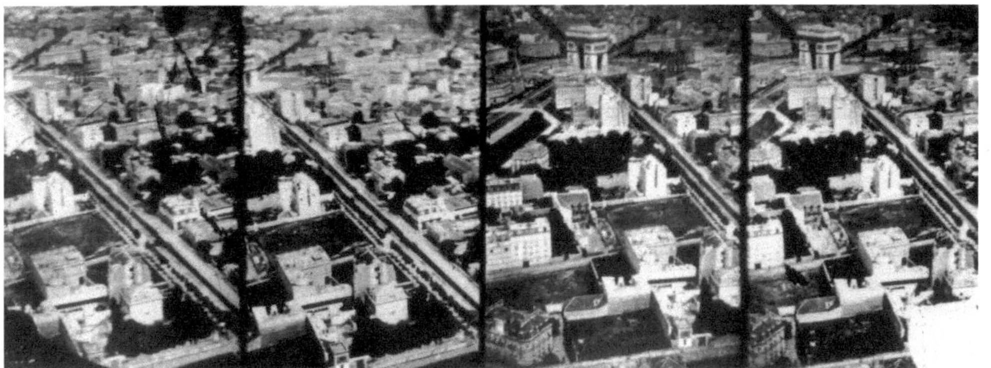

astonishing height of 300 meters (984 feet) created an impact on visual perception clearly detectable in art and design of the period. As Roland Barthes later pointed out, the Eiffel Tower's "panoramic vision added an incomparable power of *intellection*: the bird's-eye view, which each visitor to the Tower can assume in an instant for his own, gives us the world to *read* and not only to perceive; this is why it corresponds to a new sensibility of vision."[24] Sharing their elevated vantage points, the map and the aerial image simultaneously freeze life and mobilize the gaze in order to "see things *in their structure*."[25] This reading of the city is the modus of cartography, a simultaneous freezing and mobilizing of the gaze that stretches sight's capacity to discover places and patterns.

Here, we can see how the city as image converges with the transformative power of cartography understood as drawings on paper that are being implemented in idealist urban renovation projects. With the ideas of a cityscape, followed the practice of cityscaping—at times, in its most violent flavor. The radical reshaping of the French capital during the so-called "Haussmannization process," which was most intense between 1850 and 1870, would finally fully convince citizens of the city's inhuman character, as Benjamin pointed out.[26] As a result, the view from its point of creation turned out to be the best point from which one could hope

FIGURE 2.5

Nadar. *Aerial view of Paris* (1868).

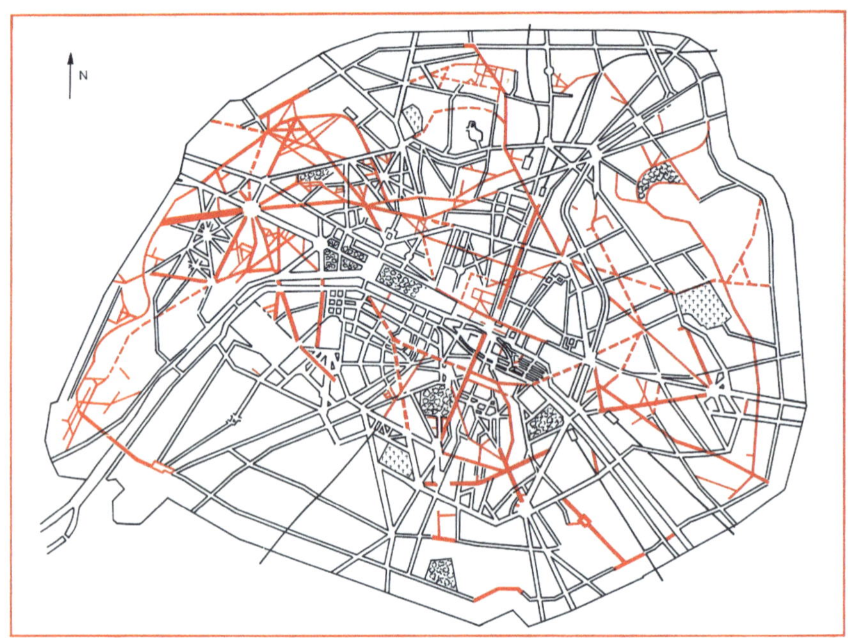

to experience it.[27] Largely produced as an idealized map, Haussmann's Paris existed as a timeless image from above, with giant boulevards and buildings, sketched out in perfect geometrical and symmetrical patterns.

This city is returned to the alienated citizen as a spectacular overview, a homogenized and totalizing surface that hides the conflicts and violence of the changes on the ground. Here we can see how the spectacularized view from the Eiffel Tower starts to take on some of the ethical problems articulated in Nadar's statement earlier, blinding the spectator from the real motion within the urban structure. On the way up to such a vista, one could experience the cinematic motion provided by the elevator's proxistant outlook.

FIGURE 2.6

Schematic plan of Paris indicating in red streets developed during the Haussmannization process (1853–1870).

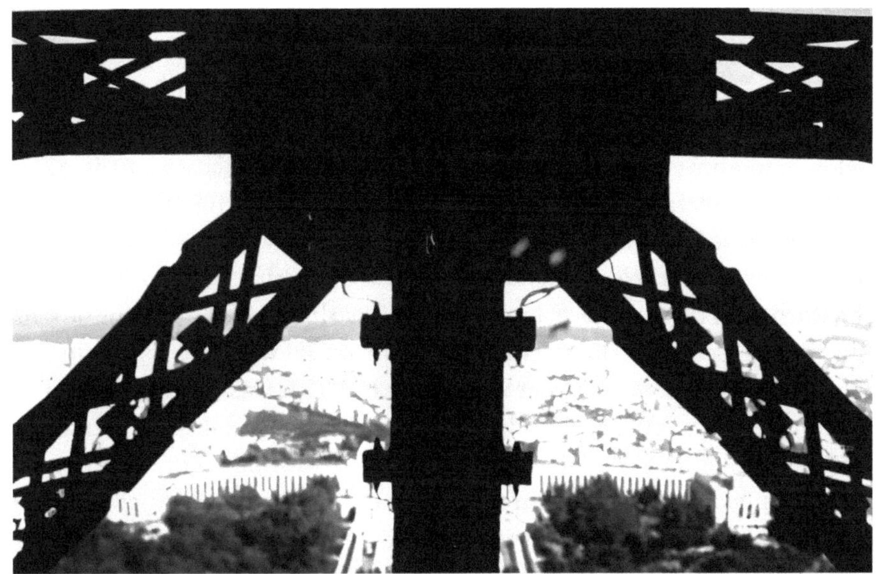

This cartographic vista of Paris from the Eiffel Tower was seen as Ferris's main inspiration in 1893. Yet, even if the elevator and the Ferris wheel mobilized the passengers by way of a smooth proxistant ride, it did not make the perceptual city less cartographic in the sense of showing it as a timeless structure. Rather, as we have argued previously, the wheel's mechanical motion heightened the sensation that the city existed in a different dimension, a cine-cartographic dimension of proxistant vision. Such insight is highly relevant today as observation wheels and similar grounded observation machines continue to flourish within urban centers around the world.[28]

FIGURE 2.7

Bull.Miletic. Video still from *Par Hasard* (2009) showing the view from one of the ascending elevators in the Eiffel Tower. Copyright © the artists.

CHICAGO 1883 AND PROXISTANT CITY PLANNING

The cinematic dimension of the wheel's proxistant vision is also what links it to a cartographic sensibility, in terms of a city plan seen from below and above. The aerial view's role in relation to city planning is a well-known narrative, as it incorporates relations on the ground. It was from an aircraft that Le Corbusier saw how the city was in need of a radical replacement, later realized as high-rise living machines in the outskirts of the European metropolis.[29] Jane Haffner has shown how aerial photography played a crucial role in connecting the social with the spatial in the interwar period as well as after World War II.[30] This was also the subject of Henri Lefebvre's thorough studies, arguing that the social space produced by the close-up knowledge of everyday life should be incorporated into the distanced operations of architects and city planners.[31] Such distancing structuration for the governing of cities was illustrated in the previous era by Ambrogio Lorenzetti's fresco cycle *The Allegory of Good and Bad Government* on the walls of Siena's Palazzo Pubblico, painted between 1337 and 1339, an insight also shared by Cosgrove in his invaluable book *Photography and Flight*.[32]

Ambrogio Lorenzetti's immersive aerial rendering across three walls in the Sala della Pace lays the Sienese world before one's feet. Even though the painted walls stretch above one's head when entering the room, the view is of an aerial perspective of towns, palaces, mountains, and fields, surveying the area of government, sometimes from low and at other times high oblique angles, and thus articulating a decidedly proxistant vision already in the early Renaissance.[33]

Lorenzetti's painting anticipates later ideas about city government by way of the view from above, exemplified by the Scottish architect Patrick Geddes's scientifically minded mapping and survey techniques, implemented through the famous *Outlook Tower* in Edinburgh from 1892 to 1932 in which an embedded camera obscura helped survey the practices of the citizens below. Cosgrove has pointed out how Geddes' ideas reached widespread application across city planning and governance throughout the Western world.[34] During the 1820–1890 period of the establishment of colonial settlements in North America and Australia, such mapping and survey techniques were in high demand, attempting to order the highly

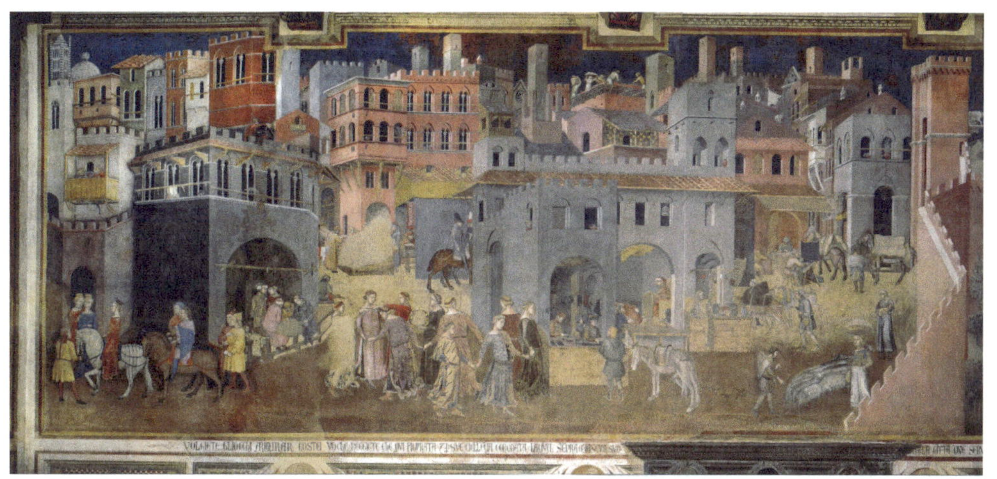

disorganized and unordered places of rapid urban growth and subsequent disorder.[35] Regarding the introduction of the 1893 Ferris wheel, we can see that this was a time when the need for control of the expanding North American metropolis became manifest through a variety of mapping practices. One such concept was the White City's idea of "associational functionalism," where exposure to elevated thinking was seen as instrumental to well-behaved social interaction. According to historian James A. Schmiechen, this previous European ideal was extended to North American city planners, who were faced with cities sprawling in uncontrolled expansion.[36] Utopian planners such as Edward Bellamy and others associated with the beautiful city movement met the challenge of the large cultural diversity of the haphazard sprawls with the need for an urban focal point. Such city development was conceived as an effective disciplinary maneuver and a lasting asset of the upper middle-class establishment, as John R. Mullin and Kenneth Payne further point out.[37] In

FIGURE 2.8

Ambrogio Lorenzetti. Detail of *The Allegory of Good and Bad Government* (1337–1339). Courtesy of Palazzo Pubblico, Sienna.

what was left of a Victorian tradition, historicism rather than futurity was fronted as the style of choice, and the White City's neoclassic architectural ideal served to suppress the growing pressure of the commercially oriented functionalist designs.[38] With this urban focal point, a part of the city was made to stand in for the whole. A unified visual coherence served as an example of how the city in its entirety should be conceived and understood. As we shall see, such focus on a central urban point later became part of the contemporary city's urban proxistant regime.

Operating amid cultural turmoil and industrial expansion, however, the proponents of these political and social urban ideals soon lost faith in the idea. New infrastructural development made city planners gradually let go of notions of elevated European harmony, turning instead to the development of the suburb. Progressive minds such as Frank Lloyd Wright imagined the city away from "the timeless community on a hill" to adopt more uniform and expandable structures.[39] Here, a newfound and expandable grid system took precedence, a system that had existed as the simplest and most widespread form of urban planning since the earliest Hellenistic colonies.[40] Hence, the production of a unified urban core simultaneously resulted in the emergence of the suburb, budding the centerless city so characteristic of our own time.[41] This expansion of life beyond the urban center was premised upon an extraordinary advance of mobility infrastructure, providing easy access to and from the city. As Gilbert points out, a good example of one such development was Frederick Law Olmsted's Riverside community, one of Chicago's earliest planned suburbs, which was established in 1868 directly in response to the Chicago, Burlington, & Quincy Railroad. This resulted in the itinerary so common today, with the city as a proxistant machine producing highly mobilized subjects in a constant loop between the suburb and the city center.

Such mobility orchestrated Chicago itself as a proxistant map, with its far-stretching flat surface. Wide streets in a gridded structure continued in straight lines without the physical obstacles in the terrain or change in elevation. At the center, a cluster of skyscrapers rose straight into the sky, providing panoramic views to employees as a part of everyday life. In addition to the proxistant vision produced by the Ferris wheel, a highly proxistant city map was also part of the Chicago World's Fair paraphernalia.[42] By depicting a vertical overview with a three-dimensional oblique

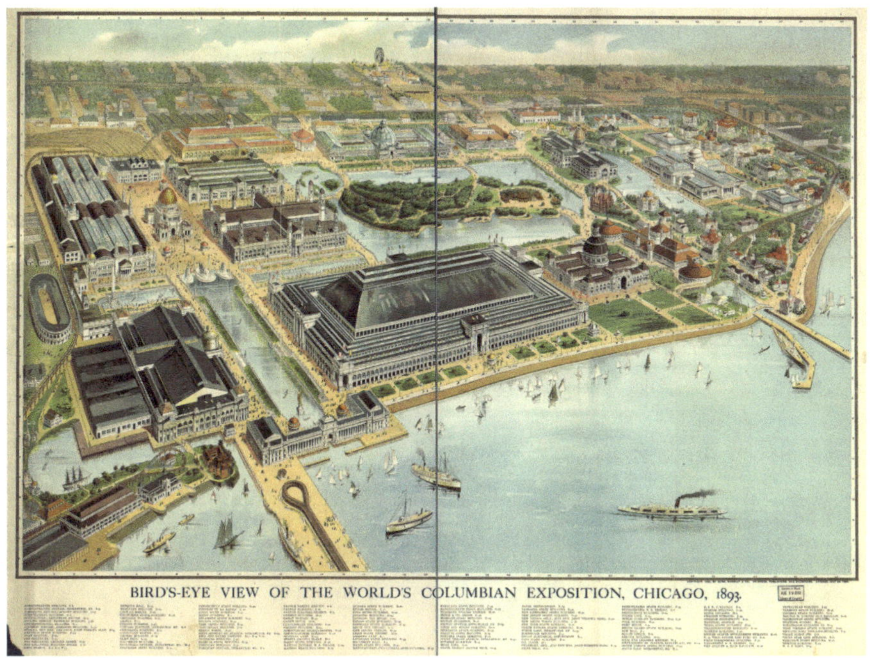

rendering of the Fair, it enabled an emphasis on the most important features, such as the White City constructions.

Such proxistant maps produced a perceptual movement on behalf of the audience, in which a mental journey between oblique proximity and vertical distance was implied.[43] As we point out in section 2, such proxistant cartographic renderings were common in earlier Renaissance descriptions of European city views, exemplified by the nineteenth-century collection by Braun and Hogenberg's *Civitates Orbis Terrarum* (cities of the world).[44]

FIGURE 2.9

Rand McNally and Company. *Bird's eye view of the World's Columbian Exposition, Chicago.* [S.l, 1893] Map. https://www.loc.gov/item/98687181/. Courtesy of the Library of Congress.

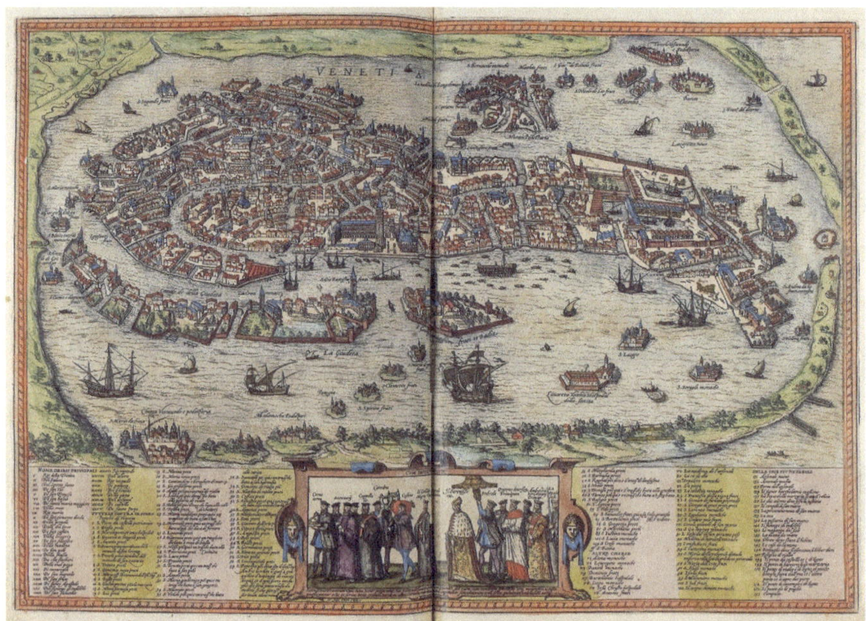

The proxistant vision of the observation wheel articulated these cartographic itineraries in kinetic architectural terms. The seemingly liberating motion of flight of the observation wheel evolved through the means of mechanical mobility from the ground to the air. Yet, its vertiginous expanse quickly looped back into an equally repeating pattern between proximity and distance, stabilized and mapped out as a pre-constituted cinematic experience. It is this smooth trajectory of an all-seeing pattern that constitutes some of the cartographic contingencies articulated in the proxistant vision.

FIGURE 2.10

Venice in *Civitates Orbis Terrarum* (1572).

MOBILIZING THE CARTOGRAPHIC CITY

We have seen how the observation wheel's formation of the cityscape as an image of attraction was culturally tied up with the technological transformations of modernity that propelled travel, mobility, and the search for an elevated vista. In his article, Dorrian points out how the connection between landscape and cityscape is detectable in the earliest accounts of the term "cityscape," found in the Oxford English Dictionary. Here, a citation from William Thackeray's letter in 1856 describes the experience of a sleigh journey in Albany, New York as "[a] fairyland of frozen land, river, and cityscape, where all the trees were glistering with silver."[45] What we should notice here, Dorrian points out, is how the notion of a cityscape is associated with something frozen, still and pristine, and most importantly, empty. Such a claim seems at first to stand in stark contrast to Bruno's emphasis on emotion, as previously discussed. Highlighting the much-earlier cityscape practices of the Italian *vedute* paintings, such as those by Canaletto (1697–1768) and Giovanni Paolo Pannini (c1691–1756), Bruno argues that such city views were understood as dynamic and emphasized the drama of location.

The Italian narrative dramatization of city space was different from the Dutch city views described by Svetlana Alpers, in which the canvas was inseparable from the act of seeing and describing.[46] In order to get more insight into what is at stake, therefore, we need to make a more nuanced reflection of the notion of this immobile and mobilized vision.

The aerial view always implied motion, not only in Bruno's sense of emotion but also with the activity of ascension and descent. Castro has pointed out that what the moving image adds to the view from above is the combination of description and spectacularization.[47] Although intensified by the moving image, we have already seen that such combinations were already present in the aerial view itself. What movement most concretely adds to the aerial view, therefore, is the potential mobile path to the intimacy of a detailed close-up. Present in mapping practices from the sixteenth-century bird's-eye view to nineteenth-century urban planning, such cartographic contingencies are what is played out in the Ferris wheel's proxistant vision. We have seen that late eighteenth- and nineteenth-century installations, such as the panorama paintings and

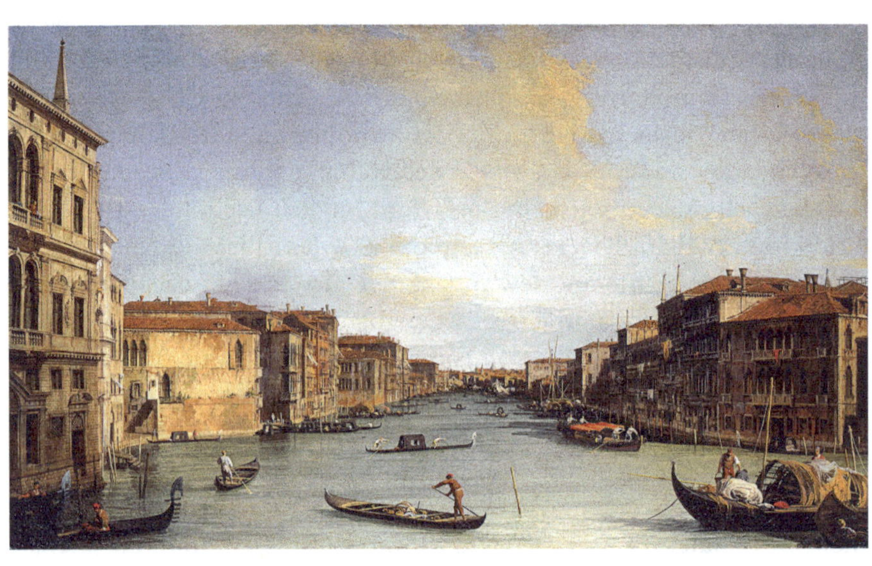

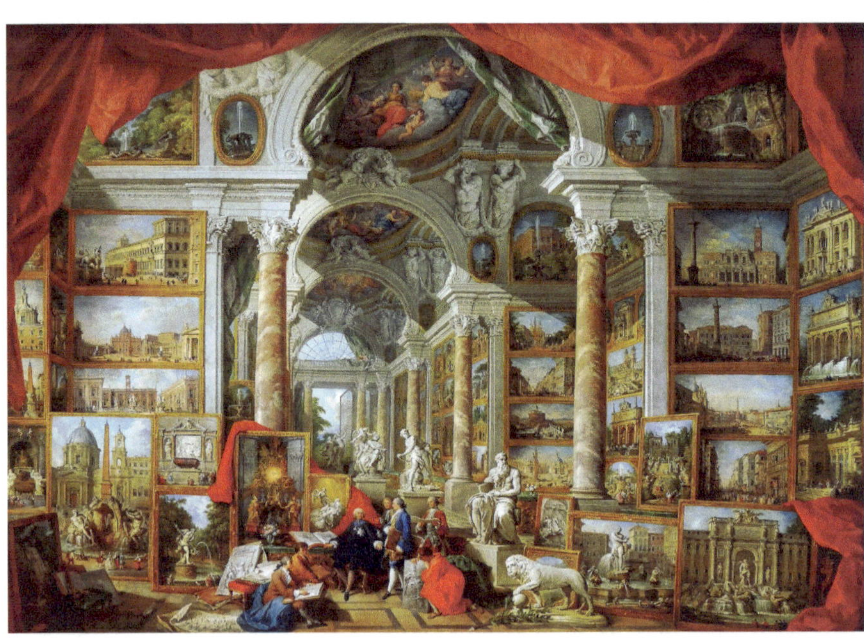

dioramas mentioned earlier, functioned as vision machines in which the effect of virtual travel combined with the structures of stabilizing repetition. As has been recognized by many, this intensifying interest in the aerial view was conditioned and formulated upon an escalation in industrialized economy and travel, with subsequent infrastructural transformations that demanded an increasingly mobilized and itinerant body. As Giuliana Bruno has noted, the notion of a view aesthetics emerging in the seventeenth century encompasses both garden views and landscaping as modes of the picturesque.[48] As life started to become increasingly mobilized and apt for rapid change, visual installations of all sorts grew more popular. Within this milieu emerged not only the Ferris wheel as the epitome of proxistant vision but also a growing tourist class.

The rapid succession of World's Fairs across the Western world throughout the second half of the nineteenth century answered to—and invited—some of this tourism.[49] The large amount of visual and informative material, such as guidebooks and maps, that followed the growing tourist industry was co-responsible for shaping the experience of the city, as historian James Gilbert and Mark Dorrian have noted.[50] On top of population growth, the railway brought hordes of a new kind of middle-class tourist on dedicated sightseeing trips, and these followed the layout of Chicago's proxistant urban planning. As visitors pursued the experience of tall buildings and their vantage points, the conventions of developing travel literature often combined such powerful vistas and maps with close-up snippets of life on the ground, tailoring every aspect of a proxistant experience. The new mobility class pursued the advertised and carefully designed tourist experiences that provided the familiar in an unfamiliar setting. This was a situation tailored to a mode of comfortable

FIGURE 2.11

Canaletto. *Canal Grande* (1697–1768).

FIGURE 2.12

Giovanni Paolo Pannini. *Gallery of Views of Ancient Rome* (1758).

bewilderment. "From the beginning to the end, the idea of tourism was a structured experience, imposed upon the various realities of the place visited," as Gilbert phrases it.[51] As a professor of landscape architecture and environmental design, Dean MacCannel generally argues that the tourist places herself intentionally in a bizarre situation with the prospect of a combined experience of entertainment and instruction. The expectation is that everything is fabricated into a "staged authenticity" to recuperate continuity from a discontinuous modernity, while still learning how different societies function. The whole conception of the tourist industry works on this basis of packaging experiences that develop a sense of a layered reality.[52]

From this we can see how, in a very significant sense, the designed tourist experience frames the world in a way that is similar to how a movie camera might capture and present it. A planned itinerary, therefore, might start with a grand establishing shot in the form of a giant Ferris wheel. This form of framing is also a significant feature inherited from the cartographic map, which prepares the terrain for later forms of premediated city experiences, and for which the cityscape is laid out as a first encounter. Rather than releasing the frozen image of the cityscape from its cartographic power, therefore, the mechanical motion of the Ferris wheel strengthens the Eiffel Tower's sense of the city as a cartographic image by turning it into a smooth proxistant model. With powerful effect, the wheel draws on combined cinematic and cartographic operations in its proxistant form, graciously circulating between vertiginous vistas and street-level perspectives, bodily stillness, and mechanical motion. The strictly laid-out path between these opposing forces firmly controls the cinematic motion within the repetitive structure of a clockwork. This cartographic contingency also operates within the smooth proxistant vision that flourishes today across media platforms of the twenty-first century.

THE PROXISTANT VISION OF LONDON

We have seen how the cinematic observation wheel inhabits a cartographic power as it journeys from proximity to distance on a smooth circular itinerary. But how does this smooth proxistance operate with cartographic and cinematic contingencies within the contemporary urban environment? Exactly a century after Ferris's steel monster majestically demarcated the transit into the twentieth century, London planned an even more spectacular entry into "the dawn of the new era" that marked the beginning of the new millennium.[53] The chosen location for the millennium monument was set in the South Bank neighborhood, a specifically challenged part of London's city center in need of a radical rehabilitation. The South Bank was a previous historic fairground site for the 1951 National Festival of Britain, but most of the festival structures had been rapidly removed and the only building left was the Royal Festival Hall. A half-century later, visitors hurried to and from the Hall, avoiding its sketchy surroundings.[54] With the construction of the millennium monument in this specific area, the city hoped to reinstate the 1951 effect and regenerate this neglected area within the otherwise glamorous urban core. The competition for the monument was announced in the *Sunday Times* on October 24, 1993, and the organizers excitedly anticipated an inflow of architectural miracles. Reminiscent of 1892 Chicago however, the competition was a fiasco as no design was recognized as worthy of the honor. Julia Barfield and David Marks's proposal for a giant observation wheel was one of many entries in the competition, but it never attracted much attention during the official campaigning. The architect couple however, continued to lobby for the idea, securing the construction of the London Eye just in time to gently transport the masses into the new millennium.[55] In a sense repeating the experience of the 1893 Chicago fair, the great observation wheel simultaneously transformed the cityscape into a main tourist attraction and became an instant London landmark. In retrospect, the Eye accomplished much more than just the regeneration of the South Bank; as Sir Richard Rogers articulates it, "the South Bank was a no-go area. [. . .] Now though, the South Bank *is* the place to go, and the Eye was a key part of that."[56]

How can we be so sure that the wheel did something good for London at large and not just for the narrow circle of corporate stakeholders in its capitalist matrix, elevating the real estate market value with a spectacular proxistant view? In its specific urban context, the construction of the London Eye participates in a trend in which urban downtowns are being shaped as shiny façades and layers of images, competing in degrees of attention. This is also recognized by Dorrian, who suggests that the

London Eye turned the South Bank into the glossy surface that Debord had rejected in his *The Society of the Spectacle*, where "the perceptible world is replaced by a set of images that are superior to that world, yet at the same time impose themselves as *eminently* perceptible."[57] The London Eye is first and foremost an "exhibitionary installation" which returns the mobile cityscape to its own advantage. The wheel's final success is undisputed, serving as the top hit on tourist attraction sites, above both the Vatican and the Sydney Opera House. Attracting more than 3.5 million visitors a year, the Eye more than doubles the number of visitors to the London Tower.[58] When passengers are transported above the turbid Thames and are gently lifted into the bird's-eye perspective, they might start to feel that the city is laid out specifically for their own visual pleasure.[59]

These points all attest to the way the London Eye operates as a giant location-establishing shot in the previously suggested itinerary for the tourist in motion. In a similar fashion to the "original" Ferris wheel, the London Eye's repetitive journey between the ground level and the sky-high vistas introduces its visitors to the cinematic experiences they can expect to encounter on their tailored tourist itineraries.[60] The wheel's proxistant vision summons the cartographically mapped-out tourist guides and attraction points and circles them up in a grand cinematic introduction. Elevated to the point of seeing the world, the wheel brings that world back to the cityscape and returns it as a commodity in a smooth proxistant layout. The sheer size of London Eye (135 meters height, with diameter of 120 meters) repeats the "original" Ferris wheel's monster sensibility, experienced in Chicago a century ago, and reintroduces its smooth and idealizing effect to the contemporary world. In a similar fashion to the industrial Ferris wheel, the London Eye encapsulates its passengers in transparent glass capsules, an important design feature also introduced by Ferris in 1893 that structures the act of observation, in contrast to the open-air thrill one gets on smaller wheels or a roller coaster.

As the gradual mechanical motion turns the cityscape into a timeless cine-cartographic structure, the city becomes unreal and frozen, transformed into the cinematic dimension of a smooth proxistant establishing shot.[61]

The present introduction of these grounded machines into the center of metropolises around the globe clearly exhibits their role as proxistant

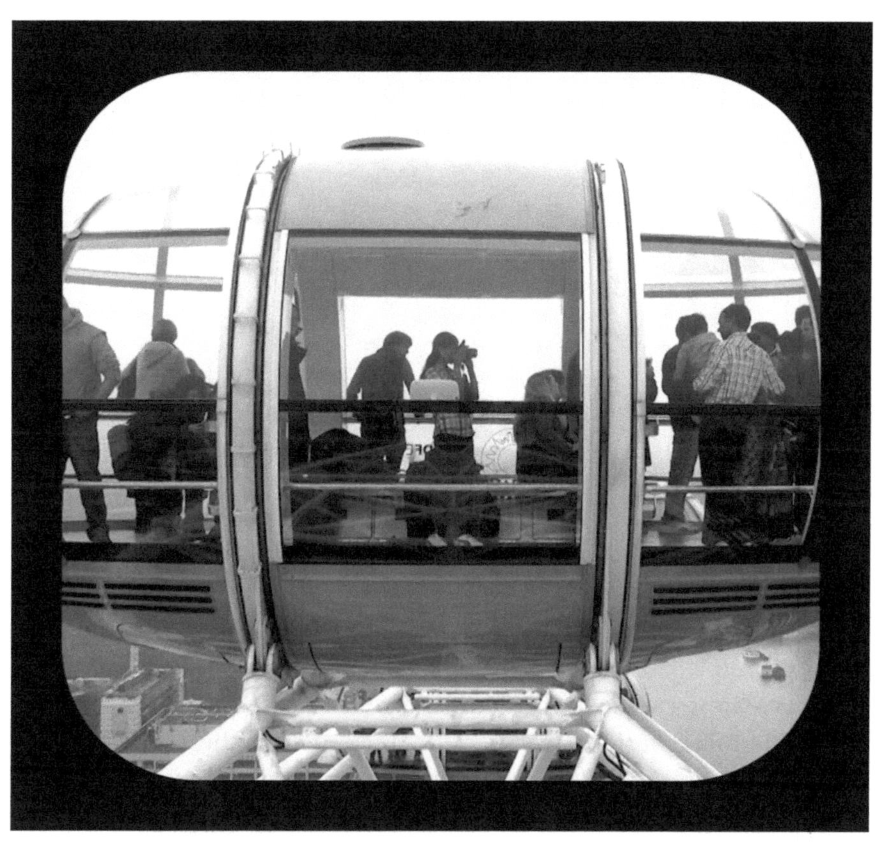

FIGURE 2.13

Bull.Miletic. Video still from *Ferriscope* (1893–2020) showing one of London Eye's ovoid glass capsules. Copyright © the artists.

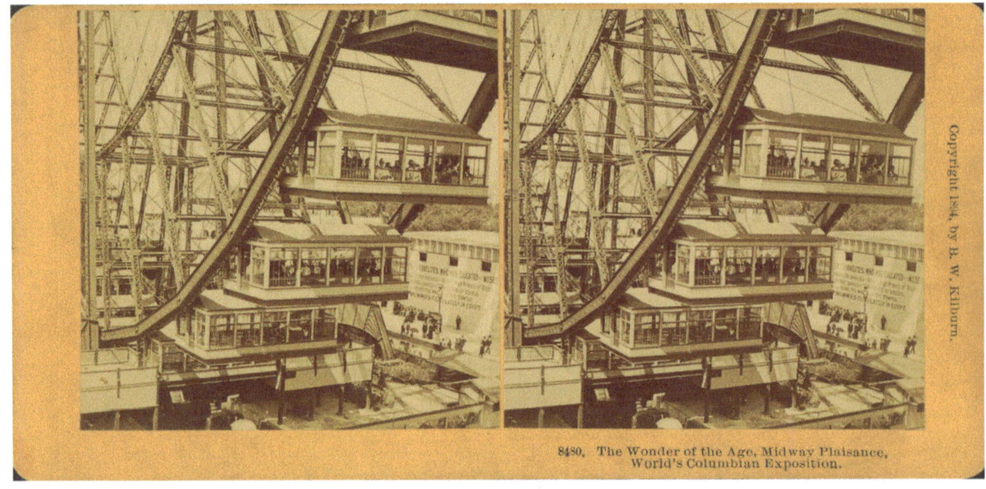

media operators of the urban flow. An excellent example of this situation is the promo video for the New York Wheel. A giant observation wheel that was planned at the northernmost tip of Staten Island, and part of the wheel-o-mania that right now seems to be circulating the world.[62] The 3D-animated flythrough video proxistantly starts out with Earth suspended in space, a computer-modeled globe "shot" from a geostationary altitude.

From this Google Earth-inspired view, the virtual camera rapidly plunges through a digital atmosphere before being smoothly transformed into an actual helicopter flight across Manhattan. Another seamless transition further proceeds back into a 3D-animated flight, encircling the computer rendering of the future New York Wheel in a dynamic composition. We seem to fly over the cityscape but, in fact, we fly over a dynamic map with multiple data points collected and composed into a coherent stand-in for the city.

FIGURE 2.14

Large glass panels on Ferris wheel's cars, World's Columbian Exposition, Chicago, 1893.

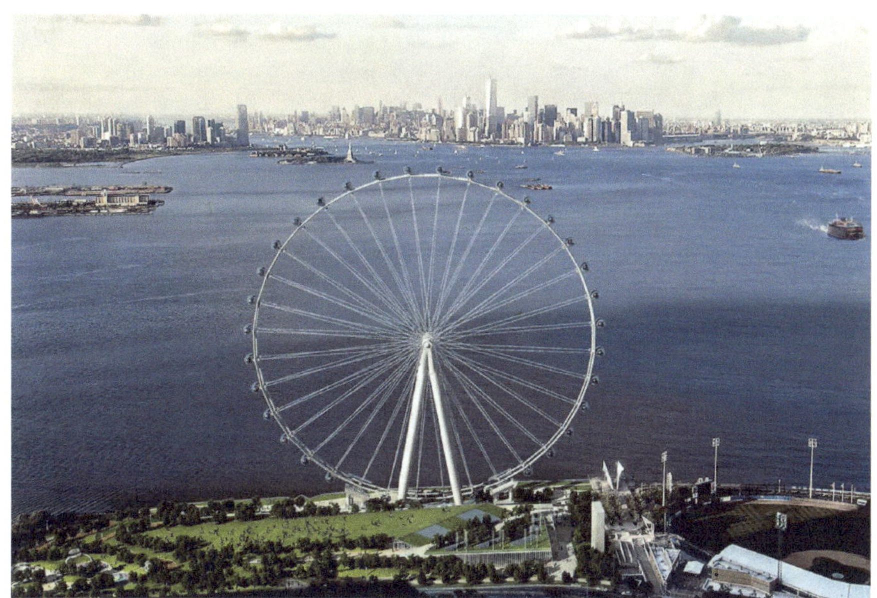

In a different text, Dorrian has pointed out how the miniature or model works on the same principle as the aerial view, its "usefulness as urban planning's most potent tool of public persuasion endures through precisely such powers of sublimation."[63] As an example, he points to the famous image depicting the model of *La Plan Voisin*, an unrealized Paris redevelopment designed by Le Corbusier between 1922 and 1925. The image shows the giant hand of the architect pointing to the miniature model city as a god-like liberator of urban space.[64]

But if the old architectural maquette was about scaling down, manually miniaturizing the structure to grasp its spatial relations, then the function of proxistant vision, with all its cartographic qualities, is to multiply

FIGURE 2.15

Video still from *New York Wheel Fly-over* (2014).

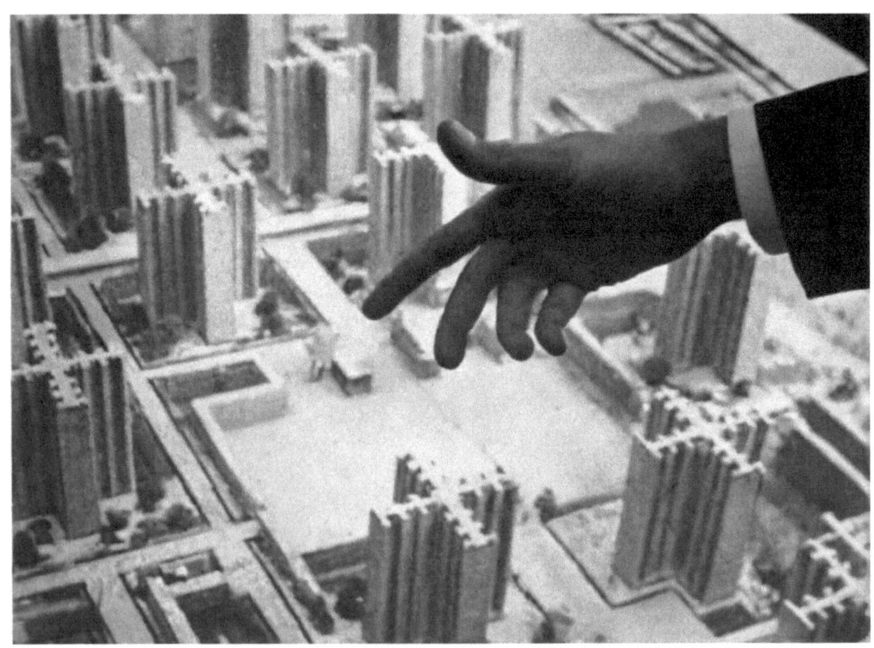

this effect as a spectacular all-seeing perspective offering empowering aerial views as well as insightful proximity within one cinematic sweep. As such, the wheel's proxistant vision functions as a way of mapping and stabilizing the city into a circulatory pattern that gives the illusion of seeing it in a model form with access to both totality and street level at once. Maintaining the close connection between cinema and cartography, it is a stabilizing form that freezes the surface of the ground as it moves above it. In addition, the smooth transition between proximity and distance recalls the flyover function pertaining to a digital model as presented in the aforementioned New York Wheel's demo video. This shows some of the contingent power with which this visual form proliferates today across the twenty-first-century media sphere.

FIGURE 2.16

Le Corbusier. *Le Plan Voisin* (1925).

Inherent to the scopic regime of modernity, vision was considered the best way to experience the city, which privileged maps and cartography as the primary medium with which it could be both known and reformed.[65] As Latour argues, influential documents such as maps and scientific drawings do not only maintain the illusion of accurately representing the world, but they also work by way of reversals, enforcing the view that this is indeed the way things themselves stand in the world.[66] Understood in its broadest sense as a device that visualizes the city into the frozen hallucination of a 3D-animated flythrough or a tourist cinema by way of proxistant location-establishing shots, the London Eye, New York Wheel, Las Vegas High Roller, and many other newly installed or planned wheels operate far beyond the modernist map as they influence everyday worldviews. Not only a smooth worldview in terms of a world without problems, ruled by the laws of investments, smiling faces, and luxurious airport lounges, but also a cartographic worldview in Latour's sense. This is the role of the immutable mobile model that produces a virtual image in the mind of the observer asking entities to stand in the world the way they are depicted.[67] As contemporary observation wheels move into the urban core, they recall the "original" Ferris wheel's emergence at the crossroads of the invention of the moving image and the ongoing trials of the new mega-metropolis. With the popularization of the urban observation wheel, we see how the cityscape turns into a cinematic location-establishing shot beyond the screen. Much like a 3D-animated flythrough, the urban wheel presents the city itself as a digital model. A model is easily operated as an object of consumption without the consideration of the social temporalities within the urban structures.

In his seminal book *Expanded Cinema*, Gene Youngblood describes the conventional narrative cinema as a policing system that enforces a "*specialized vision*, which tends to decay our ability to comprehend the more complex and diffuse visual field of living reality."[68] In similar fashion, the visual form—which we call proxistance—industrialized by the Ferris wheel on a grand scale in *fin de siècle* America, over time got locked into one (for-profit) function, becoming a major gentrifying force and a monumental instrument of corporate power. By exploring the capacities not strictly in line with the commercial intentions and the forces built into for-profit models, we approach proxistance in a media archaeological manner by bringing the combination of mechanical movement and view from the Ferris wheel to the foreground as a force of cinematic revelation and curiosity. In doing so, we reveal and expand on the genealogical relations and ongoing individuation between observation rides, cinema, and aerial imaging and how this impacts worldviews and views of the world. In the words of visual artist and robotics engineer Jan C. Schacher describing his own artistic research practice, this research too belongs to the tradition which "results in an art-form that can show the potential but also the limits and dangers of giving too much weight to technology."[69] As we will see in the third and last chapter of this section, our kinetic video installation *Ferriscope* takes a closer look at this relationship between cartography, cinema, and the city.

3

GROUNDED MACHINES AS *CINÉMA TROUVÉ*

The large urban observation wheel operates today as a twenty-first-century tool of gentrification within the global metropolis, emphasizing a glamorous and marketable location-establishing shot between the urban center and the skyline. In this chapter, we set out to investigate how the proxistant itinerary of the observation wheel could be explored through artistic practice. Here especially, we also ask how the proxistant visual paradigm obtains its effect through bodily interaction. To address these questions, it will be necessary to revisit our earlier research on kinetic architecture and consider the work of other artists who explore similar themes. As we have already seen, our argument concerning the cinematic experience of observation wheels started with our initial interest in the revolving restaurant in the project *Heaven Can Wait* (2001–ongoing.) This research helped identify the combination of mechanical motion and elevated view as ready-made cinema, or what we have come to call *cinéma trouvé* after Duchamp's *objet trouvé*.[1] This is a perceptual phenomenon that both observation wheels and revolving restaurants share with other grounded machines, such as glass elevators, cable cars, and gondolas, to name a few. We study how the moving panorama travels across architecture and cinema from earlier forms of panorama theatres and landscape painting imbued with contested traces of imperial ownership and colonial power. Artistically, we have developed a method to utilize these structures as a support mechanism for our camera. The footage obtained in this way resembles extensive tracking shots, typically achieved with dollies, cranes, or aerial equipment.

As we have seen with the example of Edison, the experience provided by kinetic architecture and mechanical rides appears early in cinema as part of "the cinema of attractions" in the form of non-narrative phantom rides and exhibitions such as Hale's tours.[2] The mechanical sensation of movement has continued to fascinate artists and experimental filmmakers, and several recent artworks approach grounded kinetic structures to probe the perceptual effects inherent to the moving image in a manner reminiscent of early cinema's explorations. Films such as *Railroad Turnbridge* (1976) by Richard Serra; *Side/Walk/Shuttle* (1991) by Ernie Gehr; *Descent* (2002) by Catherine Yass; *Time Lines* (2005) by Runa Islam; *A Memorial to Failure* (2013) by Mahmoud Khaled; and *Manakamana* (2014) by Stephanie Spray and Pacho Velez can be highlighted here. These works can be analyzed as retro-remediated practices, reformulating the cine-cartographic operations of proxistant vision inherent to the observation wheel as well as panoramic elevators, cable cars, and other visually oriented kinetic urban infrastructures.[3] There are similar affinities between examples of structuralist film and the single-shot proxistant vision from cinema's first decade.

The artworks we analyze here are based on the aspect of *cinéma trouvé* we have discussed in the introduction of this section and, as such, operate with concerns similar to those of the Structuralist filmmakers in the early 1970s. Common in these works are the attempts to grasp what Rosalind Krauss termed to be not so much a thing but "a relationship, a transitivity." Like several of the early cinema of attraction films, Krauss recognizes in Richard Serra's work *Railroad Turnbridge* (1976) "a space made visible in and of itself by the fact that [the bridge] is in motion."[4] Camera movement is highlighted here both in the way it operates differently to editing and as a cartographic vision of proxistance. The Structural/Materialist film movement of the 1960s and 1970s is a movement that, as Gunning has shown, often turned to techniques from early cinema as a form of countering the classical cinematic conventions of illusionism, idealism, and representation.[5] But how do contemporary artworks utilizing proxistant grounded machines pick up similar retro-remediating ideas and concerns? Experimental film theorist and filmmaker Peter Gidal has pointed out how the fundamental concerns of Structuralist/Materialist films are "[t]he structuring aspect and the attempt to decipher the structure and anticipate/record it, to clarify and analyze the production-process of the specific image at any specific moment."[6] Here, Gidal emphasizes how each film "is a record (not a representation, not a reproduction) of its own making."[7] This anti-illusionist practice means that viewing such a film is "viewing the 'coming into presence' of the film, i.e., the system of consciousness that produces the work, that is produced by and in it."[8] Hence, "Structural/Materialist films are at once object and procedure."[9] That is to say, its own becoming is simultaneously the film's content and form—if it ever made sense to separate the two—or better yet, what the film is produced by, meaning its material support, equals that which it seeks to discuss. Finally, as defined by Malcolm LeGrice, "it is a project towards extending clarity about the material and perceptual phenomena of film, but one which realizes the continuing development of the phenomena being studied."[10]

Structuralist filmmakers found inspiration by turning to a time before the moving image's dominant path was colonized by theatrical conventions in the service of literary narrative.[11] The avant-garde discovered many roads not taken in early cinema, which offered a moving image multiplicity that avant-garde filmmakers could draw from in their effort to counter established cinematic conventions. These insights regarding early cinema's influence on avant-garde cinematic practices are useful for understanding how *cinéma trouvé* operates in the contemporary artworks mentioned earlier. Emerging within the past three decades, these artworks all exemplify how the visual effect of proxistant vision operates at the intersection of cartography and the aerial moving image. Yet, moving beyond the pure fascination of such affinities articulated by filmmakers of cinema's first decade, these artworks can, in their different ways, be seen as retrograde remediations of such cinematic and cartographic contingencies. The American structuralist filmmaker Ernie Gehr's film *Side/Walk/Shuttle*, for example, is structured around a similar grounded machine to that of the observation wheel, namely the panoramic elevator.

The forty-one-minute-long 16 mm color film comprises twenty-five shots, with an average duration of about ninety seconds each, showing the view from rides up and down the glass elevator of San Francisco's

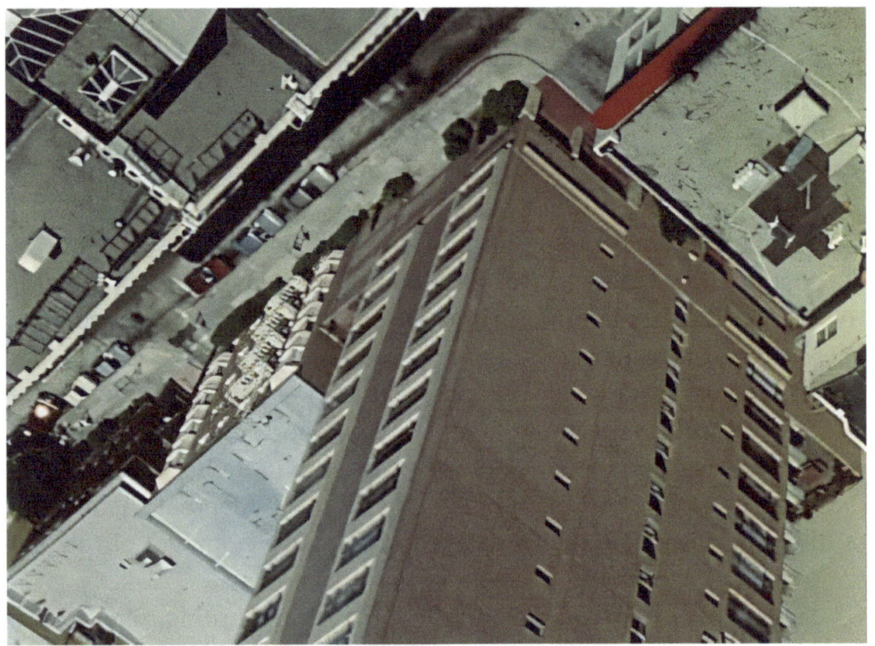

Fairmont Hotel. In line with the structuralist film movement, it follows the panoramic elevator's slow proxistant path from the ground floor's sidewalk view to the top floor's grand panoramic vista of the city and the bay. The film records these views according to the elevator's mechanical movement, highlighting how the elevator itself can be understood as a moving image machine. As we have seen, the panoramic elevator's mechanical visual movement recalls the memory of a cinematic establishing shot, of which the entry sequence from a descending window cleaning rig in Antonioni's *La Notte* (1961) is a landmark example.[12]

Side/Walk/Shuttle adopts the structural path of the elevator, moving in a straight line between the hotel floors. Gehr himself recalls that when

FIGURE 3.1

Earnie Gehr. Film still from *Side/Walk/Shuttle* (1991). Copyright © the artist.

producing the film, the outdoor glass elevator simply presented him with "visual, spatial, and gravitational possibilities." But the film also articulates how movement and transition have come into the center of everyday life experience, Gehr continues, as the work is "tempered by reflections upon a lifetime of displacement."[13] The actual duration of the elevator ride is conceptually important as it provides a fundamental structure for the film. Each shot is the total length of the ride without cuts or edits. In terms of temporality, the cinematic experience of the elevator is additionally highlighted as the elevator has only one stop, from the hotel lobby to the Crown Room at the top and back, traversing the elevation of no less than twenty-three floors in a continuous journey. Furthermore, the film maintains the alternating logic of the elevator, up-down-up-down . . . In this sense, the elevator and camera can be said to co-produce the film, since the elevator is the one deciding the overall structure, while the camera records the motion. As a structuralist film, *Side/Walk/Shuttle* can furthermore be seen to point back to the moving image's material base as film frames in the way these frames of movement are mirrored in the concept of the elevator passing by windows of the adjacent buildings.

While *Side/Walk/Shuttle* provides a perspective from within the urban environment, and rarely offers a full panoramic overview of the cityscape or even a glimpse of the sky, *Time Lines* by British artist Runa Islam gives the exact opposite.

The press release states that the film investigates "three early twentieth-century structures in Barcelona: the once-iconic cable car of Montjuic [. . .], and two rides at the antiquated Tibidabo fairground—a plane that moves in a fixed circle overhead and a crane that rotates upwards to what was formerly the highest point in the city."[14] The framing consistently excludes any view of the ground. Only the uppermost part of the cable car structure is visible as the film pins the actors to the blue-sky backdrop. In the instance where we do see the city below, it is presented as an unfocused distant abstraction. The film also differs in its structure from *Side/Walk/Shuttle* in the way it switches between two different camera modes. In addition to recording a *cinéma trouvé* experience on film, *Time Lines* also occasionally cuts to a static shot that shows the ride without being in it. These static shots are composed of vast and elevated overviews, thus highlighting the cable car's fragile structures. As the White Cube Gallery

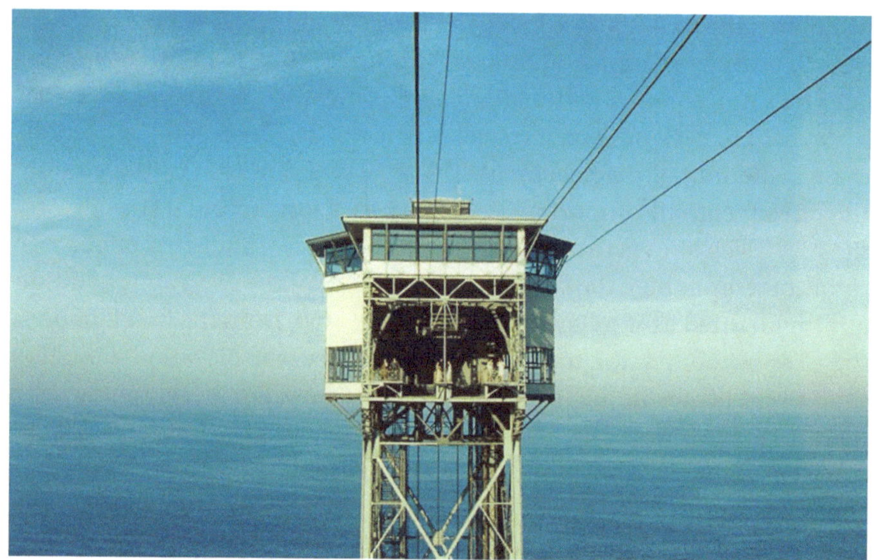

points out in their presentation of *Time Lines*, the kinetic infrastructure "provide[s] both the subject and the method of the filmmaking process."[15] Yet these perspectives from the outside never offer a totalizing view or control of the setting. The framing continues to provide the sensation of suspended disconnection from the ground. Everything remains fragile and radically unstable.

In a similar fashion to the two aforementioned works, *A Memorial to Failure* utilizes cable cars to form a simple but powerful retro-remediation of these grounded machines' proxistant vision. The roughly twenty-minute-long high-definition color video by Egyptian artist Mahmoud Khaled features two different cable car perspectives from two different cities, namely Rio de Janeiro, Brazil, and Jounieh, Lebanon.

Yet, these two very different demographically and geographically located cities seamlessly blend in the work and summon a thought of *A Man*

FIGURE 3.2

Runa Islam. Film still from *Time Lines* (2005).
Copyright © the artist.

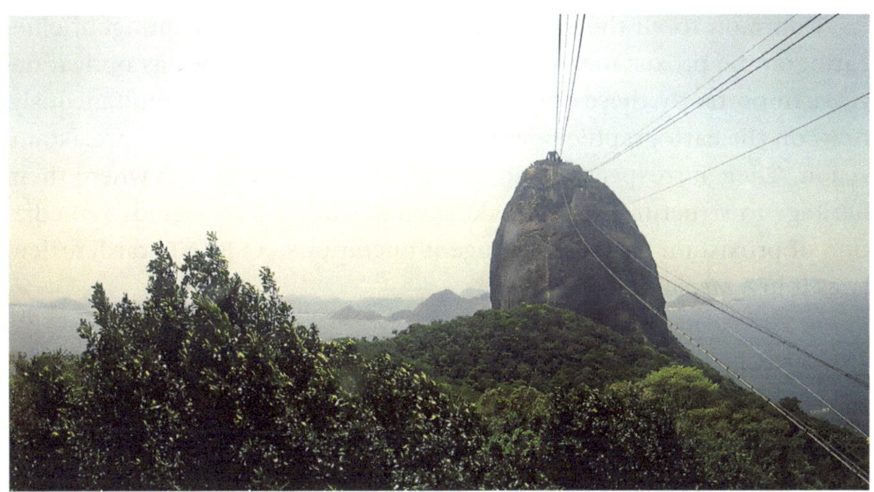

With a Movie Camera, Dziga Vertov's city symphony that combined footage from Kharkiv, Kyiv, Moscow, and Odesa into a singular urban experience. We quickly understand that *A Memorial to Failure* is not about a particular city or even a particular structure, like in the previous examples by Gehr and Islam. Rather, this work seems more philosophically to reflect on the experience of being suspended in motion between the grounded and elevated view. It simply records the views offered by the two cable cars in the direction of their slow forward-moving trajectories, one after the other. Presented as four trips up and down the two different mountains, the views are very similar to the way Edison in 1900 kept the view of Paris at center stage in the elevator ride up and down the Eiffel Tower, retrospectively in a proper *cinéma trouvé* manner. The counter-mapping aspect of this work is found in the soundtrack, which is comprised of several short verbal reflections on subjects regarding failure, social change, and activism by the Italian Marxist theorist and activist Franco "Bifo" Berardi.

FIGURE 3.3

Mahmoud Khaled. Video still from *A Memorial to Failure* (2013). Copyright © the artist.

Common to all these artworks is how they revisit contingent cine-cartographic proxistance by treating grounded machines as optical devices. Importantly, these works reveal how grounded rides simultaneously draw on the cartographic power and cinematic dimension of proxistant vision. Their introspective and anti-illusionist form is also where their heritage to structuralist filmmaking comes in, as a retrograde remediation of proxistant vision's contingent operations. As Bifo Berardi articulates it in *A Memorial to Failure*:

> Artists can be seen as those people that perceive in a different way; they see something that the common perception does not see. They listen to the noise of the city, and they find a bling that before was not perceived. So, if they are able to transform that bling into another way of producing, consuming, making love, and occupying the space, they are starting a media activist process.[16]

It is in this manner of perceiving again, but differently, that the works mentioned here achieve their effect, liberating proxistant vision by returning to early cinematic explorations of perceptual displacement. Through their different methods, these artistic endeavors open proxistant vision to its own emergent formation to approach differently the dynamic relationship between the aerial view and the detail. Common to these works is the intention to produce proxistant vision that redirects our sense of cartographic space from the totality of the *plan* as an all-seeing surface, to the folded space of artistic retrograde remediation, from the illusion of spatial stability to foregrounding the open-ended processes of becoming.

The examples discussed illustrate a shared artistic interest in the cinéma trouvé phenomenon and its possibilities for a creative investigation into how the moving image intersects with spatial disciplines, such as architecture and geography. Returning to our own artistic research, we have further studied this perceptual phenomenon through the technique of mobilizing moving image projectors in space.[17] Part of our ongoing investigation of these multiple dimensions of movement is to study and analyze contemporary affective and subconscious operations of moving image media. The pivotal role of empirical experimentation within physical spaces in this study cannot be underestimated. Such experiments yield unexpected insights that defy prior predictions. Results are achieved through the ongoing process of probing, observing, and testing in the physical exhibition space. The concurrent analysis of physical motion within the space and the recorded movement within the imagery serves as an inquiry into the dynamics of how the moving image moves thought through perceptual uncertainty.[18] Furthermore, the deployment of kinetic moving image projectors seeks to disrupt conventional spatial perception, thereby foregrounding movement and process as intrinsic elements of experiential becoming. Within the scope of this artistic exploration, the exhibition space is transformed into both an apparatus and an active component of the installation itself. The conceptual underpinnings of our empirical exploration and technological experimentation are rooted in a new materialist and process-oriented philosophical paradigm, accentuating the continuous processes of technical mediation.[19] This investigation prioritizes the construction of novel expressions and mediators, fostering the emergence of new realities and experiences that provoke fresh inquiries and innovative patterns of thought.

This media archaeology-inspired artistic method is driven by new avenues of thinking and questioning that explore contemporary issues through historical and genealogical contexts, both in practice and theory. The theoretical investigations are informed by the aesthetic practice, and vice versa. Philosopher and theorist Henk Borgdorff has described three different concepts related to research and art that have been widely referenced in recent years regarding the growing field of artistic research. These are:

- research on the arts (. . . investigations aimed at drawing valid conclusions about art practice from a theoretical distance . . .)
- research for the arts (. . . applied research in a narrow sense . . .)
- research in the arts (. . . the artistic practice itself is an essential component of both the research process and the research results . . .).[20]

Here we see that the last point, "research in the arts" lists artistic practice as an essential component in knowledge production. While such positions have been widely accepted and further developed by universities and research institutes across Scandinavia and Northern Europe, it is also a field that has been criticized for its possible negative effect on free artistic exploration.[21] One example here is artist and philosopher Tom Holert, who critiques the current knowledge economy's influence on art, warning against the potential for standardization and the subsuming of art into formats dictated by a capitalist agenda, which risks aligning artistic work too closely with the metrics of learning and research rather than with creative independence and innovation.[22] While this is a valid concern, anthropologist Tim Ingold sees research in the art as a possibility to restore the notion of research from developing into "an industry of knowledge production, dedicated not to truth but to novelty and impact."[23] Here he advocates for a practice-oriented approach that transcends conventional academic boundaries, emphasizing the importance of an integrated, experiential understanding that unifies different modes of engaging with the world. Our own position on this issue is aligned with media artists such as Hito Steyerl and Trevor Paglen, who, through a combination of practice and theory, mark a commitment to examining and critiquing the intersections of art, media, and politics, by exploring how these realms influence and inform one another in the context of our increasingly digitized and globalized world.[24]

As we redirect our attention from the horizontal structures of the revolving restaurant to the vertical structures of the observation wheel, we recognize the emergence of a paradigmatic shift beyond the wheel that proliferates across the twenty-first-century media sphere. This is the combination of proximity and distance in one visual form, a quest as old as imaging itself but intensified today with specific technological advancements. As such, *Proxistant Vision* identifies the emergence of a new visual paradigm, which has led to the invention of the descriptive words *proxistance* (noun) and *proxistant* (adjective). Most prominently exemplified by Google Earth's "digital ride" from a global perspective to street-level view, proxistant vision identifies this combination of proximity and distance experienced as a unified visual form. The "original" industrial-sized Ferris wheel built for the Chicago World's Fair in 1893, just in time before cinema itself was properly invented, presents itself as a pertinent historical trace from which we can begin to trace the impact of the urban observation wheel's proxistant journey in operation within the urban metropolis today. This does not present an origin story or any such teleological historical narrative. Rather, the "original" Ferris wheel (1893), invented one year before conventional cinema, is one of many genealogical traces of proxistance. It is studied here to understand some of the power with which today's large observation wheels operate across globalized urban spaces. This media archeological study shows not only how the wheel relates to cinema but also how the current surge in wheels globally can be analyzed as part of a larger visual paradigm across screens, digital geography, and other visualization platforms. As we return to the space of the *Ferriscope* kinetic installation, we reflect on the artistic processes and practical experiments that have both informed and been informed by previous research.

THE *FERRISCOPE* JOURNEY

Although some early moving image recording experiments were invented while Ferris's "original" wheel was still running at the Fair, the ride was never documented by a moving image. However, among countless photographs *of* the wheel at the University of Chicago Special Collections Research Center, we also located a few photographs taken *from* the wheel in close to sequential settings.[25] Hence, the *cinéma trouvé* experience of the ride on the "original" Ferris wheel could be made possible by proxy, using scarce photographic documentation stowed away in miscellaneous folders of random special collections.[26]

Currently, we have located thirty-nine photographs of this kind across various collections, of which twenty-four are in use in *Ferriscope*. An imaginary recording in the fashion of *cinéma trouvé* is established by sequencing them as if still frames extracted from a hypothetical recording of the ride. Such recording would have been nine minutes long, matching the duration of one uninterrupted revolution on the wheel, which would translate into 12,960 individual frames with a standard twenty-four frames per second shot. The imported photographs as single frames in a moving image editing software, according to this layout, could be loosely defined as a one-second compression of that ride. The entire sequence is framed within a vignette derived from the lantern slide, honoring the magic lantern as an important antecedent to the projected moving image, as meticulously studied by scholars, including Artemis Willis.[27] The vignette,

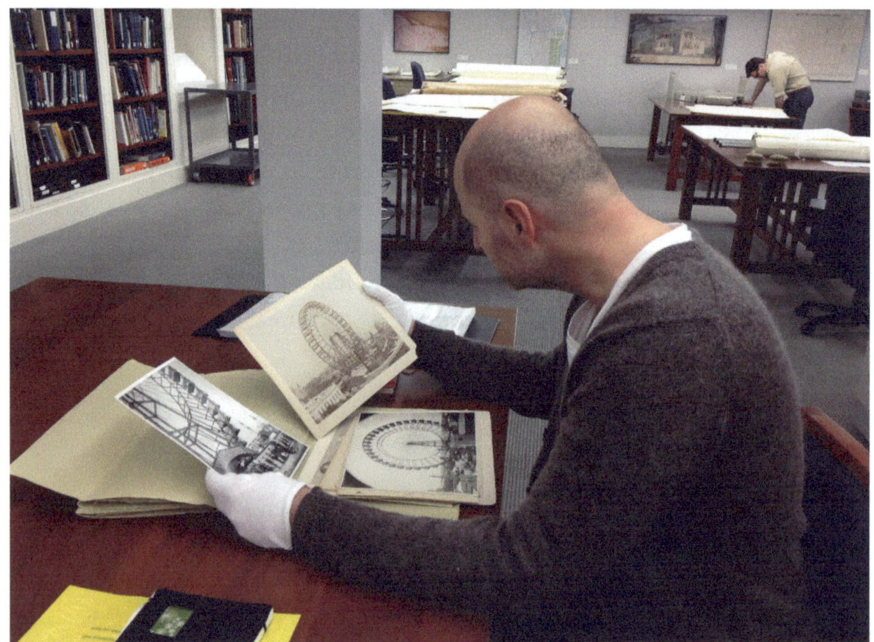

moreover, serves a dual purpose; in addition to evoking the zeitgeist and visual richness of the Victorian era, it also harmonizes the differing aspect ratios of the twenty-four photographs, a solution we found after a long struggle with the archival photographs. Aside from this little intervention, all the photograph's distinct qualities, such as resolution, tone, medium specificities, original modifications, and aging marks, are kept as originally scanned.

The wide variety of the images, combined with the speed at which they are presented, challenges the eye-brain perceptual system, which strives to both fuse them and see them as separate frames. As discussed

FIGURE 3.4

Research at the Library of the Chicago Historical Society (2012). Photo by Bull. Miletic. Copyright © Bull.Miletic.

earlier, the thaumatrope was an optical instrument that not only entertained but also conveyed a Cartesian rationale in the early nineteenth century, asserting that sensory perceptions are unreliable, and it is only with reflective reason that one can discern the illusion created by the merging of images on opposite sides of the paper. Although this image does not physically exist, it is nonetheless observable and can be communally acknowledged. Thus, the fused image is often referred to as an illusion, but it can also be seen as a perceptual affordance, as a kind of magic. This is also the very nature of the moving image, an event at which images, machines, and bodily interaction produce perceptual movement. Hence, the thaumatrope, the recorded live-action moving image, and the 3D-animated image rely on the same principle—a certain threshold of frequency ignites the eye-brain coordination to produce the in-between movement between the still frames. It is a fusion of body and machine that exists only at this moment when the machine is turned on and the eye is looking. Further experimentation with this visual phenomenon suggested that increasing the speed of a moving image projector's vertical circular motion within an exhibition space could potentially produce an optical illusion of a continuous circle of light, reflecting the circular shape of the wheel.

Through continuous dialogue with engineers and more than three years of probing and testing, the assembly of a basic prototype, which utilized a motorized mirror for the swift pivoting of the projected image, resulted in a remarkable effect.[28]

As the mirror that bounced the projector into a circle in the room accelerated, it turned the black-and-white projected image into a full circle with a spectacular rainbow-colored pattern. What we saw was a meeting between the Ferris wheel and the color wheel in a single-chip Digital Light Processing (DLP) video projector.

When physically moved, the image projected by a single-chip DLP projector acquires a peculiar *rainbow effect*.[29] The effect is observable by some even if the projection is stationary, for example, in scrolling credits, and has been addressed by engineers since the introduction of the DLP projector on the market in 1997.[30] This effect arises from the sequential color production method (red, green, blue) employed, by which a red image is flashed and superseded by a flash of a green image, which is

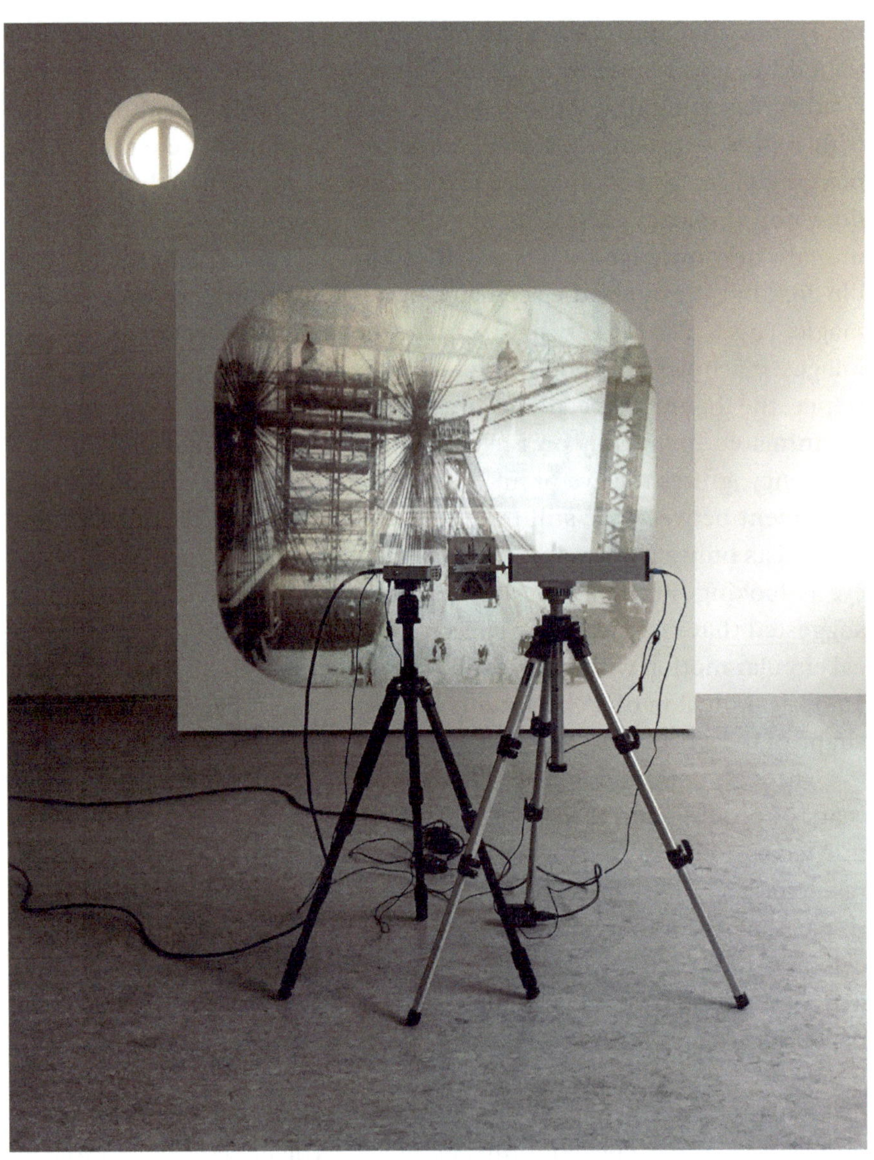

FIGURE 3.5

An early prototype of *Ferriscope*, presented at Aritistic Research Forum, Kunstnernes Hus, Oslo (2017). Photo by Bull.Miletic.

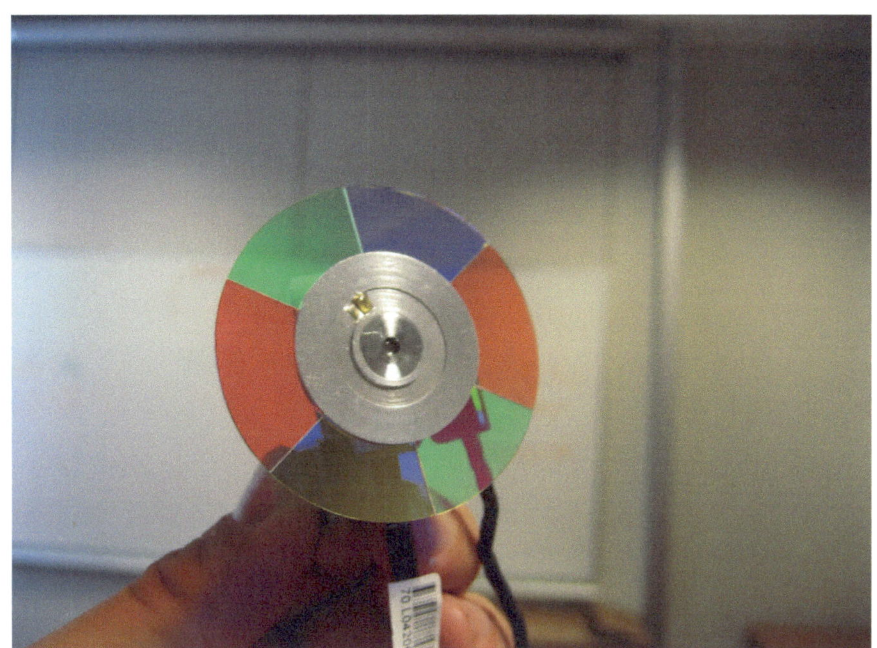

superseded by a flash of a blue image, successively. Thousands of such monochromatic images can be sequentially flashed in a second. Human visual perception is unable to distinguish between the rapid flashes of monochromatic images and blend them into a perfectly coherent color composite.

To get even more technical, the DLP technology operates with a white light emitted from a light source, often a Light-Emitting Diode (LED), which passes through a revolving color disc (or wheel), spinning at rates of 7,200 revolutions per minute and higher, with red, blue, and green filters on its way to a Digital Micromirror Device (DMD).[31]

The DMD is comprised of millions of tiny mechanized micromirrors arranged in a grid. These micromirrors or DMD pixels can tilt twelve

FIGURE 3.6

DLP® color wheel.

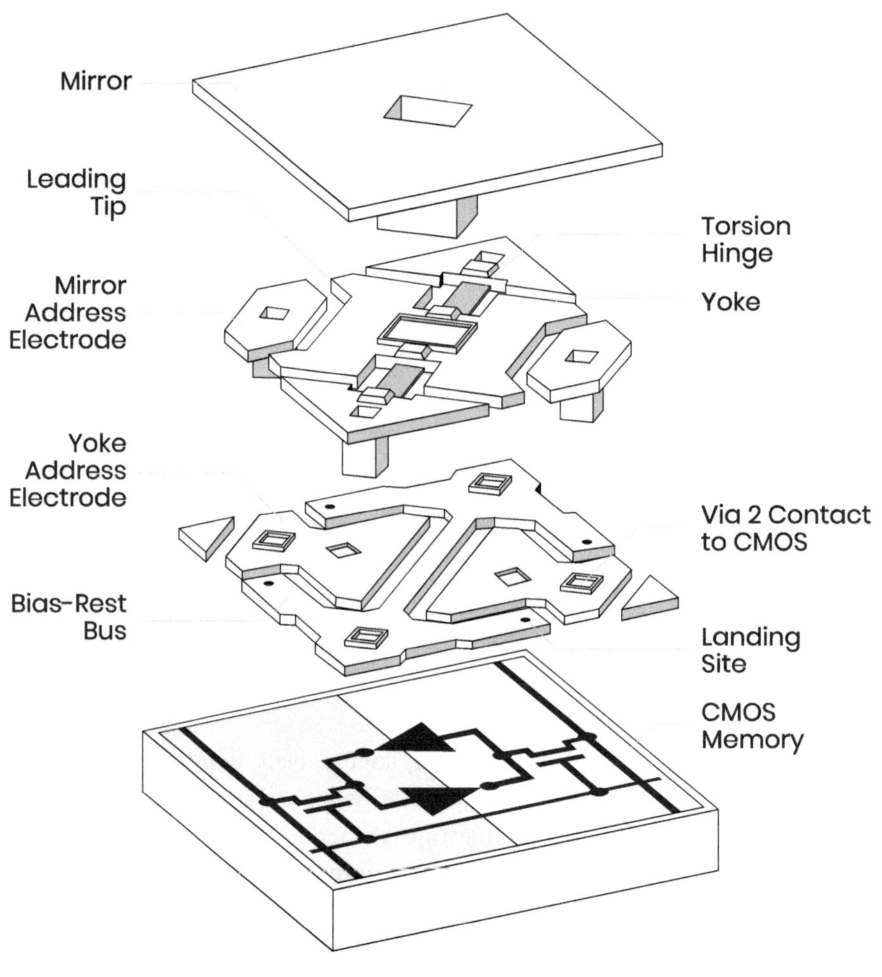

FIGURE 3.7

Diagram of a single micromirror assembly in a DMD.

degrees in either direction. By flipping between these two positions, also known as stable states, the DMD pixel determines the direction in which the light is deflected. By convention, the positive (+) state is tilted toward the illumination and is referred to as the "on" state. The negative (−) state is tilted away from the illumination into a *light dump* within the projector and is referred to as the "off" state. If, for example, a red light is deflected while the micromirror is on, a red pixel shows on the screen. When red and blue lights are deflected sequentially off the same micro-mirror at high speed, human perception fuses the rapidly alternating colors, resulting in the visual impression of a solid purple pixel. Now, to produce a particular hue of purple, the machine needs to find another way to trick the viewer. As is the case with most magic tricks, this one, too, is all about speed. The ability to alternate between on and off states over 1,000 times per second means that these tiny mirrors can deflect sequentially red, green, and blue light in extremely rapid flashes. The frequency of light flashes is proportional to the pixel's luminosity—the higher the deflection frequency the brighter the pixel. In this way, each micromirror can produce 1,024 shades of luminosity, or 16.7 million colors, by combining red, green, and blue lights. To see the projected image, the observer enters a symbiotic relationship with the machine, which meticulously coordinates micro-temporal events with the body's sensorial faculties.

Knowing how DLP operates makes it easier to understand how the rainbow effect works in the installation. As the rotation accelerates, the supposed overlapping flashes of colored light become increasingly misaligned in spacetime, and the eye catches some of this unruly behavior, perceiving it as an iridescent spectacle. As with the thaumatrope, the embodied eye sees how it sees. Black-and-white images turn into patterns of pulsating colors, revealing that the image was never projected in black-and-white but as a composite of red, green, and blue hues rapidly flashing on the screen. Experiments with different motors showed that 1,000 revolutions per minute is the point of the effect's climax. Faster rotation dilutes the effect, turning the projection into a greyish strip of light. The reason for this can be attributed to the body's specific perceptual abilities and the characteristics of light. Much like putting a physical hypothesis into space, artistic research entails observing and learning and, by this process, entering the unknown to expand artistic potential. The desired outcome is that the work takes over and shows the future direction. Much like a book sometimes starts writing itself for an author or a painting emerges from within the canvas for a painter, a kinetic video installation can also take on a life of its own, finding its final form through the process of visual and technical experiments (see figure I.1). The intention of this process has been to articulate how the proxistant visual paradigm moves between total overview and control on the one hand, and vertigo and instability on the other (see figure I.2).

An artistic thought process sometimes results in elaborating technical complexity that only the most expert engineering team can help navigate. After several prototypes, the current Ferriscope apparatus comprises an electromechanical device with a 4.7-by-4.7-inch or 120-by-120-milimeter first-surface mirror attached at a forty-five degree angle at the end of a horizontal axle powered by a stepper motor. Unlike a regular household mirror, also known as a second surface mirror, the reflective silver coating on the first surface mirror is, as the name suggests, the uppermost layer. This design eliminates the refraction or bending of a light beam as it enters a slab of glass—a physical characteristic responsible for the so-called *ghosting* effect. First-surface mirrors are made for applications requiring a strict reflection, such as precision instruments such as telescopes, periscopes, and Single-Lens Reflex (SLR) cameras. The Digital Micromirror Device in a DLP projector also consists of millions of tiny first-surface mirrors, each measuring 16 micrometers by 16 micrometers (see figure 3.7).[32] When a one kHz sine tone is played in the video, the motor starts to rotate, and the projection begins to travel vertically across the room—just like in the case of micromirrors, the light has been spatially modulated. The acceleration and deceleration curves are preprogrammed so the one kHz audio signal controls only the length of the rotation interval. This high-pitched tone is not heard in the installation, but its function is reminiscent of the sound of a golden whistle, which Ferris blew to officially start the turning of his wheel on June 21, 1893.[33]

In addition to conveying the shape of the wheel in the exhibition space, the idea of the circular movement of the projection was also triggered by the need to challenge conventional ways of observing moving image projections. Thus, the video projection continuously alternates between static and kinetic modes with the assistance of the motorized mirror, as described earlier. Hence, during the static mode, the video is conventionally projected straight onto the wall. At a certain point in the video, the motorized mirror starts to rotate gradually, causing the projected image to slowly travel vertically around the darkened room. As the projection accelerates, black-and-white video optically transforms into a continuous light strip of pulsating color patterns. The maximum speed of 1,000 revolutions per minute is achieved after one minute of acceleration when the "rainbow effect" reaches its highest intensity. Upon briefly revolving at maximum speed, the rotation begins to decelerate, affecting the gradual desaturation of the color effect. Ultimately, the mirror locks in the original position, and the black-and-white video is again conventionally projected straight onto the wall. The projection continues to alternate in this manner endlessly.

During the seven-and-a-half minutes of conventional projection between the spinning cycles, the video combines the image sequence from the "original" wheel with *cinéma trouvé* recordings from the contemporary wheels London Eye and Las Vegas High Roller but also the much older Wiener Riesenrad. Opened to the public in 1897, just three years after the giant Ferris wheel was taken down, Wiener Riesenrad is the oldest observation wheel in operation. Considerably smaller, with a height of 213 feet, or sixty-five meters, its characteristic design, craftsmanship, and the materials used for its construction very much resemble that of the "original" Ferris wheel. In a way, Riesenrad becomes a time machine, allowing the recording of an imagined previous experience in conditions very similar to the original. When imported into the editing software and desaturated, the footage indeed appears as a moving version of the archival photographs from Ferris's "original" wheel. Turning the room into a white cube for projection purposes produces an additional side effect for the installation, evoking for some the buoyant sensation of a zero-gravity chamber. As articulated by visual artist Edvine Larsen, this evokes a strange feeling of "an experience of vertigo standing on a normal floor without any height involved."[34] It is exactly this spatiotemporal approximation between proximity and distance—the power of seeing from a high vantage point combined with a street view through technological motion—that forms the artistic knowledge base from where a grounded machine's architectural proxistant vision can be studied. This visual form produces the complex sensation of simultaneous clear-sightedness, dizziness, bafflement, and wonder as the journey between proximity and distance repeats. The emphasis is on revealing by which power the urban observation wheels operate within contemporary globalized cityscapes, by exposing the contingent operative chains engrained in their outlook. Wondering *how*—not only what—one sees is the key element in this research. In the pursuit of liberating both vision and imagination from the chains of subjugating mechanisms imposed with escalating degrees of proxistant sophistication, *Ferriscope* is a reminder that the image is never a fixed entity but an incessant process of becoming—a disturbance in a habitual techno-sensorial event.

The work has led an investigation into the combination of mechanical movement and the aerial view from the Ferris wheel as a force of cinematic revelation and curiosity. Through practical experiments, it has revealed and expanded on the technical mediation between rides, cinema, and aerial imaging. The installation became a testing ground to expose how bodily participation produces proxistant vision as part of its underlying power, the way the body, before the rational mind and thus precognitively, is affected. This practical manner of working has moved the research questions into the exhibition space. The goal is to understand how the various proxistant modalities affect the human body's relation to space and the physical environment. This is an investigation into how such imaging takes place in the body, and how the body becomes, in a material sense, a constitutive part of the image. Today, proxistance materialized as giant observation wheels across many of the world's global metropolises, turning lived urban space into gentrified cinematic establishing shots. Studying this phenomenon through a combination of artistic and practical experiments identifies a larger twenty-first-century visual paradigm beyond the wheel. In this project, we have studied its genealogies and multiple historical appearances as well as its theoretical implications. Most importantly, we have shown how this research was made possible through its artistic potential.

The motion between proximity and distance makes up the cinematic contingencies of proxistant vision. Grounded machines such as observation wheels and cable cars articulate this twenty-first-century paradigm in architectural form. Seen as optical devices, these kinetic structures are characteristic of their shifting natures that oscillate between the seemingly intrinsic stability of architecture and the flux of cinematic motion. We have seen how the giant observation wheel turns the city into a location-establishing shot by launching spectators into mechanical motion between detail and overview. When Gehr, Islam, and Khaled reveal and expand on the cine-cartographic contingencies and ongoing individuation between rides, cinema, and cartography in their artworks, they reinvoke a forgotten sensitivity towards cinematic motion and produce an open-ended urban experience. Motion is here finally seen as a potential opening for experiences as well as critical views regarding a smooth proxistant establishing shot of the city. This insight lets us explore how artists approach the capacities not strictly in line with the commercial intentions and the forces built into for-profit proxistant models. Treating kinetic infrastructure as a form of camera movement, these artists approach such structures as potentials for artistic exploration of proxistant vision. Motion is here finally seen as a potential opening for the experience as well as critical views of the ongoing individuation between moving image media and grounded kinetic structures.

The analysis presented here shows the importance of considering artistic research as part of a broader scholarly investigation in the age of the Anthropocene in which understanding open-ended becoming is crucial. Coming back to Latour, it has become increasingly important to realize that entities do not stand in the world the way they are represented.[35] The tools of media archeology and artistic research have shown how the current surge of observation wheels today figure as proponents of a twenty-first-century visual paradigm materialized in architectural steel and mechanical motion. Most significantly, however, these practices and tools reveal some of the contingencies with which this visual paradigm operates as grounded machines within urban environments today. In the next part, we will lift off from these predetermined urban paths to explore the more expansive navigation between proximity and distance offered by airborne machines.

II

AIRBORNE MACHINES

Venetie 11111100110 (1500–2022)

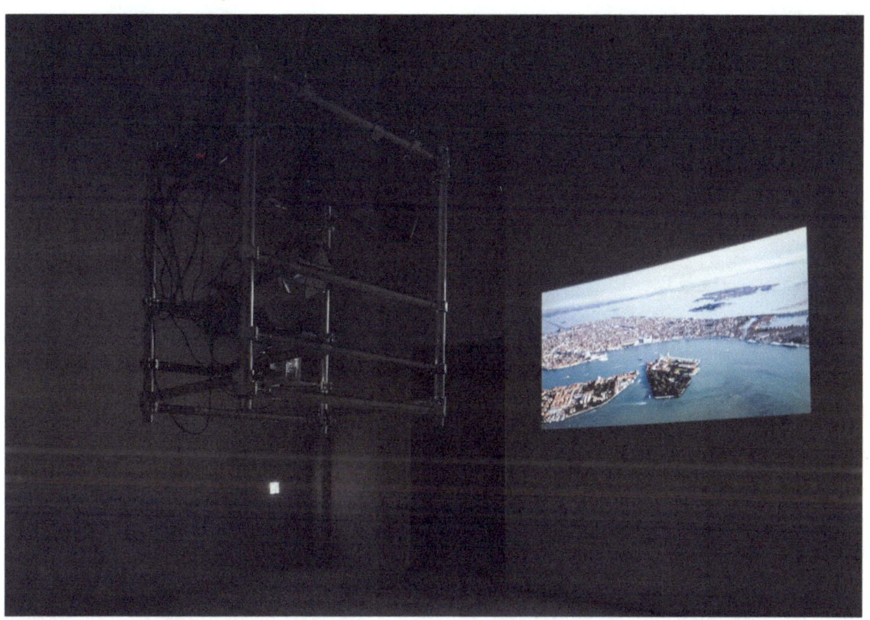

FIGURE II.1

Bull.Miletic. Installation view of *Venetie 11111100110* (1500–2022) at the Museum of Craft and Design, San Francisco. Photo by Henrik Kam. Copyright © the artists.

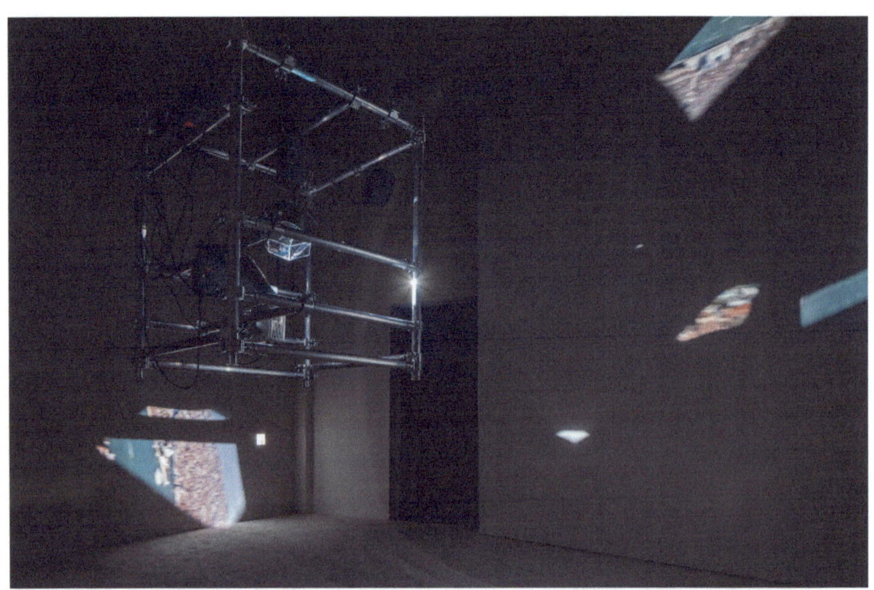

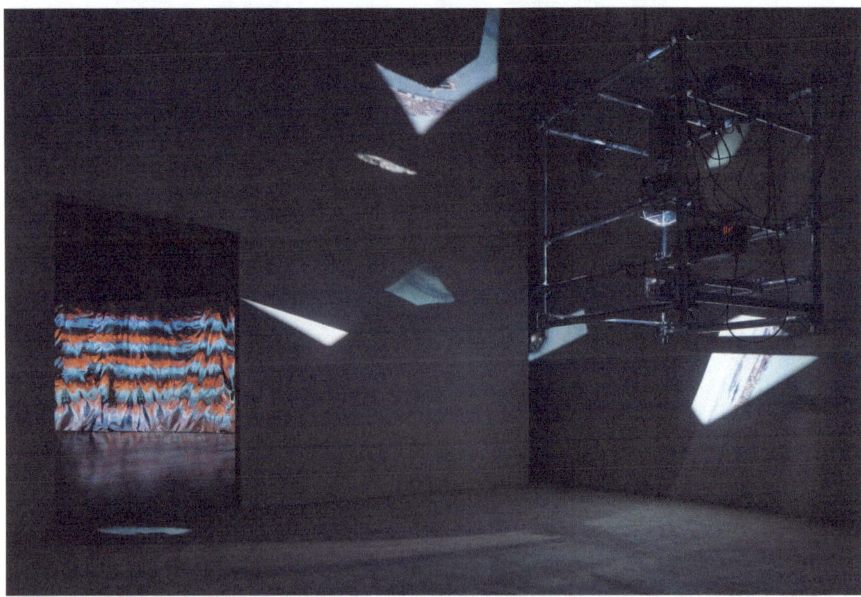

FIGURE II.2

Bull.Miletic. Installation view of *Venetie 11111100110* (1500–2022) at the Museum of Craft and Design, San Francisco. Photo by Henrik Kam. Copyright © the artists.

FIGURE II.3

Bull.Miletic. Installation view of *Venetie 11111100110* (1500–2022) at the Museum of Craft and Design, San Francisco. Photo by Henrik Kam. Copyright © the artists.

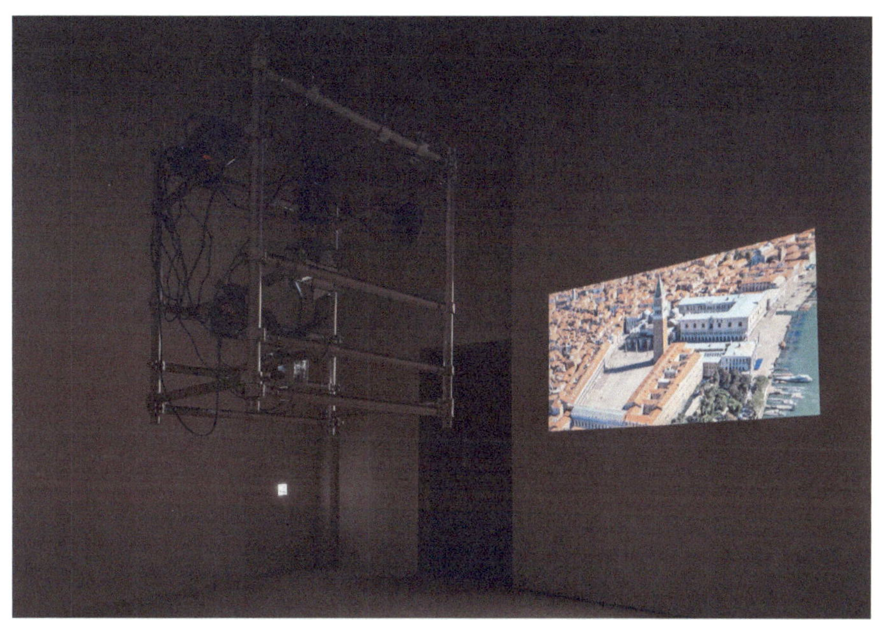

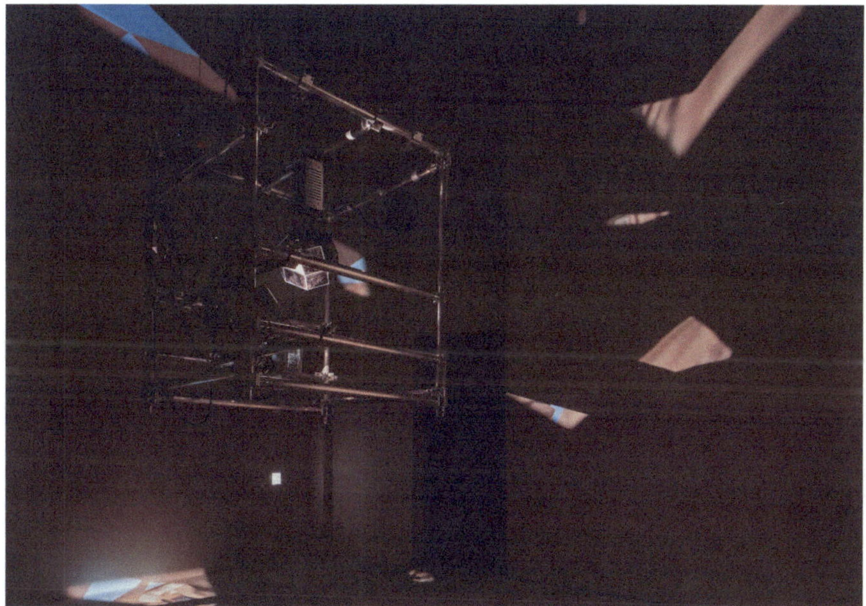

FIGURE II.4

Bull.Miletic. Installation view of *Venetie 11111100110* (1500–2022) at the Museum of Craft and Design, San Francisco. Photo by Henrik Kam. Copyright © the artists.

FIGURE II.5

Bull.Miletic. Installation view of *Venetie 11111100110* (1500–2022) at the Museum of Craft and Design, San Francisco. Photo by Henrik Kam. Copyright © the artists.

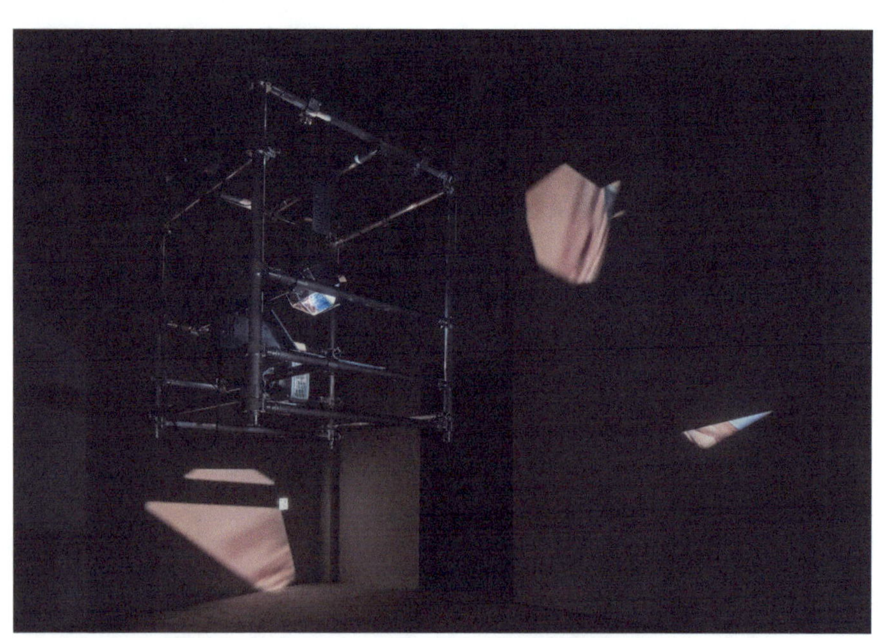

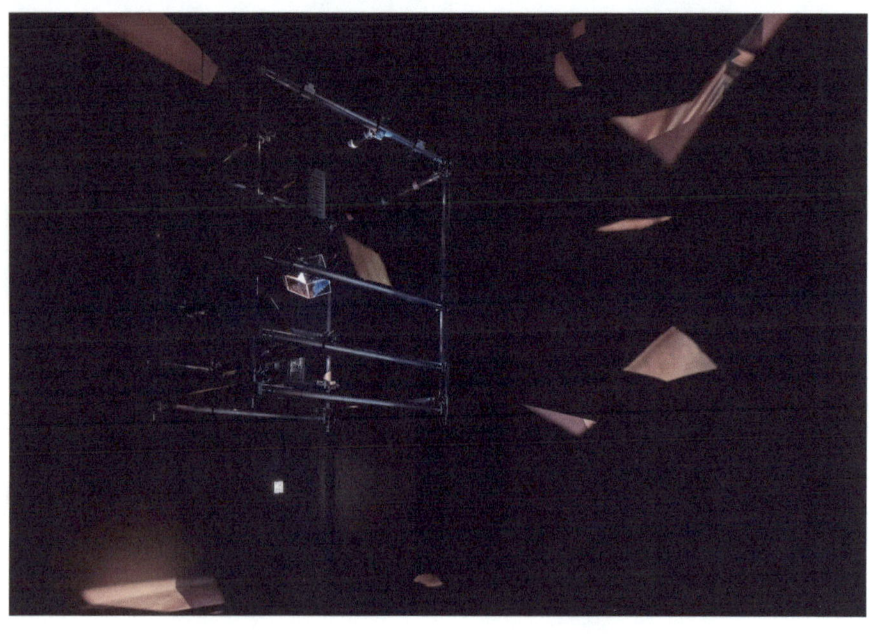

Venetie 11111100110 is a single-channel kinetic video installation wherein the projection perpetually oscillates between static and dynamic modes in a white cube with a white floor and ceiling.[1] This seamless transition is orchestrated by a system of motorized mirrors suspended in mid-air above the projector. In the static mode, the video is traditionally projected onto a suspended wall via a first-surface mirror positioned at a forty-five-degree angle directly above the projector lens. At an arbitrary moment, the projected image ascends as the slanted mirror gradually pivots away from the lens. During its slow, approximately ten-second ascent, the image shatters into kaleidoscopic fragments, permeating the room by reflecting off a gently revolving mirrored rhombicuboctahedron suspended roughly forty centimeters above the projector's lens. After approximately one minute, the image methodically transitions back to the conventional wall projection as the slanted first-surface mirror pivots back towards the lens, and the mirrored rhombicuboctahedron's rotation ceases. This alternating cycle of projection persists indefinitely.

The initial segment of the video commences with an approximately one-minute black-and-white sequence, showcasing the digitized cartographic marvel, *Venetie MD*, the grandiose birds-eye view woodcut ascribed to the atelier of the renowned Italian artist Jacopo de' Barbari. This sequence begins with a blank white frame, from which de' Barbari's panoramic vision of Renaissance Venice gradually materializes.

FIGURE II.6

Bull.Miletic. Installation view of *Venetie 11111100110* (1500–2022) at the Museum of Craft and Design, San Francisco. Photo by Henrik Kam. Copyright © the artists.

FIGURE II.7

Bull.Miletic. Installation view of *Venetie 11111100110* (1500–2022) at the Museum of Craft and Design, San Francisco. Photo by Henrik Kam. Copyright © the artists.

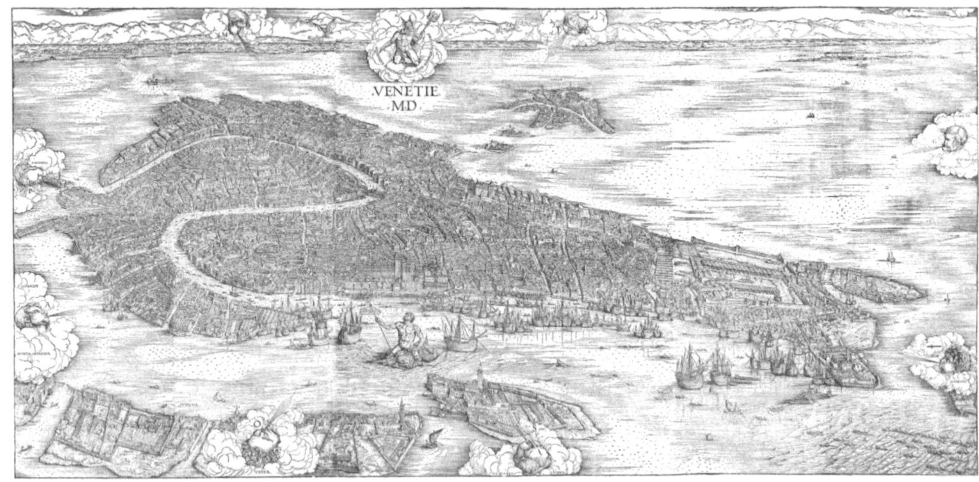

After a prolonged phase of static imagery, *Venetie MD* progressively morphs into more pixelated forms through three distinct phases. The final phase retains only faint echoes of the original, more reminiscent of flickering analogue television static than a coherent aerial depiction. The ensuing sequences present a dynamic blend of photographic aerial views of Venice, captured at varying speeds. This footage combines historical images from the Fotopiano archives, 3D-animated flythroughs, contemporary aerial photography, and drone cinematography, from here on refered to as "dronematography." This vibrant segment culminates in an aerial close-up of glistening waves, capturing the expansive vista of the Venetian lagoon from a nadir perspective.

The gradual ascent and lack of geographical markers obscure the filming location, until the camera gently tilts upwards, incrementally revealing an aerial panorama of twenty-first-century Venice, vibrant with maritime activity.

FIGURE II.8

Jacopo de' Barbari. *Venetie MD* (1500), first state, woodcut print, 53 × 110 in (135 × 280 cm).

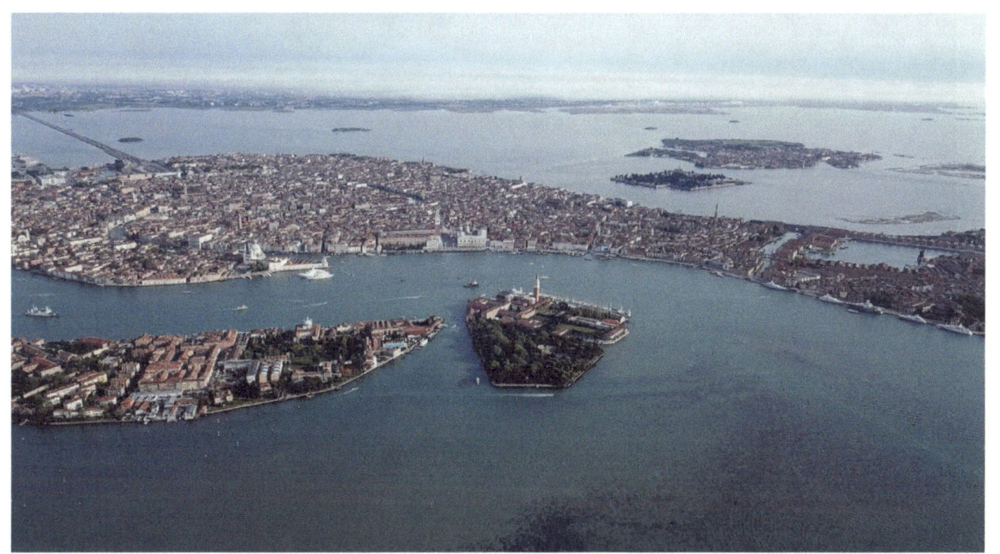

The camera's altitude and orientation align with the imagined vantage point of *Venetie MD*. In the foreground, the islands of Giudecca and San Giorgio Maggiore appear, evoking the layout seen in the 500-year-old woodcut. Central to the composition are the Giudecca Canal, Piazza San Marco with its Basilica, Palazzo Ducale, and the Campanile. The Grand Canal weaves through the city, bisecting it into two distinct halves that collectively form a unified urban entity. In the background, the Island of San Michele, the Island of Murano, Ponte della Libertà, Marco Polo Airport, and the faint outlines of the Venetian Prealps stretch into the distance. As the camera leisurely retreats from the city, the city's distinctive shape becomes increasingly discernible, almost miraculously corresponding to the form meticulously depicted in *Venetie MD* at the cusp of the fifteenth century. The image then fades to black, symbolically marking the conclusion of the video's first part.

FIGURE II.9

Bull.Miletic. Video still from *Venetie 11111100110* (1500–2022). Copyright © the artists.

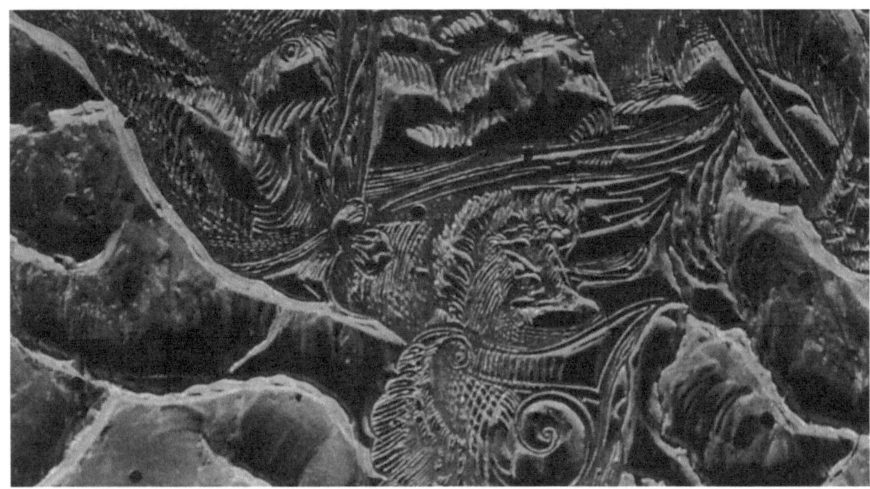

The second part of the video, which is significantly shorter, opens with close-ups of intricate wood carvings, pockmarked with woodworm holes and dust-filled pockets, emerging from the darkness. The carved shapes gradually reveal details reminiscent of *Venetie MD*. As the camera gently glides over the mirror image of *Venetie MD* carved into the darkened wood, a direct connection to de' Barbari's masterpiece is established.

It becomes evident that the meticulously examined wood carvings are segments of the six large pearwood matrices used to print *Venetie MD*. Extended sequences of these carvings are interspersed with fleeting aerial and terrestrial views of Venice, as the camera darts impulsively in all directions, attempting to capture everything at once. The presence of water becomes increasingly pronounced over time. The sequence culminates

FIGURE II.10

Bull.Miletic. Video still from *Venetie 11111100110* (1500–2022). Copyright © the artists.

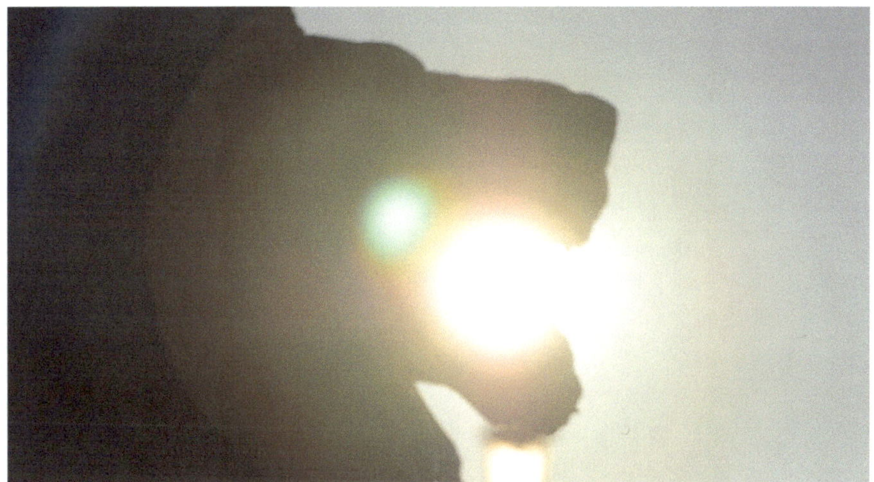

in a brief, ten-frame shot where the sun appears within the jaws of the Venetian lion on Riva degli Schiavoni.

This shot swiftly transitions to a white screen, from which *Venetie MD* re-emerges, perpetuating the endless cycle. Please consider a different front for this art work descriotion for section II in similar style to Ferriscope in section I.

FIGURE II.11

Bull.Miletic. Video still from *Venetie 11111100110* (1500–2022). Copyright © the artists.

4

FIRST-PERSON VIEW DRONEMATOGRAPHY

"Everything is movement, imbalance, crisis."
—Jean Epstein and Stuart Liebman[1]

We brush swiftly in a low flight across the beach's sandy surface. Gravity is defied. In the blink of an eye, a graceful ascent narrowly misses the rapidly approaching lifeguard station. Santa Monica's dunes curve across the screen as we rise further, extending the airborne view to a soaring vertical angle high above the beach. Within seconds, soaring altitude transforms into a speedy descent. The scarlet sunrise swirls into the far-right corner of the frame. Stability is shaken, and wobbly scalar movement clings unevenly to the screen. Once more, the lifeguard station towers in front of us. This time, we slip through a small gap beneath it, quickly transiting between sand and wooden lattice. The beach bulges and swells with wavy parallax effects. Pliable warping sand and water morph with the radical distortion of the wide-angled field of sight. From these incessant bends and folds forms yet another soaring ascent. The spokes of the Ferris wheel at the beach fairground slice sand and sky into asymmetrical wedges as we pass in between them. Ground and planar surfaces disappear from stable spatial coordinates. Perspective is no longer vertical or horizontal, but disorienting, bending, and, stretching. A novel spatial discovery is made visible by way of elevation and unobstructed movement—oscillating vision in a fusion of close-up and mesmerizing overview.

Robert McIntosh's aforementioned drone video was the winner of the "FPV/Proximity/Technical" category at the very first edition of the New York City Drone Film Festival in 2015.[2] As the title of the category suggests, this video was shot by a camera mounted onto an airborne drone, navigated via wireless video downlinks sourced to a pair of video goggles. As an acrobatic spatial navigation with no explicit plot or narrative, McIntosh's four-minute piece is exemplary of the first-person view (FPV)–navigated video's growing popularity. The drone type used in these videos is a small, often custom-made quadcopter, fitted and assembled to serve the need for speed and acrobatic maneuvering. The dynamic spatiality by way of FPV drone vision is made possible by way of an extremely agile aircraft and the expert navigational maneuvers of an experienced pilot. The airborne navigation through and around spatial obstacles exhibits precision and control, combined with reckless altitudes and near-crash excitements. Vectors of seemingly malleable and elastic space are stretched and warped across the visual field.[3] By 2016 the category adopted the name Freestyle FPV and this time it was won by Carlos "Charpu" Puertolas who was also a winning FPV drone racer at the time. McIntosh then won two consecutive years 2017 and 2018 before other pilots started climbing to the top. In 2019 the category was renamed again, this time to Cinematic FPV, a renaming that reflects the development of the sector.

When McIntosh and Charpu made their names in the FPV world, one could see that aside from a growing number of dedicated drone film festivals, this new cinematic genre reached its audience primarily via YouTube and Vimeo, allowing popular content to be shared among devoted fans on blogs and FPV-dedicated websites.[4] Hence, the rapidly expanding FPV community has emerged from an unorganized group of DIY enthusiasts and a large number of "how-to" online tutorials. This is a culture that still exists and most great FPV pilots share their know-how as well as their sponsor's equipment through their YouTube channels. FPV dronematography is experiencing growth due to several key factors. Technological advancements have made FPV drones more accessible and capable, enhancing their appeal. The popularity of drone racing and freestyle flying, particularly through professional leagues like the Drone Racing League, has attracted a wide audience. Social media and online communities play a vital role in promoting the activity, while its use in film and photography opens new professional avenues. The field's growth is additionally influenced by varying regional regulations, with some areas embracing more drone-friendly policies than others.[5] The increased use of smaller FPV systems in war and conflict contributes to this trend, as we see in the current use of drones in Ukraine.[6]

While studying the proliferation of vernacular drone videos on YouTube, Anna Munster found that "[a] mode of aesthetic experimentation opens up, resulting in a novel style of aerial videography."[7] It is this notion of experimentation that we will be taking further in our investigation of FPV videos. By addressing these somewhat diverse and undefined practices of remote-controlled flights, we enter the second strata of our investigation into the visual paradigm of proxistance. Here we examine proxistant vision's navigational capacities, as we scrutinize these extraordinary acrobatic paths between tight close-ups and high vantagepoints. The untethered becoming—but never arriving—to any of the proxistant vision's outer limits, was already suggested by the observation wheel's circular motion as a ride without a destination. While the observation wheel makes up a decisive geometrical loop, FPV dronematography introduces an undecided and vacillated track of indeterminant movement that holds the potential of going both high and low while oscillating everywhere between. How can such aerial acrobatics be theorized through the lens of navigation? In other words, which distinct practices pertaining to navigation—that have perhaps thus far gone unnoticed—come forward when proxistant vision is analyzed through the prism of FPV dronematography? We will offer some reflections on these questions in this chapter.

The histories and current practices of drones are rapidly getting more complex and variegated as ceaseless innovations in this domain draw out different archaeologies and historical contingencies.[8] At Madison Square Garden in 1898, one of history's earliest examples of drones was exhibited by Serbian-American inventor Nikola Tesla, who appeared to command an unmanned vessel to change directions simply by using his voice. Secretly, he was using radio frequencies to switch the motors on and off and to control the rudder.[9] Since then, drones have come to designate a multiplicity of different remotely operated vehicles that continue to conquer new areas of application from military and reconnaissance to commercial services, agriculture, photography, cinema, entertainment industries, and a variety of rescue missions.[10] The fast development of drones saw a surge in 2015 and spurred an expanded field of operation to the point where scholars at The Center for the Study of the Drone at Bard College suggest we are facing a drone revolution.[11] This was also the year Grégoire Chamayou published his *Drone Theory*, which aligns the powerful metaphor of the drone as the "eye of God," with the assets of being both panoptical and omnipresent.[12] While the news media cover the most diverse stories of how drones develop into disparate fields and are changing our everyday lives, we cannot escape their more obscure but steadily growing dark side, namely reconnaissance operations and target killings, exemplified but not limited to the ongoing "everywhere war" initiated by the attack on the World Trade Center in New York on September 11, 2001.[13]

The growing number of countries acquiring unmanned defense systems impacts the role these systems play in wars and conflicts across the globe. Hence, descriptions of drones as "the most important weapons development since the atomic bomb" and "the signature device of the form of contemporary power" give strong signals to how drones are perceived in contemporary culture and society.[14] The recent anthology *Life in the Age of Drone Warfare* (2017), edited by Lisa Parks and Caren Kaplan, reflects exactly this situation.[15] Parks and Kaplan argue that the current proliferation of drones in civil and commercial fields reveals the far reaches of the military-entertainment industrial network.[16] The FPV dronematorgaphy we address in this section has usually been contextualized within the history of radio-controlled hobby vehicles and model aircraft development.[17] However, in their article "Droneism," independent writer Joanne McNeill and artist and writer Ingrid Burrington bring critical attention to how the consumer or hobby drone market attempts to free itself from the dystopian image of drone warfare and military surveillance systems. They effectively point out that "it is not merely the Hellfire missile that makes drones so powerful. It is the vantage point they offer, it is the data they collect from that vantage point, and it is the power afforded by that data."[18] Such potential misuse of a hobby drone's vantage point was recognized already forty years ago, in Raymond Abrashkin and Jay Williams' juvenile science fiction story *Danny Dunn, Invisible Boy*. Here, a private drone invention ends up in the wrong hands and becomes a tool for civil surveillance and government overreach.[19]

When one begins tracing the political dimensions of such drone use, one quickly encounters the old dream of total vision, which is linked to governmental, military, and religious as well as economic structures of power. Such domination through an all-seeing panoramic view was already implemented architecturally in Jeremy Bentham's eighteenth-century ideas of the Panopticon. Power can see but not be seen. The knowledge of being visible has a disciplinary effect in which an external relation becomes internalized and habitual. Explicated by French philosopher Michel Foucault in his book *Discipline and Punish* (1975), Foucault saw this structure repeated in bigger social machinery that extended state power over physical and political bodies.[20] This is again linked to the built-in tracking and surveillance aspects of digital technology, be they intended or unintended, in their design protocols.[21] As algorithms are employed to handle the steadily increasing amount of big data ticking in from artificial intelligence queries, smart cities, and the Internet of Things (IoT), proxistant vision is what systematizes this data into predictive models for effective drill downs and overviews.

While the social sciences and cultural studies have focused primarily on the drone's military and intelligence operations, others have tried to expand this narrow address.[22] "Drones kill, yes, but they also rescue, research, and entertain," New York Times journalist William Grimes asserts.[23] And it is exactly this flexibility that "makes the drone different from other military technologies," according to independent writer Naief Yehya. The fact that drones are rapidly evolving in multiple areas outside military use makes it comparable to the computer. As such, drones can also be understood as "a liberating tool, a technology with a potential for social appropriation and reconfiguration."[24] On the basis of these and other reflections, we agree with media scholar Maximilian Jablonowski, that "it is pivotal to have a close look at the ambiguous ways in which drone technology is taking part in everyday life to further an understanding of what it means to enter the 'Drone Age' or to live in a 'drone culture.'"[25] Such claims are underlined by history of science scholar Brad Bolman, who proposes that "if we want to understand the *bad* drones hovering above contemporary battlegrounds, we need to think very hard about the *good* drones surveilling fields, forest fires, and film sets."[26] Accordingly, these authors argue, although far from the dominant trend, investigating non-military drones can offer important perspectives on emergent issues within a growing drone culture.

Robert McIntosh's prizewinning shot from the Santa Monica Pier takes the viewer smoothly across the sandy beach, softly slipping through narrow architectural structures such as a lifeguard tower and between the spokes of a Ferris wheel as if the video exhibits its own airborne freedom from such grounded structures. The immensely popular drone video *Left Behind* -FPV (2015) by Carlos "Charpu" Puertolas showcases significantly quicker flight patterns.[27] With over two million views on his YouTube channel ChapruFPV, this popular 2′48″ FPV video explores a derelict building from all possible camera angles, interior as well as exterior, via distinct acrobatic flight maneuvers, including multiple 360-degree flips and dives—the signature style that has earned Charpu his fame.[28] We also find *Abandonado* (2015) on this channel, the video that secured Charpu the New York Drone Film Festival Freestyle FPV prize in 2016.[29] Here, the flips and loops performed within three-dimensional structures return a seemingly plastic and stretchable spatiality to the screen. Judging by the number of views online, Robert McIntosh and Charpu were among the most popular FPV at their time. Forming part of several excellent pilots in an ever-growing FPV and drone racing milieu, their videos stand out partly due to outstanding post-production treatment such as meticulous editing, carefully selected soundtracks, and for McIntosh, a considerable effort invested in digital stabilization through his own software Reel Steady™. In this regard, it is interesting to note that they also both work as 3D animators in the Hollywood mainstream movie industry.[30]

The proxistant videos produced by McIntosh and Charpu and many other highly skilled pilots, are dependent on the FPV system, where the flying is navigated through a real-time video feed. As was mentioned earlier, FPV dronematography follows from the older remote-piloted hobby aircraft. As video cameras have come down in size and price, fitting one onto the aircraft to capture its unique point of view is both desirable and easily achievable. The game changer, according to Charpu, was sourcing that camera's video feed in real-time to a pair of goggles on the ground. However, "[p]iloting, by first-person view at 65 miles per hour is not only fun, it's very challenging." First off, the point of view of the pilot is from an on-board camera. As Charpu explains, "[w]hen you are flying FPV you may feel disconnected initially. Then, with time, you become one with the machine."[31] Through FPV goggles, pilots only see the drone camera's perspective, navigating space with newly acquired, radically disentangled electronic eyes. Observing the drone from the ground via line of sight (LOS) does not allow the type of acrobatic performance we see in these videos. McIntosh offers a similar comment regarding his video *Rise & Shine* (2015), where the drone is flying underneath a park bench and through a small opening in a metal structure on Venice Beach, "[u]sing a 250-sized mini quad for aerial cinematography is not only possible, but [is] the *only* way to achieve this shot."[32] McCosker has pointed out how, for an FPV drone operator, the camera's visual feed is crucial to the craft's steering and maneuverability. As such, FPV drones extend the camera operator's visual capability, transforming it from a mere recording tool to an apparatus for real-time visual navigation and observation.[33]

What we have here is moving a step further from previous ideas of camera vision as investigated in the early 1920s by Moholy-Nagy and Dziga Vertov among others, which sought to release human vision from earlier constraints, to function as a replacement for human eyes in real-time.[34] As Samuel Weber's notion of "differential specificity" concerning television noted, the nature of television abolishes the whole idea of distance by rendering it "invisible" in a real-time transmission. Rather than looking at images one "looks at a certain kind of vision," namely the ongoing abolishing of distance.[35] The FPV dronematographer utilizes this television to navigate and tease out the proxistant in-betweens of spaces, shaping the atmosphere into cartographic spatial volumes. Charpu and McInstosh form assemblages with their drones of which novel screen-spatial expressions are the emergent property. A media archeological perspective on the FPV drone video, however, will also entail an investigation of how the drone's mode of operation impacts the FPV dronematographer's ability to navigate highly dynamic and original proxistant flights. What is the role of the drone in the assemblage it forms with its pilot? Typically, FPV dronematographers use small quadcopter drones, which, in addition to the remote control, consist of a lightweight frame with a miniature action camera (GoPro or similar) strapped at the front of the copter's body.[36] Although FPV drones are many and varied, their capability of producing dynamic flights largely depends on four main components: the drone's computational potential, the size and weight of the aircraft, the processes behind its digital imaging, and the relay of real-time video feed for human navigation.

The first component in our analysis of the FPV drone is the flight controller (FC), which constitutes the electronic chief command of the aircraft. The FC is basically yet another assemblage composed of microchips, sensors, and other electronic components—a time-critical infrastructure that responds to the physical flight environment's extensive and intensive parameters, such as winds and air pressure, in speeds far beyond human perception.[37] The concept "time-critical" here is adopted from media scholar Wolfgang Ernst, and describes how the "medial operations under the conditions of digital signal processing must be processed in strictly predefined time windows in order for them to succeed and for a message to materialize at all."[38] This time-critical quantization of time is an "essential feature of the digital" and draws on a computer lineage of faster switching.[39] The most explicit example of this is the superior ability of some drones to autonomously keep a steady course in rough weather. This remarkable performance depends on so-called sensor fusion, meaning that the FC fuses information obtained by onboard sensors with the pilot's ad hoc or preprogrammed commands and relays the adequate instructions to the motor controllers that regulate the power supply to the electric motors. Basic FC types used in mini quadcopters include a gyroscope and accelerometer, while other more advanced FC types might include sensors such as a barometer (barometric pressure sensors) and a magnetometer (compass), as well as global positioning system (GPS) and sonar sensors, among other technologies.[40] All in all, an assemblage of navigational measurement technologies translated into electronic pulsations of machine-to-machine communication. Although FPV drone pilots usually put their FCs in acrobatic (ACRO) mode—a very modest type of preset that allows for flips, sharp turns, low-altitude flights, and dives—the FC still performs essential operations on which the drone pilot relies. Flying without the FC's ongoing calculations at lightning speeds does not offer great control of the drone.

The second technical component of great importance for the FPV drone system is the size and weight of the aircraft. As we have stated earlier, FPV racing and freestyle drones are often custom assembled by the pilot, a process that includes ongoing tuning and optimization for extreme aerial acrobatics. Weight and size are the currencies in this configuration and provide the variables upon which pilots base their choices. While the copter must be small enough to fly through narrow openings, the extra weight of the camera demands larger propellers, which in turn calls for a bigger frame.[41] To address these challenges, Charpu, for example, has worked directly with his sponsor and FPV drone parts manufacturer Lumenier on a design for a "stripped down" airframe for racing copters.[42] Robert McIntosh, on the other hand, has experimented with disposing of the high-definition camera's non-operational parts, such as the camera's casing, distributing the remaining parts across the drone's skeleton to balance weight. The result is a miniature drone with only two-inch propellers that measures "about 5 inches wide and 3 inches tall."[43] These miniature drones could challenge even the most inventive 3D animators about what kind of spatial experience they can draw into vision.[44]

The third important contributor to the proxistant drone flight is a digital video camera with the characteristic spherical shape of the wide-angle lens. Here, the slight radial distortion makes objects closer to the lens appear unnaturally rounded and disproportionally larger than those farther away.[45] An additional booster for the proxistant experience is the wide-angle aesthetics, which enables the action to take place within an expanded field of vision.[46] This spatial plasticity is further enhanced due to the time-critical process inherent in digital camera operations. A digital video camera captures pixel data through a sequential readout of the camera's photosensitive areas arranged in a grid. The sheer amount of data constituting the high resolution in high-definition cameras causes significant delays. Rapid camera movements can therefore often cause the image on the screen to appear squashed or skewed if the camera moves before the readout is complete.[47] For the same latency reason, full high-definition resolution cannot be used for FPV navigation. This brings us to the fourth component in the FPV drone system—the real-time video feed transmitted via radio waves (typically 2.4 GHz or 5.8 GHz frequency) to goggles worn by the pilot. While recording the flight in high definition, the FPV set-up relies on an additional analogue video camera for navigating the flight. It is this low-resolution, much faster transmission of an analogue video camera that provides the point-of-view (POV) of the drone to the pilot. In a sense "blinded" from physical space by a technological replacement, the FPV pilot navigates physical space by way of video signals, radio waves, and computational algorithms.[48] The analogue video camera causes (virtually) no delay but its transmitted signal contains a tremendous amount of noise in return.[49] Speeding through a noisy forest of fluctuating (analogue video) interferences, FPV navigation is thus distributed between autonomous sensor fusion and semi-reliable radio waves.

Piloting a drone by way of FPV goggles is often described by practitioners and fans as "a real-life video game," where the only true difference is in the respective technological construction of the environment one is flying through. Evident in FPV video by Robert McIntosh, *Rise & Shine* (2015), this creates the illusion of a 3D-animated environment, as the camera thrusts forward, moves around or floats in seemingly unobstructed space.[50] When the camera passes in front and behind, under, and above spatial obstacles in this way, the viewer perceives the becoming of rounded, voluminous, and unfolding shapes, much like a 3D model captured by a virtual camera in a computer-grenerated environemnt. As one commentator describes it, Robert McIntosh's "drone video makes real life look like a video game [. . .] The fly-through is most reminiscent of [. . .] the hovering of a camera in a digital space—but in real life!."[51] Similar comments were voiced regarding military drones as well.[52] Focusing part of his energy on developing his stabilizing software, McIntosh does much to remove the remaining bits of aesthetic dissonance between physical quadcopter flight and 3D-animated flight through digital space. Here, he smoothens out irregularities such as jags and bumps to facilitate a total smoothness, a suave soaring from close-up to panoramic height. Such smoothening and postproduction touch-ups might be considered a transitional state between the physical space of FPV dronematography and the digital space of 3D animation. This alignment between digital and physical flight is also emphasized by Charpu who, after working in the film industry as a creator of 3D-animated worlds, claims that FPV piloting offers a much more powerful "real virtuality," than the virtual camera flight experience in 3D-animated computer-generated environments.[53]

While McIntosh and Charpu dominated the FPV Freestyle genre between 2015–2017, we now see new talents coming up. Steele Davis, also known as "Mr. Steele," started early but is still considered one of the best freestyle pilots in the world, known for his precise close freestyle flight and daring dives.[54] The 5,500 subscribers to his YouTube channel and 6.6 million views on his most popular video *Why Should you fly Freestyle at 800mW?* testify to this.[55] While Mr. Steele keeps his FPV freestyle action aesthetics in the tradition of Charpu, another popular FPV pilot, Johnny Schaer, also known as "JohnnyFPV," works more cinematically and can be seen as continuing the line of McIntosh. Like McIntosh, he has created software for postproduction of FPV shots and an example of how he effectively combines FPV flights with postproduction can be seen in the Porsche Tycan Cross Turismo promotional video *Drive2Extremes* (2022), directed by Nick Schrunk, which has reached nearly one million views to date.[56]

It could be argued that FPV dronematography, through a very particular engagement with remote-controlled flight, provides a spatial mediation that introduces a new chapter in the long history of camera movement and aerial cinematography.[57] The latest commercial video posted on Instagram by McIntosh's newly established company Proxcinema shows how the technique of FPV dronematorgraphy is perfected to look like the smooth virtual flythrough models that have become increasingly popular across cinema and data visualization.[58] A well-coordinated indoor flight through a Kohl's store interior snaps through shelves and clothes hangers' narrow openings while circulating happy shoppers and smiley sales clerks as if flying through a live 3D-animated model.[59] As McIntosh states, "What you want to do is to take the viewer on a ride, one way to do that is to slow down, take in the scenery, feel more like you are floating than ripping through the scene." Recalling the ride on the observation wheel, we can start to recognize how proxistance as a visual paradigm is contagious across platforms.[60] This is taken a step further in the drone video "A World Artists Love," in which Proxcinema worked with director Ani Acopian and an additional staff of twenty-five on one of the most elastically smooth commercial to date. Ducted propellers and additional advancement of the ReelSteady software combined with expert editing capabilities make the environment both elastic and highly controllable.[61] Such an elastic form equally comes into the presence by way of the virtual camera in 3D-animated flythrough models.

To sum up, we can see that current practices of acrobatic FPV dronematography offer an opportunity to study the becoming of proxistant vision across several intersecting feedback loops. We have seen how FPV dronematography entails a particular engagement with FC computation and RC navigation. This is also an adaptation of the human body to a technical environment of video feedback and sensor controls. When the FPV dronematorgraphers adapt the drone towards their needs—smaller frame, smaller propeller, lightweight, and so on—this adaptation also adheres to a part-to-whole relationship. The employment of smaller propellers, for example, generates further modifications of the adjacent parts of the drone, such as the overall weight. As such, drone flight constitutes an ongoing feedback process between the organic and the technical, a pulsation from which both humans and the technical object are affected and modified.[62] Highly differentiated technological operations underpin the proxistant volumes drawn by FPV drone videos and the virtual camera of computer-animated models. Yet, they are similarly imbued with navigating extraordinary spatial dynamics, offering tight close-ups, and dizzying overviews in extraordinarily dynamic combinations. Considering these new conceptions and types of spaces that can be drawn into preexistence, how do the FPV drone video and 3D-animated flythrough equally seem to challenge established conventions of territory and navigation? As we navigate further on the proxistant path of airborne machines, this will be our guiding question.

VOLUMETRIC TERRITORY

As we have seen, mini FPV drones can bring vision into out-of-reach areas through tiny openings under, behind, and above infrastructural installations, and can move rapidly from ground level to soaring heights, be it by thrusting forward, spiraling, lifting off, dropping off, or another motion. Accordingly, FPV drones, like computer games, can be potent tools to control complex environments through technological coordination and complex navigation techniques. As Regina Dugan, then director of Defense Advanced Research Projects Agency (DARPA), explains in her 2012 TED talk, "When we design mini drones, we seek to learn flying from the ones that know it best. [. . .] A hummingbird is the only bird that can fly backward. It can fly up, down, forward, backward, even upside-down."[63] If the focus is to fly places where humans can't go, "we'd need an aircraft small enough and maneuverable enough to do so."[64] Copying the nano hummingbird's maneuverability, therefore, the hummingbird drone supposedly flies in all directions. Weighing less than a single AA battery, it can hover and rotate, and most importantly, it can record and transmit video signals for real-time or post-flight contemplation throughout its journey between close-ups and overviews. Since Dugan relocated to deploying the "same research tactics" at Google and then Facebook, we can assume that this ongoing development found good company among similar research initiatives, firmly situated between military defense strategies and cartographic entertainment.[65] Here we see how we are moving from a military-industrial complex to what Bruce Sterling has called the "security-entertainment complex," via large global corporations massively entangled in both arenas.[66] Taking the proxistant vision of these drones back to the non-accessible spaces they navigate, we can begin to see how they shed new light on the notion of territory as a volume rather than the flat vertical image produced by large military drone systems.

The hummingbird drone is perhaps answering to the so-called volumetric territory, which has become a recent preoccupation of several scholars in the field of political geography. Responding to Eyal Weizman's comment that geopolitics pertains to the "flat discourse" of two-dimensional maps, this discussion has generated different scholarly accounts regarding the notion of volume and volumetric space to account for a territorial claim beyond the simply vertical and horizontal planes produced by cartographic and satellite technologies.[67] Even if the airspace is missing from maps, Weizman argues, this space remains of critical importance for states. Political geographer Stuart Elden furthermore shows "how we need to think volume, think about volume, through volume, with volume, rather than simply the vertical to make sense of the complexities of territory today."[68] Through the provocation "secure the volume" rather than secure the area, Elden addresses the simple fact that air space counts as a part of a territory and underwrites the need to think of territory as volume, which cannot be understood through the lines on a two-dimensional map. Yet, two-dimensional maps continue to serve as the primary means for comprehending political borders.

In a response to Elden's paper, geographer Peter Adey highlights how Elden's concept of volumetric spatiality prompts a rethinking of "surfaces, planes and areas into something more." This shift, Adey explains, brings attention to the political depths that are not just abstract spaces but are filled with tangible elements—rocks, minerals, fossils, bridges, bunkers, airwaves, airplanes, and infrastructure."[69] Thinking about space and territory alongside philosophers such as Peter Sloterdijk and Paul Virilio, Elden points out the importance of seeing territory as a political technology. Territory always comprises the technical activity of measurement and the legal implementation of control and this needs to be thought with and alongside not only land and terrain but complex aerial and underground levels as well.[70] The advanced capabilities of the FPV drone, akin to a hummingbird in its agility, could indeed fulfill the objectives of volumetric territorial mapping and oversight. Such drones operationalize Elden's provocative phrase by effectively "securing spatial volumes."

The issue of the two-dimensionality of vertical perspective, however, was long problematized in the employment of such perspectives for the history of reconnaissance technologies, dating back to the first use of airborne perspectives at the very beginning of World War I. Newhall narrates that the French army hastily reactivated the photographic section of its air service upon the discovery of a camera in the enemy's Zeppelin captured at Badonvillers in 1914.[71] During World War I, aerial reconnaissance primarily yielded vertical and, on occasion, oblique photographs. However, the adoption of stereoscopic methods soon became crucial in identifying topographical elements on the battlefield. This technique also played a pivotal role in unveiling the enemy's ground installations and infrastructures. Such "hyperstereographic" images, art historian Beaumont Newhall points out, were extended beyond the normal stereoscopic distance of 6.3 centimeters (2.5 inches) away from the eyes of the observer to perceive the exaggerated depth of field. The result was a translation that produced "hummocks as hills, gulches as deep chasms, normal houses as skyscrapers," and so forth.[72] Thus, extending the already highly specialized navigational gaze of the trained reconnaissance eye, a gun or a soldier under a bridge would pop up in the scene.

Originally invented in 1838 by Charles Wheatstone to prove his claim about binocular vision, the technology of stereoscopy became a highly popular form of visual entertainment before it disappeared from the market in 1893.[73] Again, we see how the displacement of one medium opens possibilities for another. Importantly, however, stereoscopic vision kept its position outside leisure and entertainment applications, as media scholar Jens Schröter has pointed out.[74] Schröter especially notes how, due to its intuitive representation of spatial relations, such volumetric imaging was highly applicable for volumetric spatial control.[75] A quick look at the main developers behind what Schröter also refers to as the "transplanar image," (an image that presents a three-dimensional volume rather than a two-dimensional surface) within the military, the sciences, and medicine, supports this claim.[76]

The ongoing research on transplanar imaging reflects the need in defense research for three-dimensional spatial mapping. FPV acrobatic drones might answer to such needs in the way they navigate close-ups and overviews within spaces not so easily accessed by other means. During the last decade, the transplanar image in terms of a variety of 3D imaging has re-entered the mediasphere via the new digital 3D in CGI-heavy mainstream cinema. As exemplified by Martin Scorsese's film *Hugo* (2011), the 3D-animated flythrough was produced by constructing a detailed physical set of the Paris train station and capturing it with traditional camera techniques. Photogrammetry was then employed to translate these physical elements into a digital 3D model. Visual effects artists extended the digital environment with elements like clocks and machinery. A virtual camera was animated within this digital space to create the flythrough, and the sequence was completed by integrating the live-action footage with the computer-generated imagery. This integration was polished with realistic lighting, shading, and texturing to ensure consistency between the virtual and physical components.[77] In VFX Artist Rob Legato's explanation online, we can get a sense of the shot's proxistant intentions: "This particular shot lets you see the entire world, [. . .] get more and more realistic as you go along and you finally end up on the star of the movie."[78] This is part of a highly proxistant development that, according to some, reflects a larger military-industrial entertainment.[79]

Continuing the military logic of governance and visibility, we can see how the FPV drone could be utilized in layered and complex environments that defy revelation from a vertical perspective. However, the most pressing political issue—yet perhaps the one least reflected upon—might be that the cartographic spaces drawn up by this acrobatic FPV dronematography present the world itself as a digital model, to which the notion of a volumetric territory is a reply. As drone views and 3D flythroughs start to look similar, they simultaneously produce a model approach to the world. Hence the world itself is seen as a model and is approached accordingly, as evident in everything from gentrified city planning and extraction industries to geo-engineering. That this worldview must be navigated instead of fully and uncritically adopted is crucial.

THE 3D MODEL FLYTHROUGH

The online showreel by Lifang UK, a company that specializes in "CGI renderings, animated flyovers, and virtual reality maps," exemplifies the proxistant similarity between 3D-animated flythroughs in computer-generated environments and FPV dronematography in the physical world.[80] The showreel starts with the view of Earth suspended in space before rapidly diving into the core of a modern city fabric, adopting an acrobatic flight mode reminiscent of the aforementioned FPV videos.[81] The virtual camera of Lifang UK glides through a digitally rendered three-dimensional space. It moves beneath skyscrapers and through narrow corridors, over streets, under bridges, and smoothly navigates around minute details, capturing "everything" from every conceivable angle. Such 3D-animated flythroughs find widespread utility in diverse domains, including architectural visualization, video game development, film, virtual and augmented reality, and scientific simulations, enabling effective spatial communication and immersive visual experiences for audiences or users. While the 3D-animated flythrough has become the key means by which data is currently visualized across twenty-first-century screens, FPV dronematography produces similar volumes through remote-controlled navigation in the physical world. How are these elastic, "all-seeing" forms of close-ups and overviews connected beyond their aesthetic similarity? Following the thread of navigation, can we unravel how these smooth proxistant shapes of cine-cartographic surfaces produce the physical world as a digital model?

The article "Entering a Risky Territory: Space in the Age of Digital Navigation" by Valérie November and co-authors explores the relationship between maps, territory, and risk. The article shows that a map, and in our case, a 3D-animated flythrough of a computer-generated environment, "is not a representation of the world but an inscription that does (or sometimes does not) work in the world."[82] Maps and models have always been more than mere representations of territory; they actively participate in producing it. Hence, there might be a difference between how the 3D-animated virtual camera navigates a model through flight and the way this visual expression is understood and interpreted as a map.[83] The authors distinguish between what they call a navigational and a mimetic interpretation of the map's correspondence to the terrain. While the mimetic understanding of a map's correspondence signals the resemblance between map and territory (in philosophical terms, "word" and "world"), the navigational interpretation points to "the establishment of some relevance that allows a navigator to align several successive signposts along a trajectory."[84] The mimetic interpretation of maps imagines that there exists a resemblance between two images, the map and "the virtual image of the map's territory," which is the map-like conception of territory produced by the map.[85] The navigational approach, on the other hand, makes a connection between one set of signposts and the multiple dissimilar signposts that come before and after it.[86]

The authors argue that the convention of mimetic interpretation of maps derives historically from the field of fine art, from the introduction of the central perspective in the Renaissance, and especially from Dutch painting. Writing from the field of geography, these authors here rely on art historian Svetlana Alpers and her book *The Art of Describing*, in which Alpers shows how a visual culture, through changes over time, gives a material meaning to the expression of a worldview. What Alpers calls the mapping impulse in Dutch art belongs to the close relations between mapping and depiction at the time, a phenomenon based on the common notion of knowledge gained and asserted through pictures. Johannes Vermeer's *The Art of Painting* (1666–1668) is one such example, where the map is transported onto the painted canvas. Mapmakers were referred to as "world describers" and their maps or atlases as the world described.[87] Observation is not distinguished from the notation of what is observed.[88] As Alpers puts it, "[i]t is the capacity of the picture surface to contain such a semblance of the world—an aggregate of views—that characterizes many pictures in the North."[89] Alpers argues that the collective evolution of science, art, theory of vision, the structuring of crafts, and economic forces reshapes the understanding of vision as well as the range of observable subjects. In a different article, Bruno Latour elaborates on this aspect of Alpers scholarship, which, building on Michel Foucault's epistemic thought, shows how the art of describing at the time conveyed the knowledge of the world through representation. With the mapping impulse—the accurate inscription of the world on the surface of paper—a two-way relation was established as if the world itself was exactly this picture, the Euclidean space in which subjects and objects reside.[90]

The striking point with what Alpers has called "the art of describing" is that the similarity between scientific inscription and art also conceals an important difference.[91] While maps are made up of several reference points, painting works with only two points of reference: the painting and its model.[92] The problem arises in the Renaissance period of perspective techniques, and for cartography, the Dutch "art of describing" is especially important. Paintings of maps—as maps or that include maps—shifted the cultural imagination toward the interpretation of maps over to the "one-copy—one-model mode."[93] Thus, "[m]aps have been aestheticized and fused with the emerging culture of 'realist' painting."[94] In this way, the second mode of mimetic interpretation has colonized the first mode of navigation. Navigators always experience maps as complex variegated interfaces of calculation. "A heterogeneous set of data points from one signpost to the next," as November and her co-authors put it.[95] This is also where we can see the connection between maps and other scientific practices and the whole notion of the technical image. "[N]ot only maps but all scientific inscriptions may be framed in two orthogonal ways: the mimetic one [. . .] and the navigational one."[96] In order to better understand what is at stake, we need to include in our comprehension the *practice* of making land and map correspond, which is done through the activity of navigation.[97] Importantly, we are not here talking about a lack of exactitude in mapping techniques or the "nonexistence" of a physical world. Such questions will only bring us back to an understanding of the map in a mimetic way. It is only when we stop asking the mimetic question that we see how connected we are to the world.[98] The article discusses the historical construction of space and territory, suggesting that these are not objective realities but rather the result of cultural and technological processes. In this view, the very notion of space is contested, and the traditional division between "physical" and "human" geography is called into question.

The article thus advocates for a navigational approach to maps, viewing them as interactive platforms for real-time data navigation, not mere representations of physical space. The authors also convey a great trust in the new era of digital maps that allows for the integration of data such as risks alongside traditional geographic features. By offering dynamic, customizable mapping experiences that accommodate a broad spectrum of user needs and purposes, digital technologies supposedly enhance this navigational interaction. Yet, the various information overlays do not free the so-called base map from serving a mimetic dimension. By analyzing the proxistant vision of the 3D-animated flythrough feature, we see how it rather emphasizes a mimetic approach. When the world is mapped into a three-dimensional space with the help of agile FPV drones, adding ever more details through dynamic combinations of close-ups and overviews, the model can easily become a stand-in for the world itself. The viewer is provided with a persuasive and effective tool of proxistant spatial control. At the same time, this highly detailed and accessible model is never more than a map of collected signposts that requires a navigational approach to its data. Now, how does the distinction between the mimetic and the navigational interpretation of maps play out in 3D-animated flythrough models such as the envisaged city neighborhood flashed over by the virtual camera in the aforementioned showreel by Lifang? The 3D-animated flythrough visualization is constructed as a gracious move from detail to overview via countless in-between steps. This is a visual expression fixed to a set parameter to simulate a flight through Cartesian space. While we will return to the operation of such models later, let us first specify the mimetic dimension of these virtual flights. The current proliferation of the 3D-animated flythrough is often referred to as zooms or deep zooms, especially when in relation to Google Earth's dynamic interface.[99] However, the mimetic relation we see here is fortified not by a zoom but rather a flight that combines the aerial view with the double motion of camera movement and the moving image.

In film theory, we find a similar distinction between camera movement (dolly, crane, helicopter, and so on) and zoom. The camera movement establishes the articulation of three-dimensional space in cinema and was revolutionized already in 1914 by Giovanni Pastrone in his legendary film *Cabiria*, which is considered a landmark in cinema history for its epic scale and innovative use of tracking shots.[100] Zoom, on the other hand, works purely by optics.[101] The human body cannot zoom but it can move. Unlike physical camera movement, the zoom is an optical change of focal length, which moves the point of view in or away from the image without changing the physical vantage point. By simply enlarging the detail in the image, the zoom technique emphasizes the image's intrinsic two-dimensional nature. In contrast, 3D-animated flythrough models produce a bodily affect through a sensation of physical motion in a digitally composited three-dimensional space.

The notion that the sensation of flight is central to the digital model is emphasized by the Google Earth interface. Upon accessing the Google Earth web version, we are invited to explore "[t]he world's most detailed globe,"[102] with several choices in the software settings menu that alludes to the notion of flight. By taking a closer look at the "fly and animation" settings, we discover three distinct options for "arrival" at one's desired destination.[103] The "orbital animation" sets the virtual camera in a continuous clockwise orbit around the point of interest while maintaining a constant altitude and a fixed angle. In the "Cinematic animation" option, by contrast, the camera continues to revolve clockwise around the point of interest in oscillating velocities, meticulously synchronized with smoothly shifting angles, altitudes, and distances. Finally, in the "No animation" option, the camera freezes in the nadir position over the point of interest. Such options produce a mimetic dimension of flight, where the viewer simply embarks on the cinematic ride on a dynamic site-seeing itinerary across the many data points plotted between street view and globe suspended in space. The sense of flight enforces the mimetic dimension of the map by way of cinematic affective means, and this is an important but overlooked point that is left out in the zoom discourse.[104]

This distinction between zoom and flight is important because, as we have demonstrated in earlier chapters, the sensory-motor flight from a high altitude to a close-up works on the cartographic principle of an all-seeing motion view. The proxistant vision of airborne machines circulates a vast area from multiple angles and is not a single linear trajectory of zooming in and out. Utilizing the visual effect of a camera movement rather than a zoom, the 3D-animated flythrough reproduce a well-known visual form derived from cinema by way of tantalizing helicopter shots. Flight engages the bodily capacity for immersion, making the audience "believe" what they see (one "feels" that one flies), employing the principle Giuliana Bruno calls the *e-motion* of the moving image.[105] Proxistant vision can circulate and access a detailed journey from below the ground to outer space as a perfect geometric construct. This mobilized vantage point operates with cine-cartographic e-motion to support the point the model is meant to convey and thus affect decision-making processes. Such combination of the forces of cartography and cinematic appeal have gained persuasive significance in the growing field of data visualization, as exemplified by the United Kingdom-based company Carbon Visuals. On its website, this company defines its main task as to make "the invisible *visible*."[106] In the award-winning visualization of New York City's 2010 emissions, Carbon Visuals transformed carbon dioxide emission data into a rising numbers of digital balloons, steadily over-populating a digital 3D model of Manhattan. The 3D-animated flythrough starts from a close-up of a few balloons popping up at street level before the virtual camera ends up with a spectacular birds-eye view of the entire scene. The shot then continues to encircle the model of the, by now, skyscraper-high mountain of carbon dioxide balloons.

As pointed out by climate visualization scholar Heather Houser, "Carbon Visuals make data experiential by giving data virtual materiality and employing cinematic genre conventions."[107] However, "[t]hese commercial products deemphasize knowledge of scientific processes in favor of overt emotional appeals [. . .]. The data itself does not come under scrutiny in these commercial visualizations." Hauser argues that by simply citing an online encyclopedia provided by Air Liquide America Corporation for their information on carbon dioxide mass, Carbon Visuals' model rather limits understanding of the complexities of climate science. "[Carbon Visuals'] energy goes explicitly into inventing a world to harbor the data," Houser concludes.[108] The earlier example shows how the proxistant mimesis of a 3D-animated flythrough takes precedence over the more complex navigational aspects that concern climate change data. Rather than considering this complexity, Carbon Visuals' award-winning model simply partakes in the spectacularizing proxistant regime that currently compresses possible modes of operation and engagement in everyday life. Acting simultaneously as a map, a cinematic shot, and a dynamic ride through 3Danimated space, this model convinces the viewer of the validity of the presented data through the e-motional mimetic representation of proxistant vision. The affective moving image flight suspends a navigational approach to the sources of the data by way of a sensory-motor experience of total vision, smoothly articulated across multiple in-between points from the building's minute details in a circulating panorama of the city.[109]

Proxistant vision takes shape as it travels from early vistas and geographic images to grounded kinetic structures and cinematic flights. Its cine-cartographic e-motion operates on the mimetic rather than navigational principles when facing the challenge of visualizing ever more complex data. Data visualizations, such as the effects of global climate change, market prediction, or any kind of graph analysis, operate in a very basic sense like mapping—a translation from the world of multiplicity to the one of compression and order. Yet rather than navigating back to complexity, the viewer of the 3D-animated flythrough model becomes bodily immersed into its mimetic dimension. Science historian and designer Orit Halpern observes that visualization of data is first and foremost a process of transformation of phenomena invisible to the human eye into a perfectly seeable and concrete image.[110] With increasingly advanced and automated technological systems, collecting ever-more complex data, the need for simplification of this data in terms of so-called intuitive visualization models grows exponentially. The all-seeing attention-grabbing proxistant vision answers this need by constructing a mimetic line of flight that can move back and forth between the overview and the close-up.

Proxistant vision thus works by way of cinematic sensory-motor realism, as discussed by Bazin and Deleuze, in which the spectator is trained and ready to accept a large number of irregularities—such as apparent gaps or unrealistic events in the storyline—as long as such irregularities are smoothened by a coherent form.[111] This well-rehearsed argument by Bertolt Brecht also appears in the writings by Walter Benjamin, among others.[112] The smooth proxistant vision provided by 3D-animated flythrough models operate as data visualization's adaptation of the mainstream Hollywood mode, one that is in need of a major disruption. Exemplified by the case of Carbon Visuals, the affective e-motion of such proxistant flights effectively underwrote the insufficient criticality with which the data was scrutinized. The same proxistance prevails across the board, be it conventional cinematic narrative or precarious data analysis. These questions are crucial to keep in mind when it is well known that data visualization can form public opinion and steer the entire civilization astray, even in cases where the data itself does not even exist.[113] The audience forgets about the complexities with which the 3D-animated flythrough model draws heterogeneous data into coherent paths in order to simplify patterns and predict a future scenario.

Hence, we can conclude that data visualization's utilization of proxistance can be seen as a mode of cinematic persuasiveness. It is this virtual flight—a digital phantom ride of sorts—that currently fosters the most powerful effect of persuasion of data visualization.[114] The movement between close-up and overview in these models manifests itself as a tantalizing virtual flight, operating on principles similar to the proxistant vision of both the observation wheel and the FPV drone video. As an intensification of the mapping impulse, proxistant vision turns the world into a model, a simplified, less complex, pliable, and accessible world, ready for a flythrough by the click of a mouse or touch of a finger. With the world fully circulated and digitally connected, one can be misled to believe that entities reside in the world the way they are depicted. To turn to the navigational interpretation of the 3D-animated flythrough model, however, we avoid what November and her co-authors referred to as the daring jump from words to worlds or from maps to territory. In the next chapter, we will see how a navigational mode of proxistant vision can be approached through the media archeological investigation of the Renaissance bird's-eye view.

5

A BIRD'S-EYE VIEW ESTABLISHING SHOT

A media archeology of airborne machines, incarnated as a virtual camera in the previously discussed 3D-animated flythrough models, points us to a very special example of the Renaissance bird's-eye view. The masterpiece at stake is the famous *View of Venice* from 1500 (*Venetie MD*), a large-scale woodcut attributed to the workshop of the celebrated Italian artist Jacopo de' Barbari. Alongside other proxistant masterpieces, such as Jacques Callot's *Siege of Breda* (1627), this map stands out as a significant leap in the technological accomplishment of both printmaking technique and representational detail. De' Barbari's astonishing example of early proxistant vision sets one's mind in motion between detail and overview in its presentation of multiple perspectives on the same plane, producing a vision that summons both totality and close-up at once. As an example of Ptolemaic chorography, the Renaissance city view or bird's-eye view has been understood as an artistic rather than a scientific enterprise.[1] According to many scholars, it is a view of "imagination," which does not belong in any real sense to the history of airborne imaging. A great example of such attitude can be found in art historian of photography Beaumont Newhall's legendary book *Airborne Camera: The World from the Air and Outer Space* (1969), in which the bird's-eye view is offered a minimal reflection, compacted into a single paragraph at the very beginning of his otherwise detailed historical narrative.[2] Newhall's attention to the bird's-eye view is mostly occupied with the differences it offers to the documentary photograph in depicting the view from above, thereby establishing flight and photography as something new and revolutionailry different.[3]

While the differences between aerial photography and Renaissance bird's-eye views are obvious, we find that the prism of proxistant vision requires a different approach. The proxistant vision of the bird's-eye view often incorporates the power of multiple angles at once, something that has contributed to the interpretation of these views as primarily having served a didactic role in their time.[4] The relevance of *Venetie MD* for our investigation is its decidedly proxistant modality, in which vertically and horizontally positioned elements are rendered side-by-side on the same visual plane. As pointed out by cultural historian and theorist of cultural techniques Thomas Macho, practices and techniques emerge much before the concepts that define them.[5] Navigation is one of the earliest such practices.[6] With this in mind, we trace this early forms of proxistance, not as a concept but as a practice that emerged before the concept of it, as central to the logic with which such volumetric views operate today as a visual paradigm.

Quite contrary to Newhall, Cosgrove is interested in the aerial view across different mediums, based on what he sees as a basic cognitive capacity that evolved across species linked to the lifesaving precarity of navigation.[7] Cosgrove lists several prehistoric examples of such aerial perspective renderings, where no elevated point of observation was possible. For humans, this cognitive capacity of navigation is linked to the possibility of imagining in the mind a spatial layout of a particular place or thing as seen from above. This is supported by the discovery by the Nobel Prize winners John O'Keefe, May-Britt Moser, and Edvard I. Moser, who showed how navigation, as the practice of spatial understanding, is essential to the way the brain operates.[8] Rather than simply an aesthetic inclination, the view from above links directly to the navigational and spatial relations humans develop at a very young age. As Cosgrove puts it, "[f]rom the moment a child first picks up an object and tries to turn it in its hands, it begins to develop the skills to rotate first the micro-environment—things that are smaller than the body—and, with time, the macro-environment."[9] This so-called procedural knowledge—which differs from declarative knowledge—is based on the coordination of the eye, body, and brain, and is a knowledge that can be transferred to similar objects even though only seen from afar.[10] Over time, Cosgrove points out, the same procedural knowledge teaches us to effortlessly imagine space from many different viewpoints. Cosgrove refers to this ability as our geographical imagination, a feature of our cognitive capacity that is expressed in maps, architectural drawings, and plans. This also answers to some of the popularity of aerial images, Cosgrove concludes.[11] Although culturally and contingently produced as a desire based on modernity's scopic regime of imperial power, when presented with an aerial image, it also activates a navigational capacity. The aerial view answers to a spatial curiosity that is "hard-wired" to navigation.

The earliest examples of cartographic inscription feature a proxistant layout. While scholarly accounts do question what Cosgrove lists as the first terrestrial map found at the Neolithic Site of Çatalhöyük, others identify the so-called Bedolina Map of the first millennium BC as a proper candidate.[12] The latter is a much-celebrated petroglyph found at Capo de Ponte, at the site of Bedolina in the prehistoric area of Valcamonica in Northern Italy.[13] The petroglyph comprises of several crossing lines in what looks like a vertical sectioning of the space interspersed with several rudimentary depicted dwellings suggesting a frontal view. The glacier-washed flat stone upon which the cartographic-like rendering is carved is located forty meters above the valley for which it provides a plan of the property's occupation and distribution. Archeologists warn us, however, about understanding such petroglyphs based on modern Western conceptions of cartography. Rather than territory, Christina Turconi explains, it could just as well be a tribute to religious power or ritual.[14] Yet the proxistant layout of the habitat nevertheless underlines the power with which proxistance has operated along with other forms throughout history as one of the earliest techniques of mediating spatial relations. It is only later in the modern time of Western civilization that we have come to define cartography within a very limited rendering of flat vertical space and territorial claims, as pointed out by several geographers as well.[15]

Italian cities were among the earliest and most prolific motives for the increasingly popular bird's-eye views of cities in the Renaissance, according to Paul D. A. Harvey.[16] De' Barbari's *Venetie MD* from 1500 however, stands out as the most remarkable example of its time. City views from an imagined airborne perspective grew increasingly prevalent in the early Renaissance and figure prominently within the context of Western art history. Constituting part of the emerging view-aesthetics discussed in our previous chapter, it preceded the dominant central perspective of spatial representation promoted by Filippo Brunelleschi and Leon Battista Alberti, among others.[17] The largely different proxistant layouts of these early views are unified in their depiction of a city from an imagined aerial viewpoint. They were first popular in the depiction of the Holy Land of Palestine and its cities. An example is the outstandingly detailed view by Pietro Vesconte's of the Holy Land and city plans of Acre and Jerusalem (circa 1321), made for inclusion in Marino Sanuto's *Liber secretorum fidelium cruces*.[18] Another early bird's-eye view of Vienna and Bratislava from circa 1421 is highlighted by Harvey for its early use of a temporal scale of distance.[19] Other early examples include Fra Paolino da Venezia's woodcuts of *Venice and Rome*, mid-fourteenth century.[20] A good indicator of the popularity of the city view is furthermore present in the *Civitates Orbis Terrarum* (*Cities of the World*), first published by Braun and Hogbenberg in 1572.[21] Claiming to offer individual views of the world, this astonishing volume collected bird's-eye views of mostly European cities and by its latest edition in 1617, the number of cities included 546.[22] These early geographic images were all highly proxistant. That is, they utilized a combination of detail and overview in their cartographic rendition of physical space, often presenting buildings and people in a frontal and oversized proportion on an otherwise more homogenous and flatter surface.

At approximately the same time as the bird's-eye city view grew into popularity, we also see an interest in the earlier mentioned view paintings discussed by Giuliana Bruno and the early use of the central perspective in pictorial techniques. Such landscape views first appeared as backgrounds, as we have seen in Ambrogio Lorenzetti's fresco cycle *The Allegory of Good and Bad Government* on the walls of Siena's Palazzo Pubblico, painted between 1337 and 1339. While also credited for using the central perspective technique prior to the aforementioned Renaissance artists in his *Presentation at the Temple* (1342), Lorenzetti's immersive aerial rendering across three walls in Sala della Pace lays the Sienese world before the viewer's feet. Even though the painted walls stretch above one's head when entering the room, the view is of an aerial perspective of towns,

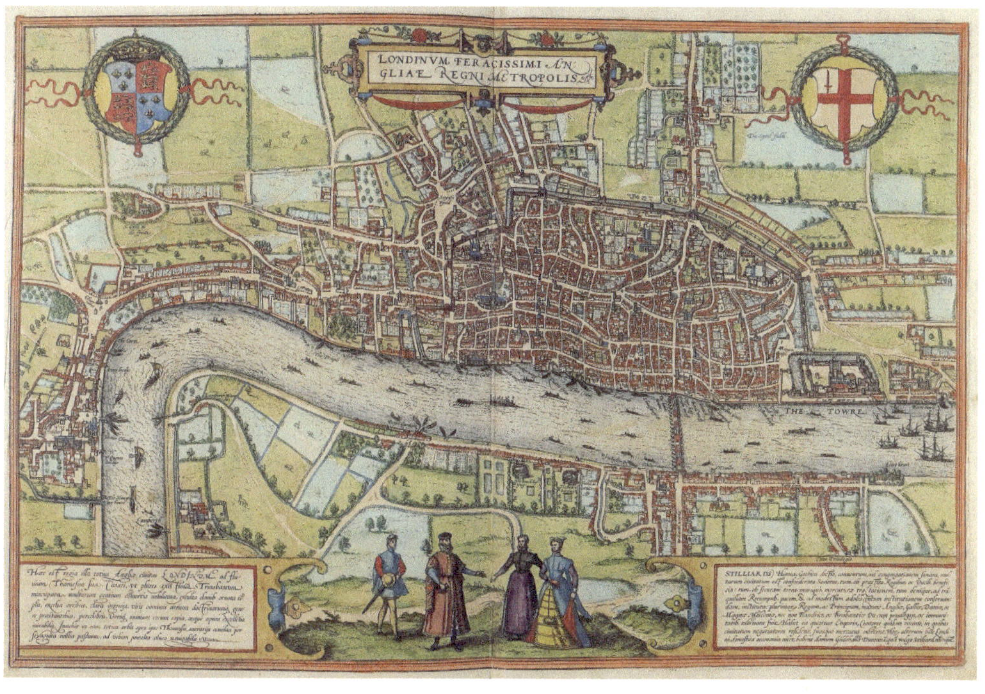

FIGURE 5.1

London in *Civitates Orbis Terrarum* (1572).

palaces, mountains, and fields, surveying the area of government, sometimes from low and sometimes from high oblique angles.[23] An aerial view indeed figures in the *Mona Lisa* (1503) by flight enthusiast and cartographically minded Leonardo Da Vinci, before the view appeared as painterly scenery in and of itself in Italian *veduta* paintings by Canaletto (1697–1768) and Giovanni Paolo Panini (circa 1691–1765).[24] As is commonly the case within an art historical narrative based on style and realistic representation, the early bird's-eye view's combination of horizontal and vertical perspectives were seen as little more than baby steps that prefigure a perfected and full-blown landscape tradition. The bird's-eye view signals an in-between state between the representation of space by way of the central perspective and prospective overviews in painting and the proper measurement surveys of scientific maps based on two-dimensional orthogonal projections. This is a division already dictated in the interpretation of Ptolemy's concept of *Geographia* and *Chorographia*.[25]

Architectural historian and renowned Venice scholar Jürgen Schulz's classic narrative similarly highlights how the city of Venice was a maritime and economic center favorably located on the Adriatic's northern shores, and as such, one of the earliest cities to be mapped and surveyed in Europe.[26] More systematic and methodical uses of maps in Europe were only gradually coming into presence with the re-discovery and distribution of Ptolemy's *Geography* in the early fifteenth century. With the introduction of the central perspective technique in painting and architecture, city views started to change in character from earlier abstract and more generalized renderings to exhibiting a growing interest in mimetic descriptions and scientific measurement.[27] This well-known trajectory is exemplified in Schulz's article about Rosselli's aforementioned city view.[28] Roselli's view of Florence exhibits the city's aerial view as seen from the surrounding Tuscan hills, rendered as a complex three-dimensional structure. The shape of the city and attention to the details of buildings and streets represent a change from earlier, more idealized city views. Yet, aside from the most important landmarks, the overall urban fabric in the view is still represented as a generalized structure, and important thoroughfares and waterways have been ignored.[29] In this respect, Schulz's claims that *Venetie MD* represents a qualitative change with regards to employing new technology and scientific measurement as a means to achieve its goal of accurate representation of a panoramic overview of the city and every detail within it. The absence of any nearby points of elevation makes the achievements even more remarkable. With the perspective of cultural techniques, however, we will show a slight displacement of this classic narrative of the bird's-eye view.

Attributed to the workshop of Jacopo de' Barbari, *Venetie MD* (*View of Venice 1500*) (see figure II.8) is an utterly astonishing example of the bird's-eye view genre due to its remarkable dimensions and exceptionally detailed rendering of the urban fabric. The size and detail stand out in historical context from other bird's-eye view renderings and indicate a major innovation in technical production of both mapping and printmaking techniques.[30] The grand scale of the woodcut, measuring 135 centimeters by 282 centimeters (4.3 feet by 9.3 feet), is achieved by a combination of six engraved pearwood blocks measuring sixty-six centimeters by ninety-nine centimters (2.17 feet by 2.25 feet). Upon printing on a special order of six equally sized sheets of paper, a composite aerial view of the maritime empire capital was "stitched" together. When approaching *Venetie MD* today, it is remarkable how this five-century-old geographic image still corresponds mimetically to the urban structure. In this special edition of the bird's-eye view, the characteristic dolphin shaped outline of Venice, graciously sliced by the S-shaped Grand Canal, frames a detailed rendition of Piazza San Marco and its majestically decorated Campanile.[31] It is not only the architectural specificities of the Rialto Bridge and the Arsenale complex of state shipyards and armories that is being carefully drawn out, but De' Barbari's view also, more surprisingly, seems to render every individual house and street in the city's characteristic overlapping structure, including details such as the shape of windows and doors and the number of bridges and chimneys.

Finally, this amazingly proxistant view incorporates the surrounding islands of Murano, Torcello, Burano, and Mazzorbo as well as the Venetian Alpine foothills with the Dolomites in the far distance. So much detail of the city is represented on the map, according to Schulz, that it is highly surprising to find that it is the only known such detailed view of its kind from this period.[32] Its production was maximized in every way possible by the German merchant and commissioner Anton Kolb who secured the largest available paper sheets and woodcut plates. The final composition was a technological leap in aesthetic and scientific output, ascribing attention to detail and proportion that far exceeded any known comparative examples at the time. There are eleven known surviving prints of *Venetie MD* today, located at archives and art institutions around the world, one of which is exhibited together with the six woodcut plates at Museo Correr in Venice.[33] In addition, images of *Venetie MD* appear on memorabilia items in the Venetian souvenir shops. The view is printed on everything from teacups to aprons, tote bags, and keyrings. Highlighting its astonishing resemblance across the 500 years, the map also lives on as a digital navigational online map.[34] In addition, Musei Civici Venezia recently produced a contemporary 3D-animated flythrough of de'Barberi's *Venetie MD*, using computer-generated techniques that further articulate the proxistant vision already inherent in the 500-year-old map.[35]

Venetie MD is widely known to represent a major technological leap in the genre of Renaissance city views, breaking precedent in terms of both mimetic resemblance and the technology of large-scale printmaking. Yet, some of the characteristics of other more stylistic or idealized bird's-eye views are still present. This is especially visible in the representation of Neptune and Mercury, as well as certain buildings and ships, which are horizontally rendered. Important religious places, such as the Basilica of San Marco and Arsenale complex—distinguished sites of state power—are proportionally enlarged, while private housing sections and gardens are miniaturized. As we move away from the main landmarks, the rest of the city seems to suffer from a great deal of overlap in what looks like a gradual lack of available space. Moreover, houses and streets are distorted with different shadings, which disclose the lack of a systematic survey.[36] This feature suggests a movement on behalf of the viewer in which, for some buildings, one is positioned below and in front, while for others at an oblique angle or vertically above. As Giuliana Bruno remarks about this map, "the observer is not fixed to a position or a set distance but appears free to wander in and around the space."[37] Thus, *Venetie MD* stands out as an early dynamic motion view that can be productively studied through the prism of proxistant vision. Media scholar Juraj Kittler and geographer Deryck W. Holdsworth have similarly argued that the sixteenth century *Venetie MD* was already a digitally constructed spatial representation that, with its realistic three-dimensional rendering of space, challenges the concept of "new media" in our own time.

Although exact knowledge of the making of the de' Barbari's city view remains unknown, Schulz, Kittler, and Holdsworth sum up several studies that indicate the process of making *Venetie MD* to have taken part in four significant stages. The first stage entails the construction of a basic plan of the city. Here, Schulz has argued that a simple water regulation plan might have been available to de' Barbari.[38] Computer studies of *Venetie MD* further show gradual amplification of distortions relative to the distance of the city's tallest campanile at Piazza San Marco. From this, one can conclude that a basic plan of the view was informed by this vantage point, as well. The second stage entails the manipulation of this plan through the techniques of foreshortening to obtain the correct outline of the city as seen from an imaginary vantage point southwest of the city at roughly 500 meters altitude.[39] The third stage is assumed to entail a small "army" of surveyors, utilizing the perspective techniques by way of portable perspective frames and alidade triangulation techniques, recording both street view details and the multiple partial overviews from the city's 103 bell towers.[40]

As we can see from this description, *Venetie MD* is assembled from multiple vantage points within the city. The practice of recording the details is dependent on a physical navigation and movement across and around the urban structure, rather than a static view from a hill, as suggested by Newhall. This navigational method allows the inclusion of the amazingly detailed city view, incorporating no fewer than 10,312 chimneys, 114 edifices of churches, forty-seven convents, and 253 bridges.[41] The details produce the effect of accuracy, such that the city view becomes "so astonishingly and brilliantly detailed that one is apt to accept it unquestioningly as a record of fact."[42] However, as we have seen, this truth production of mimetic resemblance is a subject for navigation. The final fourth stage suggests that the details from elevated and street point perspectives recorded by the assistant drafters were brought together into de' Barbari's workshop, which is likened to the equivalent of a Central Processing Unit (CPU) in a modern computer, where bits come together to be assembled as an image. From this description, we can see that the production of de' Barbari's map closely resembles the way digitally composited three-dimensional proxistant flythrough models are constructed today.

Among the various digital analogies discussed by Kittler and Holdsworth in their essay, it would have been easy for them to introduce the dynamic 3D-animated flythrough models offered today by Google and Apple maps, as well as other data visualization software that produce the characteristic proxistant vision suggested by de' Barbari's view. This would take us to the navigation between proximity and distance, as exhibited by the virtual camera, navigating geometric space around multiple viewpoints to create a three-dimensional volumetric view, a vision that can move around and about, under, and above without the constraints of a fixed vantage point. However, Kittler and Holdsworth maintain a fixed vertical perspective in their analogy, comparing de' Barbari's *Venetie MD* to the 320 gigapixel panoramic image of London, commissioned by British Telecom (BT) Group for the 2012 Olympics. The limits of this comparison are illustrated by the fact that all the individual photos for this composition were taken from the same vantage point, namely the BT tower.[43] Even though the astonishing number of 48,640 individual frames were composited into one giant interactive panoramic photograph of London, this analogy hardly captures the dynamic spatial relations present in *Venetie MD*.[44] While Kittler and Holdsworth provide an insightful study of the digital precursors to this 500-year-old view, reexamining the relationship once more through the prism of proxistance reveals an additional layer of digital connections.

A remarkable feature of *Venetie MD* is the way it suggests movement through a highly detailed fragment-to-whole composition. Also, the layers and folding of graphical elements in the woodcut resemble the construction principle of the 3D-animated flythrough model. Constructed through the navigation of multiple viewpoints within the city, *Venetie MD* illustrates in quite literal terms why such models cannot be understood mimetically from a single vantage point. The most important point about this map therefore is the question of movement and navigation. Kittler and Holdsworth could have further developed their observation that de' Barbari's dynamic perspective exhibits the true *volo d' uccello* [bird flight] within the Greco-Roman tradition.[45] Ancient masters used the bird's-eye view to give the impression of the continuous flight of a bird. "With each stroke of the wings, the bird gets an opportunity to coast for a moment and to relish the scene below."[46] They furthermore refer to Bellavitis and Romanelli, the co-authors of the book *Venezia*, who challenge the idea that the view presents a unified vantage point and instead emphasize the multi-focal collage of images.[47] Kittler and Holdsworth agree that one quickly discovers the multiple perspectives and points of view embedded in the picture, where items are depicted from below as well as above, from different sides and levels of elevation. Through a proxistant lens, we can see the additional relevance of this aspect for digital environments today. To get a full media archeological picture of de' Barbari's *Venetie MD*, however, it is necessary to address not only how the map was made but also how the bird's-eye view genre in general, and this one in particular, operated with these dynamic, multifocal perspectives within their own time.

Schulz's major claim is that de' Barbari's *Venetie MD* was an artistic rendering and a didactic map, that it was based on communicating an abstract idea rather than geographic data.[48] The subject was the commonwealth of Venice rather than the physical city—a celebration of Venice as a premiere trading and maritime power, an emblem of the city crowned by the favorable forces of Mercury and Neptune. The subject of the map is not the physical city, Schulz argues, but its operation as the leading maritime and economical power of Europe. "Her physical features are exhibited as the material manifestation of this state just as the figures of Mercury and Neptune are the incarnations of its numen."[49] *Venetie MD*, therefore, is something of "a visual metaphor for the Venetian state," Schulz concludes.[50] The purpose of *Venetie MD* was celebratory—to celebrate the fame of the city. Schulz lists both Francesco Roselli's and de' Barbari's views as what he calls "moralized city views," which continued as a trend to the early sixteenth century. Until the 1530s, such bird's-eye views functioned as depictions of "topical events or abstract ideas," Schulz explains.[51] In his nearly fifty-page, densely researched essay on how de' Barbari's view differs from earlier bird's-eye views, Schulz concludes, somewhat surprisingly, by drawing them all together in the same category. It is as if Schulz suddenly forgot his argument earlier in the text, where he states that, contrary to Roselli's views, *Venetie MD* represents a major leap in techno-vision in so far as technology helps us see beyond our bodily capacity with a pair of human eyes. Without properly identifying the way the technological leap in the map bears any significance with regards to a longer tradition of the bird's-eye view, Schulz rather confirms the conventional interpretation of Ptolemy's concept, that such views were artistic endeavors rather than scientific cartographic surveys.

If we follow the previously discussed thought of November and her co-authors, however, it is possible to embrace a rather different narrative that detaches itself from this Euclidean-based worldview. A navigational approach shows that the in-between spaces seem to linger, both in terms of the map's production methods and in its articulation of urban volumes. Media scholar Bernhard Siegert has addressed an epistemic shift involving the Renaissance conception of ocean space that is relevant here.[52] Starting from the 1601 painting *The Battle with the Spanish Armada* by Dutch artist Hendrick Cornelisz Vroom, Siegert traces the emergence of the early seventeenth-century ocean space in painting with the arrival of a disorderly swarm of pirates, known as the sea beggars.[53] Here we can see how the transition from traditional navigational methods to the dominance of central perspective techniques comes to play in geographical imagery. Investigating these overlooked and silenced contributors of skilled navigation, Siegert show their instrumental place in the initial phase of a maritime spatial transformation. Such navigational superiority brings about the notion of a seascape, which was later integrated into painterly representation and eventually converted to symbolize state power according to the mimetic approach mentioned earlier. Siegert documents how the horizon, which gradually loses its navigational reference, still bears traces in this transition. By scrutinizing the horizon line in Cornelisz Vroom's painting, Siegert identifies the mountain tops and topographical references that become apparent through the movement into the bay. The central perspective technique eventually displaces this mobile line of sight with which such spatial knowledge first became valued. A rendering of the ocean line, once based on mobile navigation, was thus transformed into a centrally located and fixed point of view, a power structure based on mimesis rather than navigation.

Siegert thus reveals a different genealogy of the mimetic approach to cartography. We saw with November and her co-authors earlier that the map lost its navigational correspondences by being included in a style of painting characterized by Alpers as the art of describing. Rather than a question of style in painting, Siegert in contrast, sees this transformation of the map from the point of view of a politics of space. The cartographic representation of space evolved into a mechanism for asserting ownership, as cartography itself transitioned from a tool aiding in dynamic navigation to a fixed, mimetic visual form. According to November and her co-authors, this transformation is a byproduct of an evolving artistic style that originated from the economic and scientific epistemological shifts of the Renaissance period. During this time, the polymathic Renaissance figures, adept in both art and science, were perceived as capturing an authentic vision of the world through their artistic expertise. In his divergent view, Siegert perceives the emergence of the ocean into a central perspectival framework as indicative of the incremental extension of state sovereignty over the seas. This emergence signified the ocean's transition into a commodified space, a valuable entity to be dominated and controlled via maritime warfare, and thus a space that required depiction in the central perspectival style, the recognized emblem of imperial claim to ownership. Hence, realism in painting did modify the navigational dimension of cartography; however, this was not a question of style but rather a transition that emerged through a navigational practice.

Emphasizing and giving new insight into the practices of "line of sight navigation," Siegert situates the bird's-eye view into an entirely new light and changes the way we might come to understand and interpret the operational capacities of such city views. These chorographic city views were based not on the visual logic of mimetic central perspective, but rather on a mobile line of several visual correspondences operating as guides for navigation. The lines and markings of physical topographical references characteristic of the bird's-eye view, such as church spires and mountain heights, corresponded to a navigational mode of movement through space. Seen in this new light provided by Siegert, we have a new reason for understanding why bird's-eye views emphasized major features within the city, and why a mixture of the oblique and horizonal rather than the vertical perspective was employed. As such, de' Barbari's *Venetie MD* can be seen as the first in a transitional period between 1500 and 1729, when the fixed pictorial techniques of the central perspective mix with the mobile navigational mode of the bird's-eye view convention. *Venetie MD* combines the previous navigational convention of city views with the pictorial central perspective techniques to map out the various details of the city as a celebration of its commercial and military power.

Hence, contrary to November and her co-authors, as well as Siegert, *Venetie MD* shows that the emergence of the mimetic approach to cartography does not happen with the transfer of the map onto the canvas of a painting, but rather as a development within the *Venetie MD* itself—the map becomes an image, a celebrated view. In the eighteenth century, the map turns to the vertical plane, as exemplified by Lodovico Ughi's *Venice* from 1729, in which the frontal close-up features of the city are relegated to the side panes, later to be replaced by pure textual references in 1847 by Bernardo and Gaetano Combatti in *Pianta Topografica Della Citta*.[54] It now becomes clear why we need to trace *Venetie MD* back not only to how it was made but also to grasp its operative logic within its own time as a bird's-eye view. This points back to how first-person view dronematographers and virtual cameras navigate physical spaces between high and low altitudes of the urban fabric today. *Venetie MD* not only prefigures digital geography and 3D-animated flythrough models through its assemblage of fragments onto a carefully rendered wireframe by way of perspectival techniques and measurement. Through the prism of proxistant vision, it also highlights the tension between navigational logic and the mimetic approach, providing a critical foundation for understanding the power dynamics at play in the contemporary use of these models across cartography, cinema, and the general media sphere. It is through this operational logic that *Venetie MD* maintains its relevance today.

6

THE AERIAL VIEW IN MOTION

Parallel to our earlier examination of grounded machines, our engagement with airborne machines was shaped by a methodology that emerged from artistic exploration and spatial experimentation. During a teaching residency at the Nordland School of Arts and Film in 2016, our investigations involving drone technology led to an unexpected historical encounter: a perspectival map crafted by Kirstine Colban, the first female Norwegian cartographer, in 1816. This map seemed to foreshadow the proxistant spatial articulation we were researching with our drone. Further research revealed insight into how pre-scientific maps operated by a conscious relation between close-up and overview in the same image. Following this line of inquiry, we identified *Venetie MD* (see figure II.8) as an outstanding example, not only by its articulation of close-ups and overviews on the same two-dimensional surface, but also as an example of a proto-digital 3D model. Encountering the map during a commission for the Artistic Research Pavilion at the Venice Biennale in 2017, we identified it as a key to unlock media archeological insights into the contingent powers of proxistant vision. Our goal was to scrutinize its cine-cartographic principles, with a particular focus on composite imaging and spatial control.

What characterizes the airborne machines is that they not only combine both perspectives but, more importantly, they map out every perspective in between.[1] Thinking cartographically, however, we can see that the combination of vertical and horizontal views in one visual form was

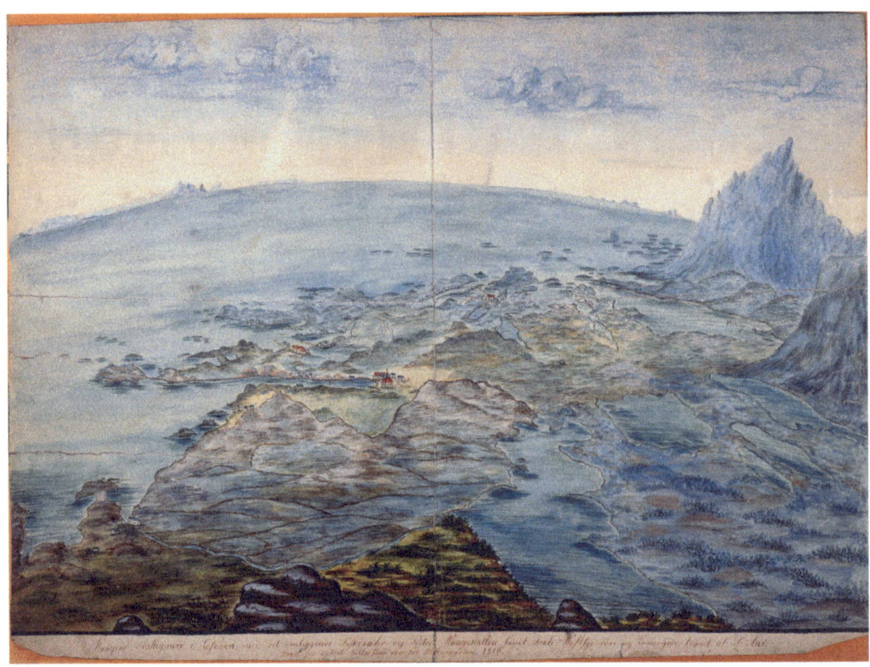

commonplace in popular bird's-eye views of Renaissance cities. In parallel with technological development in the context of war and power, artists have made use of such innovative leads by working through implicit critiques. Concerned with the spatial renderings that emerge between close-up and overview across diverse technical operations, we have conducted a media archeological investigation of the Renaissance bird's-eye view that reveals the cine-cartographic contingencies underpinning the contemporary proliferation of proxistant vision. We will return to the bird's-eye view, but first, a detour through the technological and artistic evolutions of the twentieth century is needed. These developments

FIGURE 6.1

Kirstine Colban (Stine Aas). *Perspective Map of Kabelvåg* (1816). Courtesy of Lofotmuseet, Kabelvåg.

expanded the possibilities of spatial representation, leading to new forms of dynamic, proxistant vision.

Cinema's co-emergence with the conquest of the skies simultaneously realized two of the oldest human desires: making images move and being able to fly, as described well by philosopher and sociologist Edgar Morin.[2] The way these two technologies mediated each other offered a significant contribution to the development of proxistant vision, and this was quickly utilized towards cine-cartographic means. Proxistant vision has arguably developed into its extraordinary perfection today, but a significant surge of proxistant spatial articulation in art was already present from the earliest influences of the co-evolution of cinema and flight. Pioneer aviator Wilbur Wright invited a cinematographer on a low-altitude flight as part of his flying machine promotion in Italy.[3] Furthermore, the novel aerial perspectives that became available to World War I reconnaissance operations influenced with the same force a new generation of artists, as well.[4] The Suprematist's revelation of the aerial view into objectless painting, as Malevich articulated it, is well documented in the insightful work by art historian Christina Lodder.[5] Even more relevant to the proxistant modality are the volumes and dynamic forms developed by Cubism's articulation of a multiplicity of perspectives on a two-dimensional surface. As Gertrude Stein pointed out, it was when she cast her eyes upon the world from onboard an airplane for the first time, that she could fully comprehend the issues at work in Cubist thought: "I saw there on the earth the mingling lines of Picasso, coming and going, developing and destroying themselves, I saw the simple solutions of Braque, I saw the wandering lines of Masson [. . .]."[6]

Furthermore, the Italian *Aeropittura* (Aeropainting), a combat and stunt flying-inspired painterly expression of the second-generation Italian Futurists operating between 1929 and 1940, explores a high degree of proxistant vision reminiscent of the cinematic sensation of flight.[7] Fueled by Italy's predominance in aviation during the period, Futurists of this later generation shifted the focus of their mechanophilia from the automobile to the airplane. Artists such as Benedetta Cappa, Gerardo Dottori, and Tato, signed the "Manifesto dell'Aeropittura futurista," (Manifesto of Futurist Aeropainting) in which they astutely proclaimed that "the principle air perspectives and consequently the principle of aeropainting, is a perpetual advanced multiplicity of forms and colors with the crescendo and diminuendo of intensely elastic space, giving birth to new shades of colors and shapes."[8] Visible in paintings such as *Spirale Tricolore su Roma* (*Tricolor Spiral over Rome*) (1923) by Roberto Marcello Baldesari and *Aeroritratto di Mussolini aviatore* (*Aerial Photo of Mussolini the Aviator*) (1930) by Alfredo Ambrosi, the genre is highly proxistant in its Cubist-inspired layering of painterly shapes and techniques. Curved and spiraling three-dimensional volumes—often combining an aerial perspective with multiple angles of view on the same picture plane—celebrate the domination of flight and motion by the unprecedented power of the airborne machine over fragile grounded structures.

Aeropainting's style partially adopted the dynamic movement of flight mediated by the moving image as the popular aviation movie continued to develop in the wake of World War I. The Italian film director and actor Elvira Notari's early aviation movie *The Heroism of an Aviator in Tripoli* (1912) set the standard for the cinematic aviation hero who defeats the enemy and returns to civic life and romance. This convention quickly became a staple narrative, according to film scholars Mary Ann O'Farrell and Lynne Vallone.[9] The repetition of a more or less similar narrative in a number of aviation films the following years, such as *Marriage by Aeroplane* (1914), *Aerial Revenge* (1915), *Dizzy Heights and Daring Hearts* (1915), and *The Great Air Robbery* (1919) attests to this claim.[10] As better and more secure camera mounts combined with ever more daring flights, these films became more proxistant. Amazing performances combined vertiginous overviews with rapidly approaching close-ups of Earth's surface as the stunt pilots assumed ever more audacious crash-landings. As aerial cinematographer Stan McClain points out, the growing film and aviation industries both established their operations in Hollywood in the early 1920s, and many film directors and producers used this opportunity primarily for stunts and special effects.[11] The spectacular aerial shots in *Wings* (1927), directed by William A. Wellman, earned the first Academy Award for Best Picture in 1929.

This silent World War I aviation movie, which perfectly fits the aforementioned heroic aviator narrative, featured highly realistic air combat sequences, and was only superseded by the dogfight scenes in *Hell's Angels* (1930), directed by Howard Hughes. According to McClain, Hughes

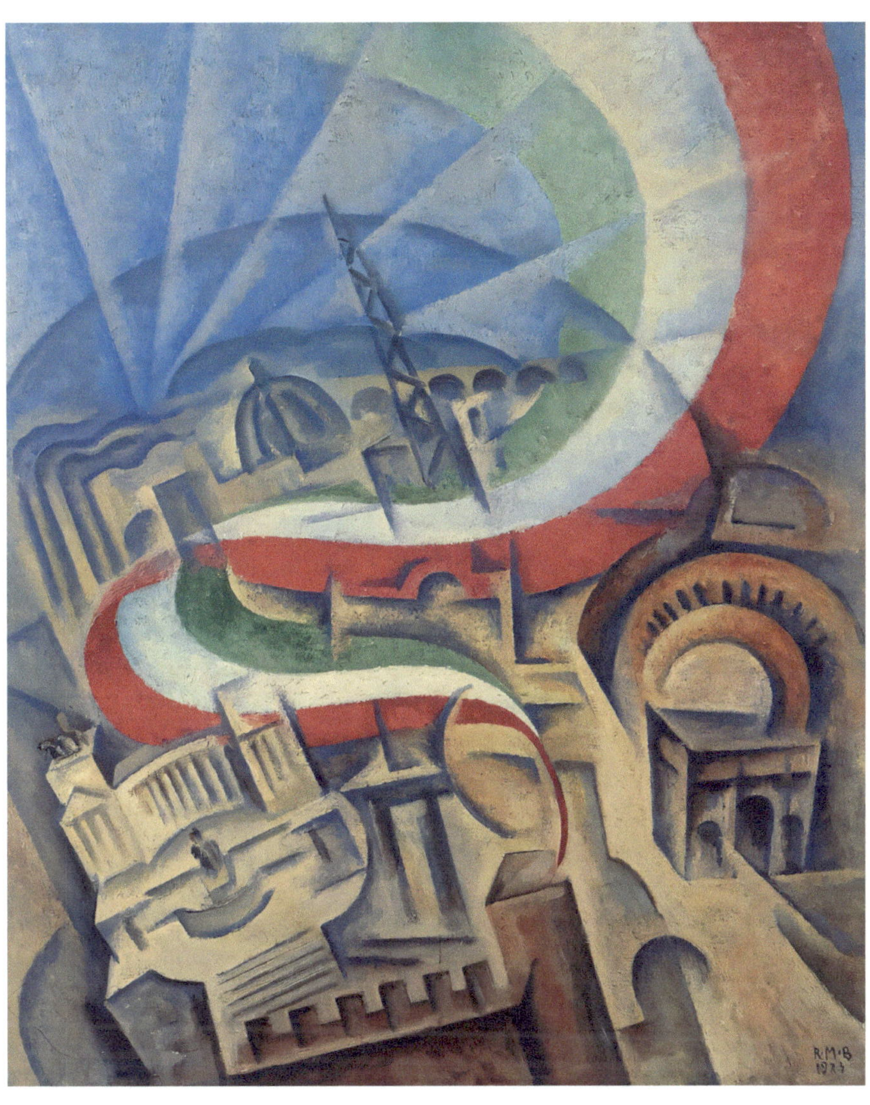

FIGURE 6.2

Roberto Marcello Baldessari. *Spirale Tricolore su Roma (Tricolor Spiral over Rome)* (1923).

hired aviation experts to traverse the world in search of planes to be used in his film, ending up with more than fifty World War I aircrafts in his holding, setting a new standard for the largest-budget aviation show at the time.[12] Pioneering aerial cinematographer Elmer Dyer together with stunt pilot Paul Mantz were leading the rest of the aviation team, which numbered up to 137 in one scene and was mainly comprised of actual World War I pilots.[13] The aerial photography in this movie is daring even by today's CGI standards and offers several exhilarating proxistant shots. The battle scenes of these aviation movies are where proxistant vision most prominently figure, often featuring the point-of-view of a struck plane falling to the ground.[14]

Yet, the most significant amplification of proxistant vision in aerial cinematography was introduced with the helicopter. The conception of the helicopter as an idea goes back to as early as 1483 Leonardo Da Vinci's "aerial screw." Nevertheless, fully operational aircraft helicopters appeared only recently in the skies. Struggling with issues of stabilization in a period of intense innovation between 1843 and 1939, a practical model was finally developed in Igor Sikorsky's VS-300, featuring the most elementary parts of modern helicopters: "a single main three-bladed rotor, with collective pitch, and a tail rotor."[15] After World War II, the helicopter developed rapidly and assumed many roles, one of which was to offer cinema exceptional proxistant vision. TV series such as *Highway Patrol* (1955–59), and *Whirlybirds* (1957) properly introduced the dynamic flight capabilities of the Bell 47 helicopter with pioneering airborne camera work. As camera mounts improved, helicopters offered cinema the ability to design a "dolly" movement in the air, exaggerating previous crane shots to a vertiginous vantage point, while gracious maneuvers and halts could be performed in the same shot. This post-World War II period also firms up the convention of the aerial establishing shot, a form already contingent on earlier view aesthetic practices and early cinema experiments. This smooth proxistant shot sometimes opens films, but can also be employed anywhere in the narrative to elevate the perspective of the action in a quite literal way, as well as to situate it in a particular geographical location.

One of the earliest uses of such aerial establishing shots is found in *The Bandit of Sherwood Forest* (1945), directed by George Sherman and

Henry Levin. Another early helicopter shot is featured in *They Live by Night* (1949), a film directed by Nicholas Ray, in which the camera follows a car in the tight airborne tracking shot of the entry sequence. *The Naked City* (1948), directed by Jules Dassin, is remarkably early in the use of such proxistant vision shots with combinations of different aircraft.[16] The helicopter ending scene of Jean Negulesco's *Johnny Belinda* (1948) suggests a move that will come to be used in later films in its reverse version. As the press release succinctly puts it:

> The ability of a helicopter to fly backwards and gain altitude at the same time was employed in photographing the final scene of *Johnny Belinda*. The scene is a traveling shot showing a buggy being driven along the rugged coastline. The camera pulled back and up going out to sea. The buggy reduced further and further in the distance leaving as a final impression only a small segment of earth on which the story was played.[17]

Such proxistant vision as the final shot in a narrative film has later been codified to suggest the small life of man in the grand scheme of things, as described by Nick Pinkerton.[18] *Japanese War Bride* (1952) by King Vidor follows a similar track as *Jonny Belinda*, when the helicopter pulls out from the main characters' rejoining embrace as they are reunited at the very end of the story.

The proxistant vision offered by the helicopter was further perfected in the famous shot of Barbara Streisand on a tugboat crossing the Hudson River in William Wyler's *Funny Girl* (1968). Shot by celebrated cameraman Nelson Tyler, who constructed a helicopter camera gimbal to stabilize the camera, this famous helicopter shot starts with a wide view of New York City before it navigates towards the Hudson River and eventually smoothly closes in on a close-up of Streisand's face, just as she hits the high note in her song. Subsequently, and without edits, the camera pulls back out to the grand overview before the film ends.[19] Tyler first developed his camera mount for John Sturges' *The Satan Bug* (1964), inspired to smoothen the shaky opening shots of the three-year earlier *West Side Story* (1961), directed by Robert Wise and Jerome Robbins.[20] Although this path was crude, it suggested the proxistant vision from an elevated overview to a close-up of the characters in the movie, later adopted by Tyler.

A parallel stabilizing technique, the so-called "ball mount," was developed for military purposes by a Canadian division of Westinghouse. This was a stabilized sphere, four feet in diameter that was attached to the nose of the copter.[21] The continuous refinement of these initial techniques started the race towards smooth helicopter scenes soaring across the screen, with *Grand Prix* (1966) and *Ice Station Zebra* (1968) as prominent examples. Newer and better exterior mounts were developed for the legendary helicopter shots towards the later 1960s and 1970s, exemplified by *Capricorn One* (1978), directed by Peter Hyams; *Apocalypse Now* (1979), diected by Francis Ford Coppola; and the stunning aerial flight above Glacier National Park in the opening shot of *The Shining* (1980), directed by Stanley Kubrick. The aerial location establishing shot, now firmly a convention, was largely abandoned towards the 1990s before it saw a revival with the new possibility of 3D-animated virtual flights such as in Martin Scorsese's *Hugo* (2011) and Alfonso Cuarón's *Gravity* (2013). Today, the highly popular 3D-animated flythrough model figures widely beyond the realms of cinema, transporting proxistant vision over to other digital realms, such as data visualization, digital cartography, architectural modeling, and computer games.

A media archeological study with a focus on the concept of navigation, however, takes us to the problems encountered by the earliest aerostats and their sole dependency on natural forces. As a lighter-than-air form of transportation, the balloon presented significant challenges to the skill of navigation. "The forward motion of a balloon is affected by the wind alone; navigation is a prayer that the wind is blowing in the desired direction," as Beaumont Newhall put it.[22] As such, the aerostat flight presented an unpredictable journey full of possibilities, where one's outlook is always on the move. With the balloon's close connection to the surface and its constant movement of elevation and descent according to the shifting winds, it belongs to the long list of cultural techniques that turned vision into the proxistant register. But the experience of such a flight was not easily communicable. Thomas Baldwin, author of the detailed and richly illustrated book *Airopedia* (1786), pondered how to mediate what he described as the "'white floor of Clouds,' the 'exquisite and ever-varying Miniature' of the buildings, and the look of the rivers, 'infinitely more serpentine' than ordinary maps would have you believe."[23] Drawing maps and images based on sketches made while he was in a balloon flight, Baldwin rolled up a paper into a telescope-like tube and moved it about over one of his balloon maps. This technique perhaps anticipated how the moving image was able to mediate flight on the level of physical sensation.

The earliest combinations of flight and moving image into a proxistant vision were most prominently explored within the non-narrative cinematic genres, both before and most significantly after 1914.[24] As we have seen in the section on grounded machines, proxistant vision was articulated through the early cinematic phantom rides and city views. It also found its airborne visual expressions in the baskets of the tethered balloon, as seen in the previously mentioned Lumière brothers' balloon film experiment. The implementation of kinetic train cars for the maximum effect of the phantom ride as a fairground entertainment in Hale's Tours and Scenes of the World attests that a moving image recording of a journey through space, such as a flight, in the cinema was much like being on that journey itself.[25] The visual extravagance of the Ferris wheel's proxistant vision was amplified to its fullest potential with the multiplicity of dynamic vantage points offered by the untethered balloon ride. Now, finally disconnected from Earthly constraints, the camera had the potential to go everywhere where the winds would take it, connecting close-ups with overviews in new and unusual angles.

Culture studies scholar Kaplan has shown that most of the military aerostatic initiatives were canceled due to the lack of navigational precision in lighter-than-air vehicles.[26] Yet the dirigible balloon soon entered the arena, serving both leisure and military needs. Smooth proxistant vision came along with this invention from the very beginning and it could well be argued that it also served a specific role. The navigational possibilities of the dirigible aerostat also presented new possibilities to the operation of the airborne camera, producing close-ups and overviews as the balloon descends and ascends. That the effect of this proxistant vision saw its early utilization in the nation-state's reunification projects after World War I is exemplified by Teresa Castro's reading of the film *En dirigeable sur les champs de bataille* [*In airship on the battlefield*] (1919.)[27]

Castro points out how, early on, the aerial moving image was recognized both as a useful cartographic technology and as a powerful emotional expression, utilized as such toward instrumental means. Produced

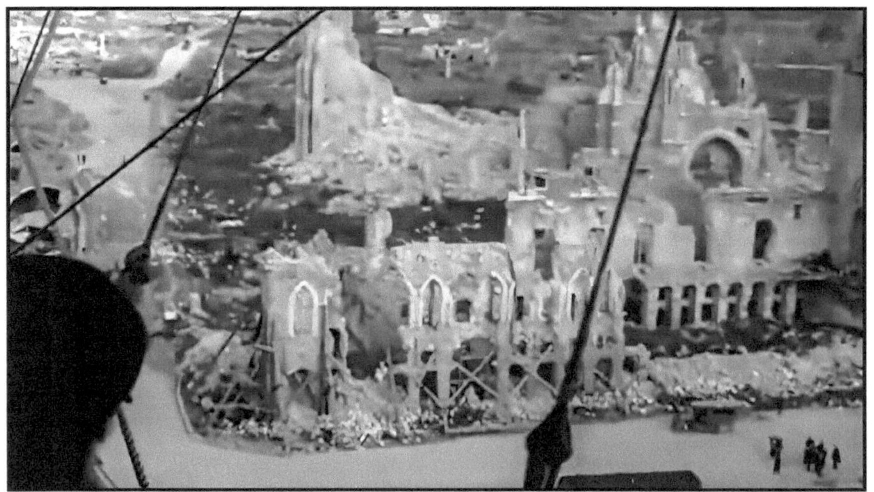

by the Cinematographic Service of the French Army, the film was imbued with the patriotic power viewers needed to enter the long period of major post-war reconstruction. "The cinematographic specificity of these images is crucial," Castro adds, "since no assemblage of aerial photographs could convey, in such an immediate and effective way, the intense sensorial stimulation brought about by the double kineticism of flight and film."[28] Through a proxistant prism we can see how the flight's descriptive combination of close-ups and overviews produced additional emotional effects.

En dirigeable comprises multiple shots from the aircraft in a low flyover across the bombarded landscape, powerfully articulating the vast devastation through a seemingly endless succession of bomb craters, free-standing walls, and roofless buildings.[29] This double kineticism is precisely the affective expression that is being radically intensified

FIGURE 6.3

Lucien Le Saint and Camille Sauvageot. Film still from *En dirigeable sur les champs de bataille* (1919). Courtesy of Musée Albert-Kahn, Boulogne-Billancourt.

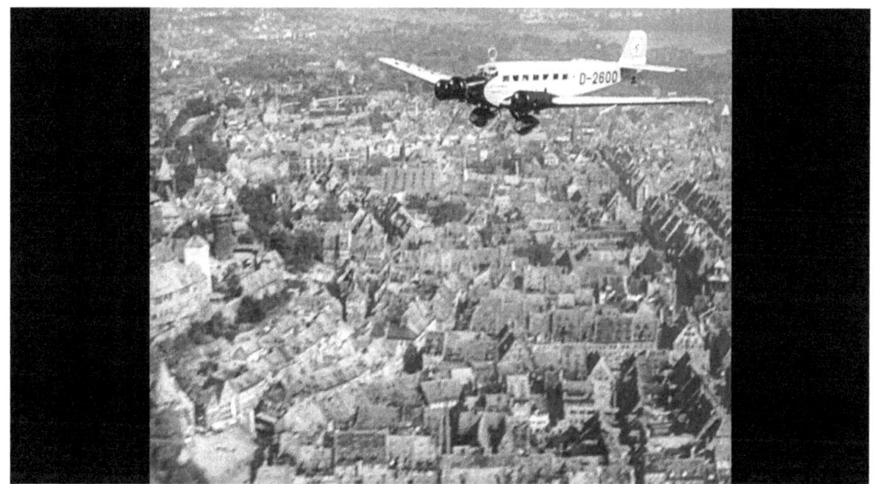

through the current proliferation of proxistant vision. As this visual form moves into the center of visual culture today, it exercises inherent mimetic capacities and e-motional charge by turning softly articulated cartographic terrain into 3D flythrough models. Moving from this early military articulation to the cinematic avant-garde operating in the wake of World War I aerial technology, proxistant vision by way of the airborne moving image was thought of as an artistic potential in city symphonies and related artistic films by Moholy-Nagy and others. This practice clearly demonstrated a newfound expression by way of dynamically combining high and low angles as artists were probing the possibilities this technology opened. Yet, the airborne moving image simultaneously continued to inhabit what Kaplan has described as the shadow of the wartime aftermath.[30] The aerial opening scenes in the Nazi propaganda film *Triumph of the Will* (1936) by Leni Riefenstahl potrays Hitler in a divine descent from Heaven to Deutschland in his Junkers 52.[31]

FIGURE 6.4

Leni Riefenstahl. Film still from the opening sequence in the *Triumph of the Will* (1936). Copyright © the artist.

As Jay Griffiths points out about this shot, "[f]ascism begins as something in the air. [. . .] and invests heavily in performance."[32] The aviator is the navigator of the proxistant in-between—the inhabitant of airborne freedom and an unobstructed view. It is precisely such airborne fascist aesthetics that figure as a backdrop for the attentive spatial concerns of Italian neorealist filmmaker Michelangelo Antonioni, as he navigates between poetic consciousness and the potential utilization towards national myth creation.

Film Scholar Noa Steimatsky has pointed out that Antonioni's cinematic oeuvre is marked by the transposition of background spaces into the foreground, thereby animating the environment with a complexity that imbues it with the vitality of a living character.[33] To add to this, we suggest that in the films of Antonioni, we are presented with the awareness of the camera eye as the agent of cinematic construction. It is never us the viewer, but the camera that observes. The camera is the navigator of a perceptual becoming that happens in the gaps between the cinematic and the pro-filmic environment. This aspect of technological agency obtains a significant proxistant dimension in one of Antonioni's latest works, *Noto, Mandorli, Vulcano, Stromboli, Carnevale* (1992). This ten-minute short film, shot on 70 mm film, was commissioned by the Italian electricity company ENEL for its exhibition at the Italian pavilion at the Seville Expo the same year. Expected to show a celebratory and commercially oriented cross-section of the Italian wonders of material and cultural excess, the film fittingly utilizes the dynamic possibilities of a helicopter-borne camera in the two sections *Vulcano* and *Stromboli*. Far from purely celebratory framings, however, these airborne sections exhibit a highly dynamic proxistant vision that navigates and teases out the spatial dimensions of an active volcano. In *Stromboli*, the helicopter starts with a circulating panoramic overview of a more conventional celebratory style before a few shots closer to the volcano reveal parts of its overwhelming cavity at the distant bottom of the crater. While gliding by the fuming volcanic surfaces in a close-up camera movement across the ridge, we can observe in detail a multiplicity of tiny semi-circular "valves" energetically spewing out streams of white smoke to release the volcanic pressure. The breathing character of the giant volcano is revealed as a time bomb of geological

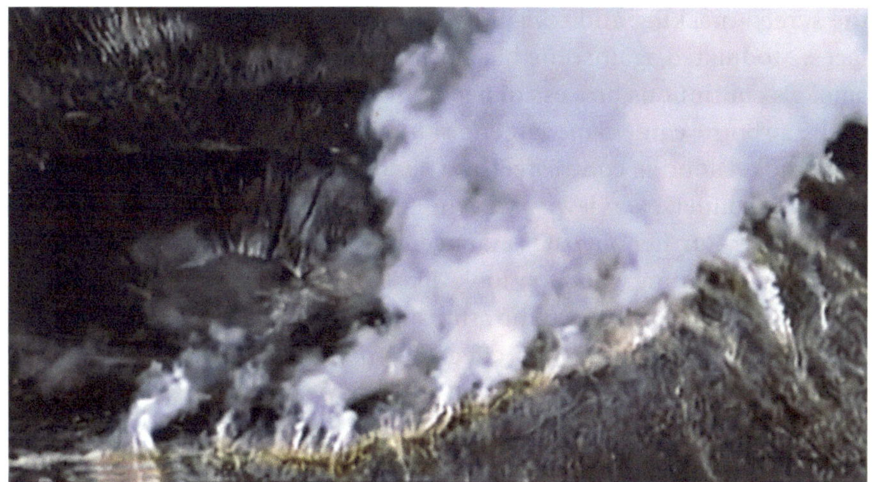

proportions, with millions of outlets struggling to keep pace before the massive pressure turns into a violent eruption.

In the next section of the film, titled *Stromboli*, we follow the dynamic point of view of a helicopter-mounted camera that gradually reveals the dimensions of a differently shaded mountainscape reminiscent of black dune formations. Occasional glimpses of sky and ground reveal the camera's elevated position, while the presence of swirling white smoke alerts us to the unfriendly habitat. As the helicopter camera moves closer to the mountain, it tilts down to a vertical angle, losing sight of the sky while delving into bare rock formations. The disentangled movement of the camera probes and navigates around the black sand and smoky atmosphere, as if searching for the camera angles best suited between close and distant views. Abstract shapes of sand and smoke dance across

FIGURE 6.5

Michelangelo Antonioni. Film still from *Noto, Mandorli, Vulcano, Stromboli, Carnevale* (1992). Copyright © the artist.

the screen masking and revealing a variation of organically shaped surfaces. Modulated against the blackness of the mountain ridge, the white smoke's continuous process of becoming and disintegration is followed by the airborne camera movements' kinetic articulations. A final close-up of a smoke cloud is contrasted by a sudden burst of vertiginous height. With this sudden overview, we see the shape of the volcano and the mountains below. Further out, the camera encircles the volcano as an island in the ocean, revealing what now looks like a tiny mound with a single outlet steadily puffing smoke into the atmosphere.

Antonioni's camera thus effectively navigates the intensive forces at work in the two volcanoes through dynamic airborne movements between close-up and overview. Rather than portraying an abstracted vertical plane, the helicopter camera moves into a close connection, searching out the paths of the volcanic spatial dimensions. As the camera slides up closely along the ridge of the pulsating volcano, proxistant vision is rearticulated as vibrant materiality. The volcano's rock formations glide by as we encircle the steaming crater. The camera shows us an unknown yet referential spatiality—a cinematic potential between proximity and distance. Hence, ENEL's commission of a celebratory corporate-national film is balanced by a curious navigation of a spatial becoming between the heat-producing volcano and its proxistant vision equivalent. The film thus subverts and rearticulates the potential of proxistant vision from the dominating agenda by futurist propaganda. Rather than a celebratory vista, the camera is immersed and overwhelmed by the intensive forces of nature—an energetic complexity that cannot be mimetically tamed.

RANIERI'S PROXISTANT VISION

Turning closer to our time, we can see that Antonioni's volcanic intensity can be contrasted with the gracious proxistant vision of the 3D-animated flythrough models and CGI environments emerging as an artistic potential during the first decade of the new millennium. Contemporary artist and filmmaker Mark Lewis's film *In Search of the Blessed Ranieri* (2014), a roughly twenty-three-minute 5K production transferred to 2K, is an excellent example of how a virtual camera is set to investigate its proxistant potential as a detached cinematic form. Lewis is emblematic of a generation of filmmaking artists working around the turn of the last millennium who, through their disassembled cinematic displays within gallery and museum spaces, critically engaged with the waning eminence of cinema as the quintessential artistic medium of the twentieth century. Artists such as Eija-Liisa Ahtila, Stan Douglas, Douglas Gordon, Isaac Julien, Steve McQueen, Paul Pfeiffer, Pipilotti Rist, Jane and Louise Wilson, and Knut Åsdam, to name but a few, entered more seriously into conversation with the movie industry while exhibiting in a contemporary art context.[34] The introduction of digital platforms and a multiplicity of formats presented artists with readymade forms for which they investigated a *dispositif* of subjectivity and cinematic cultural formation.[35] Working in this environment, Lewis started out in the same fashion, deconstructing narrative elements, such as title sequence in *Two Impossible Films* (1995) and the role of the extra in *The Pitch* (1998). However, already apparent in the latter, which was based on one reel of film and went through all the focal length of the tele lens, Lewis gradually became more interested in the moving image's spatial articulation through its technical and stylistic capacities as a stand-alone investigation.

This evident affinity with the minimalist and conceptual strategies of the structuralist film movement of the 1960s and 1970s can be traced to the feminist experimental film *Riddles of the Sphinx* (1977) by Laura Mulvey and Peter Wollen, in which a continuous mechanical movement of the 360-degree pan was utilized.[36] The attention to micro phases of physical movement of Yvonne Rainer may also have made an impact here, as did fellow Canadian artist Michael Snow's zoom, pan, and camera movement explorations in films such as *Wavelength* (1967) and *Back and Forth* (1969).[37] The *cinema trouvé* explorations of mechanical movement, which we discussed in chapter 1, can be seen as important influences as well. Turning to drone technology and CGI environments in his later works, Lewis plays off the aesthetic similarities between these technologically different operations in a fashion that recalls early cinema's fascination with a new medium.

Lewis's film *In Search of the Blessed Ranieri* is titled after the famous painting *Blessed Ranieri Delivering the Poor from a Prison in Florence* (circa 1430) by Stefano di Giovanni.

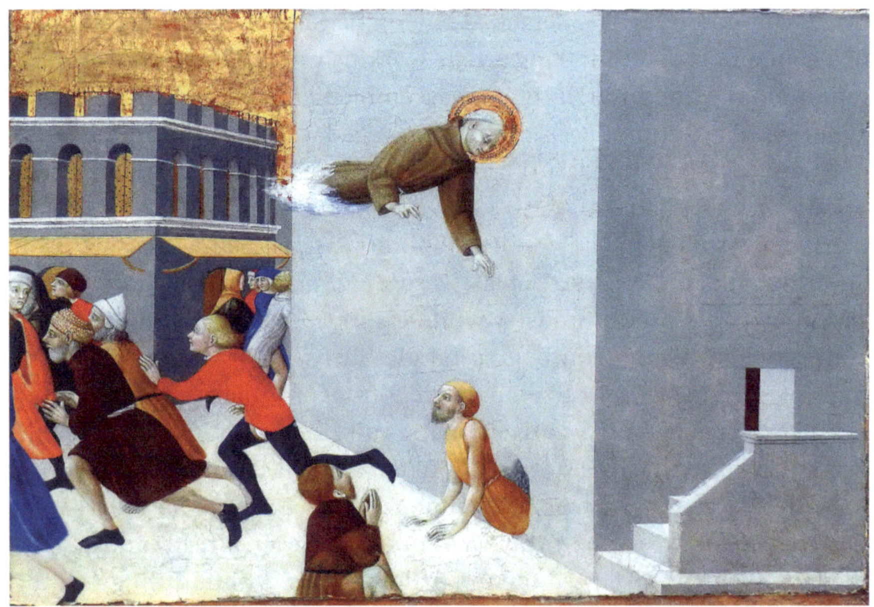

The film combines CGI with physical camera movement in its navigation of the museum space, articulating a decidedly proxistant vision across several different media operations. In addition, *In Search of the Blessed Ranieri* seems to draw attention to the intermediate states between a narrative action rather than offering a clear beginning or end. This is due to the way the film opens with a forward thrust across the interior of the Louvre, starting from the middle of the gallery space. We get the impression that the camera already traversed the museum's halls and hallways for a long time before we arrived. The forward hover-movement glides silently passed early Italian Renaissance paintings and people in

FIGURE 6.6

Stefano di Giovanni. *Blessed Ranieri Delivering the Poor from a Prison in Florence* (circa 1430). Courtesy of Louvre Museum, Paris.

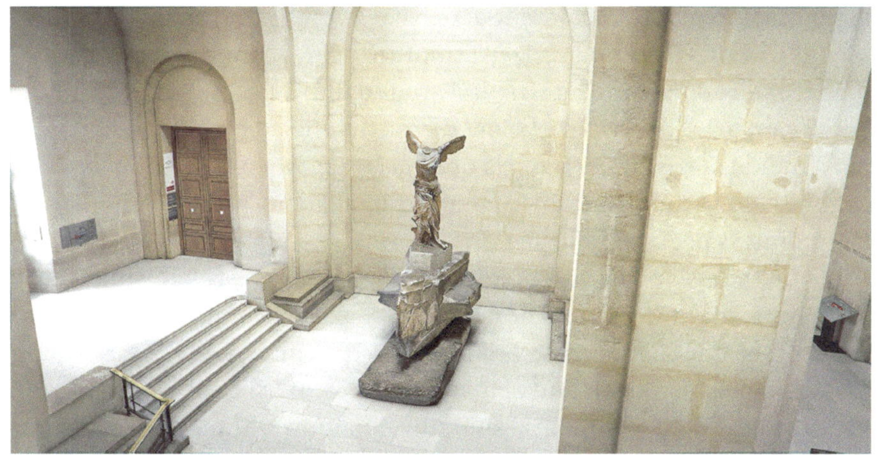

the brightly lit galleries of the Louvre before a slow gliding turn moves direction toward a close-up of a painting on the wall.

As the camera closes in on the painting, the hovering Ranieri is transferred to another hovering position between the painted surface and the cinematic frame. With the painting now translated into the moving image medium of 3D-animated CGI, this double articulation signals the thematic drama of the film itself. As if absorbing Ranieri's levitational abilities, the camera, like the detainees in the painting, is freed from the prison of Earthly constraints. From this close contemplation of the painting, we cut to a forward thrusting movement toward an oval-shaped window in a different room, later to be revealed as a ceiling window in the grand staircase hall that houses the legendary *Winged Victory of Samothrace*, a second-century BC marble sculpture of the Greek goddess Nike.

The camera, which now has turned virtual, is elevated far above the staircase, contemplating art historical levitation through its gracious

FIGURE 6.7

Mark Lewis. Video still from *In Search of the Blessed Ranieri* (2014). Copyright © the artist.

flight. As if to mirror the potential of Nike's wings, the virtual camera descends towards the miniaturized sculpture below, detailing walls and columns, before encircling into a spiral around the sculpture's rugged plinth. As the camera glides by Nike below, we see the effect of the smooth camera movement utilized in Pastrone's *Cabiria* (1914), when three-dimensional volumes are articulated on the two-dimensional screen—another in-betweenness negotiated by the film.

With the eyes of the virtual camera, we continue past Nike while slowly ascending, scanning in a panoramic swipe past the multiple arched volumes of the famous staircase vaults as they turn into malleable cascading archways between deep and shallow surfaces. With another 180-degree pan from the Nike below, in a smooth transition without cuts, we enter the densely populated dark red gallery walls of French eighteenth-century neoclassical paintings. We have now left the 3D-animated flight in a seamless transition to a steady cam float. The camera glides seamlessly through the museum's interior, as if the air was made up of a thick liquid. It moves between close encounters with the surfaces of famous paintings, such as *The Sleep of Endymion* (1791) by Anne-Louis Girodet de Roussy-Trioson and *The Intervention of the Sabine Women* (1795–1799) by Jacques-Louis David, and the observing public. As if in a constant search, the kinetic camera draws neoclassical surfaces and contemporary lives into a proxistant vision of the museum itself as a dynamic archive.[38] Upon a brief rest by the *Grande Odalisque* (1814) by Jean-Auguste-Dominique Ingres, the camera meanders further on to the large Salon Denon. While entering this space, the camera, now virtual, immediately turns attention to the incredibly detailed ceiling paintings by Charles Louis Müller, commissioned between 1863 and 66 by Napoleon III (Louis-Napoléon Bonaparte). The golden eagles, the ultimate symbol of the Bonaparte regime, crowning each corner of the squarely divided painterly composition, attract the second levitation of the camera, spurring yet another vertiginous virtual flight.

This play of surfaces and dimensions goes on for yet another spiraling flight back up before the camera comes down again to enter smoothly the eye-level steady cam float among the rest of the museum visitors. By navigating the spatial volumes that materialize between close-up and overview on the screen, Mark Lewis's *Blessed Ranieri* draws attention to the museum as a state of continuous becoming between the audience and the painting and the camera's own process of depiction mirrored in the painterly and architectural volumes. Just as figures emerge from the ground on the painterly surfaces, so emerges the volumetric dimension of the museum itself as a mediator between the artwork and spectator. Thus, the museum is navigated in the film as a ductile atmosphere articulated through digital means as a slow-moving invisible materiality. The three-dimensional volumes of sculpture and architecture offer infrastructural principles to the digital model flythrough, while the painterly surface signals a two-dimensional construction of three-dimensional volumes. The film employs a juxtaposition of close-up and overviews to explore the evolution of spatial representation from traditional painting to digital 3D models, highlighting the transformation of painterly space into geometric digital environments. The camera furthermore utilizes these processes of becoming to articulate proxistant vision as a subject matter, a cinematic space of possibility between close-up and overview. Art critic and writer Sarah Milroy has noted how "*In Search of the Blessed Ranieri* makes one wonder about the museum itself as a machine for seeing, as a lens that can focus our attention."[39] This "digital re-mastering of the real," Milroy further reflects, "delivers us from the restrictions of embodiment," offering camera positions and kinetic motion beyond human capabilities.[40]

Much to the contrary, as we have seen with proxistant vision, it is exactly the embodied visual experience that is highlighted in the film. Finally, Raymond Bellour recalls, knowing how the film was made does not help, "[i]t is rather the physical confusion offered to the eye that surprises and attracts."[41] Similarly to the thaumatrope, the brain knows, yet it sees. These reflections are valid, therefore, only for the visual experience the work exposes if we remain on a mimetic level of interpretation. It is exactly the digital composite that reveals the importance of this work, a revelation only accessible to the media archeological navigator.

What we have so far analyzed is the visible surfaces of the 3D model and its virtual camera movements that mimic cinematic space made up solely of digital code. A mimetic interpretation will rest at ease with this analysis, while a navigational approach has more to offer. *The Blessed Ranieri* offers us a smooth proxistant camera movement, yet it is the composited logic of de' Barbari's *Venetie MD* and not Antonioni's dynamic helicopter flight that underpins its technological operation. The work generates a virtual environment through 3D animation software similar to the animated flythrough maps of data visualization and architecture models discussed earlier. One way to make this work is to first perform a complete laser scan of the physical environment. This data is transferred to a digital three-dimensional point cloud in the computer software and dressed up in a composite skin made up of millions of still frames from the museum's image-mapped interior. Within this computer-generated 3D model, Lewis can position a virtual camera anywhere he likes and animate a path through it. By plotting a continuous line of coordinates across the xyz axis of the model, the computer calculates and generates the camera angles. The result, when played back in motion, is a virtual camera that navigates a motion path through the pre-plotted camera angles, generating a dynamic proxistant vision within the digital model.

The virtual camera navigates by way of simulated movement through a CGI environment, which itself is made possible by the navigation of geo-referenced image-elements within the same model.[42] If we compare this process to de' Barbari's *Venetie MD*, we see that de' Barbari's many draftsmen have turned into digital image capture.[43] Millions of overlapping images are produced and stitched together to drape the 3D wireframe of the staircase gallery and the Nike sculpture. Animated 3D modeling is nothing more than an automated perspectival image generated from multiple viewpoints.

In this technically ambitious film, Mark Lewis collaborated with Gramercy Park Studios to push the boundaries of visual effects and virtual cinematography. The sophisticated blend of live-action and virtual environments was realized through advanced digital techniques including geometry extraction, 3D modeling, and digital paint. Photogrammetry first transformed extensive photographic data into high-resolution textures and precise geometric models. Specialized software calibrated the photographs within the virtual space, allowing for the extraction of detailed point clouds to construct accurate 3D models. Moreover, the creation of these models involved a careful photographic capture of the museum's interiors with panoramic equipment, including a panoramic head, from which the team, led by VFX Technology Supervisor Francisco Lima, developed production-ready meshes for the film's CGI environments. The live-action footage, shot with a RED Epic camera, was seamlessly integrated with these digital constructs through a matchmaking process, blurring the lines between the real and the virtual. This integration allowed for a close examination of details combined with soaring panoramic overviews that contextualized art, cinema, and architecture in previously unseen ways. The film ultimately drives proxistant vision to its extreme, in the Louvre, creating novel perspectives that may be impossible to achieve through traditional cinematography.[44] The final product is a testament to the possibilities of proxistant contemporary filmmaking technology, redefining the audience's engagement with historical and cultural spaces.

If we continue our navigational, rather than a mimetic approach to *The Blessed Ranieri*, we can furthermore see how digital technologies have abolished the difference between still and moving images. Lewis is influenced by the language of structuralist filmmakers where the material specificities and technological operations dictated the form and content of the film, such as sorting to one continuous tracking shot without perceivable edits. *The Blessed Ranieri* continues this mode by launching a virtual camera into physically impossible trajectories, spectacularly articulating the spatial construction of the famous museum through a digital wireframe. What looks like a single shot is rather a composite of several shots by way of the CGI models discussed earlier. We have seen that impossibly smooth proxistant flights are made possible through the logic of *Venetie MD*'s composite mode. If we move beyond this cultural interface, however, we see yet another fusion between still and moving images, since the digital image on the screen simply consists of a grid of pixels that are controlled by the computer code executed in particular microtemporal sequences.[45] In their digital formats, the difference between the still and the moving image is merely a variation in the code that controls the behavior of the (sub)pixels on the screen. As such, the *Blessed Ranieri* not only showcases the freedom of the virtual camera that has left the terrain of physical constraints of older moving image practices by moving through a digitally constructed wireframe dressed up in still images, but it also demonstrates the capacity of virtual cinematography to replicate traditional artistic styles, bridging the unfamiliar with the familiar in a process of proxistant persuasion.

No longer restrained to abstract graphs, statistical information can be animated into these photorealistic models with the e-motion of a cine-cartographic realism that produces a powerful virtual image of the map in Latour's sense. The digital composition of environments based on a wireframe dressed up in pixels is further reflected upon in Lewis' more recent work *Museum* (2018). Here we see how the virtual camera slowly traverses another collection of paintings from a different century in a fragmented digital environment, where bits and pieces of the architectural and painterly surfaces have been texture-mapped and the remaining space is black. The camera navigates through the dark abyss encountering suspended lumps and fragments of pixels that resemble half-constructed paintings and pieces of walls or columns. Fragments of 3D elements, such as ceilings, floors, and walls, appear to float disconnectedly in an expansive void. It suggests, only in its abstraction, a museum environment suspended in a half-texturized coordinate system of an otherwise invisible grid. With this image of a half-composed, half-destroyed, and fragmented digital 3D museum, it becomes apparent that the digital environment can re-mediate older visual forms while simultaneously operating in a mode of self-reflexivity. By adopting the logic of cinema, 3D-animated flythrough models visualize the process of constructing a digitally composed environment and the fragility of such construction.

This section has developed along the logic of navigation by mapping out an acrobatic path between proximity and distance. The proxistant spatiality drawn up by the daring flights of first-person view dronematography and the aesthetically similar yet operationally different virtual flights offered by 3D animation has been scrutinized across their aesthetic similarities and operational differences. The focus on navigation brought up the principal issue in cartographic discussion about the relation between the map and the terrain. While the FPV dronematographer navigates near reel-time physical space in collaboration with multiple sensor-fusing technical operations, the 3D-animated flythrough navigates a previously recorded path, a future prediction calculated based on past events. Finally, we saw how the operationally different yet aesthetically similar smooth proxistant vision is further investigated through the work of Canadian artist Mark Lewis, whose extended camera movement combines traditional and 3D-animated techniques in its navigation through older forms of two- and three-dimensional representations at the Louvre. If one should pinpoint a single characteristic of Lewis' films, it could be the way the camera operates as a compositional navigator, constantly searching for new possibilities in what seems best described as a dynamically articulated investigation between the new possibilities of digital cinema and early cinema's curiosity for a new medium. This is a curiosity and probing that draws into vision a significantly smooth proxistance that projects both forward and backwards in a cine-cartographic self-reflexive mode. What we see here is a cine-cartographic navigation between the outer limits of proximity and distance. The aerial moving image studies itself and its own historically contingent conventions by way of extending and rearticulating a smooth proxistant capacity.

This media archeological trajectory helps us read and understand the contingency with which such proxistant vision operates across practices and fields today. As already suggested, the proliferation of proxistant vision moves beyond the entertainment industries of FPV drone videos and digital cinema's 3D-animated flythroughs discussed earlier. Proxistant shapes currently figure across medical imaging, data science, urbanism, and architectural planning to name a few practices with similar cinematic contingencies. Here, we can begin to understand how the seemingly insignificant FPV drone videos of McIntosh and Charpu partake in a larger paradigm of a visual paradigm that penetrates deep into the formation of worldviews. Through the historical example of Jacopo de' Barbari's map *Venetie MD* (1500), we identified the cartographic and technical contingencies with which such smooth proxistant vision operates today. This also highlight the importance of a navigational approach to the physical correspondences of a representation, not only for maps but for visual surfaces altogether, which includes those made up by our very own eyes. Returning now, to de' Barbari's new life as a digital interface in the artwork *Venetie 11111100110*, we will explore how artistic research into this motion between close-up and aerial view can further attest to such self-reflexive modes.

DIGITAL VENETIE

The ground-breaking woodcut *Venetie MD* combines an overview of the imperial city with unprecedented detail of its convoluted urban fabric in a dynamic visual form. The key to our interest in *Venetie MD* is its implied

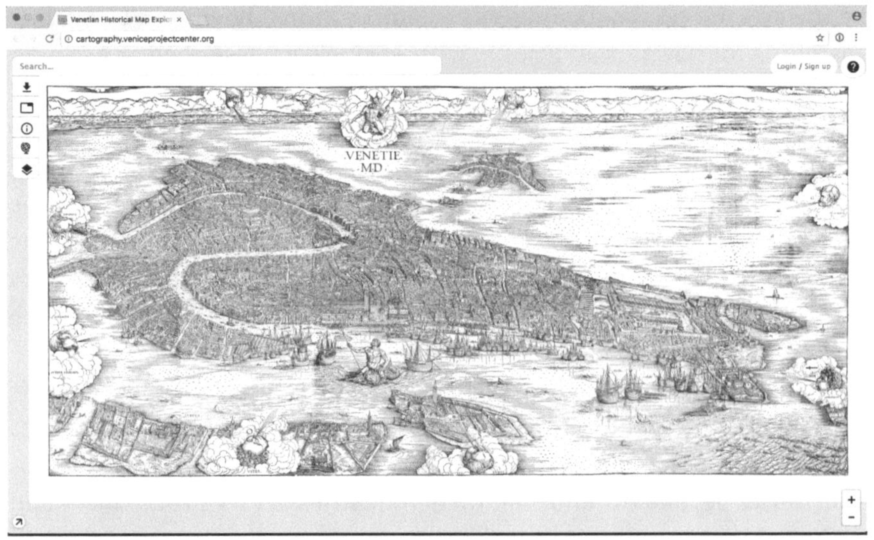

motion visible in the multiple perspectives, which pre-dates later cartographic standardizations and aerial imaging technologies. As we have seen, *Venetie MD* shares qualities with digital maps of our time, where diverse elements are synthesized into a seamless 3D-animated flythrough experience. The new life of de' Barbari's map as a digital interface further attests to such a comparative mode. The digitized version of *Venetie MD*, found on the Venice Project Center's website, is a composite interface that can be navigated by streets and buildings, allowing users to explore Venice's intricate layout in a way reminiscent of contemporary digital maps such as Google or Apple Maps.[46]

The map's intricate level of detail closely resembles that of a Google Maps interface, demonstrating its continued utility for navigation in present-day Venice. While navigating the digitized *Venetie MD* online interface, we noticed that the toolbar offers a feature to "download what is currently visible." However, the downloaded image differs significantly

FIGURE 6.8

Screenshot of http://cartography.veniceprojectcenter.org (February 14, 2019).

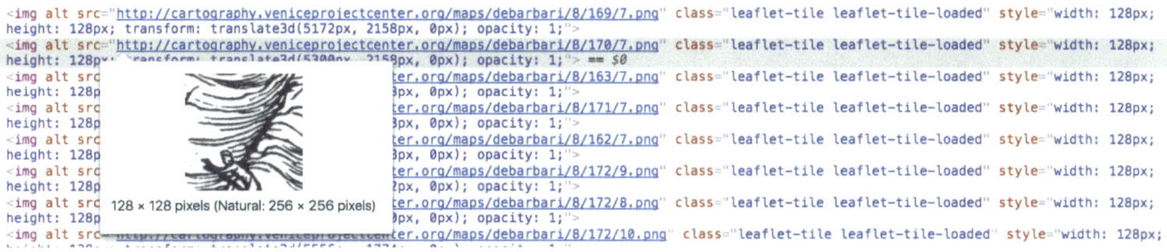

```
<img alt src="http://cartography.veniceprojectcenter.org/maps/debarbari/8/169/7.png" class="leaflet-tile leaflet-tile-loaded" style="width: 128px;
height: 128px; transform: translate3d(5172px, 2158px, 0px); opacity: 1;">
<img alt src="http://cartography.veniceprojectcenter.org/maps/debarbari/8/170/7.png" class="leaflet-tile leaflet-tile-loaded" style="width: 128px;
height: 128p                                 158px, 0px); opacity: 1;"> == $0
<img alt src                                 ter.org/maps/debarbari/8/163/7.png" class="leaflet-tile leaflet-tile-loaded" style="width: 128px;
height: 128p                                 3px, 0px); opacity: 1;">
<img alt src                                 ter.org/maps/debarbari/8/171/7.png" class="leaflet-tile leaflet-tile-loaded" style="width: 128px;
height: 128p                                 3px, 0px); opacity: 1;">
<img alt src                                 ter.org/maps/debarbari/8/162/7.png" class="leaflet-tile leaflet-tile-loaded" style="width: 128px;
height: 128p                                 3px, 0px); opacity: 1;">
<img alt src                                 ter.org/maps/debarbari/8/172/9.png" class="leaflet-tile leaflet-tile-loaded" style="width: 128px;
height: 128p                                 2px, 0px); opacity: 1;">
<img alt src                                 ter.org/maps/debarbari/8/172/8.png" class="leaflet-tile leaflet-tile-loaded" style="width: 128px;
height: 128p                                 0px, 0px); opacity: 1;">
<img alt src=                                ter.org/maps/debarbari/8/172/10.png" class="leaflet-tile leaflet-tile-loaded" style="width: 128px;
```

128 × 128 pixels (Natural: 256 × 256 pixels)

from what we see on the screen. The 14,196 image tiles of the de' Barbari's digitally encoded map are organized in a grid of 169 columns and eighty-four rows. Each tile is a 256 × 256-pixel image.

This tiling technique optimizes the user experience on the web and minimizes web traffic. However, a closer examination of the downloaded section reveals that the algorithm in the download function produces an image file that populates 256 × 256-pixel images (tiles) in a 128 × 128-pixel grid without resizing them. This misalignment is most likely due to a syntax error—a bug—in the server-side code, and this bug could be as tiny as just one misplaced character. The result is a defective map displaying only one-fourth of each tile, leaving three-fourths of each image tile obscured. This fragmented visual output, though unintended, highlights the complexity of rendering the map digitally, setting the stage for further exploration.

While the maximal magnification of *Venetie MD* has been segmented into 14,196 distinct image tiles, these tiles cannot be completely visualized due to the inherent display constraints of computer monitors. Viewing the complete tile assembly as a single composite image requires individual downloading and manual compilation. To streamline this process, we deployed a script to automate the assembly. However, when the images were downloaded section-by-section in full resolution, the resulting composition resembles not the bird's-eye view of systematic access and navigation, but the topological space of a computational process repeatedly executing a glitch. Taking this electronic event as a hypothetical turning

FIGURE 6.9

Inspecting the source code of the user interface.

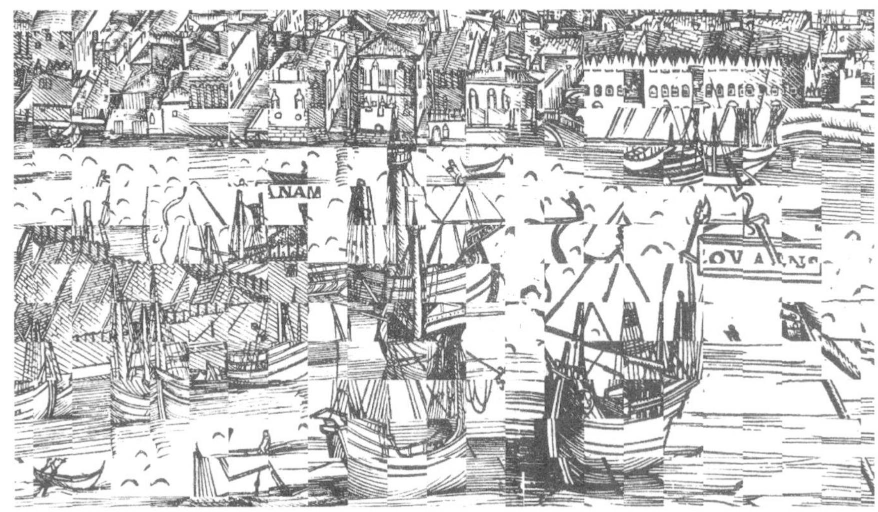

FIGURE 6.10

Downloaded image via "Download what is currently visible" function.

point in the life of the artwork, we deviced an algorithm that replicated the logic of the glitch. This algorithm was used to generate *Venetie MMXVII*, a project comprising three distinct states that increasingly diverged from the original map. By adjusting certain parameters within the assembly algorithm, we controlled where and how much each image tile would be exposed. In the final state, we opted for a complete random assembly resulting in a fully abstract composition. The three states reflect the three versions of *Venetie MD* created by de' Barbari, mirroring the evolution of the city over time.

Hence, our artistic investigation continues our navigational, media archeological approach to shed light on the map's newly scanned material life as an assemblage of digital micro-temporal events. This is an attempt to talk about the life of an artwork and its continued modulation through various infrastructures, eventually ending up as an occurrence of electromagnetic pulsation. This line of exploration is furthered

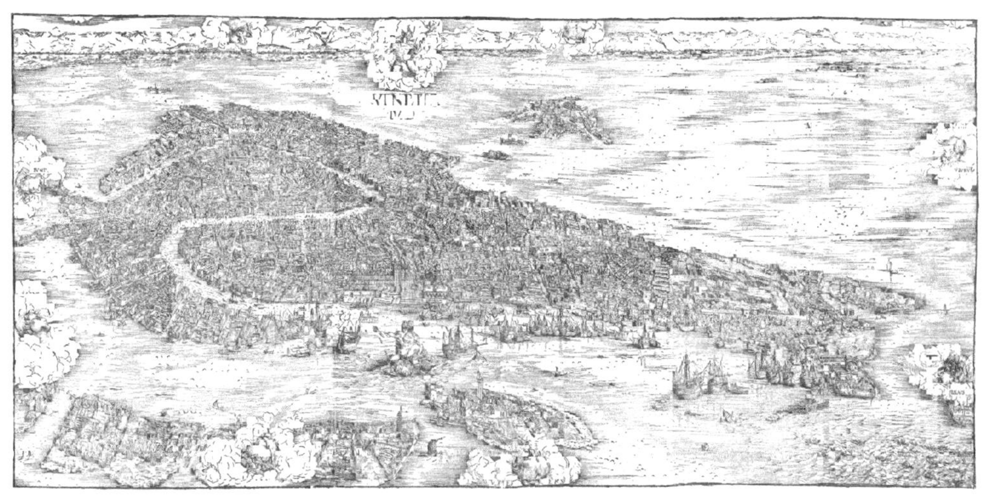

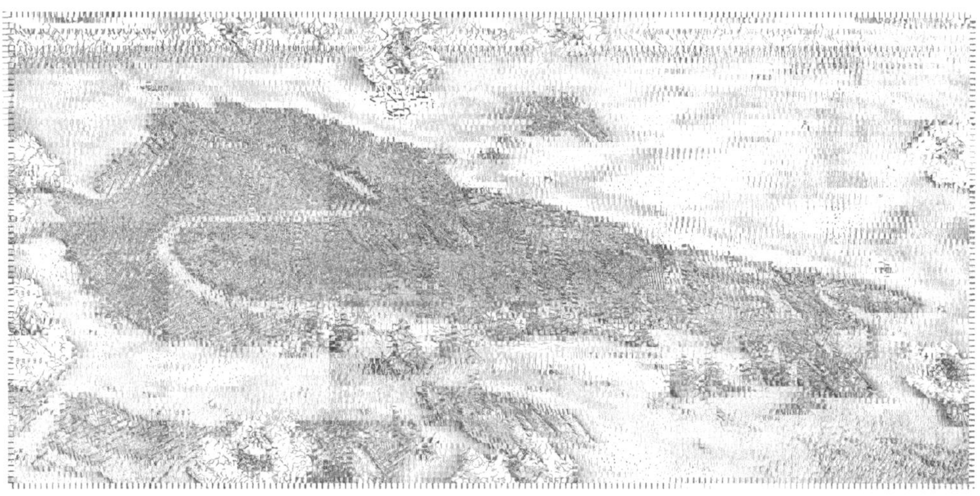

FIGURE 6.11

Bull.Miletic. *Venetie MMXVII* (1500–2017), first state. Copyright © the artist.

FIGURE 6.12

Bull.Miletic. *Venetie MMXVII* (1500–2017), second state. Copyright © the artist.

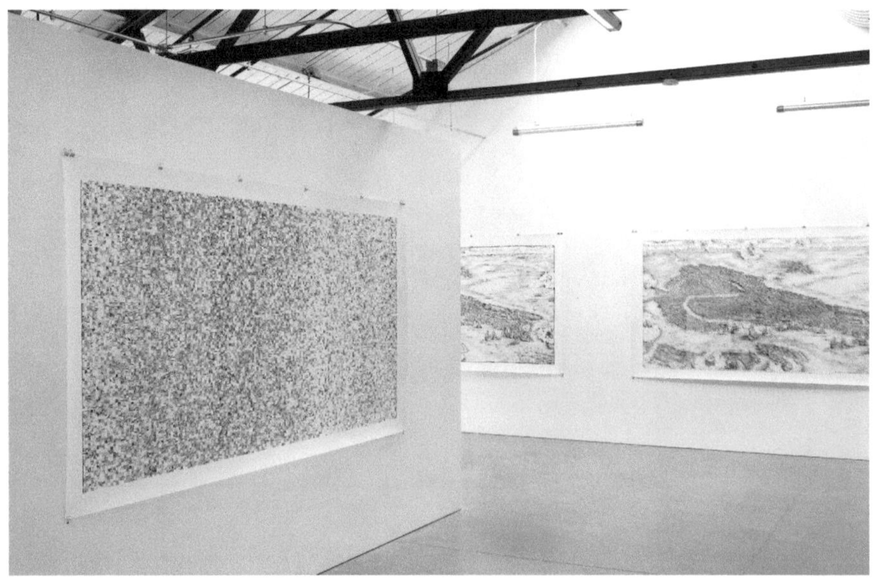

by employing the moving image, exploring the cine-cartographic contingencies inherent in the map's proxistant layout. The research entails extensive aerial footage captured via drones in Venice, alongside digital cartographic tools, including Google Maps and other mapping services. The video utilizes proxistant vision as a method of exploration, allowing for navigation without a predetermined plan. This approach further explores the logic of *cinéma trouvé* discussed in part I, where the camera operates independently to highlight the technological operations in the process. Mark Lewis has reflected similarly on his work, in which his interest is to understand how, metaphorically speaking, the camera might have a will of its own: "That the shot, the composition, might be

FIGURE 6.13

Bull.Miletic. *Venetie MMXVII* (1500–2017), third state at Anglim Gilbert Gallery, San Francisco. Photo by Anglim Gilbert Gallery. Copyright © the artists.

determined by something which is not human, [and] does not operate according to the laws of human consciousness."[47] This interest of Lewis is one we share, in which the emphasis in the film is what the camera sees, trying to free up the subjectivity that associates a camera movement with a POV of a human character. For Lewis, this type of camera work resembles a form of collaboration rather than direct control: "You can put the camera on the computer and allow the computer to generate the move. The feel is that the camera operates on its own."[48] This method, therefore, could be understood as self-reflexive on behalf of the camera, in that it foregrounds the agency of nonhuman vision. Such thoughts are further explored through theoretical frameworks that explore how technology integrates and operates autonomously.[49]

This is also how we operate when we pull our camera over the vitrine at Museo Correr or when we navigate a 3D-animated model of Venice using Gooogle Maps. Proxistant flythrough models, such as those produced by Google Maps, Apple Maps, and similar programs, promise to "see it all" by providing a seamless, uninterrupted virtual flight from a global perspective to a detailed street view of choice. In the *Venetie 11111100110* video however, as the camera moves in for a close-up, the image loses its clarity and shifts into geometric abstraction, driven by glitches encountered in the detailed views.

This reveals the inherent limitatons within digital archival processes, as exemplified by the proxistant flythrough model's difficulty in rendering the appropriate details during close-up. Such moments expose the underlying instability of networked digital archives, which rely on dynamic data processing and transmission.[50] Although these CGI environments effectively producie film-like, immersive experiences, they are nothing more than numerical constellations that translate into visual forms through recursive computational processes. The software of a certain encoding makes these numerical constellations visible in the process of operation, but the 3D model, as an image, does not exist prior to or after the event of executing the code. This is critical from the perspective of archiving and storage since what is stored in a digital file does not presuppose its visual materialization. In the digital version of *Venetie MD*, therefore, we encounter not only the smooth proxistant vision created by multiple perspectives but a further modulation of spatial principles—where the map

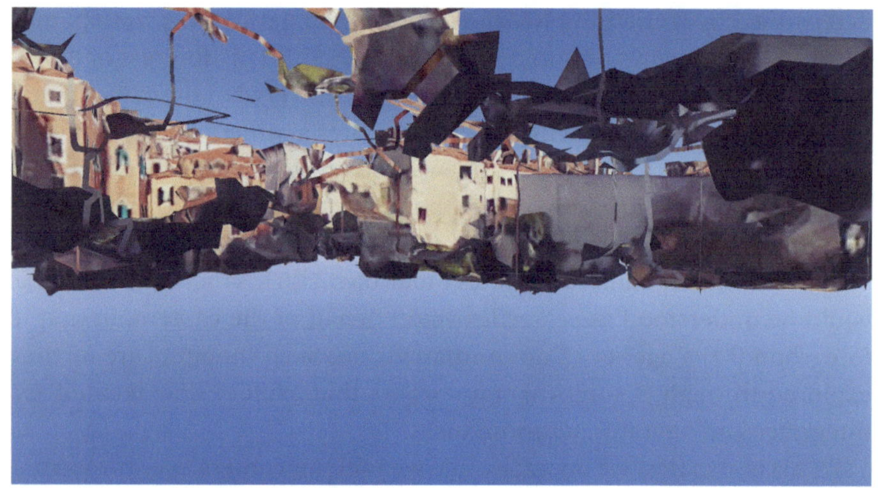

transistions from a cohesive whole into an assemblage of fragments, first as 14,196 individual image tiles, and further down to millions of pixels encoded in binary form. This artistic process reflects the map's original creation as an assemblage of fragments, now reconfigured in a digital abstract form. Through the prism of proxistance, the map's navigational qualities emerge, moving beyond its mimetic representation to navigate underlying structures of power and control. This approach, rooted in media archaeology, points back to how historical contingencies shaped the map, where maritime navigational principles intersect with static perspectival techniques, embedding dynamic routes and connections within the image space.

Through our research on *Venetie MD*, we discovered a reference in another work attributed to de' Barbari, the *Portrait of Luca Pacioli* (circa 1495–1500). The painting's depiction of a transparent archimedean solid with eight triangular and eighteen square faces, known as rhombicuboctahedron, inspired us to develop this artistic research into a kinetic installation.

FIGURE 6.14

Bull.Miletic. Video still from *Venetie 11111100110* (1500–2022). Copyright © the artists.

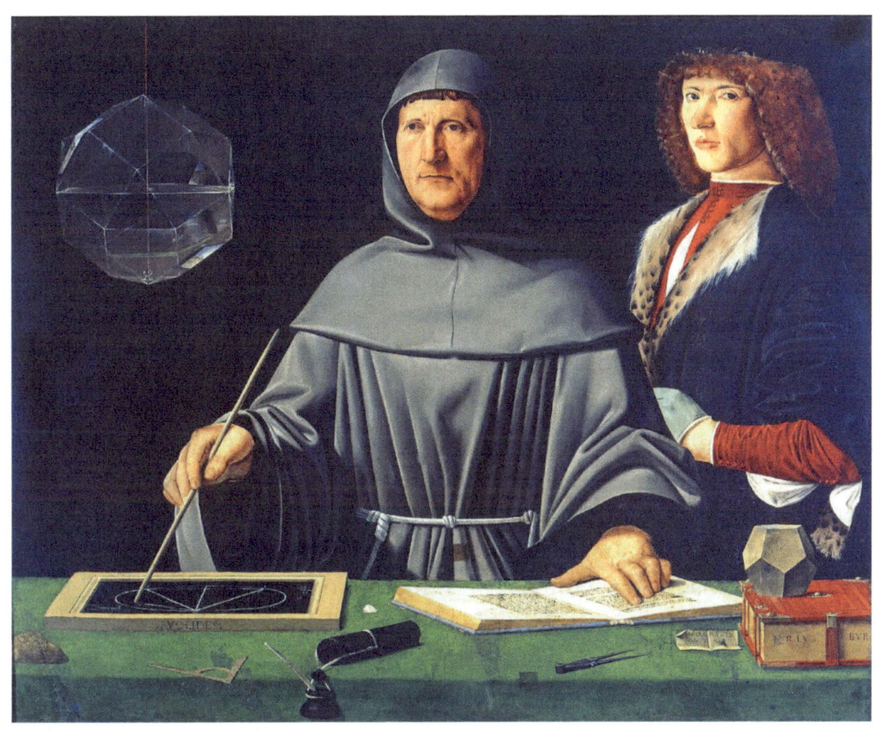

FIGURE 6.15

Jacopo de' Barbari. *Portrait of Luca Pacioli* (c. 1495–1500), tempera on panel, 99 cm × 120 cm (39 in × 47 in). Courtesy of Capodimonte Museum, Naples.

Our initial idea was to facilitate a fragmentation of the video across the exhibition space. This setup was enabled by a custom-designed robotic mechanism, which directed the video projection to periodically reflect off a mirrored rhombicuboctahedron. The mirrored rhombicuboctahedron dispersed geometrically abstracted reflections across the room in a way that resembled the fragmented visual forms generated in our video of the 3D-animated model of Venice created using Google Maps. Scaled based on proportions from the *Portrait of Luca Pacioli*, the motorized rhombicuboctahedron enhanced perceptual instability by setting the shapes afloat aimlessly around the space. The flipped back-and-forth movement of the mirror was mechanized with a linear actuator, allowing the projected light to pass through or reflect at a ninety-degree angle. A modular control unit with a spectrum analyzer, developed for *Ferriscope*, enabled continued experimentation in this composition and its alterations between conventional and kinetic modes (see figures II.1–II.7). Bernhard Siegert's philosophical concept on remediation maintains that a critical goal of cultural techniques is to identify instances in which media engage in self-reflection or interact with other media forms. When one medium reflects on another medium, it can show us something about its operation that we can study further.[51] Such a study through re-mediation is key to our investigation of *Venetie MD* from an artistic research perspective. The bug is the starting point for understanding the difference between the material base of the map's physical paper version created in 1500 and its contemporary online existence as electronic pulsation. Equally fragile, equally material.

Encountering the digitized map and the subsequent digital bug introduces a discussion on preservation and the archive. The archive, as a technology of reference, embodies proxistant qualities, where one can effectively navigate from a perceived totality to specific details. With digital archives, this technology is translated into an accessible shift between overview and close-up. This visualization, however, does not operate according to human reference systems but is governed by the computational logic of algorithms. Contemporary culture increasingly relies on such algorithms to access essential data, a situation made additionally complex by rapidly developing generative AI systems.[52] As noted by Deleuze and Guattari among others, representation is not a second-grade reality but has an active role in its continuous construction. Mapping functions not merely as a reflection of reality but as an active process that reshapes the worlds where diverse species and matter coexist.[53] Considering the age-old discussion of the correlation between map and territory, Venice today is actively conserved in defiance of the natural progression of decay and the entropic forces of time. The enactment of preservation has allowed a 500-year-old map to remain functional for navigating Venice today. Contemporary Venice is more than a tourist destination; it has become a self-replicating model of itself, continuously reimagined by visitors, despite the impinging threat of rising ocean levels. The glitch inherent in the digitized map on the Venice Project Center's website serves as a metaphor for the equal instability of digital and physical worlds. Just as the digital map deteriorates, so does the material city it represents.

The instability of such a storage principle points back to the fragility of Venice itself as a cultural archive. As Stoppani has noted, "Venice is often identified with the images that represent it."[54] In the desperate effort to keep up its virtual image, the city of Venice is in a constant state of preservation. That the 500-year-old *Venetie MD* still functions as a map for Venice today testifies to this fact. As we have seen with Latour, perspective establishes a "four-lane freeway" between reality and its representation.[55] If we forget the navigational approach to maps, and indeed, all imaging, we are quickly left with a worldview in which we believe that separate objects exist in empty geometric space. Similarly to the city of Venice, the Louvre Museum is itself a virtual image of a previous age, an architectural black box of recursive rehabilitation, remaking the old with the new. To repeat November and her colleague's point about maps, "an isolated image has no scientific referent—but it generates, of course, like all images, a virtual image, the 'what' that it is said to be the representation 'of.'"[56] With a navigational approach we can see how proxistant vision is constructed, which also gives us insight into how it operates.

This chapter has developed along the logic of navigation by mapping out an acrobatic path between close-up and overview. The proxistant spatiality drawn up by the daring flights of first-person view (FPV) dronematography and the aesthetically similar yet operationally different virtual flights offered by 3D animation has been scrutinized across their aesthetic similarities and operational differences. The focus on navigation brought up the principal issue in cartographic discussion about the relation between the map and the terrain. While the FPV dronematographer navigates near real-time physical space in collaboration with multiple sensor-fusing technical operations, the 3D-animated flythrough navigates a previously recorded path, a future prediction calculated based on past events. Through the historical example of Jacopo de' Barbari's map *Venetie MD*, we see the cartographic and technical contingencies with which such smooth proxistant vision operates today. This also underscores the importance of a navigational approach to the physical correspondences of any form of representation, not only for maps but for all visual surfaces, including those shaped by our own perception.

If one should pinpoint a single characteristic of Lewis' films, it could be the way the camera operates as a compositional navigator, constantly searching for new possibilities in what seems best described as a dynamically articulated investigation between the new possibilities of digital cinema and early cinema's curiosity for a new medium. This is a curiosity and probing that draws into vision a significantly smooth proxistance that projects both forward and backwards in a cine-cartographic self-reflexive mode. The aerial moving image studies itself and its own historically contingent conventions by way of extending and rearticulating a smooth proxistant capacity. This media archeological trajectory helps us read and understand the contingency with which such proxistant vision operates across practices and fields today. This is a larger visual paradigm that penetrates deep into the formation of worldviews. Perhaps the most hyperbolic version of proxistant vision is Google Earth, in which a virtual camera effortlessly travels between an orbital perspective and a detailed street-level view. When we ascend out from the local to the extremely far away, we get the sense that we can be everywhere and see it all. However, proxistant interfaces such as Google Earth in fact "see" very little because they harvest highly specialized data.[57] As Latour has emphasized, this exemplifies how each instrument produces only one perspective and, importantly, simultaneously excludes all the other. As we move on to the orbital machines, we will follow this line of argument, for which the analysis of the current proxistant paradigm is crucial.

III

ORBITAL MACHINES

Zoom Blue Dot (1990–2020)

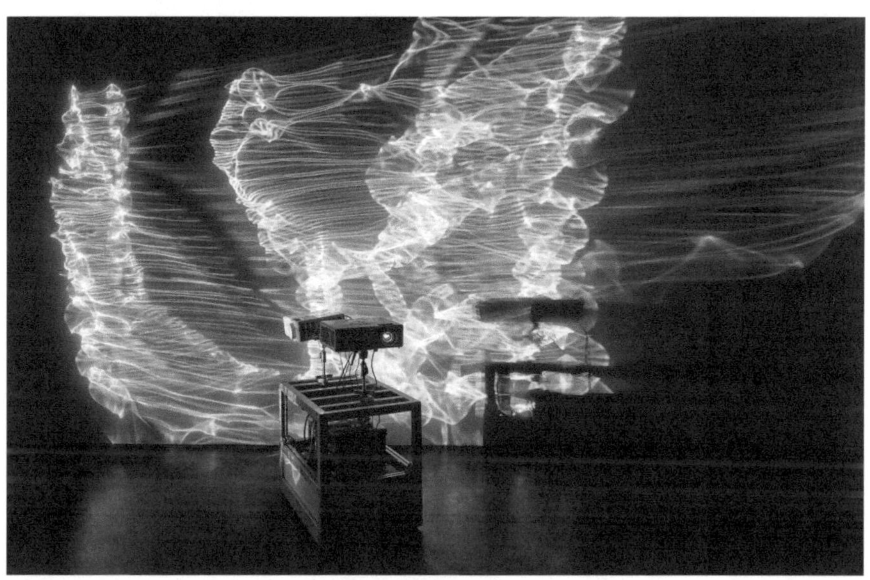

FIGURE III.1

Bull.Miletic. Installation view, *Zoom Blue Dot* (1990–2020) at the Museum of Craft and Design, San Francisco. Photo by Henrik Kam. Copyright © the artists.

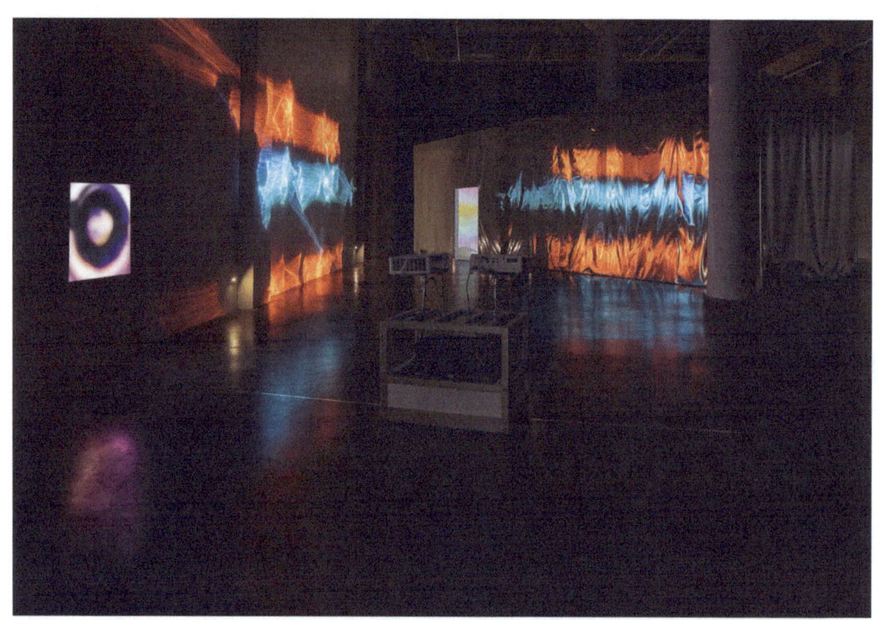

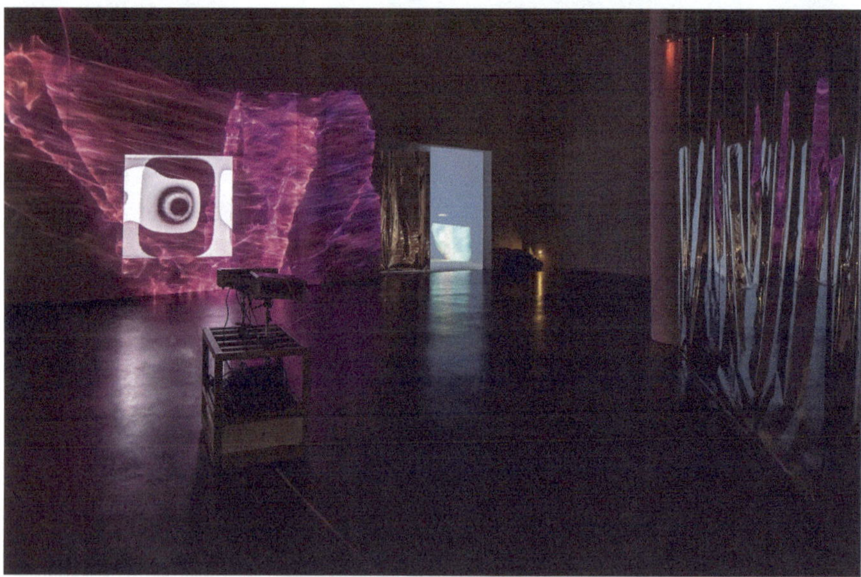

FIGURE III.2

Bull.Miletic. Installation view, *Zoom Blue Dot* (1990–2020) at the Museum of Craft and Design, San Francisco. Photo by Henrik Kam. Copyright © the artists.

FIGURE III.3

Bull.Miletic. Installation view, *Zoom Blue Dot* (1990–2020) at the Museum of Craft and Design, San Francisco. Photo by Henrik Kam. Copyright © the artists.

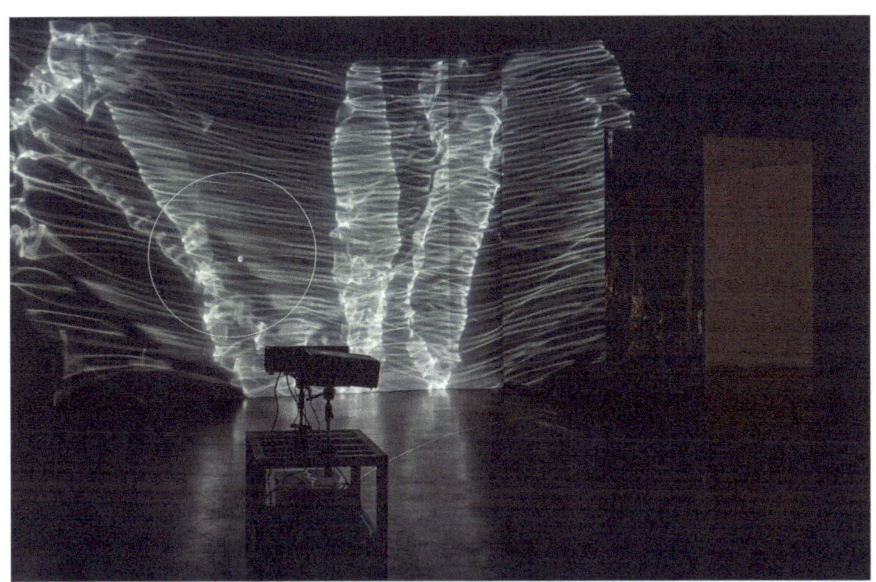

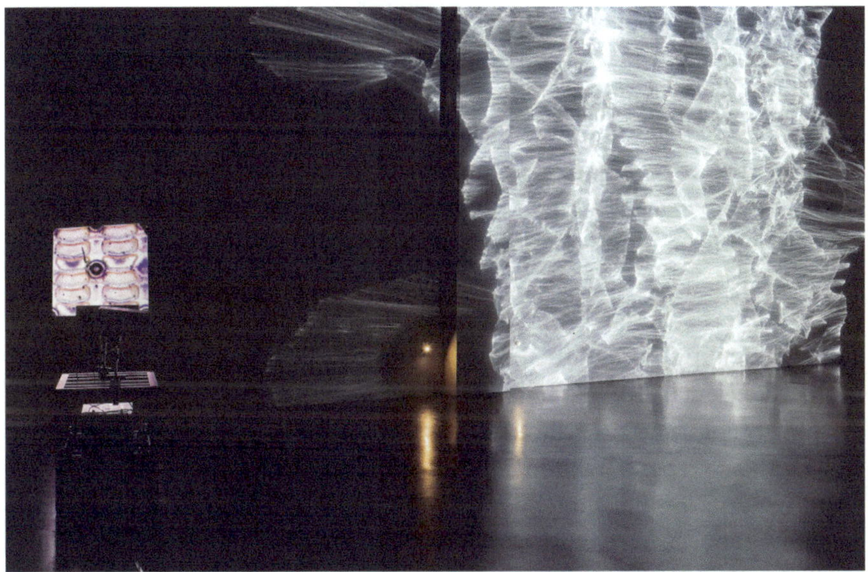

FIGURE III.4

Bull.Miletic. Installation view, *Zoom Blue Dot* (1990–2020) at the Museum of Craft and Design, San Francisco. Photo by Henrik Kam. Copyright © the artists.

FIGURE III.5

Bull.Miletic. Installation view, *Zoom Blue Dot* (1990–2020) at the Museum of Craft and Design, San Francisco. Photo by Henrik Kam. Copyright © the artists.

Zoom Blue Dot is a two-channel kinetic video installation featuring a custom-made robot equipped with two video projectors positioned in opposite directions, slowly navigating a darkened exhibition space along a curved trajectory.[1] The robot's perpetual back-and-forth movement results in continuous alterations in the projections' shape, size, and intensity. The two videos' content is not synchronized with the robot's spatial position, ensuring that no projection occurs at the same angle and distance from the projection surfaces. The videos also differ in duration (channel A is seventeen minutes long and channel B is twenty-two minutes long). A large reflective Mylar curtain, suspended from ceiling to floor and tailored to the venue's specific architectural features, further destabilizes the spatial relations within the installation. Each time the beam of projected light strikes the curtain, a unique reflection is cast into the space. As the curtain gently sways due to the airflow generated by visitors' movements, the randomness of the reflections increases, causing further "deformations." As the robot moves, the entire venue—with its distinctive architecture, infrastructure, and varying configurations of engaged spectators—becomes an active participant in the artwork's composition. The path leads to the walls on either end, where the robot pauses momentarily before resuming its endless journey in the opposite direction.

The repetitive motion of the robot in the exhibition space sets the stage for the two videos, each commencing with an identical sequence lasting approximately three minutes. In this sequence, the camera, as if descending from outer space, smoothly approaches the surface of Earth. The journey begins from a vantage point where Earth appears as a single pixel within the frame. Gradually, the camera draws closer, and Earth expands to occupy more of the image. At a geostationary altitude, an almost perfectly circular dry lakebed in Nevada's vast arid landscape emerges as the landing target. As the descent continues, Earth looms larger, and just as the lakebed's whiteness fills the view, a tiny black dot appears at its center. The dot grows larger and more defined as the camera descends further. Eventually, it becomes clear that what initially seemed a single black dot is, in fact, a pair of smartphones positioned perpendicularly, with their screens facing the sky. The phones lie unattended, arranged in a position reminiscent of the two amorous picnickers in the film *Powers of Ten*.

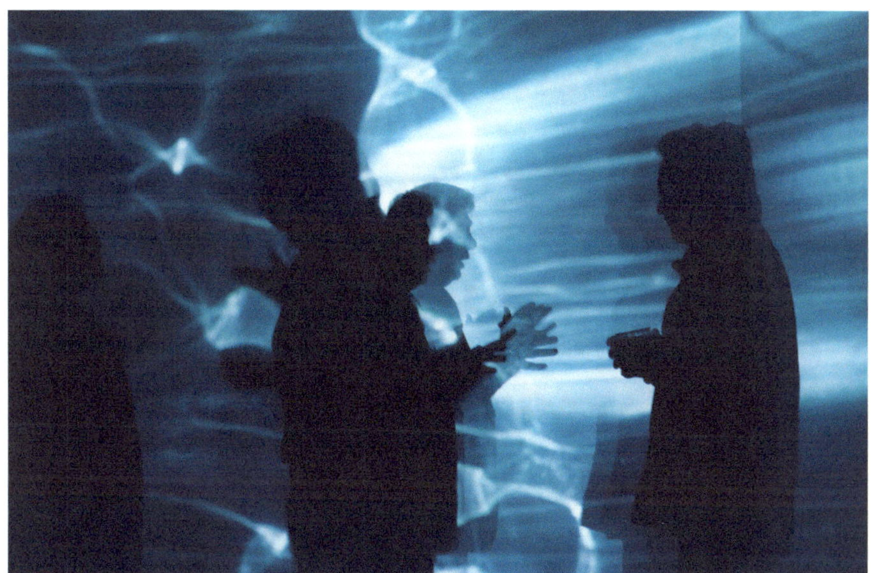

If the two videos were played in sync and displayed side by side, this is the point where they would diverge. Here, the camera metaphorically splits in two, each part directed towards the tiny white dot displayed on both smartphone screens. Subtitles indicate that this dot is the *Pale Blue Dot*, a photograph of Earth taken by the *Voyager 1* space probe in 1990.

The camera continues its descent in both videos, with the only difference being the orientation of the smartphone screens and the display of the Pale Blue Dot in portrait and landscape formats, respectively. The first major divergence occurs as the camera moves closer to the screens, revealing their distinct liquid crystal display (LCD) architectures. The dot quickly morphs into jagged fields of colored light as the camera plunges into the screen. As the camera delves deeper into the seemingly infinite expanse of the LCD assemblage, the differences between the two videos

FIGURE III.6

Bull.Miletic. Installation view, *Zoom Blue Dot* (1990–2020) at the Museum of Craft and Design, San Francisco. Photo by Dallis Willard. Copyright © the artists.

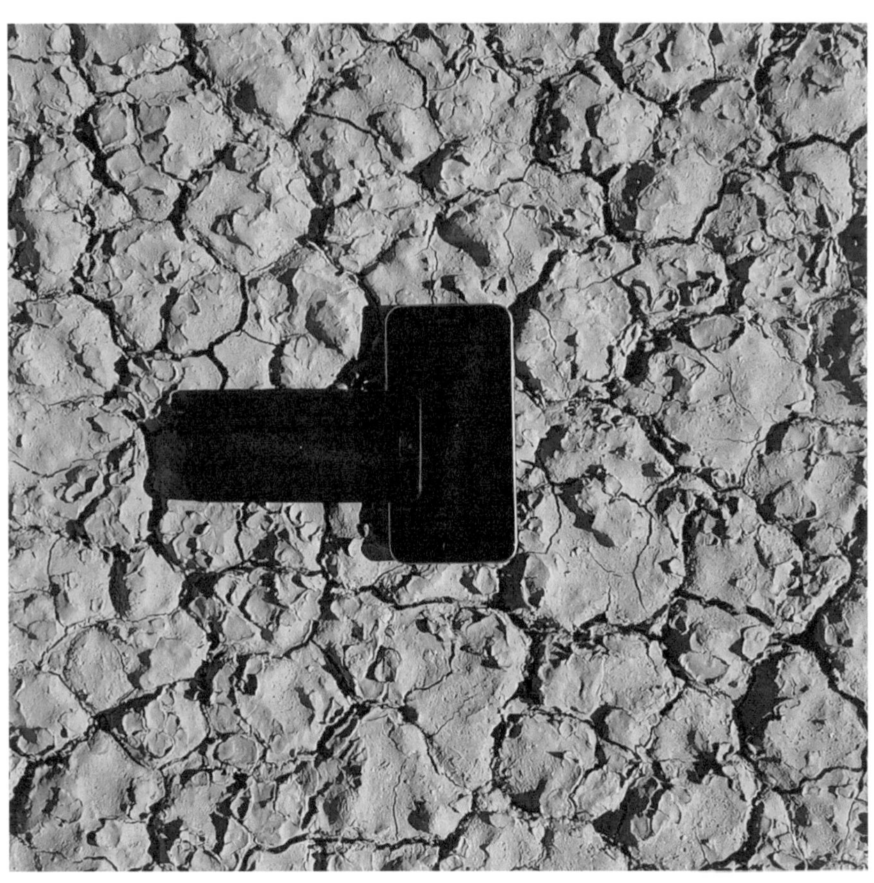

FIGURE III.7

Bull.Miletic. Video still from *Zoom Blue Dot* (1990–2020). Copyright © the artists.

FIGURE III.8

NASA image PIA00452 also known as *Pale Blue Dot* captured by *Voyager 1* on February 14, 1990. Courtesy of NASA/JPL.

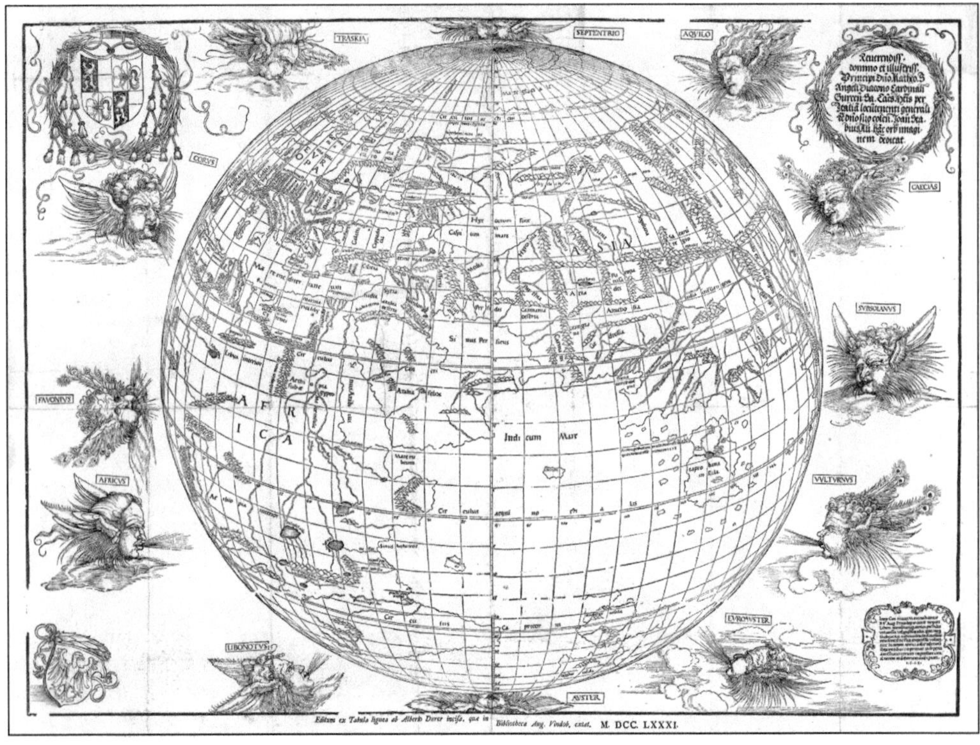

FIGURE III.9

Johannes Stabius, Albrecht Dürer. *Stabiussche Weltkarte (The Stabius World Map)* (1515), woodcut print, 34 × 25.5 in (86.5 × 65 cm). No examples from the sixteenth century are known to exist. This edition was published by Joseph Elden von Kurzbeck under the supervision of the scholar Johann Adam von Bartsch in 1781.

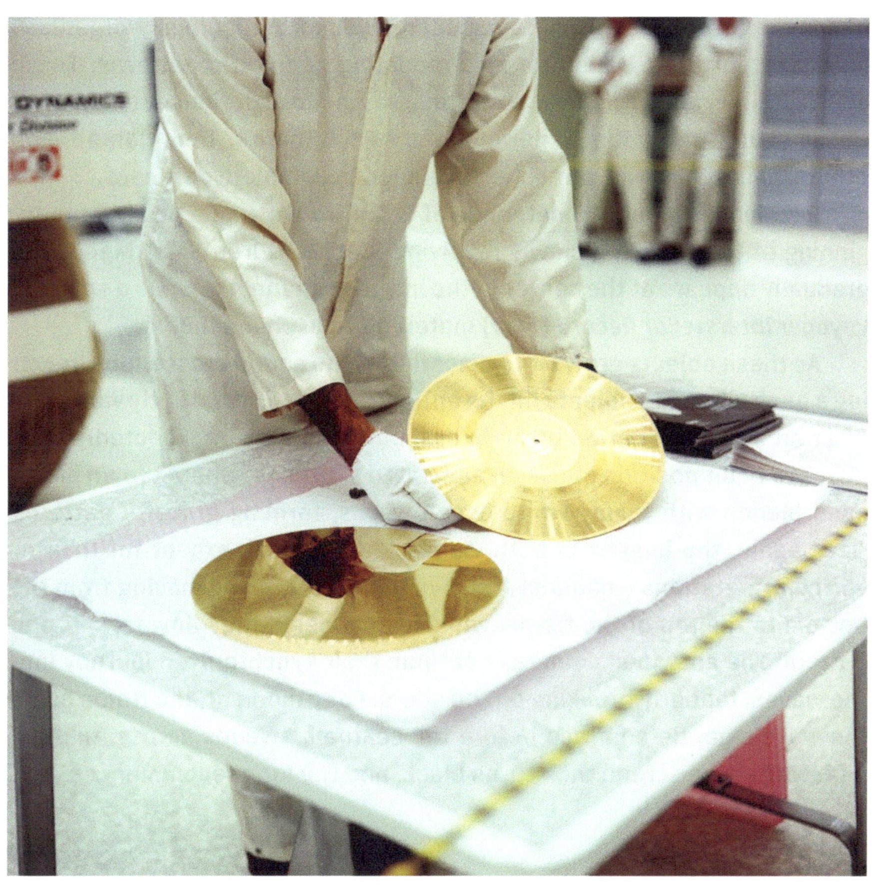

FIGURE III.10

Voyager Golden Record and the gold-platted cover. Courtesy of JPL/NASA.

become more pronounced. Layer upon layer of meticulously organized lines and surfaces transform into repeating geometric patterns. These abstract lines and grids form a shifting, rhythmic experience reminiscent of the structuralist film experiments by Paul Sharits, Tony Conrad, and others. Eventually, the screen is enveloped in complete darkness.

Recalling the initial emergence of Earth from a single pixel at the beginning of the videos, a slowly revolving Stabius-Dürer World Map (1515) gradually appears at the center of the image in channel A, while a spinning *Voyager Interstellar Record* (1977) materializes in channel B.

As these objects grow more discernible, the sound crescendos, reaching a peak when the objects fill the entire frame before abruptly vanishing. After an extended period of darkness, both cameras unexpectedly reappear in a nadir position above an elongated shoreline, where brown beach sand blends with foamy white ocean waves, forming graceful patterns. Once again, the images in both videos are identical, except for their inverted orientations—channel A shows the ocean waves moving from the bottom to the top of the frame, while in channel B, they flow from top to bottom. The entwined cameras continue their synchronized journey into the waves, tenderly breaking on the shore. For a moment, the frame holds the wave's gentle embrace before the seafoam sweeps across, filling it with white. The screen then turns black, and the loop recommences.

7

PROLOGUE (*PALE BLUE DOT*)

"Look again at that dot, [. . .] every saint and sinner in the history of our species lived here—on a mote of dust suspended in a sunbeam."
—Carl Sagan[1]

In 1990, the *Voyager 1* space probe pointed one of its cameras towards Earth to snap one last photograph. This image, shot from a distance of roughly four billion miles, depicts Earth as a crescent only 0.12 pixels in size.[2] Poetically described by one of the initiators of the event, astrophysicist and space explorer Carl Sagan, the Earth appeared as a glimmering speck of dust, "a pale blue dot suspended in a sunbeam."[3] In the long cultural history of Earth imaging, this photograph is often bypassed, and perhaps rightfully so, since the Earth occupies less than 0.00015625 percent of the image.[4] Nevertheless, capturing this image represented a significant challenge for the scientists of the *Voyager 1* mission. Before its realization, the image had been a decade-long dream originally proposed and fought for by Sagan himself, then-Planetary Society President and Voyager Imaging Team member. As Sagan later reflects in his book *Pale Blue Dot: A Vision of the Human Future in Space*:

From Saturn, I knew, the Earth would appear too small for *Voyager* to make out any detail. Our planet would be just a point of light, a lonely pixel, hardly distinguishable from the many other points of light *Voyager* could see, nearby planets

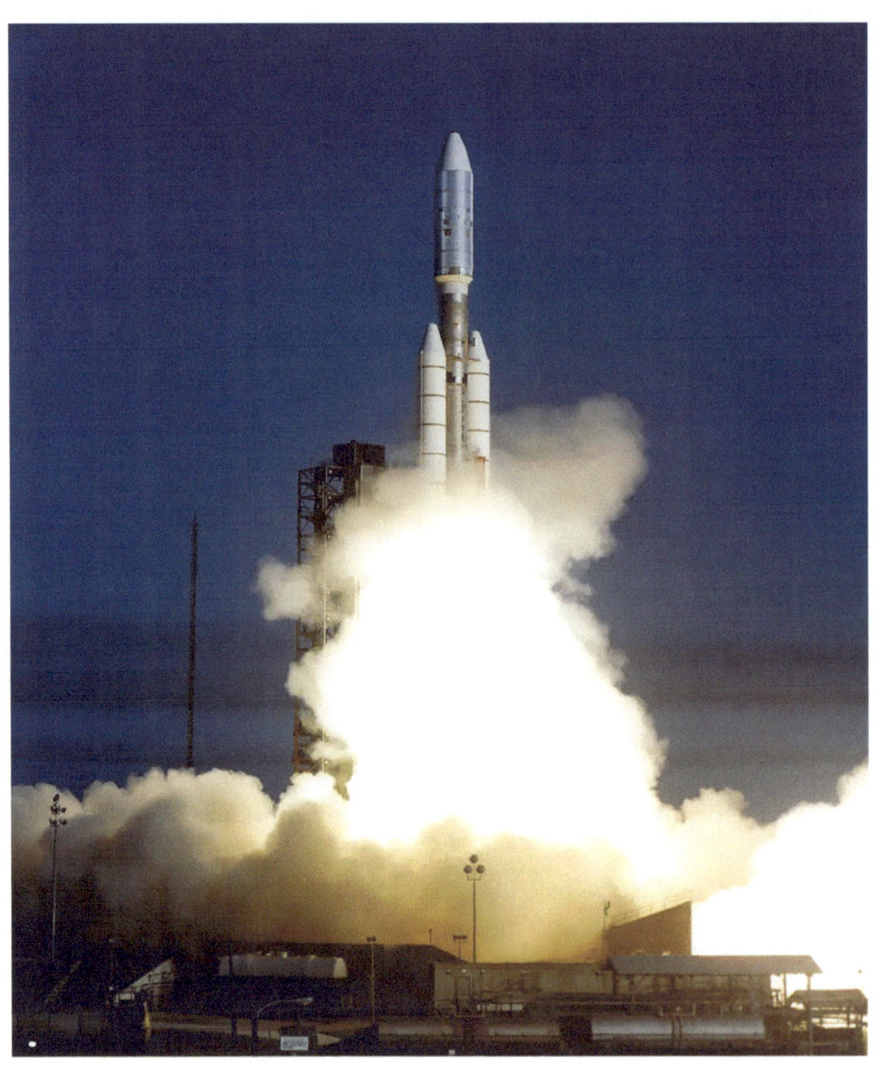

FIGURE 7.1

Voyager 1 launches aboard Titan III/Centaur on September 5, 1977, 12:56:00 UTC. Courtesy of NASA.

and far-off suns. But precisely because of the obscurity of our world thus revealed, such a picture might be worth having.[5]

The moment before the entire imaging system would be shut down and the space probe was to continue its blindfolded journey into the vastness of outer space presented a symbolically charged last opportunity.[6]

Voyager 1 started its epic journey thirteen years earlier, in 1977, from Cape Canaveral, Florida, when NASA launched two identical spacecrafts, *Voyager 2* and *Voyager 1*, on August 20 and September 5, respectively (see figure 7.1). The planned five-year assignment, as described on the NASA Jet Propulsion Lab (JPL) website, was "to conduct close-up studies of Jupiter and Saturn, Saturn's rings, and the larger moons of the two planets." The mission went on successfully, and both spacecraft were reprogrammed for new missions. On August 25, 2012, *Voyager 1* became the first spacecraft to enter the interstellar medium.[7] Even though Earth was never officially identified as an "observation target" for either *Voyager* probe, their cameras have taken some of the most iconic and wondrous images of our planet, such as the first image of the Earth–Moon system in a single frame from a distance of 7.25 million miles.[8]

The onboard Imaging Science Subsystem (ISS) consisted of two cameras. One low resolution camera with a wide-angle 200-milimeter focal length lens and a higher resolution camera with a 1500-milimeter narrow-angle lens.

Both cameras were modified versions of the slow-scan vidicon-based camera designs that were used in the earlier Mariner flights and included a commandable eight-filter wheel.[9] In the specifications, we can read that "[u]nlike the other onboard instruments, operation of the cameras [was] not autonomous, but [. . .] controlled by an imaging parameter table residing in one of the spacecraft computers, the Flight Data Subsystem (FDS)."[10] However, in 1990, astronomical calculations suggested that *Voyager 1* was unlikely to pass by any photographable objects and the power preserved by turning off the ISS could prolong the operation of the remaining scientific instruments.[11] Hence, the proposal to shut down the cameras did not generate a large debate, but it did resurrect a decade-old idea brewing in the minds of some of the involved scientists to turn the cameras toward Earth before they were shut down. Aside from Carl Sagan,

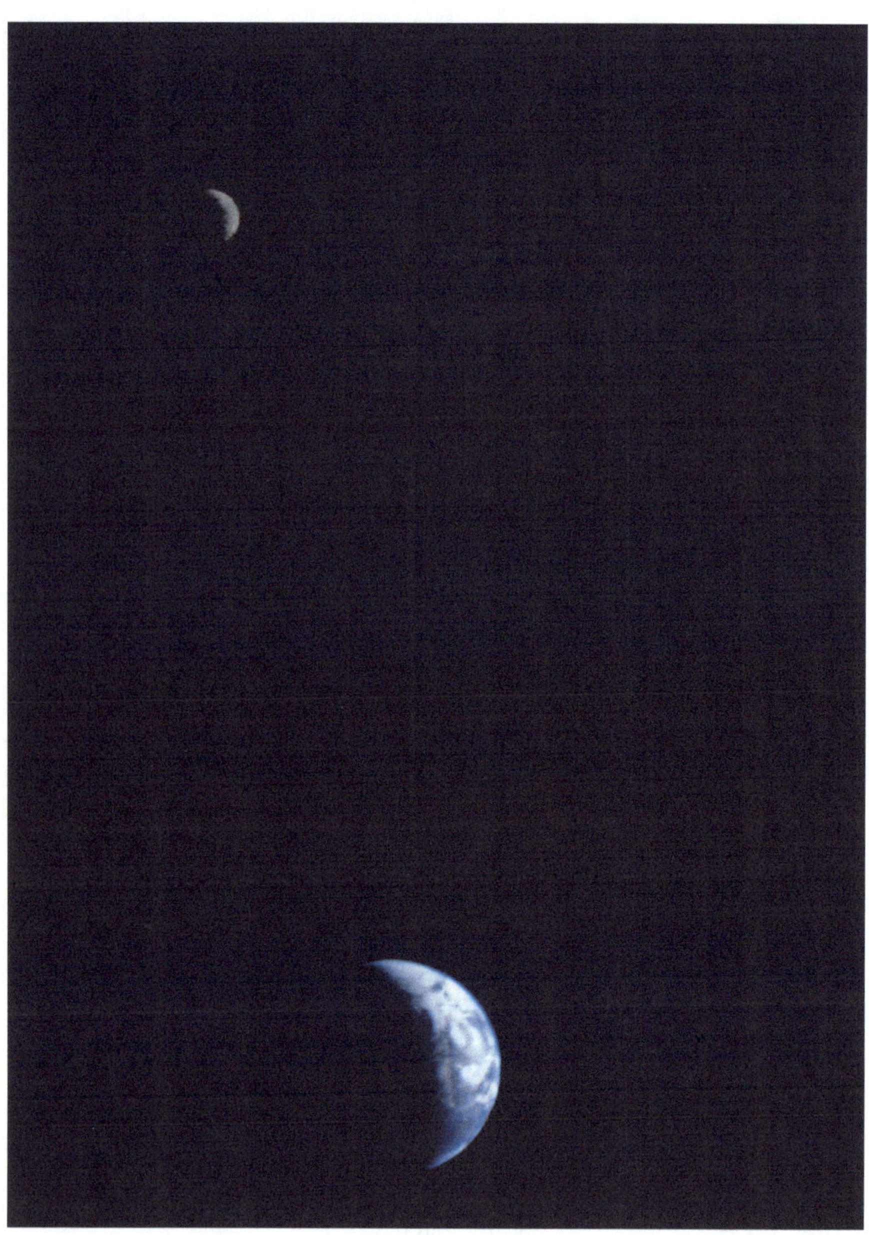

FIGURE 7.2

NASA image GPN-2002–000202. On September 18, 1977, at 16:13:00 UTC, *Voyager 1* captured the first picture of the Earth and Moon in a single frame. Courtesy of NASA.

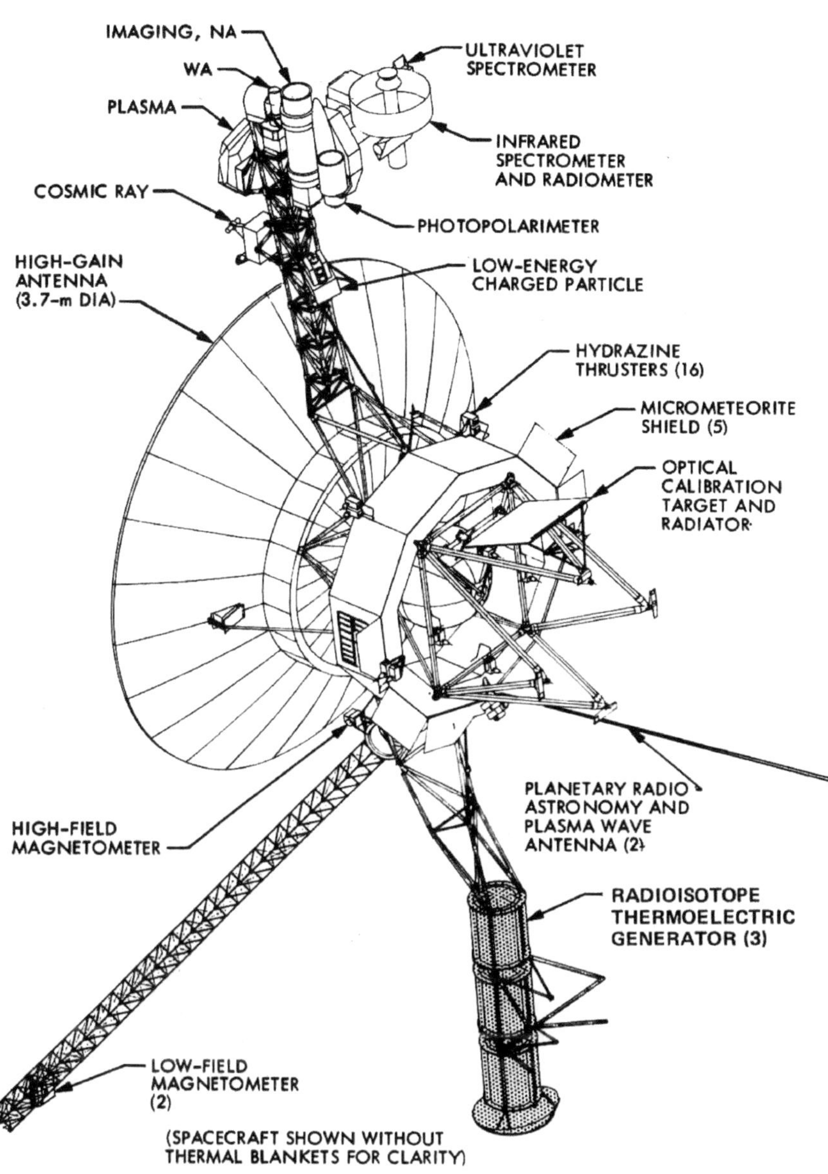

FIGURE 7.3

Diagram of *Voyager 1* shows ISS with narrow-angle (NA) and wide-angle (WA) cameras at the top. Courtesy of NASA/JPL.

Candy Hansen of JPL and Carolyn Porco of the University of Arizona were engaged in this pursuit. A considerable portion of the mission's scientific personnel, on the other hand, questioned the lack of scientific grounding for the initiative, regarding it as a mere waste of resources. Nonetheless, the limited timeframe generated enough force and determination to pursue the decade-long dream. Aiming the camera from *Voyager*'s position perched at the threshold of our solar system and whizzing 40,000 miles per hour away from its even faster moving target was not an easy task. With the expert knowledge of Candy Hansen and Carolyn Porco designing the command sequence and calculating the camera exposure times, the protocol was written, transmitted, processed, and executed by the onboard ISS.[12]

As a Valentine's greeting card, the Earth was photographed by *Voyager*'s high-resolution camera on February 14, 1990. The ISS used three different exposures for the blue, green, and violet filters. The component video signal was encoded as a pattern of differently oriented magnetic regions on a half-inch tape waiting in cue for transmission time.[13] Several months later, when transmission slots opened in the Deep Space Network, signals to describe each pixel traveled in the speed of light to NASA's ground-based radio telescopes. After about five-and-a-half hours, all the 1,920,000 pixels arrived on Earth, making Earth's self-portrait as a "Pale Blue Dot" emerge on the computer screen.[14] One of the biggest challenges *Voyager*'s image sensors were facing when recording this photo was the weak sunlight reflecting off Earth, some four billion miles away. Many regions of the sensor got excited by Sun-emitted photons entrapped in the camera's optics during the three exposures, producing the characteristic lens flare in the picture that looks like a beam of light in which our tiny planet shyly glimmers.[15] This "beam of sunlight," Sagan cautioned, "underscores our responsibility to deal more kindly with one another, and to preserve and cherish the pale blue dot, the only home we've ever known."[16] Created by a massive assemblage of the brightest scientific minds using the most advanced scientific means—but without a strict scientific objective—this tiny rendering of our planet was interpreted by Sagan and his collaborators as a persuasive reminder of the interconnectedness of all living beings.

With questionable scientific value but significant cultural impact, the *Pale Blue Dot* refocused attention to Earth's fragility amid vast outer space. As professor of public affairs and aerospace historian Howard E. McCurdy notes in his review of *Pale Blue Dot*, with this image as a starting point, Sagan attempted to convince audiences around the world that space exploration could "revitalize the human spirit made somber by astronomical discoveries."[17] In Sagan's view, humans are made to explore, and uninhabitable planets might therefore be made inhabitable in the future. He went so far as to suggest that "[h]umans take a foolish risk by binding themselves to Earth. In the long run, . . . every galactic civilization is obliged to become spacefaring for the most practical of reasons: staying alive."[18] Sagan explained this view on the basis of "the inevitability of asteroid strikes, whose potential force far exceeds the destructive power of all the nuclear weapons left on Earth."[19] Outer space is presented as the savior of humanity. Earth is a fragile and ultimately unreliable spot in the vastness of the universe, unsuited and rapidly surpassed as a future refuge of humankind. As we can see from McCurdy's 1995 review, Sagan's mantra is thereby closely tied in with the myth of the "saving power of the frontiers,"[20] where the achievement of ingenuity and democracy were seen as coexistent with the acquisition of new territory, a quintessentially colonial enterprise.[21] As we zoom in from this most distant vantage point towards our present time, we see Earth distributed across multiple platforms, elastically contracting and expanding. As a three-dimensional model behind two-dimensional screens, its spinning surface responds to our touch and generates a smooth proxistant interface. With the *Pale Blue Dot*—and the strenuous efforts it took to create it—in mind, we might ask how this ubiquitous proxistant view of the world exposes a deeper relation of worldviews. As we will show in the next chapter, this is a question of scale.

8

PROXISTANT EARTH MODELS

"The disappearance of the outside is certainly the defining trait of our epoch."
—Bruno Latour[1]

Networked geospatial models of Earth, most prominent in the example of Google Earth, present a hyperbolic version of proxistant vision, in which a virtual camera effortlessly travels between an orbital perspective and a detailed street-level view.[2] As such, this digital globe accesses age-old dreams of panoramic overview combined with unobstructed perceptual control. The exponential growth of orthophoto-mapped models of Earth, created through cinematized datasets, produces an effective scalable planet far from the vibrant ecosystem that travels at 60,000 miles per hour around the sun.[3] Like this, Earth today exists primarily as a mediasphere in which various visualization systems provide us with functional models of the world. This pertains in particular to the multiplications of aerial and orbital imaging technologies from which data is sourced to generate scalable interfaces across military, corporate, and civilian screens, feeding geospatial datasets into aggregates of computational calculations and prediction. The default screen layout in 3D-animated models such as Google Earth often features the image of a gently spinning Earth as seen from a geostationary position, from where one plunges into the close-up of the desired destination within one continuous sweep. Vittoria Di Palma has pointed to how such visual access "spawned unaffiliated websites such

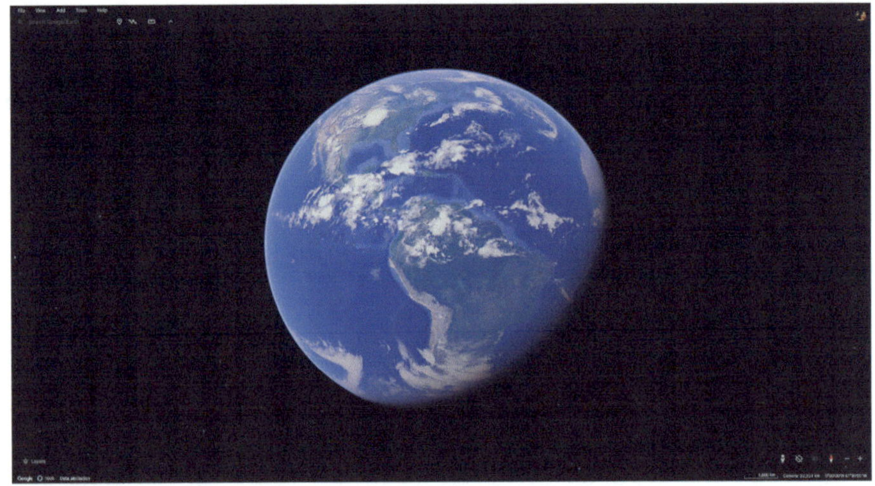

as Google Sightseeing," in which the motto "why bother seeing the Earth for real?" directs attention to the global influence of this vision machine.[4] Hence, the current proliferation of proxistant 3D-animated Earth models not only provides views of the world but also generates worldviews.

Several authors have linked the current surge in Earth modeling to the earlier Earth imaging paradigm of the Apollo moon landing era, epitomized by the iconic images *Earthrise* (1968) and *The Blue Marble* (1972).[5]

These images are widely recognized to have generated ethical debates regarding the significance of (human) life on Earth and humanity's responsibility toward the environment. Somewhat unnoticed in these debates, however, are similar issues picked up and exaggerated in 1990 in Carl Sagan's meditation on the *Pale Blue Dot* in which Earth appears as a speck of dust, a tiny pixel to which humans should assume the greatest

FIGURE 8.1

Screenshot of https://earth.google.com (Version 10.55.0.1). Maps data: Data SIO, NOAA, U.S. Navy, NGA, GEBCOLandsat / CopernicusIBCAOU.S. Geological SurveyPGC/ NASA. Copyright © 2023 Google LLC.

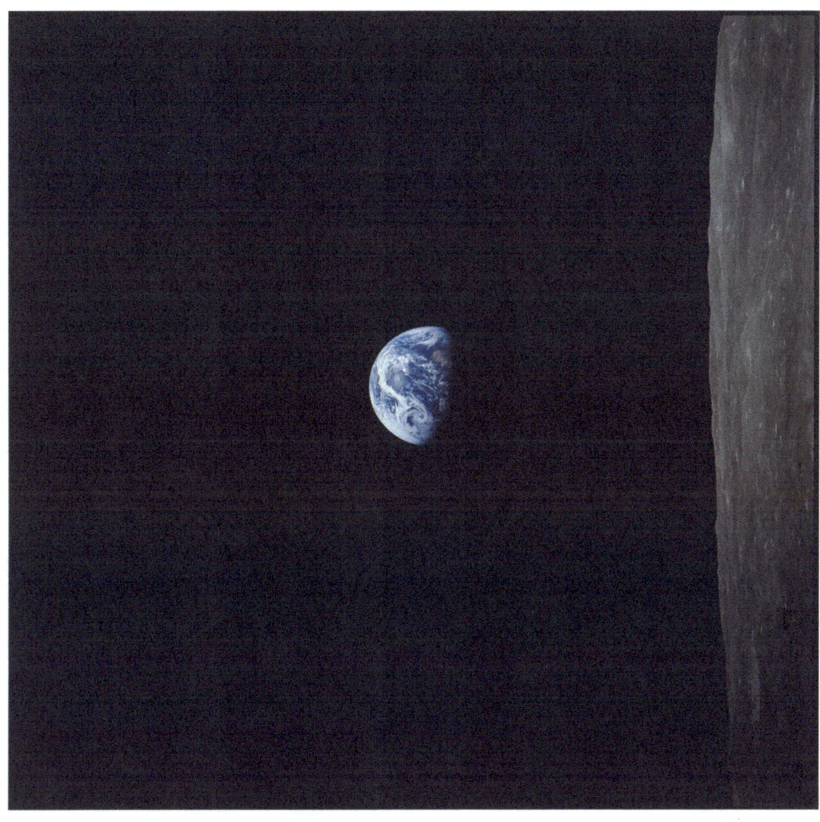

FIGURE 8.2

NASA image AS08-14-2384 also known as *Earthrise* (1968) taken by William Anders at 075:49:09 during Apollo 8's orbit 4. Courtesy of Image Science and Analysis Laboratory, NASA-Johnson Space Center.

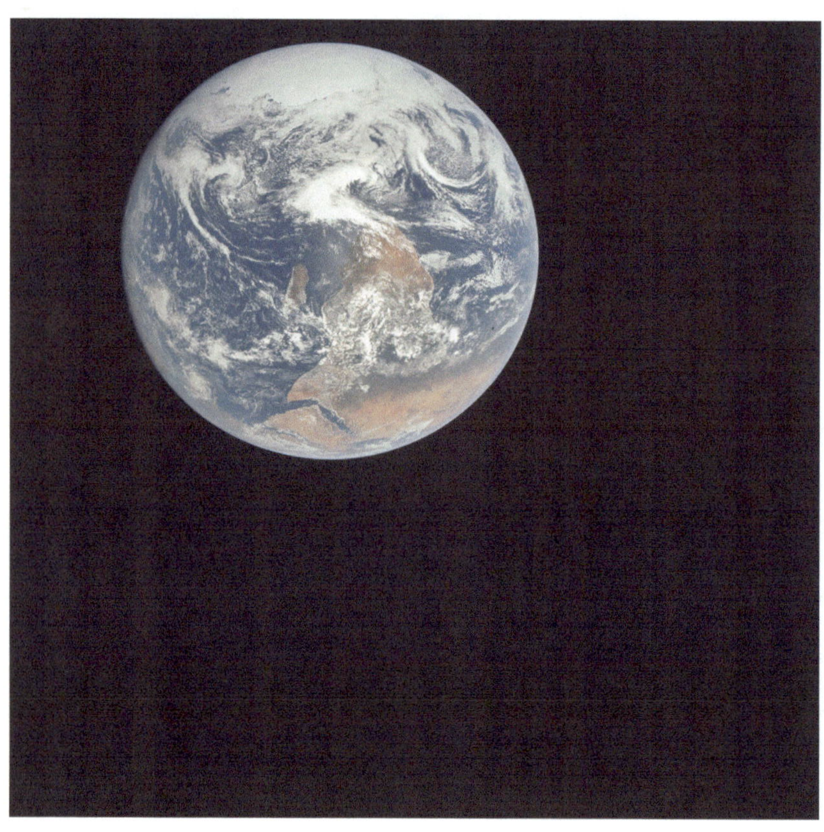

FIGURE 8.3

NASA image AS17-148-22727 also known as *The Blue Marble* (1972) by Apollo 17 crew, original framing and orientation. Courtesy of NASA.

responsibility. Liberated from cartographic codes and cultural borders, the globe became a powerful symbol of humanity's shared destiny on a common planet and alluded to renewed thinking around issues of ecology and sustainable development.[6] Yet, as Cosgrove has noted, *Earthrise* and *The Blue Marble* equally propelled a "language and imaginary of globalization."[7] They effectively visualized a unified globe over which multi-billion-dollar companies could assume power. Such ambiguities, it is commonly argued, continue to inhabit, with exaggerated strength, the digital globe, figuring across the multiplicity of screens, devices, and platforms today.[8]

A study of Earth models reveals the historic effort to visualize, identify, and control the world as a unified globe. As signaled in the prologue regarding Earth's depiction as a speck of dust, this last inquiry into proxistance is concerned with the question of scale. We address the concept of scale in this section because we see a need for an epistemic shift of awareness brought on by the concept of the Anthropocene or, as Donna Haraway rather refers to it, the Capitalocene or the Chthulucene.[9] Proxistant Earth models are produced with data obtained by orbiting satellites, in which the principle of remote sensing operations corresponds to those described in the recording of *Pale Blue Dot*. Lisa Parks has noted how "of all communications technologies, satellites perhaps paradoxically, have the tightest grip on our world."[10] Mobilized through portable devices, and operated through societies of control, these technologies control their users as much as the users control them.[11] As mentioned, one of the most illustrative examples of a smooth proxistant vision today is Google Earth's convention to plunge from geostationary altitude into Earth's atmosphere before gently easing in on the details of a house or a street.[12] But what kind of worldview operates beneath this extended visual continuity across scales? How can an analysis of an earlier Earth imaging craze expose the technological and historical contingencies fueling the proxistant Earth models we see proliferating today? Before we can begin to answer these questions, however, we need to understand how scale itself is anything but a straightforward concept. Scale, it turns out, is fundamentally bound up with mediation and difference, but to see this requires an extra step by the beholder, releasing long ingrained mimetic views to adopt a navigational approach.

SCALING EARTH TO *THE POWERS OF TEN*

As we have already seen, Google Earth presents a hyperbolic version of proxistant vision, letting its user effortlessly move between orbital overviews and street-level close-ups. Serving trillions of proxistant rides to its global users daily, how can studying this model foreground the question of scale to the paradigm of proxistant vision? How can analyzing these models' scalar operations help us understand this paradigm's challenges for contemporary worldviews? In his recent book, *The Cosmic Zoom: Scale, Knowledge, and Mediation*, Zachary Horton elucidates how scale is conceptualized across different disciplines. Geography focuses on measuring and representing physical space, often through cartographic methods that divide large areas into smaller units. Physics involves precise measurement of physical sizes, aiming to understand the fundamental laws of nature from the subatomic to the cosmic level, with an emphasis on quantitative analysis. Engineering applies these physical measurements practically, focusing on designing and constructing structures and systems that emphasize functionality and safety. Mathematics approaches scale abstractly, using dimensions and the concept of infinity to explore relationships beyond physical constraints, aiding in the development of theoretical models. Finally, biology examines the relationships between parts and wholes within living systems, focusing on functional dynamics across various biological levels. Importantly, scale also exists as an intrinsic quality of matter, independent of these epistemological frameworks. This fundamental form of scalar dynamics is one of intensity, where scale is understood as internal differentiation, embodying the concept of difference in its very act of differing.[13] Therefore, the mediation of scalar access, especially in ways that engage scalar difference, is a central concern. The endpoint of such mediation results in a scalar collapse, defined as the speculative merging of various scales within a single medium.[14] Horton emphasizes the need to recognize these disciplinary differences to avoid conflating them, as this can lead to oversimplifications and misunderstandings, hindering effective problem-solving in complex contemporary issues. However, within the current paradigm of proxistant vision, achieving this goal proves particularly challenging.

Historically, Google Earth originated from Keyhole Inc.'s "Earth-Viewer 3D," a pioneering geospatial visualization application developed in 2001 by John Hanke and his team, including key engineers such as Avi Bar-Zeev, Brian McClendon, and Michael Jones. Keyhole Inc. was funded by the CIA's venture capital arm, In-Q-Tel, highlighting the strategic importance of geospatial technology in national security contexts. In 2004, Google acquired Keyhole Inc., and the software was rebranded as Google Earth, officially launching in 2005.[15] Concurrently, Google Maps was introduced in 2005 as a web-based mapping service, developed by a team including Lars Rasmussen and Jens Eilstrup Rasmussen. It offered detailed road maps, local business information, and driving directions.[16] The launch of Google Maps marked a significant shift from static, paper-based maps to interactive digital navigation tools. In 2007, Google Maps introduced Street View, an innovative feature developed by Luc Vincent and his team, providing panoramic street-level views captured by specially equipped vehicles. This feature allowed users to virtually navigate through cities and view locations in detail. Over time, the functionalities of Google Earth and Google Maps became increasingly integrated, with Google Maps adopting virtual flythroughs and Google Earth incorporating Street View, enabling seamless transitions between different levels of geographic exploration. This integration reflected ongoing advancements in data processing, machine learning, and cloud computing, driven by the collaborative efforts of Google's development teams.[17]

Back in 1969, when Laura and Jack Dangermond came up with the Environmental Systems Research Initiative (ESRI) and laid the ground for digital geography, the most powerful microchip on the market contained only a few thousand transistors.[18] Today, microchips containing billions of transistors are housed by smartphones alone.

This dwarfs the processing powers of the state-of-the-art computers that paved the path into the Space Age.[19] Being such a processing power-thirsty piece of software, Google Earth until recently existed only as a so-called native client, or a stand-alone application that had to be installed on a computer. In 2017, a new technology based on ESRI's ArcGIS Explorer enabled Google Earth's transformation into an online application.[20] This event additionally boosted proxistant vision across platforms and devices.

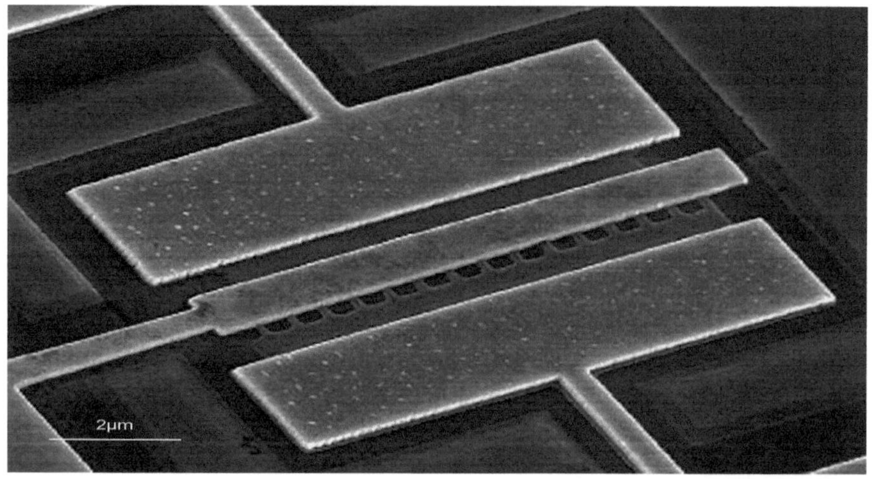

In Jeremy Crampton's interview with Keyhole developer Avi Bar-Zeev, it became evident that Google Earth was influenced by the film *Powers of Ten* (1977) by American design couple Ray and Charles Eames.[21] The prototype of this film titled *A Rough Sketch for a Proposed Film Dealing with the Powers of Ten and the Relative Size of Things in the Universe* was made in 1968, the same year NASA released the Apollo image *Earthrise*, and is often referred to as the most famous extensive zoom of the Cold War and Space Race. Both films were adaptations of the innovative children's book *Cosmic View: The Universe in 40 Jumps* (1957) by Kees Boeke.[22]

This film is also an important historical reference for the current paradigm of proxistant vision, acting as a forerunner and inspiration for Google Earth. The film starts with a vertical framing of a couple picnicking on a lakeside green in Chicago. The opening title card announces that this is "a film dealing with the relative size of things in the universe and the effect of adding another zero."[23] Philip Morrison's voiceover explains that we are one meter above the ground and that the scene we

FIGURE 8.4

Single transistor in a microchip seen through a scanning electron microscope.

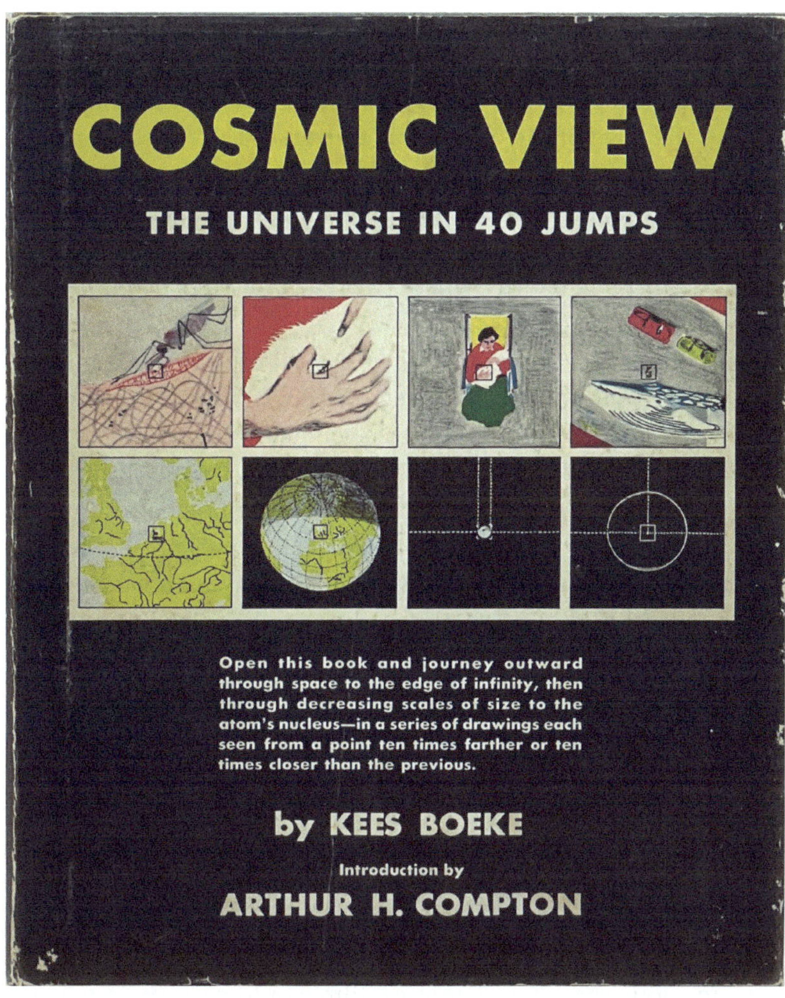

FIGURE 8.5

Kees Boeke. Book cover of *Cosmic View: The Universe in 40 Jumps* (1957).

see measures one-by-one meter. “Every 10 seconds we will look from 10 times farther away,” Morrison continues.[24] By way of visual effects, artistic impressions, and infographics, the film constructs the illusion of a camera moving to the edge of the observable universe at 10^{24} meters, or one hudred million light years away.[25] At this point, the virtual camera starts its descending journey back *into* the sleeping man’s hand, penetrating the microscopic level of the “vast inner space” until 0.0000010 ångströms or 10–^{16} meters, as Morrison tells us, where “we reach the edge of our present understanding.”[26]

Reviewing this film scale critically, we see that the visual transition posited—from a specific point in Chicago to the expansive limits of the Big Bang and then further into the minutiae of quantum physics via incremental magnifications of tenfold—is fundamentally flawed in its premise.[27] Rationally, we know that no camera can travel trillions of kilometers and come back to a microscopic position like the Eameses present it. This visual argument is impossible to sustain, yet the idea that one does have access to an optical continuity between the detail and the big picture not only persists but is reiterated exponentially through proxistant Earth models like Google Earth. The fantasy that one can move from a local to global view is convincingly reproduced visually with proxistant vision without recognizing that this is, in fact, a mediated fallacy. A more realistic version of the Eameses’ film would be navigating from one institution to the next, from satellite control center to telescope, from surgery room to microscopy lab, which would result in a very different film from the smooth proxistant camera moving seamlessly between the galaxies millions of light years away and the carbon molecules of a human hand. This scale conscious version of Eameses’ film would present an entirely different view of the world.

That this trans-scalar ride is an illusion can be effectively illustrated through a peek into the “geology” of Google Earth’s web version, which reveals that a simulated flight through geospatial data is made up of an assemblage of several interacting components.[28] The vectorial nature of this model infinitely simplifies computations as the geospatial coordinates maintain their intrinsic relationship to each other, regardless of the model’s size and/or its orientation. Leveraging this principle, the model smoothly enlarges when zoomed in and the distances between

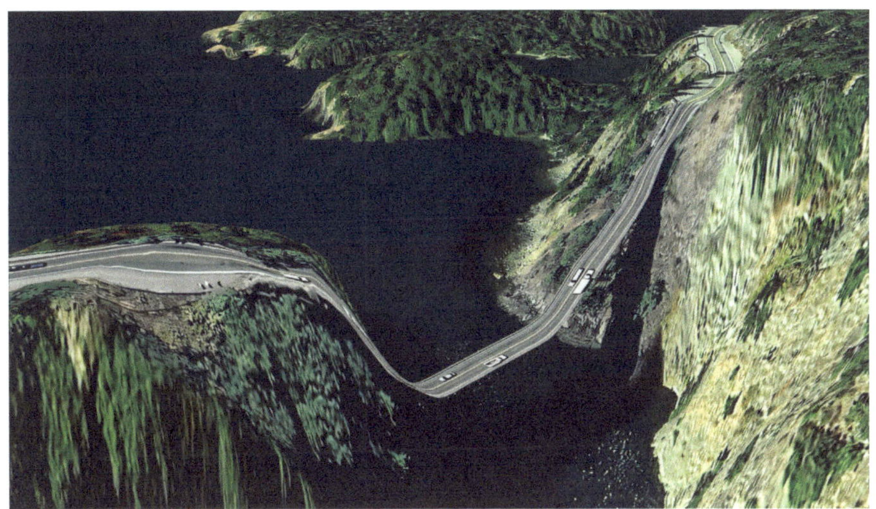

the geographical coordinates on the screen increase proportionally. The texturing technique of 3D-animated models, discussed in part II, also applies to Google Earth, which is dressed up in layers of countless images of the globe taken from a variety of angles and distances.[29] The visual effect of the zoom function is thus enabled by the combination of layers of images in different resolutions, where each layer corresponds to a particular power of magnification or altitude of the virtual camera. If the image layer or texture of Earth's surface appears perfectly seamless at first, a closer inspection might sometimes reveal numerous imperfections or glitches.[30] These anomalies are a direct result of the diverse image data collected from different sources at different times and exposed to different manipulations.[31]

Google, which previously owned a set of satellites, now acquires most of its Earth images from specialized companies such as Planet, which

FIGURE 8.6

Clement Valla. Screenshot made on Janaury 23, 2019, for *Project Postcards from Google Earth* (2010–ongoing). Copyright © the artist.

launched over 500 satellites since its start-up in 2012 and serves companies with an evolving repository of over 10 billion square kilometers of satellite imagery, updated daily.[32] Google Earth, furthermore, claims to provide "the world's most detailed globe," but its details are highly controlled such that sensitive data is blurred or completely erased.[33] This has been the topic of visual artist and geographer Trevor Paglen's "experimental mapping." Through elaborate processes involving fieldwork and spy photography, Paglen has traced the activity of the Central Intelligence Agency's (CIA) "black world," discovering locations and activities on the ground that do not appear on any unclassified map. Such experimental mapping productively interrogates the pervasive belief, advanced in the era of Google Earth, that the entirety of the world is subject to visibility, cartographic representation, and epistemic mastery.[34]

To provide a virtual flight between destinations around the world, however, requires additional technicalities. Data access speed (DAS), for example, is facilitated by Google's recent investment in cloud computing with an expanding network of data centers around the world.[35] Furthermore, by minimizing the number of requests from a remote server and maximizing the software's synergy with the local host, latency can be additionally reduced. JavaScript (JS) provides the capability to interpret a user's input and transform it into a tangible action on the screen at lightning speed.[36] Upon selecting a destination, the user experiences that the downward pointing camera literary "jumps" from the current location into a geosynchronous orbit (GSO) around a gently turning globe. The data for the "spinning globe effect" is prefetched at the very point of accessing the software, so this smooth effect is secured regardless of the speed of the internet connection. The trajectory of the flight is calculated easily the very moment a destination is selected. The visualization of this itinerary, by contrast, is exceptionally demanding. The animation must be produced while the flight is *en route*, and each frame is produced just milliseconds ahead of its display. While JS is crucial in this process, countless other techniques and technologies are also at work, including increasing computer processing power.[37]

As one can see in this simplified analysis of the Google Earth Engine, the key challenge for the software is to devise a seamless transition between different datasets that are integrated into the same smooth proxistant form, constructing the captivating illusion of continuous linearity between a geosynchronous perspective of the globe, all the way down to the street view. This technical explanation shows that such a move through different datasets is not optically coherent. What happens rather is a process of quick switches between framing and formatting, instruments, and data collection. Decisions are made regarding the omission or inclusion of different types of information before finally deciding on the design of different visual displays. The visual paradigm of proxistance found in contemporary proxistant Earth models carries on from Eameses' scalar continuity across the universe, infesting its human-centric view across disciplines and practices. But why is this a problem? Returning to Horton, we saw that scale functions as a basic concept that operates autonomously from human discernment and is consolidated into distinct levels via the practices associated with human understanding. The Eameses' films discussed previously illustrate what Horton calls "scalar collapse," which he defines as the reduction or oversimplification of complex, multi-scalar phenomena into a single scale or level of analysis.[38] Rather than collapsing scales, Horton emphasizes the importance of understanding these disciplinary scales to address complex contemporary issues effectively. Horton calls out for a greater scale literacy in our time of the Anthropocene, emphasizing that "[w]e must see scale in its full light, as ontological difference, construct of knowledge, and speculative ecology—all at once."[39] This scale literacy, which means recognizing and distinguishing between the different dimensions of scale and the parallel and complex ways in which they operate, is needed to resist the lure of proxistant vision with its human-centric worldview. The linear trajectory through the universe is a cinematic technique that produces an illusion of unlimited scalar access, and this is the contingent operation of proxistant vision that currently proliferates beyond the screen.[40]

The very core of the problem is that space in these models is understood based on Cartesian coordinates, that is, space as an empty container. Everything within this "whole" can be measured and scaled up or down based on aggregation. Importantly, such global views produced by smooth proxistant world models such as Google Earth never contain the world; they merely circulate within it. It is never the case that we move from local to global. Rather, we should be reminded that there is no access to the global.[41] This illusion of global visual access across disparate scales recalls the feminist criticism of the "view from nowhere" and a call for a "situated knowledge" postulated by Donna Haraway, among others, targeting the very concept of "objective knowledge."[42] The aggregation of data and its visualization into a linear scalar journey, as shown in the Eameses' *Powers of Ten*, is only exaggerated in our time with digital mapping interfaces and dynamic navigational systems such as the online version of Google Earth. By extending the horizon line of the panorama theatre to the entire scalar spectrum of the universe, these proxistant Earth models reiterate the illusion of trans-scalar access to a centrally located human observer. Like this, the mastery of space through proxistant vision extends from its precedent in *The Powers of Ten* to contemporary automated visualization systems that continue to produce the world as a proxistant model that occludes scalar difference.

CINEMATIC AND CARTOGRAPHIC SCALES

The smooth proxistant flyover of Earth is in essence a convergence between two powerful cultural tropes: the image of the entire planet suspended in space and the cinematic location establishing shot.[43] By drawing equally on these two visual expressions, proxistant vision inherits scale issues related to both cartography and the moving image, respectively. Starting in the cartographic register, proxistant models of Earth correspond perfectly to Denis Cosgrove's observation that the development of information technology over the past three decades has caused nothing less than a revolution in spatial representation.[44] The continuous manipulation and transformation of coordinates and references change the presentation of the map on the screen, creating what he refers to as kinetic cartography.[45] Scale is a central element in this kinetic cartography, as it is in cartography in general. In Jorge Luis Borges' famous story, "On Exactitude in Science," we read the tale of the empire's outstanding geographers who succeeded in accurately representing, on the most exact map measuring one-to-one in scale, the entire territory with all the houses, hills, and rivers.[46] We find a similar cartographic endeavor in the tale *Sylvie and Bruno Concluded* by Lewis Carroll, where "everything" is represented. However magnificent, the "everything-map" also proved impractical, since it covers everything and shuts out the sun when spread out.[47] Hence, it was decided instead to use the territory itself as the map.[48] Such well-known legends harbor the common concerns by which the map can accurately represent reality, which is translated into a question of scale.[49]

In his article "Towards a Plastic Conception of Scale," architect and theorist El Hadi Jazairy draws up two main concepts of scale as they exist in geography and planning.[50] First, there is the notion of an "ontological fact," where scale structures matter from the miniature to the gigantic in a sequence of gradual steps. Secondly, scale is employed as a method of measurement and framing, as in technical drawings and maps, where spatial coordinates maintain their internal coordinates. What is central here, yet missing in Jazairy's account, is an acknowledgement that this activity of mapping is the same measuring and collecting activity that structures the "ontological fact" of matter in a line of gradual steps, as in Latour's concept of the immutable mobile.[51] However, Jazairy also proposes a third conception of scale, in which he suggests thinking of scale not as "a fixed environment within which events unfold . . . [but] as the unfolding of events that produce a certain scale."[52] In this approach, scale is understood as plastic, as a relational aspect of events rather than a fixed entity of measurement. Rather than advocating scale in a global manner, this theory reconsiders the intensive and extensive relations of folding and bending. Similar ideas have been voiced by design theorists such as Benjamin Bratton and Orit Halpern, regarding how different scales interact with each other, from individual user interfaces to global networks in the context of planetary design research.[53]

Historically, issues of cartographic scale can be traced back to Hellenistic cosmology, and the effort to condense complex physical realities into simplified, manageable models to better understand their governing laws and systems. The concept of the atom was already studied by Democritus and Lucretius, while the Middle Ages produced the effort to map the entire cosmos in several *mappaemundi*. Yet the consequences of circumnavigating the world in the sixteenth century produced an immediate effect on the quantity at which new knowledge could be mapped. These new spatial dimensions were equally applied to the global or geographic scale, as well as to the regional or chorographic scale, a distinction articulated by Greco-Roman polymath Claudius Ptolemy (100-circa 179 AD) in his influential *Geographia* written in about 150 AD.[54] While geography, according to Ptolemy, was the study of the entire world, chorography pertained to a smaller part of this whole such as a province, region, or city.[55]

Chorography delineates an impression of a part from the broader canvas of geography, akin to creating an image of just an ear or an eye, according to Ptolemy. Such ideas signal that chorography could be understood as an early form of a close-up in a cinematic sense by cutting out a part from the whole and positioning it in a sensorial relation to the spatial perception expressed. Modernity and scale in the context of cartography are furthermore demarcated by technology and the dream of superseding the limitations of the human eye. The scientific revolution brought about the telescope and the microscope, together with other measuring instruments, interrogating scientific accuracy in the process of quantification of space and allowing greater control. When one starts looking at these observation instruments and technologies of visual capture, one can discern the relation between cinema and cartography most clearly. As Cosgrove phrases it, behind the invention of the microscope and the telescope was a "concern with the human eye's physical capacity to register and to visualize materiality at every scale."[56] Yet the visual techniques with which the world is captured introduce new ambiguities around the conception of scale, as film scholar Mary Ann Doane has argued.[57]

Referring to the Russian director Sergei Eisenstein, Doane shows how certain scalar ambiguities reveal themselves in the different ways in which the French, Russian, and English languages conceptualize the idea of the close-up. While a close-up in French and Russian denotes large-scale (*gros plan* in French or *крупный план* in Russian), one would say that in English, a close-up indicates nearness and proximity.[58] "The close-up thus invokes binary oppositions—proximity vs. distance and the large vs. the small," as Doane puts it.[59] In terms of scale, this formulation problematizes the notion of big and small, since a detail at the same time presents an enlargement of a tiny fragment, while distance miniaturizes the whole to fit in one frame. While Hollywood cinema identifies the frame with the point of view perspective, that is, the place of the spectator within the scene, French and Soviet cinema see the close-up as a property of the image; the image is therefore large-scale, larger than life.[60] In his canonical essay "The Work of Art in the Age of Mechanical Reproduction," Walter Benjamin understands the cinematic close-up as an answer to the modern spectator's desire for closeness, while simultaneously patching the loss of the aura which is premised on distance.[61] Closeness therefore signifies ownership and possession, while simultaneously questioning the very notion of ownership.[62] In French and Russian terms, there is no sense of possession, since the image is seen as transcending life, existing in a scale "that guarantees unattainability," as Doane puts it.[63] Doane's insight in this essay is that the close-up performs both of these conceptions at once, "simultaneously posing as both microcosm and macrocosm, detail and whole."[64] The cinematic close-up therefore exists as a "spectacle of scale," in which both a detail of a larger image and a totality in its own right perform.[65]

While we agree that the close-up performs a "spectacle of scale," we fail to see how it promises a whole or totality. While the image is referred to as large in French and Russian, this mainly refers to the mimetic scale enlargement of the detail. Whether the detail is larger than life, as in French and Russian cinema, or offers close intimacy or nearness for inspection, as in Hollywood, it does not take away from the fact that its mimetic scale relation to the world operates in the form of a detail, a chorography, in Ptolemy's sense. Whether the detail is seen as enlarged or near, it remains a cut-out detail from a larger picture. This is especially visible from a proxistant point of view, which indeed combines detail with its bigger picture, and therefore offers something quite different than the close-up. Applied to 3D-animated models of Earth, one can see how proxistant vision draws powerfully on the combined effect of the image of the whole Earth and the spectacularism of the detail, understood as enlarged, or close, or a combination of the two. Important in all of this is that proxistant vision, like maps in general, assumes reliability and consistency of knowledge by relying on information that is unstable, irregular, and incomplete. This is the nature of the multiple data sources proxistant vision depends on, which are scaled and mixed to fit a seamless integration of a coherent composite that obscures each data point's local production and actual relationship to one another. Hence, it is these ongoing scale operations, intrinsic to this smoothening of a "bumpy" world, combined with the drama of a cinematic effect, that is at work in the proliferation of proxistant vision today.

The most basic task of cartography, Cosgrove asserts, is to secure and convey spatial knowledge graphically. How this practice is carried out varies in different cultural and historical contexts, but we do have certain a priori features, which consist of "scale, framing, selection and coding."[66] From this we can see that out of these four key features, scale is the one that controls the others in proxistant vision. Or, put differently, proxistant Earth models reveal that the questions of framing, selection, and coding can be studied through the question of scale. Scale is the truth claim operator of maps. It is the mechanism with which precise measurement can scale relationally by maintaining internal coordinates that produce scientifically verifiable data about a terrain. But this is also a speculation on scale-as-size, in which the blowing up or miniaturization of a phenomenon on the map alters the meaning of the way things stand in the world, as observed in the bird's-eye view convention of a previous century. Proxistant vision operates with scale as second nature to size, confirmed affectively by way of cinematic contingencies. Hence, proxistant world models offer nothing less than the whole world combined with its tiniest detail in the form of a spectacular location establishing shot.

In a recent talk on the Anthropocene, Bruno Latour looked for a way to address Earth beyond the old totalizing concepts of "nature" or "the globe."[67] By shifting attention from "the globe" to what Latour calls the Terrestrial, Latour provides a glimpse of the critical zone, the thin surface that makes the complexity of life forms possible.[68] Here we see that there is no unity. Lifeforms have made their environment. Earth is a discontinuous patchwork of prehistoric and layered matter, of uncertain scales and emergent properties. Properties of which we are composed, even as we rapidly alter them with increasing carbon dioxide levels and a heated atmosphere. The smooth proxistant outlook that connects global vision with precise detail in a tantalizing flight falls short when it comes to articulating such connections. In the next chapter, we will see how artistic research can rethink the question of scale through proxistant world model inquiry.

9

NON-OBJECTIVE SCALES

Every art is really a miniature, and when the Earth itself becomes a miniature you can reverse it. You can look at a grain of sand as a gigantic boulder; it's just how you want to view it in terms of your scale sense. And that is why scale is one of the key issues, in terms of art.
—Robert Smithson[1]

Proxistant world models present an exponential intensification of older mapping and cartographic techniques that draw on a cinematic model of attention and spectacle to enforce spatial dominance and control. The scalar contingencies underpinning the Eameses' cosmic linearity through the universe have become a visual paradigm of our time. By tracing the proxistant vision that currently proliferates across platforms and screens back to the late 1960s, how does contemporary art respond differently to the same cultural, technological, and political shift during the moon landing era in the United States? How could such scalar experiments be reenergized through an artistic research-led investigation? While we are influenced by contemporary artists working in this domain, such as Hito Styerl, Trevor Paglen, Laura Poitras, Laura Kurgan, George Barber, Omer Fast, and others, our media archeological method allows a deeper dive into the genealogical contingencies with which proxistant vision operates today. Artistically, therefore, we take our cue from the post-minimalist practices of the post-war era that introduced perceptual twists and disruptions to such a homogenizing worldview. Here, different conceptions of scale guide a proxistant journey in which the most distant image of Earth meets the solid materials of rocks and crystals.

Like millions of people worldwide, the Eameses responded to the breathtaking appearances of Earth from space that circulated as a by-product of the Apollo missions. This image also fueled the environmental movement as a social and political critique of unsustainable environmental practices in the United States. Images of Earth from space did exist prior to the manned space travels, however. In 1946, American scientists utilized confiscated German V-2 rockets to conduct experiments in the upper atmosphere. This initiative marked one of the earliest instances of launching machines into low Earth orbit to capture images from space. Hence, several years before Sputnik inaugurated the Space Age, Earth appeared in grainy black-and-white photographs taken from an altitude of sixty-five miles above sea level and three miles beyond the Kármán line marking the boundary between Earth's atmosphere and outer space.

The first full-disk photograph of Earth, taken by the Soviet Molniya 1–3 communications satellite on May 30, 1966.[2] Another leap in Earth imaging occurred when the first color image of the full Earth was recorded by the Department of Defense Gravity Experiment (DODGE) satellite in September 20, 1967.[3] The same year, on November 10, NASA's third iteration in a series of Applications Technology Satellites, ATS-3, managed to record the image data that later was composited into a color image of Earth's full circle.[4] It was this ATS-3 image of Earth that appeared on the front cover of Stuart Brand's first issue of the Whole Earth Catalog (WEC) in 1968, a popular magazine often claimed to be an early offline version of Google.[5]

Leading up to this moment, Norbert Wiener and Ludwig von Bertalanffy introduced cybernetics and systems theory, respectively, which marked a pivotal moment in scientific thought and cultural development.[6] The impact of the cybernetic idea suggests not merely a parallel between the human mind and communications machines but, in fact, their interchangeability. As art historian James Nisbet points out, this "takes the reversal of individual agency and ecosystem to an extreme position, wherein the behavior of any individual entity within a system is capable of substitution and exchange without disrupting the integrity of the whole."[7] Hence, when the fragility of the whole Earth brings about

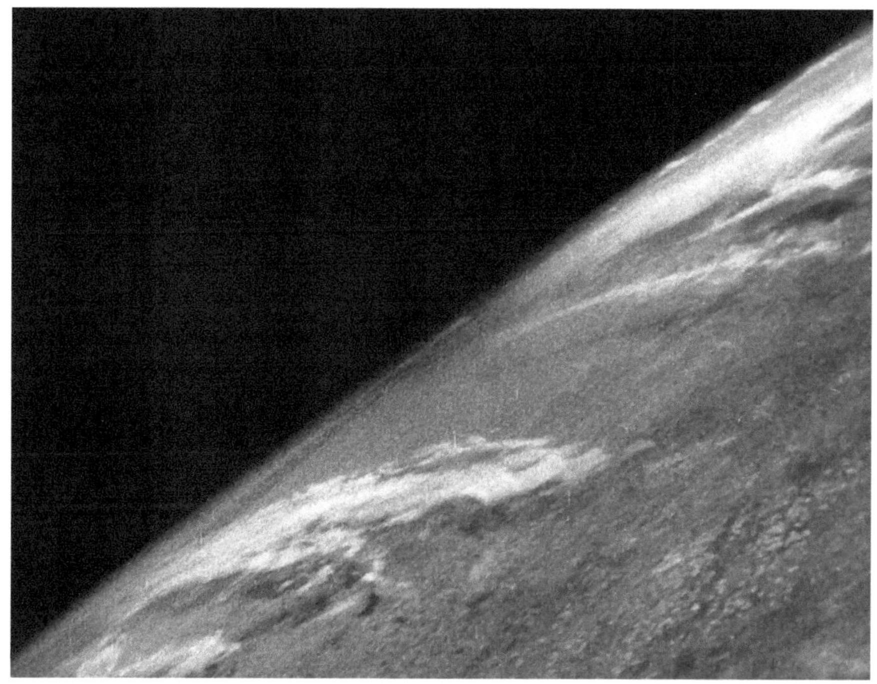

FIGURE 9.1

The first photos from space were taken on October 24, 1946, by the sub-orbital U.S.-launched V-2 rocket (flight #13) at White Sands Missile Range. Photos were taken every second and a half. The highest altitude reached was 65 miles (105 km), five times higher than any previous pictures. Courtesy of White Sands Missile Range/Applied Physics Laboratory.

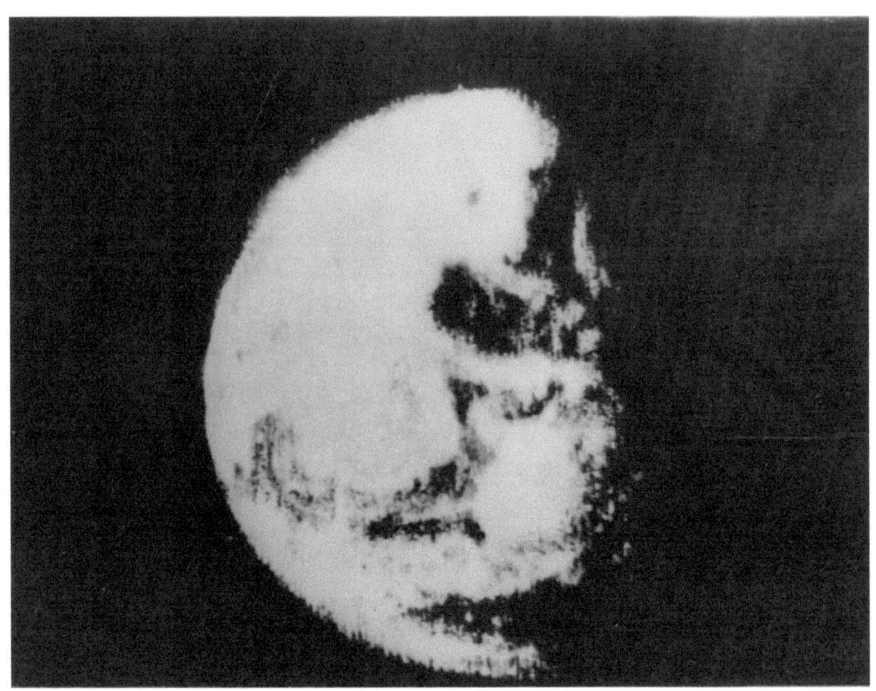

FIGURE 9.2

The first full-disc photo of Earth from outer space. This photo shows Earth as it appears from 25,000 miles away, taken by a TV camera on the Soviet communications satellite Molniya 1 and transmitted to Earth on May 30, 1966.

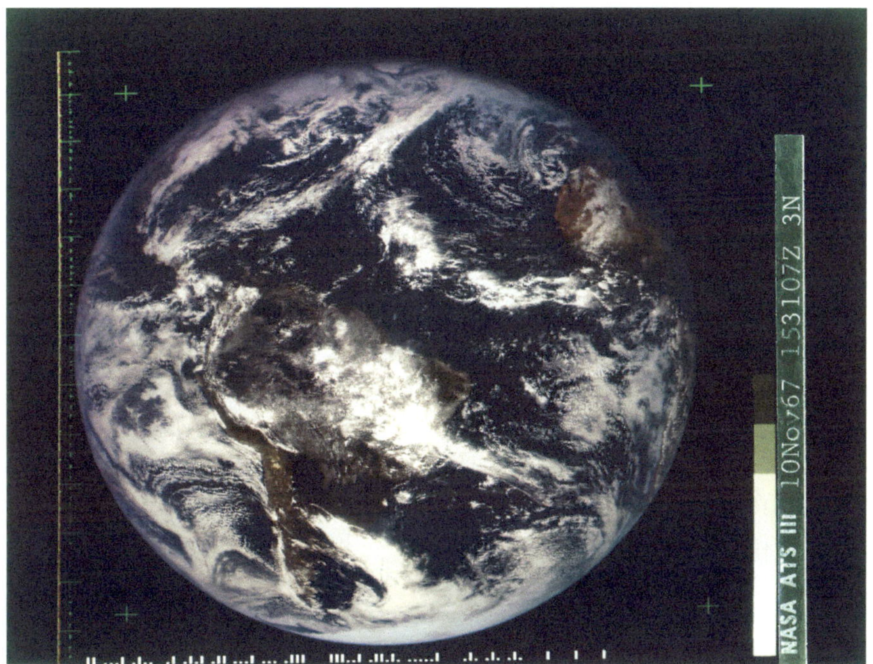

a new wave of environmental concerns, it is this systemic approach to ecology that becomes significant. WEC epitomized the American cultural transformation in 1968, and the magazine's first issue hit its readers in a similar fashion to how the overview effect hit the astronauts observing Earth from outer space.[8] Readers were struck by the image of Earth's circular shape pitched against the vastness of black uninhabitable space. Notably, it was Brand himself, a Stanford University alumnus, biologist, and social activist, who initiated the public campaign in 1966 for NASA to release the rumored image of Earth.[9]

FIGURE 9.3

NASA's first color photo (digital image mosaic) of Earth, imaged in 1967 by ATS-3, was used as the cover of Whole Earth Catalog's first edition. Courtesy of NASA.

Brand was convinced that the image of the whole Earth, as seen from space, would serve as a powerful symbol of a shared destiny. As environmental historian Andrew Kirk points out, serving the many hippie communes and countercultural movements of the time, WEC first and foremost heralded the "notion that the antimodernist desire to return to a simpler time when humans were more closely tied to nature could be achieved through technological progress."[10] The old-fashioned preservation of nature was dismissed in favor of holistic and systemic theories that considered the whole Earth and everything within it. This is further underlined by journalist Fred Turner, who describes WEC as a kind of "Hippie Bible" for a techno-liberal ideology aimed at turning technological progress away from military threats toward ideas of personal freedom. Here, WEC's goal was to produce "the cultural conditions under which microcomputers and computer networks could be imagined as tools of liberation," as Turner concludes.[11] Equally embracing both antimodernism *and* modernism, readers of WEC could find reviews of "primitive wood stoves and survivalist supplies for counterculture neo-Luddites" next to "personal computers, geodesic domes, and oscilloscopes."[12] This is the backdrop and the climate in which founding partners Larry Page and Sergey Brin formed Google while still doctoral students at Stanford thirty-five years later.[13]

Encountered in the pages of WEC under the section "Whole Systems," Buckminster Fuller's modular theories appeared with great influence. In his book *Operating Manual for Spaceship Earth*, published in 1969, one year after the release of NASA's *Earthrise* and the Eameses' *A Rough Sketch*, Fuller compares Earth to a spaceship with the Sun as its leading energy supplier. Contributing to the general rife of 1960s cultural production, Fuller's scalar ecology presents a universal modularity of isomorphic pieces operating according to systems of topological variations.[14] The image of the globe thus became the last universalistic icon symbolizing the "'great transformation' of the Western system of knowledge and order after 1945," as curator and art critic Anselm Franke formulated it.[15] Design historian Orit Halpern further notes that this emphasis on algorithms, patterns, and processes significantly reconfigured the period's cognitive, perceptual, and sensory paradigms.[16] It was here, in the blend of communal do-it-yourself ecological culture, anti-war protests, and Norbert

Wiener's theory of cybernetics, that the image of Earth turned into the very symbol of digital utopianism. The focus on computational systems and information theory influenced the period's highly modular sense of ecology and scale, expanding a cinematic convention into new proxistant dimensions.

Placing a new centrality to the question of scale, the process-based approaches of post-minimalism in the late 1960s often operated by introducing a twist on the prevalent systems discourse to pierce the glossy fantasy of a continuous and controllable universe. While these artists often appropriated scientific mapping strategies and mathematical models, they do not generally share the Eameses' and Fuller's post-war positivism. What we see here, rather, is a play of words and concepts that, while implicitly ridiculing a systems approach to objectivity, also sought to reposition and actualize art's role as a necessary antidote in the context of positivist techno-scientific utopia. The question of scale in art follows long-outmoded ideas of composition and aesthetics, altogether dismissed by the modernist avant-garde. When the question of scale resurfaces as a central concern in the post-war artistic discourse, it is altogether different. The question of scale in this period, first and foremost, makes apparent the complexities involved in the move from Minimalist emphasis on individual experience to the planetary-scale systems and information theories that permeated the post-Minimalist mindset.[17] This shift from object to system operates both as a physical dimension in the artworks themselves and as a conceptual framework for understanding ecological relations.

The rapid technological advancements and the success of wartime technologies fostered a belief in the potential of technology to solve societal problems. In addition to prosperity and progress, however, artists saw Cold War anxieties, nuclear threats, and the Vietnam War on the geopolitical horizon. The rise of cybernetics in fields such as cognitive science, artificial intelligence, and robotics saw the beginning of a serious inquiry into how machines could emulate human thought processes and decision-making. Conversely, the fear of technological domination led to dystopian narratives in literature and film, exploring themes of surveillance, control, and dehumanization. Most importantly, systems thinking promoted the idea that Earth is a complex, interconnected system with which the artworks and artists could engage and interact. This laid the ground for different conceptions of scale as artists began to approach ecological and environmental themes, shifting their focus away from the confines of the gallery to engage directly with landscape and the planetary scale. Works such as *Oakland Wedge* (1968) by Dennis Oppenheim and Michael Heizer's *Double Negative* (1969–70) can be mentioned here, as they engage directly with the negative space of a non-existent object that proposes the entire Earth as a piece of art. Furthermore, Nancy Holt's *Sun Tunnels* (1973–76) is aligned with the sunrise and sunset during the summer and winter solstices, and holes drilled in the tunnels project constellations of light inside. Finally, Agnes Denes' work *Rice/Tree/Burial* (1968) is another example, where she planted rice in a field, chained trees together, and buried a series of writings. As a logical expression of such vast spaces, artists of this era often turned to various forms of cartographic expression. Since proxistance is understood as a form of cartography, both physically and in its form of thinking, it will serve to start this investigation from the perspective of mapping.

Art and cartography have a long and intertwined relationship, evolving significantly over centuries with peaks in the Renaissance, as discussed in section 2, and the interwar period in movements like Surrealism and Dadaism. The politically activist approach of the Situationist movement's intense counter-mapping of the city of Paris, furthermore, consciously moved out of the art world to encounter the circumstances of everyday life.[18] When the map reentered the artistic center stage through conceptual and process-oriented practices in the late 1960s, it lacked the authority of the Dutch Renaissance painting.[19] This period's cartographic turn rather questioned the maps' factual nature by utilizing quasi-scientific mapping techniques to produce disturbances indicative of the social shifts of this period.[20] Compared to the Situationist approach, however, we find a rather different form of counter-mapping in the art practices that came to fruition in the late 1960s post-Minimalist art.[21] The presence of alternative maps of this period has been analyzed by geographers such as Denis Wood through the prism of a more general discourse on the nature of mapping.[22] Works such as Öyvind Falström's *World Map* (1972), *Garden (A World Model)* (1973), and *Sketch of World Map* (1973) are highlighted, but also Yoko Ono's performance *Map Piece* (1962), in which the reader was asked to draw an imaginary map and follow it, are often mentioned here. The work of Chieko Shiomi (Mieko Shiomi after 1967) can also be added to this list, in which the whole Earth was considered the stage for a series of mail-art events titled *Spatial Poems*. This work by Shiomi comprised nine events between 1965 and 1975, of which a variety of actions Shiomi mapped onto a world map.[23] The conceptual artists On Kawara and Richard Long, who both began their mapping projects in the late 1960s, are also relevant here, such as Kawara's *I Went* series in 1968 and Long's *Ben Nevis Hitch-Hike*, 1967.[24] This trajectory shows that cartography and mapping were central elements across various post-Minimalist practices.[25] However insightful such a trajectory is for the history of maps, Wood does not fully come to terms with how artists turned to mapmaking in this period.

Wood and his co-authors attempt to situate the post-Minimalist interest in maps to the growing ubiquity of maps in the visual culture of the time. In other words, conceptual art's use of maps reflects the growth of the map industry itself.[26] A similarly shorthanded claim on behalf of art and cartography comes from Peter Wollen, who has formulated a comparison between the Situationists and Conceptual artists on their different approaches to art and cartography. Despite the major differences between Situationist and Conceptual art, Wollen finds it productive to investigate these movements' interest in maps "not only as form of documentation but as a form of design."[27] The Situationists were concerned with city space and the brutal commercialization of Paris post-World War II, which was comparable in impact to the period of Haussmanization. Conversely, Conceptualists, Wollen recognizes, have a somewhat different agenda. Not directly relating their mapping practices to the governmental privatization of public space as such, although deviances occur, Conceptualists primarily address the art world.[28]

While Wollen concludes, on a somewhat generalized note, that the role of cartography can serve both political and utopian tools and that both Conceptual artists and Situationists did important work in resistance mapping, he fails to pinpoint to which extent the turn to mapmaking for Conceptual artists in the late 1960s primarily moves beyond the role maps themselves play in the world. Both Wood and his co-authors and Wollen, therefore, miss out on the question of scale and, hence, the way mapmaking points to a larger question of how scientific equations operate in the world in much broader terms. When artist Jasper Johns makes a map, he is not just casting doubt about mapmaking and maps' role in producing political borders. Rather, Johns uses the map to cast doubt about "everything." By removing color codes and names, Johns removes the map's scale reference to the world. This act can be seen to show how maps are graphic enterprises in line with other visual expressions that respond to rules and conventions in their visual layout. To their excuse, it should be added that Wood and Wollen are concerned primarily with the artworks that embed cartography into the artwork in one way or another. Principles of cartography, however, can also be recognized in the different ways in which language and photography operate in a broad number of post-Minimalist and Conceptual artworks of this era. In fact, cartography and the question of scale could very well be the framework that best articulates what is happening in many of the post-Minimalist practices of the late 1960s. While this includes but also moves beyond Wood's mapping industry argument, it works in relation to other art historical accounts for which prisms such as photography, the archive, and time-critical technologies have been highlighted.[29]

As discussed in the previous chapters, cartography proposes a particularly strong connection between an image and the world, and this stronghold is scientifically verified through the principle of scale. Extensive properties on Earth's surface are measured and scaled down to accurately represent such relations. The homogenizing scales of the Eameses' zoom through the universe along a linear trajectory amplifies the continuity in operation beneath the surface of scientific maps. Hence, mapping and cartography became favored subjects for post-Minimalist practices who sought to question the techno-utopian atmosphere across political and scientific planetary scales. As Deleuze and Guattari suggestively propose, "[a] map is essentially an experimentation in contact with the real."[30] Given the power of maps, we are encouraged to make our own maps rather than trace those already in place. This was the project that artists of the later 1960s took on as they engaged in various mapping practices, continuing in the footsteps of earlier Fluxus approaches. As art historian Ina Blom has convincingly argued, the theme of exact measurement and scale was a preoccupation of the early Fluxus explorations as well, as it follows their investigation of cause and continuity.[31] Here, we see how the question of scale in art, previously pertaining to long-lost ideals of composition, resurfaces with a new agenda.

DIAGRAMMATIC PROXISTANCE

A significant example of how the question of scale in maps takes on a bigger discussion through an arrangement of proxistant vision in the late 1960s can be exemplified by some of the Conceptual map works by Douglas Huebler. As many artists of the time, Huebler first worked in a sculptural tradition loosely associated with Minimalism before turning to Conceptual art in the late 1960s. Rather than a sculptural occupation of space, Huebler became more interested in defining space through mapping—through a form of loosely corresponding references. In the declarative conceptual statement that constituted the artwork in the famous catalog-as-exhibition *January 5–31, 1969*, arranged by art dealer Seth Siegelaub, Huebler argued that he avoided adding more objects to "a world full of objects, more or less interesting."[32] He saw it as satisfactory, therefore, "simply, to state the existence of things in terms of time and/or place."[33] Accordingly, Huebler's work was often composed of a number of photographs, a written statement or description, and existing cartographic maps, arranged in series, such as *Location*, *Duration*, and *Variable Pieces*.[34] In the next line of Huebler's statement, however, one can detect a philosophical twist to all of this since "the work concerns itself with things whose inter-relationship is beyond direct perceptual experience."[35] It is this twist of direct perceptual experience that will be our focus here as we seek to decipher how scale and proxistance operate in some of these arrangements.

A significant work by Huebler in this regard is the work *Site Sculpture Project. Variable Piece No. 1, NYC* (1968). In this piece, we are presented with a non-linear proxistant vision, in which four square maps of midtown Manhattan figure across a single page, arranged in a two-by-two grid. The maps are equal in size, and each shows an identical location at a different scale, such that it appears as if a camera started to zoom in from a high altitude and, through three distinct steps, stopped in proximity to the ground. Hence, while the top left map shows the tightly gridded pattern of midtown Manhattan, the bottom right one contains only one city block. Beneath this arrangement, a handwritten statement in capital letters reads:

> 1. All sites shown as located in Manhattan. 2. a3, b3, c3, d3, marks placed on automobiles and trucks thereby being carried into random and horizontal directions. 3. a2, b2, c2, d2, markers placed in static and permanent location. 4. a1, b1, c1, d1, markers placed in elevators thereby being carried into random and vertical directions.

At the top of the page of the catalog, furthermore, a text informs readers that the sixteen markers employed to carry out this work are one by five-eighths inch oval stickers made of fabric.[36] When reading this statement, we indeed recognize the marks indicated at each corner in the three incrementally zoomed-in maps. Within these four differently scaled maps, we are presented with twelve different perspectives by way of four vertically and four horizontally mobilized markers and four markers in stationary positions. Arguably, upon reading the statement and the variously scaled maps of Manhattan, a multiplicity of angles and views about the city start to collide.

What does this cartographic layout suggest in terms of proxistant vision? How does it differ from *A Rough Sketch*'s smooth journey between detail and the big picture? While we do have both close-ups and overviews within one field of vision, which indicate a proxistant modality, this modality is not at all linear. There is no coherent form that closely describes each spatial position between them. The space in between these different perspectives is not described but only suggested as a discontinuous and heterogeneous space of possibility. Huebler's layout, therefore, can be said to operate more like a diagram of an electrical circuit that describes connections and operations rather than spatial fixation. A diagram, as Deleuze has shown, can also be understood based on the virtual, non-actualized space of possibilities that is incarnated in emergence.[37] Huebler's initial artist's statement, cited earlier, further supports this reading when it points out that the work cannot be directly perceived. Huebler further clarifies this in one of his presentations, stating that "maps are full

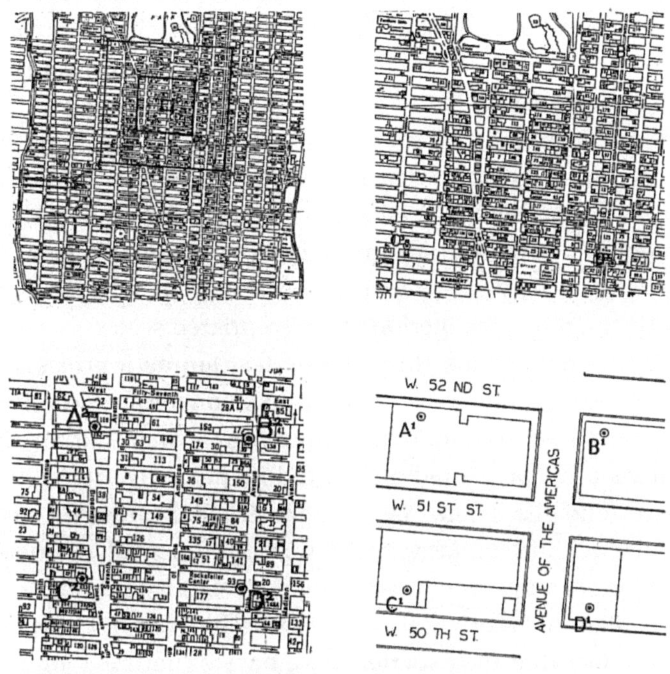

FIGURE 9.4

Douglas Hubler. *Variable Piece No. 1, NYC* (1968), drawing, ink on paper 13″ × 12″. Copyright © the artist.

of information about natural forms you believe to be true, but yet they are just scratches and words on a piece of paper. On the other hand, you can use it to make a mental relation between this room, the next relation, the building, the city." From this reflection, Huebler importantly concludes, "maps are kind of magical in this sense."[38] Here, we can see how Huebler's proxistance can serve as a form of diagrammatic thinking, infusing the motion that moves thought.[39] Huebler's arrangements establish a mental image, but this image is simultaneously being moved through the uneven arrangement of a proxistant diagram, in which the scale is open and always becoming. Proxistance here exists as an engine for such movement, fueled by the ongoing production of differentiated scales.

In more dramatic terms, through this diagrammatic proxistant vision, Huebler suggests a more fundamental limitation of the mimetic continuity to the phenomena we see. To take the example of de' Barbari, in which proxistant vision is presented on a two-dimensional surface, we can be "everywhere" and see it "all." By contrast, Huebler presents a constellation in which we cannot take up the views simultaneously. Modern vision, Huebler suggests, only reveals nature to us through a network of conventions. To explain his motives, Huebler wrote in 1968: "For me, all this is an irony, the fact that the experience we have of nature is underpinned by multiple conventions."[40] This irony refers to the notion that "what we observe is not nature in itself but nature exposed to our method of questioning," as a pioneer of quantum mechanics and a mastermind of the uncertainty principle Werner Heisenberg famously declared in his third Gifford Lecture in the winter of 1955.[41] "All that we can pretend to know about nature, through its representation, is in fact nothing more than the network of conventions that govern it."[42] This is where navigation as a strategy comes in, as we learned from airborne machines in section 2. As a diagrammatic construct, Huebler's proxistance works to destabilize the illusion of its linear and topological cousins. By arranging his proxistance as a diagram, Huebler not only moves our perception but also makes us aware of how perception is being moved.

In Huebler's work, proxistance becomes an essential element in his effort to destabilize or suspend perception to question the mimetic dimension between cartographic vision and the world. His strategy is to apply scientific objectifying techniques such as maps and descriptive coordinates to expose the shortcomings of the post-war era's formulaic conventions of a universal scale and interchangeable patterns pressed onto a contingent, plural, and always-becoming world. As such, Huebler's diagrammatic approach exists in the spirit of contemporary art of the late 1960s, which "produces the starkest possible contrast between the open-ended contingencies of fact and the synthesizing powers of truth," as Ina Blom has articulated.[43] When Huebler turns to maps with the question of scale, he not only questions the way scale operates as a highway between image and the world, but he also questions the fundamental way in which this continuity is ingrained in vision itself, since knowledge structures the way we see and perceive. Huebler presents a diagrammatic proxistant vision to suspend and make visible the unconscious epistemic operators that structure cartographic perception into a default mimetic response. As we can see, such practice is of high relevance to our current proxistant situation. Next, we shall dive into another approach of similar importance.

THE SCALE CONSCIOUSNESS OF AERIAL ART

The cybernetic atmosphere that defined the Space Age and Moon Landing era presented itself to artists as usable tools for engendering perceptual twists. For Huebler, this took the shape of the combination of photographic and cartographic scales with statements that played on the positivist flavors of logic, calculation, and control. This approach provided a side view to the era's firm belief in the power of scientific methods to produce reliable, objective knowledge. A very similar diagrammatic approach is evident in Robert Smithson's work. Smithson's conception of aerial art emerged during his engagement as an art consultant for the architect and engineering firm Tippetts-Abbett-McCarthy-Stratton (TAMS).[44] Walther Prokosch, from TAMS, asked Smithson to collaborate on the firm's proposal for the large-scale airport to be located between Dallas and Fort Worth.[45] In Smithson's later text on the airport proposal, titled "Aerial Art" (1969), he noted how "the investigation of a specific site is a matter of extracting concepts out of existing sense-data through direct perceptions," and this process of extraction could be aided by the air flight itself.[46] In other words, the aerial view from an airplane has the potential to release thought from its habitual image by framing the world anew. Here, one can think of framing as an abstracting agent. "The straight lines of landing fields and runways bring into existence a perception of 'perspective' that evades all our conceptions of nature. The naturalism of seventeenth-, eighteenth- and nineteenth-century art is replaced by non-objective sense of site," Smithson continues.[47] This non-objectivity points directly to the era's positivist view that objective, scientific knowledge is the highest form of understanding. This perceptual shift is further alluded to when Smithson explains how he sees the airport becoming nothing "but a dot in the vast infinity of universes, an imperceptible point in a cosmic immensity, a speck in an impenetrable nowhere."[48] Most importantly, Smithson points out, this is "a matter of perception. It's how you perceive."[49] The change of perspective on the ascent or descent of an airplane can aid one's ability to enter this perceptual situation, but it applies to all aspects of scale. It "is a certain kind of abstract consciousness which sets up a way of dealing with raw material and mental experience," Smithson explains.

Upon being asked about the coining of the term "aerial art" by fellow artist Dennis Wheeler, Smithson explains that he used the term as "a kind of rubric, but at the same time it connotes a certain kind of scale consciousness which I wanted to get across."[50] The rubric Smithson has in mind implies not just an aerial perspective, but also a proxistant relation that destabilizes continuous visuality between symmetric part-to-whole constellations. Smithson thus relates scale consciousness to uncertainty. The concept of aerial art became significant for subsequent works in which a variety of back-and-forth operations were set in motion. Scale here, is not intended as in the sense of big or small. Rather, it is about a certain form of consciousness. Smithson explains, "[a]lthough you are conscious of the scale, it's how your consciousness focuses." The artwork, he continues, "might appear big, but in fact it's very tiny, so that you have this telescoping back and forth from both ends of the telescope." Similarly, Smithson explains, referring to a never-realized proposal to create a massive artwork by covering a small, rocky island near the island of Nanaimo and city of Vancouver with ninety tons of broken glass: "[Y]ou can conceive of [the island] as a very large work, like one particle on the island might be conceived as being a gigantic tumulus . . . The particle on the island takes on an enormity. Whereas the island itself is just a dot."[51] This is how scale becomes the domain of art.[52]

One way in which this can be understood is to see that the artwork is not defined by its extensive properties, such as size, but by its capacities to affect and be affected. This view suggests that the artwork is an assemblage rather than a unified whole, or an ongoing actualization of a virtual space of possibility, and that scale is an emergent property of this assemblage.[53] Scale is thus uncertain because we do not have any homogenizing wholes, but only interacting assemblages from which emergent properties will be (however slightly) different at every repetition. As Horton noticed, scale is not only a primary form of differential dynamics, it is also a primary form of difference.[54] In Smithson's notes, one can find a newspaper clipping that shows the plan drawing of the Dallas/Fort Worth International Airport project superimposed on a map of Manhattan.

As we have seen, their measurement in cartographic area corresponds in size on paper.[55] Yet when thinking scale in terms of connections, the point of view changes. A scale is not delineated by fixed boundaries in space or time, Horton observes. Instead, a scale is the abstract realm of space and time where a particular set of typical events occurs. Even a scale as small as 10^{-10} meters is vast, like the universe, yet only specific events occur at this level.[56]

Smithson linked this to his much-favored Jorge Luis Borges's reading of the mathematician and Renaissance man Blaise Pascal, who had turned around the early religious notion of a divine sphere by stating that "[n]ature is an infinite (fearful) sphere, whose center is everywhere and whose circumference is nowhere."[57] Through a genealogical tracing of this statement, Borges demonstrates how this dialectic is fundamental to thought.[58] In opposition to Descartes, who constructs a whole from parts, Pascal's statement signals the essential uncertainty about our universe and the fallacy of objective measurement in trying to grasp a seamless totality. Here, we can perceive a critical perspective on the cybernetic mindset, which deconstructs complex phenomena into manageable components to comprehend their interactions, a concept that inspired the Eameses' film.

Smithson's way of working with this concept of scale and nonmechanistic worldview continued from the DFW project into artworks

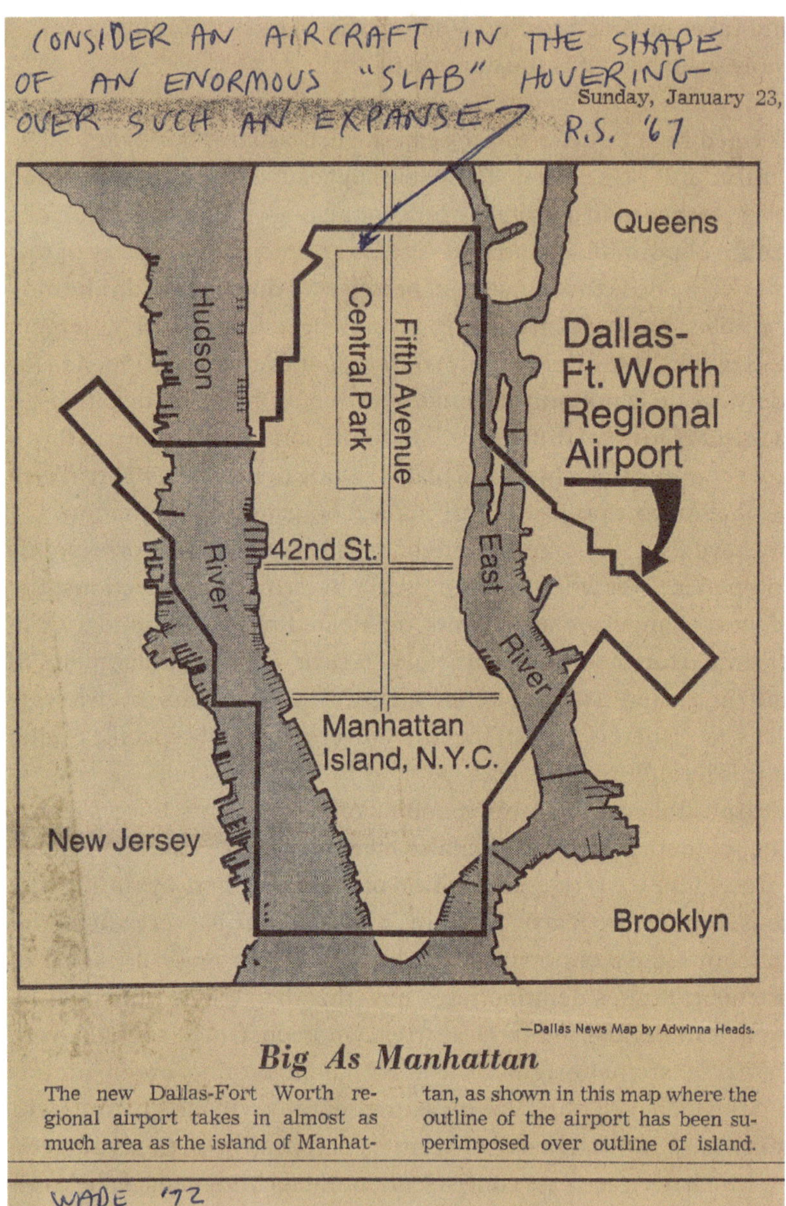

—Dallas News Map by Adwinna Heads.

Big As Manhattan

The new Dallas-Fort Worth regional airport takes in almost as much area as the island of Manhattan, as shown in this map where the outline of the airport has been superimposed over outline of island.

WADE '72

FIGURE 9.5

Illustration of Dallas–Ft. Worth Regional Airport superimposed on Manhattan. Press clippings with a personal note by Robert Smithson. Courtesy of Robert Smithson and Nancy Holt Papers, Archives of American Art, Smithsonian Institution.

that devised what Smithson referred to as site–non-site dialectic. These works further explored the cartographic approach from Aerial Art by setting up a dialogue between dialectical oppositions, such as center–periphery, outdoors–indoors, two-dimension–three-dimension, or proximity–distance. The first such artwork, according to Smithson, was *A Non-Site (an outdoor Earthwork)*, later retitled *A Non-Site, Pine Barrens, New Jersey* (1968), which was realized in relation to the smaller and less profiled airport at the Pine Barrens in New Jersey.[59] Also referred to as an Earthwork, this piece adopted the hexagonally shaped area defined by the landing strips. In the gallery, therefore, one would find a hexagonally shaped floor structure with thirty-one expanding square-shaped containers of sand. Complementing this floor sculpture was a similarly hexagonally shaped map on the wall, with a red mark in its center. Below the map, one could read the following statement:

> A NONSITE (an indoor Earthwork), 31 sub-divisions based on a hexagonal "air-field" in the Woodmansie Quadrangle—New Jersey (Topographic) map. Each sub-division of the Nonsite contains sand from the site shown on the map. Tours between the Nonsite and the site are possible. The red dot on the map is the place where the sand was collected.[60]

In this proxistant setup, we can see how Smithson responds to the cartographic scale on the map by turning it into sculptural limits. The equilibrium-state distribution of sand on the site is constrained by containers that mirror the measured and downscaled map or abstracted "air-field" on the wall pointing to where the sand was collected. The non-site can be seen as a fragment of the site outdoors. Yet, to come back to Pascal, this is not a small cut out, which can be aggregated into a bigger whole. Rather, in a similar fashion to aerial art "[t]he non-site functions like a map that tells you where the fringes are."[61] To further investigate Smithson's reasoning here, we can refer to an interview with Kenneth Baker, where Smithson explains that the site-non-site works were intended to operate as a dialectic between the condition of the site outdoors and the confinement of the gallery indoors, in an endless cycle. As we saw with Pascal, this is the relationship of the ever-present center to the non-existent circumference, a form of dialectics that is very different from the Hegelian goal-driven and teleological concept. Smithson further emphasized this in the short unpublished text "Art and Dialectics (1971)," in which he states that "[d]ialectics is not only the ideational formula of thesis-antithesis-synthesis forever sealed in the mind, but an on-going development."[62] This statement shows the process-oriented nature of Smithson's thought.

In the interview with Wheeler, Smithson alerts readers to the fact that the site in this site-non-site work was twice abstracted, first in the material structures of the non-site and secondly by the abstraction of the gallery itself.[63] This double abstraction or framing of the site gives us a point of view of the site that tells us very little about it, observed from a conventional cartographic perspective; yet, it cannot be denied that the site is materially represented in the abstraction. Through a closer analysis, one can see that the map on the wall plays a central role. The text below the map encourages trips between the site and the non-site. By this, however, we should not assume that Smithson suggests that bringing this part-to-whole constellation would complete the picture in a proxistant coherence between detail as sand and the big picture as a map. In a different text called "A Provisional Theory of Non-Sites," Smithson rather noted that traveling between the site and the non-site might be conceived as "a vast metaphor."[64] This can be said to operate with a twist on behalf of cartographic conventions that claim to present a seamless view of Earth's surface. The capacity with which the site is claimed to be represented in the non-site as a form of cartography facilitates the extraction of concepts that underpin scale-as-size and leaves scale to the realm of uncertainty.

As we have seen, this generation of post-Minimalist artists investigated processes and open-ended becoming in the face of the uncritical acceptance of technological progress and topological modes of control.[65] Today, a paradigm of proxistant Earth models consistently repeats the same scalar collapse that characterizes Eameses' *Powers of Ten* and *A Rough Sketch*. Tracing this continuous line between the farthest reaches of the observable universe and the microscopic realms of subatomic particles back to the late 1960s through a media archaeological analysis lets us scrutinize the historical and technological contingencies in operation behind proxistant Earth models today. Simultaneously, this perspective has brought new relevance to the post-Minimalist practices that introduced perceptual twists and disruptions to the homogenizing surface of such worldviews. Building upon these preliminary post-Minimalist scalar contemplations, we now return to the dynamic installation space of the *Zoom Blue Dot*. As we will see, this artistic research of orbital machines has both been informed by and reciprocally informed the preceding explorations.

IN THE SPACE OF THE *ZOOM BLUE DOT*

In the *Zoom Blue Dot* project, we question the agency of Earth models and their production of worldviews. How does Earth correspond to the images we make of it? The history of mapping is a history of territorial claims. Digital imaging is itself a process of mapping; it is a translation of electromagnetic radiation into discrete electric pulses organized in a grid of pixels. How can we depict alternative futures when the imaging technologies we have at our disposal follow the grid system of the disappearing globe? Our task in this artistic research project is to re-approach and make visible the omnipresent grid as a historically contingent limit to which both cartography and Earth models adhere. This is the starting point for a navigational approach to proxistant Earth models, a task on which we will embark with humble curiosity.

Approaching the paradigm of proxistant Earth models from an artistic research perspective mobilizes various forms of practice-based media archaeological strategies. As a starting point, we investigate and probe several proxistant Earth models on the backdrop of the historic effort to visualize the world as a unified globe. Adding to the backdrop of the 1960s world imaging craze, we find *Voyager 1*'s photograph of Earth, described by Sagan as "a mote of dust suspended in a sunbeam." This tiny dot exhibits not only that Earth itself is a detail in a larger picture, but also how technological advancement is driven by emotional effort as an unplanned production. Confronted with this tiny image of Earth, we resort to the method that inspired today's proxistant models by initiating a cinematic form reminiscent of the linear journey presented in the Eameses' *A Rough Sketch* and the *Powers of Ten*. Inspired by the 1960s post-Minimalist diagrammatic drives and scale consciousness, this form is not intended as a smooth flight of topological linearity. Rather, it is motivated by media archeological examination to understand the screen's double nature as both an image of Earth and a different composition of that same Earth as the material assemblage of the image's technological support.

Our practical testing starts from this tiny dot. However, instead of Eameses' camera that travels through the galactic constellation back to its starting point on Earth's surface and into the molecular structure of a human body, our initial idea was to enter this dot as it is presented on the screen, investigating its material support. Thus, the camera in *Zoom Blue Dot* starts its journey from the scalable media interface of Earth produced by diverse satellite views into the *Pale Blue Dot* image displayed on a smartphone screen. Through a variety of laser scanning and electron microscopes, the journey proceeds into the smartphone screen, probing the fabric of the electronic image's material support—in this case, the multi-layered assemblage of Liquid Crystal Display.[66] This method implies extending the scope from the microscope to the satellite and beyond. Like the *Voyager* space probe, with the microscope, our investigation goes deeper, beyond human capability, into the infrastructure of the image, discovering its physical components of electronics, rear earth minerals, and chemical compositions.

From an artistic research perspective, the way this was done mounted to a significant part of the research. With access to the Berkeley University Molecular Imaging Center (MIC) and the invaluable support of MIC director Holly Aaron, we utilized a Laser Scanning Microscope (LSM) to scan the surface and interior of both iPhone 5 and 6 as it displayed the *Pale Blue Dot* image. This allowed for the capture of individual frames at progressively higher magnifications, which were animated to simulate the effect that the camera was moving progressively closer to the iPhone screen.

The initial images were captured without laser assistance, relying on the smartphone's liquid crystal display (LCD) to emit photons. This method is akin to observing an LCD with magnifying glasses, revealing that the *Pale Blue Dot* comprised several multicolored pixels when magnified. This phase of imaging employed default microscope software settings for so-called pseudo coloring, paralleling both the creation of *Pale Blue Dot* and early video art techniques, where artists manipulated black-and-white video signals with custom color synthesizers. When moving on to laser scanning microscopy, individual pixels were no longer discernible;

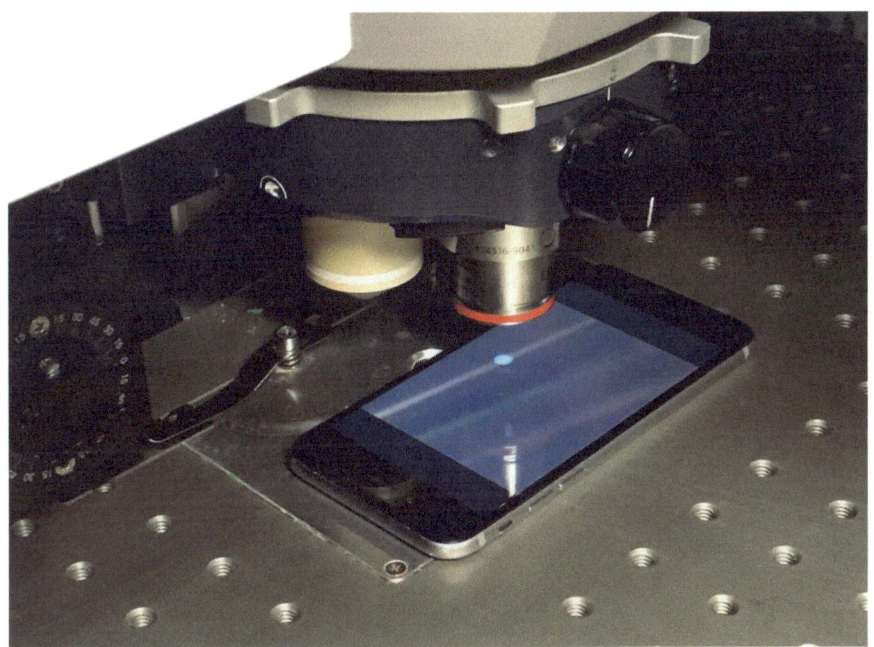

instead, subpixels arranged in a grid appeared on the screen in grayscale. This technique, which merges the smartphone display with LSM imaging, lends a new perspective to Walter Benjamin's assertion about the camera revealing a different nature than the naked eye.[67] Subpixel filters, the physical components of a screen's pixels, become discernable, with each electronic screen pixel containing at least three subpixels.

The combination of these subpixels' luminescence, optical blurring, and the human eye's perception results in the appearance of solid colors. This exploration operates below human perceptual thresholds, opening

FIGURE 9.6

iPhone 6 with PIA00452 also known as *Pale Blue Dot* on display in a LSM at the Molecular Image Center, Cancer Research Laboratory, University of California Berkeley. Photo by Bull.Miletic. Copyright © Bull.Miletic.

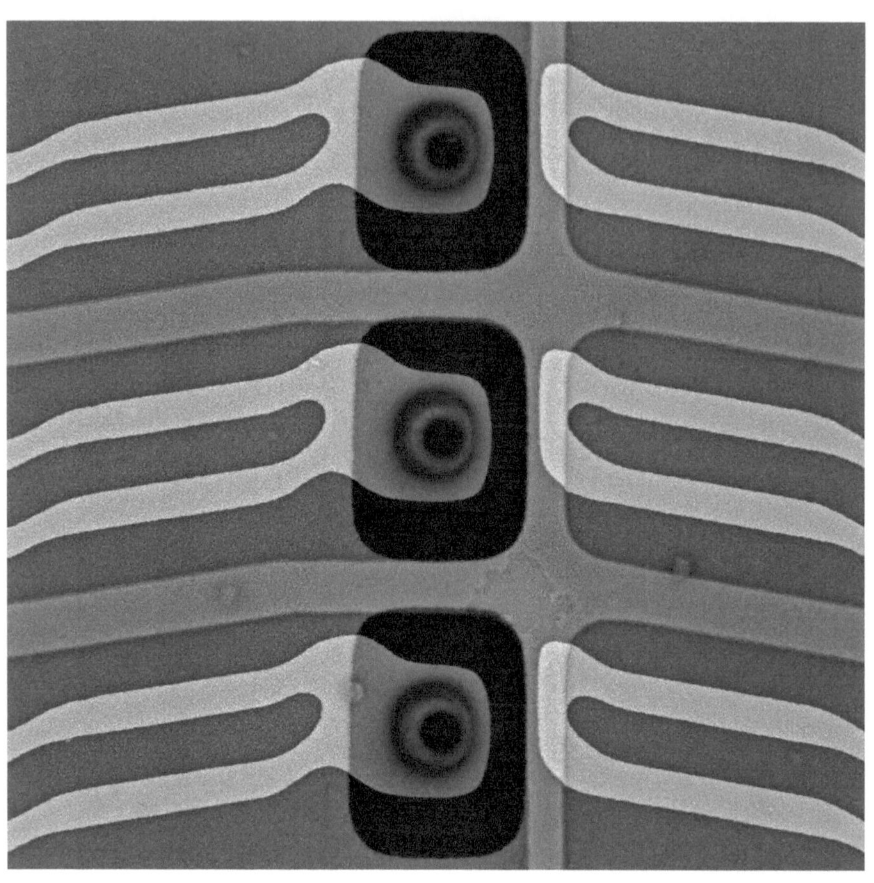

FIGURE 9.7

iPhone 6 subpixel architecture seen through SEM. Photo by Bull.Miletic. Copyright © Bull.Miletic.

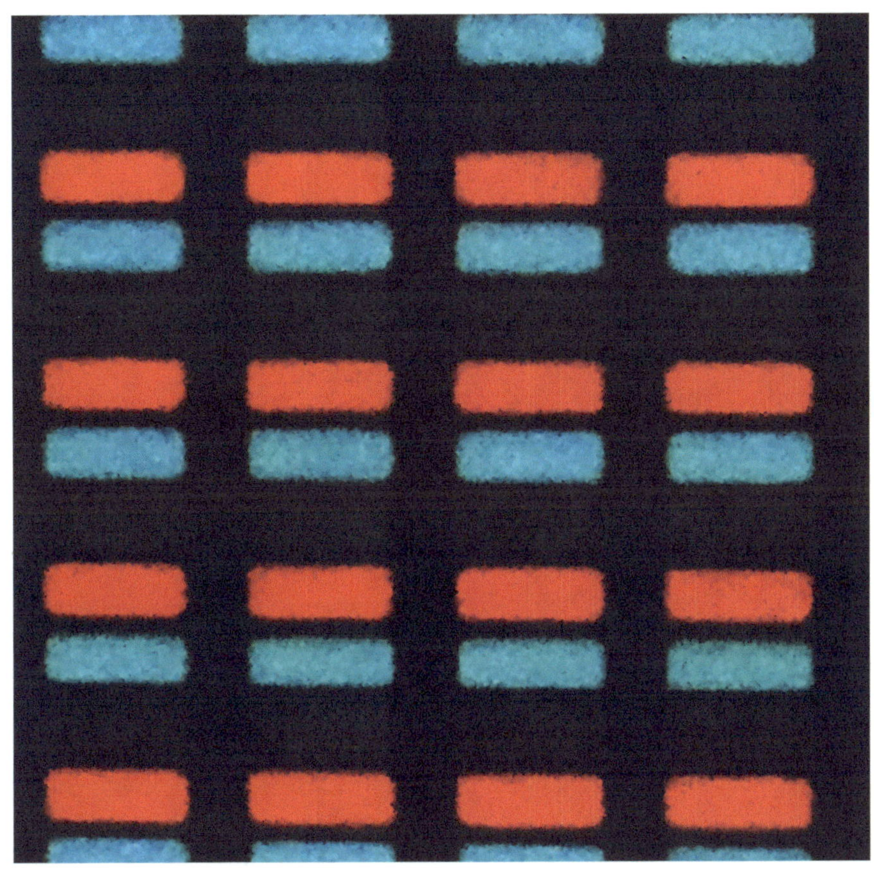

FIGURE 9.8

iPhone 5 subpixel architecture seen through LSM. Photo by Bull.Miletic. Copyright © Bull.Miletic.

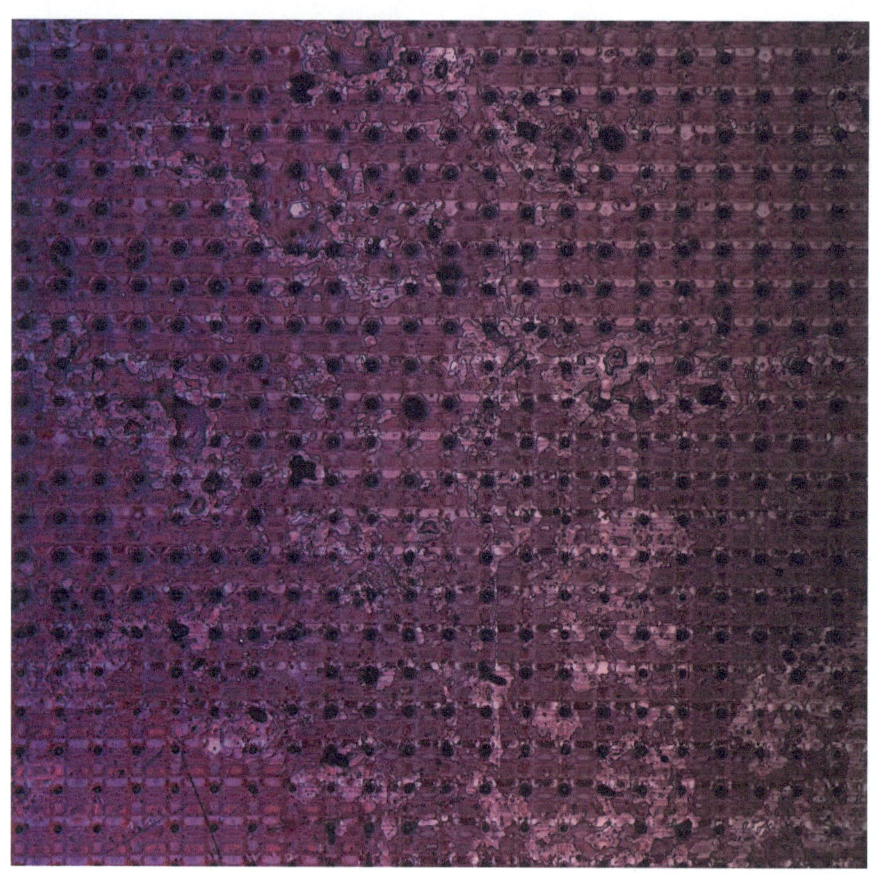

FIGURE 9.8 (continued)

a domain for potential manipulation and highlighting our imaginative, creative, and ethical engagement with technology.

Magnification through the LSM increased progressively until its limits were reached, enlarging the Pale Blue Dot region to about 2,000 times the size visible to the unaided eye, with only a few subpixels filling the screen. Considering that the iPhone's LCD screen has over three million subpixels, each about fifty-by-twenty micrometers in size, this level of detail is notable. The LSM technique not only magnifies but also scans along the Z-axis, creating "slices" of the sample at each level of magnification. In this instance, fifty-three scans of the subpixel color filter layer were made at 0.75-micrometer intervals, totaling a depth of 39.75 micrometers. To examine the subpixel color filter and other layers, an LCD needed to be disassembled, leading to the acquisition of several damaged iPhone LCDs from a repair store. The investigation proceeded with scanning at the electron microscope (SEM), which allows magnification up to 10,000 times. With immense help from Danielle Jorgens at the Electron Microscope Lab, the dissected layers were skillfully prepared for SEM analysis.

SEM operates by scanning a sample with an electron beam focused and steered by electromagnetic coils, in contrast to the light and lenses used in LSM. This process requires a vacuum chamber to prevent electron dispersion by air molecules. By hitting the sample, the electrons bounce off its surface and get registered by a detector in a similar way to how the vidicon sensor in *Voyager 1* registered photons that bounced off Earth's surface in the process of making *Pale Blue Dot.*

After initial inspections, the iPhone 5's LCD layers revealed a thin-film transistor (TFT) layer with a distinct subpixel geometry, differing from the iPhone 6's chevron-like shapes by being more rectangular. This layer, situated beneath the color filter film, consists of a TFT grid embedded in a liquid crystal substance, encapsulated between two polarizing light filters, held apart by microsphere spacers. Each TFT, about the size of a human white blood cell, corresponds to a subpixel and regulates its brightness through voltage-induced changes in the liquid-crystal orientation, thus controlling light passage through the color filter. The LCD's backlight comes from a series of LEDs at the top edge, with light diffusion and enhancement facilitated by a sequence of reflective, guiding, and diffusing components before it passes through the polarizers and liquid

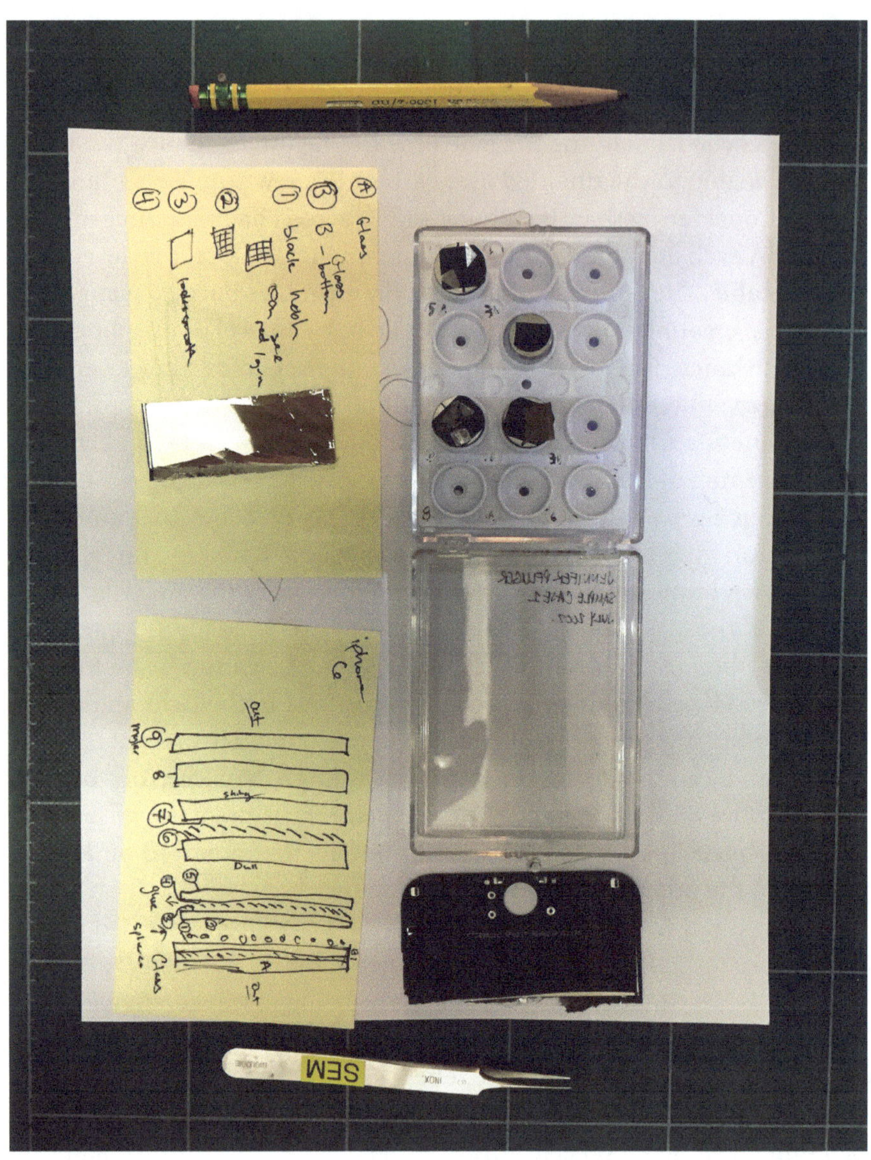

FIGURE 9.9

Diagrams of iPhone 6 LCD layers by Danielle Jorgens at the Electron Microscope Lab, University of California Berkeley. Photo by Bull.Miletic. Copyright © Bull.Miletic.

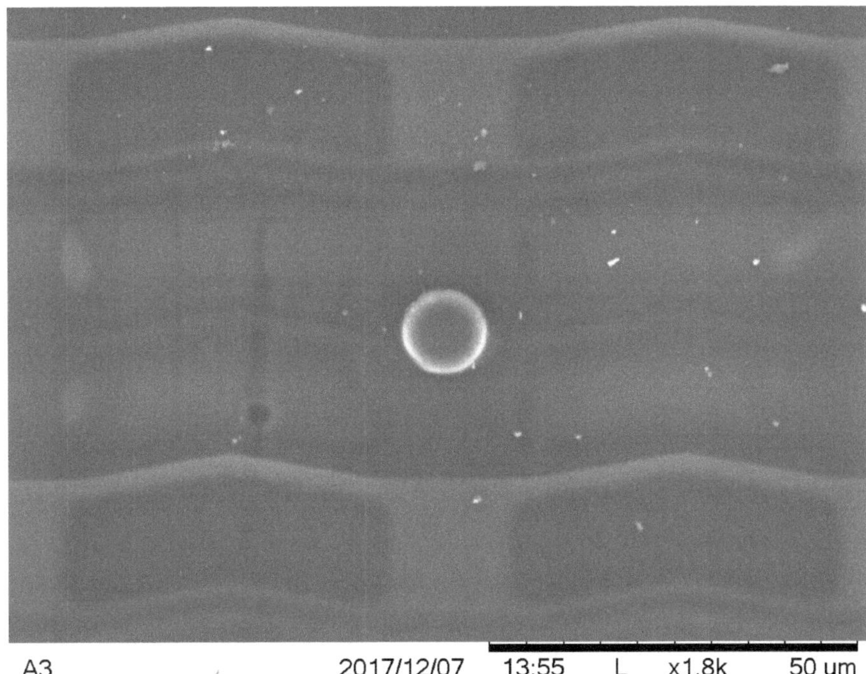

FIGURE 9.10

Glass microsphere in iPhone 6 LCD, seen through SEM. Photo by Bull.Miletic. Copyright © Bull.Miletic.

crystals. Focus on this intricate assembly led to twenty-one detailed SEM scans across magnifications from 100 to 10,000 times. The Molecular Imaging Center and Electron Microscope Lab exposes the gridded subpixel infrastructure in contemporary display systems. This pixelization of vision works hand-in-hand with the processes of spatial commodification, transformation, and homogenization of the grid across cartography and planning.[68] This eye-opening postulation became a compass in navigating the vastness of the Pale Blue Dot. Unlike the Eameses' camera that convincingly negotiates between universal scales expressed in yottameters and femtometers, *Zoom Blue Dot* aims at the material basis of Earth's self-portrait as a mote of dust simultaneously made up of and reflecting itself. Juno's flyby video, taken during the spacecraft's orbit around Earth on October 9, 2013, was used to connect Pale Blue Dot with Google Earth.[69] The transition between Google Earth and Earth dronematography was created with a vertical drone shot in a location that matched the landing "target" in Nevada. The two smartphones were positioned on the encrusted surface of a dry lakebed for a drone shoot starting at 2000-meter altitude, descending gradually until the drone's camera made physical contact with the smartphones upon landing.[70]

To further investigate the double movement inherent in proxistant Earth models, we needed a robot that could move the video projections slowly across the room (see figures III.1–III.6). The engineering experimentation took place at CITRIS Invention Lab with the diligent assistance of Chris Myers.[71] The custom-made robot with two video projectors, facing opposite directions, slowly traverses the darkened exhibition space in a curved trajectory—echoing the path *Voyager 1* took on its epic journey through our solar system. Once it reaches the gallery wall, the robot pauses for a moment before it reverses and continues its journey in the opposite direction. This perpetual movement causes the projected video to continuously shrink and expand across the gallery environment, reflecting and deforming the architectural boundaries. Micro-movements of the reflective Mylar curtain, covering multiple surfaces within the space, induce further deformations and alter the projected images, disrupting the installation's spatial coherence.

This arrangement enables a study of how the image size affects the detail or big picture alternatively across the proxistant journey. Shaping

and forming around the architectural elements in the space, this constellation of projections includes both exhibition space and its public in this investigation. The two projectors on the robot each feature a similar but slightly different video as they each pertain to the two different protagonists in their films: the iPhone 5 and the iPhone 6. To help keep the videos apart, they are titled Channel A (iPhone 5) and Channel B (iPhone 6). American composer Phill Niblock created the original soundtrack for the installation.

Niblock's layering of long durational sounds with very slight pitch distinctions generates a multitude of beats, complex overtone patterns,

FIGURE 9.11

Dronematography on location in Mojave Desert, California, for the prodution of *Zoom Blue Dot*. Photo by Bull.Miletic. Copyright © Bull.Miletic.

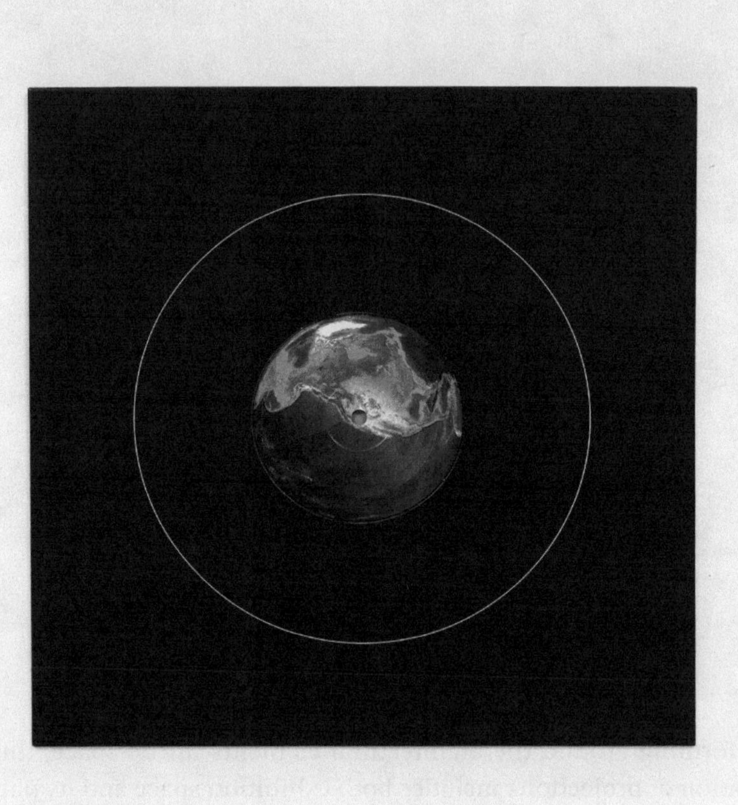

FIGURE 9.12

Phill Niblock. *Zoom Blue Dot*, 12″ vinyl, edition of 200. Production, graphics, and layout by Bull.Miletic. Copyright © Bull.Miletic.

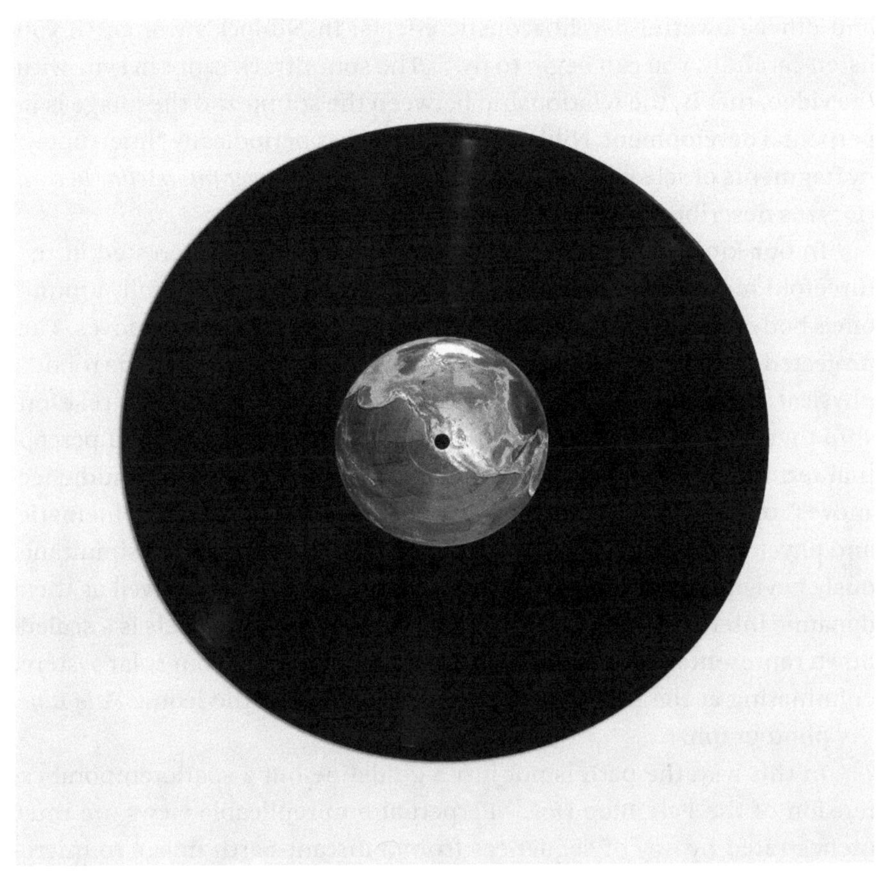

FIGURE 9.12 (continued)

and other powerful psychoacoustic effects. In Niblock's words, "if you listen carefully, you can begin to fly."[72] The soundtrack is not in sync with the video, that is, the relationship between the sound and the image is in perpetual development. Niblock's soundtrack is periodically "interrupted" by fragments of selected compositions from the *Voyager Interstellar Record* (1977) as described previously (see figure III.10).

In our kinetic video projections, we are especially interested in the threefold movement of the moving image that travels physically around one's body and the recorded space through which the camera moves. The projected moving image, which shows camera movement and the robot's physical movement in the exhibition space, enters a dynamic relationship that allows us to study this triple kineticism in artistic and perceptual terms. Unlike in normative video installations where the audience "moves" only within the projected image, in kinetic projection, cinematic and physical movements are interconnected. The spectator is simultaneously navigating the image space and the physical space, as well as their dynamic interaction. The route the robot continuously travels is a scaled-down representation of *Voyager 1*'s epic journey through our solar system, culminating at the location from which it captured the iconic *Pale Blue Dot* photograph.

In this way, the path is not just a guideline but a spatiotemporal extension of the Pale Blue Dot.[73] Perpetual non-replicable views are thus orchestrated by way of sequences from a distant Earth image to microscopic electronic details in a dynamic interplay. Here, too, the movement of the robot is highly predictable, but the exact result of its movement is impossible to foresee.

With this practice-based media archaeological approach, we are interested in opening new ways of asking questions and alternative ways of answering them. Our entrance in this project is inspired by social anthropologist Tim Ingold, in that we seek to approach the world longitudinally.[74] With the analogy of wood cutting, Ingold distinguishes between chopping up the wood into separate logs and entering it in its lines by joining its veins as you do when you make boards to construct a house. With composition rather than analysis, our artistic endeavor seeks to express rather than analyze difficult questions. This is the nature of artistic research: we employ artistic expressions in physical space to embed the

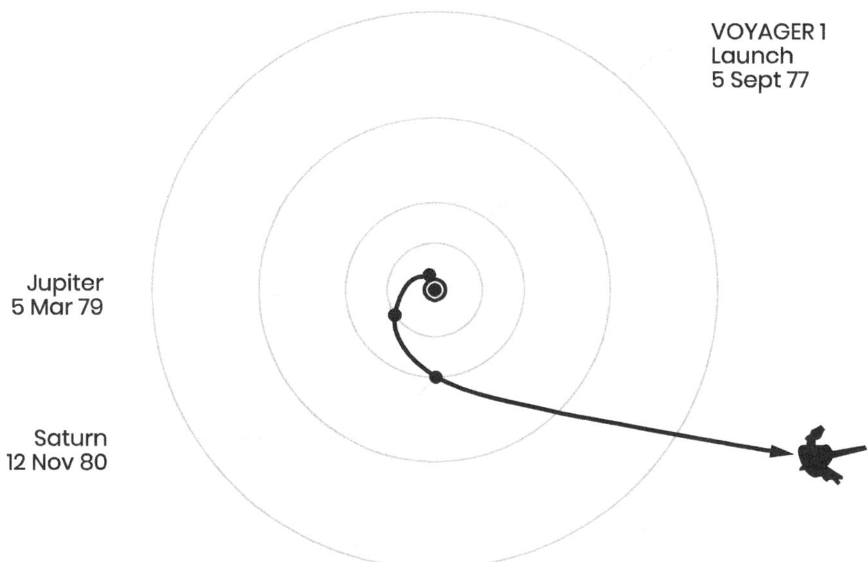

viewer in experiences that linger with vibrant pressure. The significance of contemporary art in the context of this discourse is paramount, not solely for its capacity to transcend verbal and visual communication but also for its propensity to demand sensory engagement from its audience. This sensory venture, in which we, too, are participants, necessitates a concerted effort towards understanding the world in terms of its becoming—with an acknowledgment of the heterogeneous temporalities and the interconnectedness of disparate trajectories. The involvement of the exhibition space as a testing ground emphasizes the nature of the situation in which "the conditions are set but the outcome is not."[75] This is what we mean by referring to the exhibition as a stage in an ongoing process. The exhibition space is an extension of the laboratory, which allows for the experiment to continue in real-time interaction with the public, with the range of responsibilities and ethical considerations such activity entails.[76]

FIGURE 9.13

Diagram of *Voyager 1* path.

As already mentioned across the pages of this book, we consider technology an equal player in our work, and we aim to bring forth its affordances and agencies in an increasingly globalized environment. The artwork emerges between technical processes and organic brains in assemblages of networked feedback loops between human and nonhuman entities. Every practice concerns a mode of thought. To start with practice means to address the problem artistically. For us, thinking through practice means grasping topics more intuitively to allow other types of connections to appear and flourish. Thus, open-ended experiments in artistic research are very different from scientific experiments in which the desired result should be repeatable. The artwork emerges as a diagram across dissimilar and disparate analogies, forging new ways of addressing questions and, ultimately, new ways of thinking. Here, we are pushing the logical brain to the back as we work with sensibilities such as pattern recognition and new forms of abstractions within a strictly artistic logic. This is a mode in which we try to return to the wonder of perception through processes of unlearning conventions and tropes by seeing them anew—to study how they work on us pre-cognitively.

All installations in the Proxistant Vision project have more than one state, moving from proximity to distance physically in the room as we are researching camera movement through physically moving the projectors in space. What is crucial in these kinetic video installations is how they involve the body of the visitor—displacing the bodily sensation of the physical exhibition space and the relation between body, space, and screen. By tracing the current paradigm of proxistant vision today back to the late 1960s through this practice-based media archaeological analysis, the installation enmeshes the viewer into some of the historical and technological contingencies that drive proxistant Earth models in operation today. Extending the philosophical and artistic mindset present among the post-minimalist practices at the time, the *Zoom Blue Dot* kinetic installation introduces perceptual twists and disruptions to the homogenizing scales of such worldviews.[77]

Today, Earth is a digital interface on portable devices at the tip of one's finger. Revolutionizing technological leaps in aerial imaging and mapping techniques update Earth's interface regularly to access ever tinier details. At the same time, we face the age of the Anthropocene, the current geological era marked by significant human impact on Earth's geology and ecosystems. Earth as a globe no longer exists. Gaia, or the "critical zone," is a patchwork of processes and multiplicities of which extraction politics and capitalist growth pose a major risk.[78] Satellites also turn into orbital debris, generating a critical concern for space sustainability and collision risk management in near-Earth space operations.[79] Similarly, as a digital model, the globe should not be mistaken as immaterial. On the contrary, its material substratum comprised of rare minerals, heavy metals, and toxic chemicals (as well as the enormous energy consumption caused by its operation) is one of the most controversial topics of our time, a subject of provocative scholarly works, and a key infrastructural component of the electronic image display we investigate in this research.[80] As Seán Cubitt points out, a machine can be studied as an archaeological site or a "'social hieroglyphic' [—] an ostensibly innocent artifact in which is disguised a world of complex networks."[81] With the concept of "finite media," Cubitt refers to the finite and often scarce natural resources used in the production of digital media devices, as well as the finite capacity of the environment to absorb the byproducts and waste generated by these technologies.

In this work and research, we stand by a large group of media art practitioners and a roster of media artworks in which, as Ina Blom describes it, "new media information technologies are not just deployed but are themselves also objects of thinking, investigation, and imagination."[82] The analysis through media-archaeologically informed artistic research furthers the capacities of humans and nonhumans to co-reflect on some of the technological operations that produce scale as size and the world as a digital model. On the other hand, such practices also forward imaginative alternative forms that continue to alert to scale's fundamental uncertainty.

10

AFTERTHOUGHTS ON THE ANTHROPOCENE

"The world is slowly destroying itself. The catastrophe comes suddenly, but slowly."
—Robert Smithson[1]

"Uncertainty cannot be measured."
—Dipesh Chakrabarthy[2]

In 1972, the same year *Blue Marble* was released as a conveyor of global wholeness, the artist and designer György Kepes, then founder and director of the Center for Advanced Visual Studies at the Massachusetts Institute of Technology (MIT), edited the book *Art of the Environment*, in which he wrote an introduction discussing themes that curiously resonate with the Anthropocene discourse we have today.[3] "When observed and measured with maximum precision," Kepes writes, "the environment in both its largest and its smallest realism cannot be considered an independent objective world anymore."[4] What we are faced with here according to Kepes is "[a] wildly proliferating man-made environment [that] has shrunk living space, dimmed light, bleached color, and relentlessly expanded noise, speed, and complexity."[5] The essays included in the book further express similar viewpoints and the book can be seen as a sign of growing dynamics among many artists of the time. Not surprisingly, among the included texts was Smithson's essay "The Spiral Jetty."[6]

According to Kepes, "[w]e all are now at the threshold of a new scale consciousness, a complete reorientation; we are shifting frames of reference and thus perspectives."[7] For humans living in the Anthropocene, this scale consciousness should be taking center stage, as we are forced to transcend history and take in the deep time of the planet with its volcanoes, mountains, oceans, and tectonic plates "in the routine life of critical thought," as historian Dipesh Chakrabarty importantly asserts.[8]

It is easy to recognize the influence of the Moon landing and cybernetic eras on Smithson's work. On several occasions, Smithson stated his disbelief in the technological progress underpinning the space exploration advancements occuring in his time, which he believed exhibited a mechanistic and human-centric worldview.[9] In a withdrawal letter to Kepes's technology-centered proposal for the X Sao Paulo Biennale, Smithson states that "[a]s rockets go to the Moon [. . .] the darkness of Earth grows darker."[10] The way Smithson mediated trips from distant sites back to the gallery can be linked directly to how the Moon landing events were televised across the world.[11] Smithson himself acknowledges one such comparison, made by *Artforum* editor Philip Leider.[12] However, rather than a heroic act, Smithson saw the Moon as "a very expensive non-site," and identified his practice with the technological fallacy of the neo-colonial human explorers, charting a new frontier.[13] When operating as a "geological agent" in a "landscape that suggest prehistory," Smithson asserts, "[m]easure and dimension seem to break down at a certain point."[14] This is where "man actually becomes part of the process rather than overcoming it," Smithson further explains.[15] When Baker confronted Smithson with the question about the Moon landings, Smithson replied with the following insightful statement:

> To go to the Moon means some kind of escape, trying to break out of the boundaries of the earthly prison again. And once they get up there, they're all chained into this machine and they're actually more constrained than they'd ever be in a local vacant lot on Earth. [. . .] The feedback in terms of the cameras and everything is supposed to be a great technical feat, but it comes across like a kind of bad science-fiction movie. Maybe that's what I'm trying to get at, that no matter how great our technical resources are, it doesn't necessarily mean a good movie.[16]

With Smithson's cinematic statement, we fast-forward to 2019, when we celebrate the fiftieth anniversary of the Moon landing in the middle of the epistemological scale shift that is rendered by the Anthropocene discourse. Earth escapism now takes the form of Elon Musk's plans for Mars colonization, marked in 2018 by sending one of his roadsters on an interplanetary test drive. Virgin Galactic, on the other hand, hopes to take its first paying customers onto a weightless excursion through suborbital space this year.[17] Smithson's take on the Moon landing as a technically advanced "bad movie" seems to perfectly describe these neocolonial activities, as well.[18] This brings us back to the smooth proxistant models of the world shimmering on our digital screens. Proxistant Earth models and 3D-animated flythroughs are visualization of collected states, aggregated through statistics. These smooth models expose only the most probable states, and the homogeneity becomes the future we subsequently end up enacting. The world is heterogeneous and patchy, as Anna Tsing remind us, and any smooth surface is a perceptual illusion.[19]

Latour signals how the search is on for new methods to engage with Earth that move past the outdated, all-encompassing notions of nature or the globe.[20] With the globe view, the things we care for disappear because they are so small. By redirecting our focus from the concept of the globe to what Latour terms "the Terrestrial," we gain insight into the critical zone—the slender veneer of Earth that enables the rich diversity of life.[21] Referencing James Lovelock's *Gaia hypothesis*, Latour is not here making a simple claim about the world being alive, but rather asks the question: What is the world made of? This question is at the same time a recomposite of agency because it asks: What it is to have agency? To Lovelock's Gaia hypothesis, Latour adds Lynn Margulis's concept of the *microcosmos*, in which the body is understood based on a multiplicity of microorganisms.[22] Here, we see that agency is that which acts. There is no distinction between biotic and abiotic entities—we are all linked, folded, and overlapping with each other in strange ways.[23] We see that there is no unity. Lifeforms have made their own environment. On this basis, Latour asks if we can discern the emergence of a new political subject. According to Lovelock, the sustainability of our planet implies the "human" as a democratic partner. It is when we understand how our bodies depend on microorganisms that we can understand how we have never been individual.[24] It is also here we see that these connections go beyond microorganisms to also include technological operations and the evolution of data visualization systems. We are composites and this blurs and obscures boundaries of what it means to have agency. Agency is distributed across multiple entities, and this modifies how we see the self and how we understand lifeforms.

Yet, the smooth proxistant outlook through which we see entities as finalized details aggregated into a whole continues to flourish today. The proliferation of this visual modality is perhaps symptomatic of the current oscillation between the long-lost ideals of the global and the "return to the reinvented land of old."[25] The latter is what Latour has suggested that we call the new political horizon on which the neonationalist tendencies emerge. "Flight is the right word," Latour asserts, about the notion of the other direction, the modernizing front of globalization, which is another lost hope today.[26] "Going global was a flight of imagination!"[27] The difference between such global flight and a landing on Earth is the fundamental uncertainty with which we have to come to terms in the age of the Anthropocene. Latour continues:

> Nature was indifferent to our actions, but for that reason it could be mastered. However, Earth as Gaia is terribly reactive (even ticklish, as Isabelle Stengers would say) and for that reason escapes all our hopes of dominating it. That's what it means to be facing Gaia; let's face it, we have no longer any idea of what it is composed. And now that we have learned how reactive it is by having modified it so much, we know even less than before.[28]

Gravity (2013) by Alfonso Cuarón comes to mind as a film containing a particularly smooth proxistant shot that can be seen to reverse this globalizing front in its making.[29] The film starts with a spectacular view of Earth from lower orbit, where the planet's marbled surface nearly fills the frame. The entire narrative is suspended in a weightless cinematic construct, suggesting the life-bearing interdependencies with which an Earth-escaping human explorer is interlinked. Just above the thin layer of Earth's life-supporting atmosphere, yet still covered by its protective geomagnetic field, we see the main character, Dr. Ryan Stone (Sandra Bullock), who, on her mission outside the International Space Station (ISS), struggles to comply with weightlessness as an equally physical and mental condition. A sudden hit by a zapping swarm of space debris infinitely amplifies this situation. As Dr. Stone is catapulted into the vastness of frictionless space, her utterly disentangled existence is matched by a highly disorienting camera movement in which the traces of 1960s avant-garde filmmaking stretches the by now strictly twenty-first-century gravitation-less virtual camera to its extreme capacity in a seventeen-minute continuous shot.[30]

A smooth journey through the cosmic darkness gradually brings Dr. Stone into a tight close-up.[31] As the camera enters her helmet, we see Earth flipping by in rapid revolutions spread out and magnified across the screen. In a mirror reflection overlay, we glimpse the horrified human face, gasping for the last molecules of oxygen behind the spherical visor. From this vantage point, a conventional narrative takes over by way of a heroic homecoming despite multiple life-threatening challenges. Upon Dr. Stone's water landing, we are given the film's final, title-giving shot from a frog's perspective. Here, we witness nothing less than a human "re-birth" arriving from the ocean—the primordial soup out of which all life on Earth once evolved—making a footstep imprint on Earth's surface. Earth, as a discontinuous patchwork of prehistoric and layered matter, of uncertain scales and emergent properties. Properties of which we ourselves are composed, even as we rapidly alter them with increasing carbon dioxide levels and heated atmosphere. The smooth proxistant outlook that connects global vision with precise detail in a tantalizing flight falls short when it comes to articulating such connections, even as this dynamic perspective is what flourishes across computer screens today. "The difficulty of making sense of Gaia." Latour and Earth system scientist Timothy M. Lenton reflect, "it's not clear if it's a discovery of a new phenomenon or the introduction in science, as well as in philosophy, of a new way of looking at all phenomena on Earth."[32] Dr. Stone's shallow footprint in the sand can hardly be seen to symbolize that "[w]e are not on Earth but in it," as Latour puts it, while directing our attention to "the brownish, layered, earthly character of this critical zone that we have to learn how to reconnoiter."[33] For this we finally give up on the globe-to-detail view. Entities are not situated in the world according to how a smooth proxistant vision presents them. As Smithson asserts, we must sharpen our scale consciousness—"[s]imply looking at art from eye-level is not an option."[34]

NOTES

INTRODUCTION

1. Paul Virilio, *War and Cinema: The Logistics of Perception*, trans. Patrick Camiller (London: Verso 1984), 15.
2. "VFX Artist Rob Legato Discusses the Opening Scene of "Hugo," YouTube video, 2:43, uploaded October 11, 2015, https://youtu.be/DsNQdtwWRIU, accessed January 13, 2024.
3. Denis Cosgrove, *Geography and Vision: Seeing, Imagining and Representing the World* (London: Bloomsbury Publishing, 2012).
4. Lisa Parks, "Vertical Mediation and the U.S. Drone War in the Horn of Africa," in *Life in the Age of Drone Warfare*, eds. Lisa Parks and Caren Kaplan (Durham, NC: Duke University Press, 2017); Lisa Parks, *Rethinking Media Coverage: Vertical Mediation and the War on Terror* (London: Routledge, 2018); Lisa Parks and Caren Kaplan, *Life in the Age of Drone Warfare* (Durham, NC: Duke University Press, 2017); Teresa Castro, "Aerial Views and Cinematism 1898–1939," in *Seeing from Above: The Aerial View in Visual Culture*, ed. Mark Dorrian and Frérdéric Pousin (New York: I. B. Tauris, 2013); Mark Dorrian, *Writing on the Image: Architecture, the City and the Politics of Representation* (New York: I. B. Tauris, 2015); Mark Dorrian and Frédéric Pousin, *Seeing from Above: The Aerial View in Visual Culture* (New York: I. B. Tauris, 2013); Hito Steyerl, "In Free Fall: A Thought Experiment on Vertical Perspective," in *The Wretched of the Screen*, ed. Franco Berardi (Berlin: Sternberg Press, 2012); Laura Kurgan, *Close up at a Distance: Mapping, Technology, and Politics* (Cambridge, MA: MIT Press, 2013); Caren Kaplan, *Aerial Aftermaths: Wartime from Above* (Durham, NC: Duke University Press, 2017); Sonja Dümpelmann, *Flights of Imagination: Aviation, Landscape, Design* (Charlottesville: University of Virginia Press, 2014); Jeanne Haffner, *The View from Above: The Science of Social Space* (Cambridge, MA: MIT Press, 2013), to name a few.
5. Dorrian and Pousin, *Seeing from Above*, 1; Seán Cubitt, *Digital Aesthetics* (London, Thousand Oaks, New Delhi: Sage Publications, 1998).
6. Paula Amad, "From God's-Eye to Camera-Eye: Aerial Photography's Post-Humanist and Neo-Humanist Visions of the World," *History of Photography* 36, no. 1 (February 2012): 66–86.
7. László Moholy-Nagy, *The New Vision and Abstract of an Artist* (New York: George Wittenborn, 1947); Le Corbusier, *Aircraft* (London: The Studio Publications Inc., 1935).
8. The important role of city symphonies here will be discussed in chapter 1. György Képes, *Language of Vision* (Chicago: Paul Theobald, 1944). Dziga Vertov,

Kino-Eye: The Writings of Dziga Vertov, ed. Annette Michelson, trans. Kevin O' Brien (Berkeley: University of California Press, 1984).

9. Siegfried Kracauer, "The Mass Ornament," in *The Mass Ornament*, ed. Thomas Y. Levin (Cambridge: Harvard University Press, 1995); Walter Benjamin, "The Work of Art in the Age of Mechanical Reproduction," in *Illuminations*, ed. Hannah Arendt (New York: Schocken, 1969); Walter Benjamin, "The Storyteller: Reflections on the Work of Nicolay Leskov," in *Illuminations* (New York: Schocken, 2007).
10. Martin Heidegger, "The Age of the World Picture," in *Science and the Quest for Reality* (New York: Springer, 1997), 70–80.
11. Allan Sekula, "The Instrumental Image-Steichen at War," *Artforum* 14, no. 4 (December 1975): 27.
12. Sekula, "The Instrumental Image-Steichen at War."
13. Virilio, *War and Cinema*.
14. Davide Deriu, "The Ascent of the Modern Planeur: Aerial Images and Urban Imaginary in the 1920s," in *Imagining The City, Volume 1* (2006); Kevin Lynch, "The Form of Cities," *Scientific American* 190, no. 4 (1954); Michel de Certeau, *The Practice of Everyday Life* (Berkeley: University of California Press, 1984); Haffner, *The View from Above*.
15. Kaplan, *Aerial Aftermaths: Wartime from Above*, loc. 1774.
16. Jacques Amont, "The Variable Eye or the Mobilization of the Gaze," in *The Image in Dispute: Art and Cinema in the Age of Photography*, ed. Dudley Andrew (Austin: University of Texas Press, 1997), 234.
17. Beaumont Newhall, *Airborne Camera: The World from the Air and Outer Space* (New York: Hasting House, 1969), 12.
18. Denis Cosgrove, *Apollo's Eye: A Cartographic Genealogy of the Earth in the Western Imagination* (Baltimore: Johns Hopkins University Press, 2001), 195; Amad, "From God's-Eye to Camera-Eye."; Donna Jeanne Haraway, "The Persistence of Vision," in *The Visual Culture Reader*, ed. Nicholas Mirzoeff (London: Routledge, 2001); Bruno Latour, *We Have Never Been Modern*, trans. Catherine Porter (New York: Harvester Wheatsheaf, 1993); Donna Jeanne Haraway, "Situated Knowledges: The Science Question in Feminism and the Privilege of Partial Perspective," *Feminist Studies* 14, no. 3 (1988).
19. Cosgrove, *Geography and Vision*, 12.
20. Matthew and Luke narratives (Luke 4:1–13 and Matthew 4:1–11), cited in Cosgrove, *Geography and Vision*, 12.
21. Amad, "From God's-Eye to Camera-Eye," 67.
22. Parks, "Vertical Mediation and the U.S. Drone War in the Horn of Africa." Drones have many official and unofficial acronyms. We discuss this terminology further in chapter 4. An overview of terms can also be found at "Drone, UAV, UAS, RPA or RPAS . . . ," AltiGator, accessed Januray 13, 2024, https://altigator.com/drone-uav-uas-rpa-or-rpas/.

23. Kaplan, *Aerial Aftermaths*; Parks and Kaplan, *Life in the Age of Drone Warfare*; Parks, "Vertical Mediation and the U.S. Drone War in the Horn of Africa"; Parks, *Rethinking Media Coverage*.

24. This close-up via tele-presence, however, is not proxistant vision as we define it in this book. That is, proxistant vision does not describe a real-time visual access to a "close-up from a distance," to use a phrase from Kurgan, *Close up at a Distance*. We define what constitutes proxistant vision further on under the heading "Proximity and Distance."

25. Parks, "Vertical Mediation and the U.S. Drone War in the Horn of Africa."

26. Derek Gregory, "From a View to a Kill: Drones and Late Modern War," *Theory, Culture & Society* 28, no. 7–8 (2011): 193. Such vertically proxistant layout becomes extraordinary with the combination of so-called "wide-area surveillance sensor systems" such as Gorgon Stare, a mosaic of several high-resolution cameras into one image, or the Argus-IS multi-giga pixel sensor. As Gregory has showed, this broadly cast recording of data navigates by "activity-based intelligence" in the attempt to establish a "pattern of life" that can signal unwanted activity on the ground.

27. Ian G. R. Shaw, *Predator Empire: Drone Warfare and Full Spectrum Dominance* (Minneapolis: University of Minnesota Press, 2016). See comprehensible research on drones at "About," Center for the Study of the Drone at Bard College, https://dronecenter.bard.edu/about/, accessed January 13, 2024. We offer a short review in chapter 4 as well.

28. Steyerl, "In Free Fall." László Moholy-Nagy, in his proposal for a "new vision" for the photographic medium in 1922, advocated for this change. Moholy-Nagy, *The New Vision and Abstract of an Artist*.

29. Anne Friedberg, *The Virtual Window: From Alberti to Microsoft* (Cambridge, MA: MIT Press, 2006).

30. Nicholas Mirzoeff, *The Right to Look: A Counterhistory of Visuality* (Durham: Duke University Press, 2011). We discuss the field of vision and visuality further later on in the chapter.

31. Steven Shaviro, *Post-Cinematic Affect* (Winchester: John Hunt Publishing, 2010).

32. Mark B. N. Hansen, "Algorithmic Sensibility: Reflections on the Post-Perceptual Image," in *Post-Cinema: Theorizing 21st-Century Film*, eds. Julia Leyda and Shane Denson (Falmer: Reframe Books, 2016), accessed January 13, 2024, http://reframe.sussex.ac.uk/post-cinema/6-3-hansen/.

33. Steen Ledet Christiansen, *Drone Age Cinema: Action Film and Sensory Assault* (New York: I.B. Tauris, 2016), loc 336.

34. William Brown, *Supercinema: Film-Philosophy for the Digital Age* (New York: Berghahn Books, 2013).

35. Kristen Whissel, *Spectacular Digital Effects: CGI and Contemporary Cinema* (Durham: Duke University Press, 2014).

36. Thomas Elsaesser, "The 'Return' of 3-D: On Some of the Logics and Genealogies of the Image in the Twenty-First Century," *Critical Inquiry* 39, no. 2 (2013): 241.

37. Elsaesser, "The 'Return' of 3-D," 242.

38. Harun Farocki, "Phantom Images," *Public* 29 (2004).

39. Aud Sissel Hoel and Frank Lindseth, "Differential Interventions: Images as Operative Tools," *Media Commons*, The Operative Image (2014), http://mediacommons.org/tne/cluster/operative-image, accessed June 9, 2024; Nanna Verhoeff, *Mobile Screens: The Visual Regime of Navigation* (Amsterdam University Press, 2012). Photosynth, Augmented Reality, and Google Street View have been case studies in these accounts.

40. Nigel Thrift, "Lifeworld Inc—and What to Do About It," *Environment and Planning D: Society and Space* 29, no. 1 (2011).

41. Bruce Sterling, *The Caryatids* (New York: Del Rey, 2009).

42. Tom Gunning, "The Birth of Film out of the Spirit of Modernity," in *Masterpieces of Modernist Cinema*, ed. Ted Perry (Bloomington: Indiana University Press, 2006), 13.

43. Virilio, *War and Cinema*, 21.

44. Tom Gunning, "'Nothing Will Have Taken Place—Except Place': The Unsettling Nature of Camera Movement," in *Screen Space Reconfigured*, eds. Susanne Ø. Sæther and Synne T. Bull (Amsterdam: Amsterdam University Press, 2020), 263–281.

45. David Bordwell, Kristin Thompson, and Jeff Smith, *Film Art: An Introduction*, 11th edition (New York: McGraw-Hill Education, 2017).

46. Cinemetircs measures the length and the number of individual shots across a feature film. See Mike Baxter, Daria Khitrova, and Yuri Tsivian, "Exploring Cutting Structure in Film, with Applications to the Films of D. W. Griffith, Mack Sennett, and Charlie Chaplin," *Digital Scholarship in the Humanities* 32, no. 1 (2015). The research project related to this article "Cinemetrics Across Boundaries: A Collaborative Study of Montage" can be seen here: https://neubauercollegium.uchicago.edu/faculty/cinemetrics/, accessed June 9, 2024.

47. Gunning, "Nothing Will Have Taken Place—Except Place."

48. Jakob Isak Nielsen, *Camera Movement in Narrative Cinema: Towards a Taxonomy of Functions* (Aarhus: University of Aarhus, 2007).

49. Daniel Morgan, *The Lure of the Image: Epistemic Fantasies of the Moving Camera* (Berkeley: University of California Press, 2021).

50. Teresa Castro, "Cinema's Mapping Impulse: Questioning Visual Culture," *The Cartographic Journal* 46, no. 1 (2009): 9–15; Tom Gunning, "The Cinema of Attraction," *Wide Angle* 3, no. 4 (1986); Tom Gunning, "Landscape and the Fantasy of Moving Pictures: Early Cinema's Phantom Rides," in *Cinema and Landscape*, eds. Graeme Harper and Jonathan Rayner (Bristol, Chicago: Intellect Books, 2010). See also newly published online catalog on the Lumière Brothers early films at "L'œuvre cinématographique des frères Lumière [The cinematographic

work of the Lumière brothers]," Catalogue Lumiere, https://catalogue-lumiere.com, accessed January 13, 2024. Through the concept of "the cinema of attraction," Tom Gunning has brought attention to the first decade of cinematic expressions, providing a sharp lens through which we can begin to grasp some of the most important ways in which the moving image modulate our perception.

51. Denis Cosgrove and William L. Fox, *Photography and Flight* (London: Reaktion Books, 2010), 9.

52. Tom Conley, *Cartographic Cinema* (Minneapolis: University of Minnesota Press, 2007), 1, 215 n2.

53. Timotheus Vermeulen, *Scenes from the Suburbs: The Suburb in Contemporary US Film and Television* (Edinburgh, Scotland: Edinburgh University Press, 2014).

54. Giuliana Bruno, *Atlas of Emotion: Journeys in Art, Architecture, and Film* (New York: Verso Books, 2002).

55. Castro, "Cinema's Mapping Impulse," 9.

56. François Penz and Richard Koeck, *Cinematic Urban Geographies* (New York: Palgrave Macmillan, 2017); Sébastien Caquard and D. R. Fraser Taylor, "What Is Cinematic Cartography?," *The Cartographic Journal* 46, no. 1 (2009): 5–8.

57. Eyal Weizman, *Hollow Land: Israel's Architecture of Occupation* (New York: Verso Books, 2012).

58. Stephen Graham, *Vertical: The City from Satellites to Bunkers* (New York: Verso Books, 2016).

59. Trevor Paglen, "Some Sketches on Vertical Geographies," *e-Flux Superhumanity* (2016), https://www.e-flux.com/architecture/superhumanity/68726/some-sketches-on-vertical-geographies/, accessed January 13, 2024.

60. Stuart Elden, "Secure the Volume: Vertical Geopolitics and the Depth of Power," *Political Geography* 34 (2013). Jeremy W. Crampton, "Assemblage of the Vertical: Commercial Drones and Algorithmic Life," *Geographica Helvetica* 71, no. 2 (2015); Peter Adey, "Securing the Volume/Volumen: Comments on Stuart Elden's Plenary Paper 'Secure the Volume,'" *Political Geography*, no. 34 (2013); Jeremy W. Crampton, "Cartographic Calculations of Territory," *Progress in Human Geography* 35, no. 1 (2011); Jeremy W. Crampton, "Cartography: Maps 2.0," *Progress in Human Geography* 33, no. 1 (2009).

61. Google Earth web-version launched April 18, 2017, "New Google Earth Web Version Available Now," *Google Earth Blog*, https://www.gearthblog.com/blog/archives/2017/04/new-google-earth-web-version-available-now.html, accessed January 13, 2024.

62. Rob Kitchin, Tracey P. Lauriault, and Matthew W. Wilson, *Understanding Spatial Media* (Los Angeles: Sage Publications Ltd., 2017), 2. The quote is from Eric Gordon and Adriana de Souza e Silva, *Net Locality: Why Location Matters in a Networked World* (Hoboken: Wiley-Blackwell, 2011).

63. Rob Kitchin and Martin Dodge, "Rethinking Maps," *Progress in Human Geography* 31, no. 3 (2007): 5.

64. Kitchin and Dodge, "Rethinking Maps."

65. Mary Ann Doane, "The Close-Up: Scale and Detail in the Cinema," *Differences* 14, no. 3 (2003): 89–111; André Bazin, *What Is Cinema?* Vol. 1, trans. Hugh Gray (Berkeley: University of California Press, 1967); Siegfried Kracauer, *Theory of Film: The Redemption of Physical Reality* (Princeton: Princeton University Press, 1997); Gilles Deleuze, *Cinema 1: The Movement-Image*. trans. Hugh Tomlinson and Barbara Habberjam (London: Athlone Press, 1986); Sergei Eisenstein, *Film Form: Essays in Film Theory*, ed. and trans. Jay Leyda (New York: Harcourt, 1949); Béla Balázs, *Theory of the Film: Character and Growth of a New Art*, trans. Edith Bone (New York: Dover Publications, 1970).

66. Zachary Horton, *The Cosmic Zoom: Scale, Knowledge, and Mediation* (Chicago: University of Chicago Press, 2021). Seán Cubitt, "Cosmic Zoom," lecture at the Event Horizon Symposium, Centre of Visual Arts, University of Melbourne, August 21, 2020, https://arts.unimelb.edu.au/research-unit-in-public-cultures/news-and-events/news-and-events/city-as-a-classroom-from-the-global-village-to-media-architecture-complex-with-professor-scott-mcquire3, accessed January 13, 2024. Joshua DiCaglio, *Scale Theory: A Nondisciplinary Inquiry* (Minneapolis: University of Minnesota Press, 2021).

67. Bruno Latour, "How Better to Register the Agency of Things," Tanner Lecture on Human Values, Yale University, March 26–27, 2014, https://web.archive.org/web/20240715071819/https://tannerlectures.utah.edu/_resources/documents/a-to-z/l/Latour%20manuscript.pdf, accessed June 9, 2024.

68. Related accounts, especially regarding Google Earth, have emphasized zoom and pan, but as we discuss in chapter 4 in "The 3D Model Flythrough," such concepts do not sufficiently account for the cinematic flight of this visual form. However, our concerns regarding the worldview this visual form signals do indeed relate to accounts such as Steven Johnson's and others, in which the zoom structures the way he sees the build-up of the universe. We discuss this in greater depth in chapter 3. Steven Johnson, "The Long Zoom," *The New York Times Magazine*, accessed June 9, 2024, https://www.nytimes.com/2006/10/08/magazine/08games.html.

69. Sarah Kember and Joanna Zylinska, *Life After New Media: Mediation as a Vital Process* (Cambridge, MA: MIT Press, 2012).

70. Parks, *Rethinking Media Coverage*, 182.

71. Nicholas Mirzoeff, "The Right to Look," *Critical Inquiry* 37, no. 3 (2011): 475.

72. Mirzoeff, *The Right to Look.*

73. W. J. T. Mitchell, *Picture Theory* (Chicago: University of Chicago Press, 1994); Anne Friedberg, *Window Shopping: Cinema and the Postmodern* (Berkeley: University of California Press, 1993); Friedberg, *The Virtual Window*; Martin Jay, "Scopic Regimes of Modernity," in *Vision and Visuality*, ed. Hal Foster (Seattle: Bay Press, 1988); Laura Mulvey, "Visual Pleasure and Narrative Cinema," in *Visual and Other Pleasures* (New York: Springer, 1989).

74. Gilles Deleuze, *Cinema 2: The Time-Image*, trans. Hugh Tomlinson and Robert Galeta (London: Continuum, 2005), 151.

75. Leonard Lawlor and Valentine Moulard-Leonard, "Henri Bergson," *The Stanford Encyclopedia of Philosophy*, Winter 2022 ed., eds. Edward N. Zalta and Uri Nodelman, https://plato.stanford.edu/archives/win2022/entries/bergson/, accessed June 10, 2024.

76. Henri Bergson, *Matter and Memory [Matière Et Mémoire]* (New York: Dover Publications, 2004), 38.

77. Bruno Latour, "Visualisation and Cognition: Drawing Things Together," in *Representation in Scientific Practice*, eds. Michael E. Lynch and Steve Woolgar (Cambridge, MA: MIT Press, 1990), 9; Svetlana Alpers, *The Art of Describing: Dutch Art in the Seventeenth Century* (Chicago: University of Chicago Press, 1983).

78. Latour, "Visualisation and Cognition," 9.

79. Jussi Parikka, *What Is Media Archaeology?* (Cambridge: Polity, 2012), 3.

80. Jussi Parikka, "Operative Media Archaeology: Wolfgang Ernst's Materialist Media Diagrammatics," *Theory, Culture & Society* 28, no. 5 (2011). Materialism here operates both on the level of physical operative machines and the new materialist attention to the self-organizing properties of matter. This differs from a Marxist's materialism.

81. Parikka, "Operative Media Archaeology," 65.

82. Wolfgang Ernst, *Digital Memory and the Archive*, ed. Jussi Parikka (Minneapolis: University Of Minnesota Press, 2013), 71.

83. Gilles Deleuze, *Foucault*, trans. Sean Hand (London: Boomsbury Academic, 2006), 34–35.

84. Manuel De Landa, "Deleuze, Diagrams, and the Genesis of Form," *Amerikastudien/American Studies* (2000): 34.

85. Gilles Deleuze and Claire Parnet, *Dialogues II* (New York: Columbia University Press, 2007), 69.

86. Exemplified by Aristotelian hylomorphism, which divides an object in its substance and form. See "Form vs. Matter," *Stanford Encyclopedia of Philosophy*, https://plato.stanford.edu/entries/form-matter/, accessed June 17, 2024.

87. Gilles Deleuze, *Francis Bacon: The Logic of Sensation* (London: Bloomsbury, 2005), 77.

88. Henri Bergson, *Creative Evolution* (Mineola, NY: Dover Publications, Inc., 1998).

89. Ina Blom, *The Autobiography of Video: The Life and Times of a Memory Technology* (Berlin: Sternberg Press, 2016); Matthew Fuller, *Media Ecologies: Materialist Energies in Art and Technoculture* (Cambridge, MA: MIT Press, 2005).

90. Deleuze, *Foucault*, 34–35.

91. Gilbert Simondon, "The Genesis of the Individual," in *Incorporations*, eds. Jonathan Crary and Sanford Kwinter (New York: Zone, 1992), 300.

92. Gilbert Simondon, "On the Mode of Existence of Technical Objects," *Deleuze Studies* 5, no. 3 (2011).

93. Benjamin H. Bratton, *The Stack: On Software and Sovereignty* (Cambridge, MA: MIT Press, 2016); Jennifer Gabrys, *Program Earth: Environmental Sensing Technology and the Making of a Computational Planet* (Minneapolis: University of Minnesota Press, 2016).

94. Parikka, "Operative Media Archaeology."

95. Liv Hausken, ed. *Thinking Media Aesthetics: Media Studies, Film Studies and the Arts* (Frankfurt am Main: Peter Lang, 2013).

96. Parikka, "Operative Media Archaeology," 10.

97. In this statement we draw on the insights of Bernhard Siegert, "The map *is* the territory," *Radical Philosophy*, no. 169 (September/October 2011), 13–16.

98. Thomas Elsaesser, "The New Film History as Media Archaeology," *Cinémas: revue d'études cinématographiques/Cinémas: Journal of Film Studies* 14, no. 2–3 (2004). This is an old text and Elsaesser has since voiced more critical views to the concept of media archeology. We however, subscribe to the ideas offered in the previously cited text. See Thomas Elsaesser, *Film History as Media Archaeology: Tracking Digital Cinema* (Amsterdam: Amsterdam University Press, 2019).

99. Elsaesser, Film History as Media Archaeology, 9, 80.

100. Wanda Strauven, *The Cinema of Attractions Reloaded* (Amsterdam: Amsterdam University Press, 2006); Wanda Strauven, "Media Archaeology: Where Film History, Media Art and New Media (Can) Meet," *Preserving and Exhibiting Media Art*, eds. Julia Noordegraaf, Barbara Maitre, and Vinzenz Hediger (Amsterdam: Amsterdam University Press, 2013), 59–79. A broad backdrop to this research includes Crary's *Techniques of the Observer*, Doane's *The Emergence of Cinematic Time*, and Bolter and Grusin's *Remediation*, as well Lev Manovich, *The Language of New Media* (Cambridge, MA: MIT Press, 2002). Furthermore, Pavle Levi's, Anne Friedberg's, and Giuliana Bruno's works have been central to seeing cinema outside its limitation of the celluloid. Pavle Levi, *Cinema by Other Means* (Oxford: Oxford University Press, 2012); Friedberg, *Window Shopping: Cinema and the Postmodern*; Giuliana Bruno, *Surface: Matters of Aesthetics, Materiality, and Media* (Chicago: University of Chicago Press, 2014).

101. Bernhard Siegert, *Cultural Techniques: Grids, Filters, Doors and Other Articulations of the Real*, trans. Geoffrey Winthrop-Young (New York: Fordham University Press, 2015), 13.

102. Siegert, *Cultural Techniques.*

103. Gilles Deleuze and Félix Guattari, *What is Philosophy?*, trans. Hugh Tomlinson and Graham Burchell (New York: Columbia University Press, 1994), 18.

104. Seán Cubitt, "Cosmic Zoom," lecture at Event Horizon, August 21, 2020, https://sites.research.unimelb.edu.au/cova/projects/symposia/symposia-and-seminars-2020/event-horizon/test-3/sean-cubitt, accessed June 8, 2024; Joshua DiCaglio, *Scale Theory: A Nondisciplinary Inquiry* (Minneapolis: University of Minnesota

Press, 2021); Mary Anne Doane, *Bigger Than Life: The Close-Up and Scale in the Cinema* (Durham, NC: Duke University Press, 2022); Nick Hall, *The Zoom: Drama at the Touch of a Lever* (New Brunswick, NJ: Rutgers University Press, 2018); Zachary Horton, *The Cosmic Zoom: Scale, Knowledge, and Mediation* (Chicago: University of Chicago Press, 2021).

105. Deleuze and Guattari, *What is Philosophy?*, 23.

106. As the literary third-person form as an all-knowing narrator indicates, this view is an all-seeing, everywhere view, also linked to Michel Foucault's idea that power and knowledge are not separate entities but are interlinked and co-constitutive. Michel Foucault, *Discipline and Punish: The Birth of the Prison*, trans. Alan Sheridan (New York: Vintage Books, 1995).

107. Henk Borgdorff, "The Production of Knowledge in Artistic Research," in Michael Biggs and Henrik Karlsson, eds., *The Routledge Companion to Research in the Arts*, Routledge Art History and Visual Studies Companions (Abingdon, UK: Routledge, 2011).

108. The London Eye was formally opened by the Prime Minister Tony Blair on December 31, 1999, but did not open to the paying public until March 9, 2000 because of a capsule clutch problem. "London's Big Wheel Birthday," *CNN*, http://edition.cnn.com/2001/WORLD/europe/UK/03/08/millennium.wheel/, accessed June 17, 2024.

109. This installation premiered in its full version at the exhibition Bull.Miletic: Proxistant Vision at the San Francisco Museum of Craft and Design, November 19, 2022–March 19, 2023.

110. Gabrys, *Program Earth*.

111. Carl Sagan, *Pale Blue Dot: A Vision of the Human Future in Space* (New York: Random House, 1994), 8.

112. See, for instance, Michael Tavel Clarke and David Wittenberg, *Scale in Literature and Culture* (Cham, Switzerland: Springer International Publishing, 2017).

113. Bruno Latour and Timothy M. Lenton, "Extending the Domain of Freedom, or Why Gaia Is So Hard to Understand," *Critical Inquiry* 45, no. 3 (2019).

PART I

1. *Ferriscope (1893–2020)* was preliminarily exhibited in a solo exhibition at the Trondheim Art Museum between October 13, 2018, and January 6, 2019. In the spring of 2019, the artwork was exhibited in A Video Event at Experimental Intermedia in New York. *Ferriscope* received the Excellence Award at the Japan Media Arts Festival in 2020, and it was nominated for the New Technological Art Award, Zebrastraat, Ghent, Belgium, in 2022. From November 19, 2022, through March 19, 2023, *Ferriscope* was featured in Proxistant Vision, a solo exhibition at the Museum of Craft and Design in San Francisco. The *Ferriscope* kinetic installation was acquired by the National Museum in 2021. Video documentation

of the work can be previewed online, https://bull.miletic.info/works/ferriscope, accessed June 9, 2024.

CHAPTER 1

1. Kathryn Gibbs Davis, *Mr. Ferris and His Wheel* (New York: Clarion Books, 2014), 39.
2. Dubai Eye, or Ain Dubai, closed shortly upon its opening and is currently not in operation. "Ain Dubai, the world's largest Ferris wheel, remains closed indefinitely," CNBCTV 18, https://www.cnbctv18.com/world/ain-dubai-the-world-largest-ferris-wheel-remains-closed-indefinitely-17455961.htm, accessed January 13, 2024.
3. The New York Wheel project ended in 2018 due to lack of funds. "De Blasio: No bailout for Staten Island Ferris wheel project," *New York Post*, https://nypost.com/2018/09/21/de-blasio-no-bail-out-for-staten-island-ferris-wheel-project/, accessed January 13, 2024.
4. Synne Tollerud Bull, "Kinetic Architecture and Aerial Rides: Towards a Media Archeology of the Revolving Restaurant View," *Journal of Contemporary Archaeology* 2, no. 1 (September 2015): 58–66.
5. Wolfgang Schivelbusch, *The Railway Journey: The Industrialization of Space and Time* (Berkeley: University of California Press, 1986), 64.
6. Giuliana Bruno, "Haptic Space: Film and the Geography of Modernity," in *Visualizing the City*, eds. Alan Marcus and Dietrich Neumann, *The Architext Series* (London: Routledge, 2007), 13. See also anthologies such as Laren Rabinovitz, "From Hale's Tours to Star Tours: Virtual Voyages and the Delerium of the Hyper-Real," in *Virtual Voyages*, ed. Jeffrey Ruoff (Durham, NC: Duke University Press, 2006); Linda Williams, *Viewing Positions: Ways of Seeing Film* (New Brunswick, NJ: Rutgers University Press, 1995).
7. Michel Foucault, *The Order of Things: An Archaeology of the Human Sciences* (London: Routledge, 2002), 319.
8. David E. Nye, *American Technological Sublime* (Cambridge, MA: MIT Press, 1994), xxi. Nye defines the technological sublime as "repeated experiences of awe and wonder, often tinged with an element of terror, which people have had when confronted with particular natural sites, architectural forms, and technological achievements."
9. Levi, *Cinema by Other Means*, xii.
10. Levi, *Cinema by Other Means*, 42–43.
11. Norman D. Anderson, *Ferris Wheels: An Illustrated History* (Bowling Green: Bowling Green State University Popular Press, 1992), 3.
12. John F. Kasson, *Amusing the Million: Coney Island at the Turn of the Century* (Toronto: HarperCollins Canada Ltd, 1996), 3.
13. Kasson, *Amusing the Million*.

14. Daniel Burnham, cited in Norm Bolotin and Christine Laing, *The World's Columbian Exposition: The Chicago World's Fair of 1893* (Champaign: University of Illinois Press, 2002), 23.

15. Anderson, *Ferris Wheels*, 50.

16. This involved the so-called "Bessemer process" introduced in 1855, which enabled large-scale steel production to replace iron as the most commonly used structural material.

17. Other accounts of Ferris as the sole originator can be found flourishing online as well as in booklets and other information materials from the Columbian World's Fair. Examples mentioned here are but a few: Davis, *Mr. Ferris and His Wheel*; John A. Kouwenhoven, "Eiffel Tower and the Ferris Wheel," *Arts Magazine* 54, no. 6 (June 1980); Jamie Malanowski, "The Brief History of the Ferris Wheel: Originally the American Answer to the Eiffel Tower, the Summertime Amusement Became a Hallmark of Summer Fun," *Smithsonian* 2015, no. X (June 2015).

18. Chad Randl, *Revolving Architecture: A History of Buildings That Rotate, Swivel, and Pivot* (New York: Princeton Architectural Press, 2008). Anderson, *Ferris Wheels*, 50.

19. Anderson, *Ferris Wheels*, 29.

20. Anderson, *Ferris Wheels*, 29.

21. Anderson, *Ferris Wheels*, 45.

22. James Gilbert, *Perfect Cities: Chicago's Utopias of 1893* (Chicago: University of Chicago Press, 1991).

23. Kasson, *Amusing the Million.*

24. Erik Larson, *The Devil in the White City: Murder, Magic, and Madness at the Fair That Changed America* (New York: Vintage Books, 2004), 13.

25. Indeed, it is to this date considered the most influential of its kind in history, according to Gilbert, *Perfect Cities*. Its former location in Chicago still bears the name Midway, and the concept was so powerful that this term still signifies a wide variety of amusement parks in our time. Examples are plenty, such as Midway State Park, NY, "Midway State Park," New York State Department of Parks, Recreation, and Historic Preservation, https://parks.ny.gov/parks/167/details.aspx, accessed January 13, 2024; and North American Midway Entertainment, IN, "North American Midway Entertainment," https://www.namidway.com, accessed January 13, 2024. Furthermore, Merriam-Webster's definition of midway suggests: an avenue at a fair, carnival, or amusement park for concessions and amusements.

26. Kasson, *Amusing the Million*; Larson, *The Devil in the White City*; Gilbert, *Perfect Cities*; Dorrian, *Writing on the Image*, to mention but a few.

27. The White City itself, constructed in cheap materials like plaster, plywood, and papier-mâché, was primarily built to be looked at. This practice of cheaply but convincingly putting together entire cities solely for the camera continues in

global cinematic productions for several decades before now gradually being replaced by computer-generated imagery.

28. Forming the milieu for the early "cinema of attraction" that appears a few years later, as argued by Gunning. Tom Gunning, "The World as Object Lesson: Cinema Audiences, Visual Culture and the St. Louis World's Fair, 1904," *Film History* 6, no. 4 (Winter 1994).

29. "One revolution of this wheel is made in about ten minutes, and there are two revolutions for a ride. There are six stops for every revolution, which permits the emptying and filling of six cars from twelve raised platforms, six on each side for ingress and egress." George Washington Gale Ferris Jr., *Souvenir of a Ride on the Ferris Wheel at the World's Fair, Chicago* (Chicago: American Engraving Co., 1893), 5.

30. Kasson, *Amusing the Million*, 23. Helen Lefkowitz Horowitz, *Culture & the City: Cultural Philanthropy in Chicago from the 1880's to 1917* (Lexington: University Press of Kentucky, 1976). "Little Egypt" was the stage name for a number of belly dancers and performers around the turn of the twentieth century in the US.

31. Dorrian, *Writing on the Image*.

32. Jonathan Crary, *Techniques of the Observer: On Vision and Modernity in the Nineteenth Century* (Cambridge, MA: MIT Press, 1992).

33. Jonathan Crary emphasizes the benefits of thinking with the observer and the observed rather than simply vision or spectator. This shows, according to Crary, the participatory nature on the part of the observer which is fully and actively involved. Crary, *Techniques of the Observer*, 1–3.

34. Anderson, *Ferris Wheels*, 68.

35. Marietta Holley, *Samantha At The World's Fair* (New York: Funk & Wagnalls, 1893), 620–621.

36. Robert Graves, "North Side: George Ferris, the Big Ferris Wheel," *The Alleghenian* (July 1893), http://www.info-ren.org/projects/btul/exhibit/neighborhoods/northside/nor_n105b.html, accessed January 13, 2024.

37. Ferris Jr., *Souvenir of a Ride on the Ferris Wheel at the World's Fair, Chicago.*

38. From the time we can assume that the choice of pictures included in this booklet was highly deliberate. Even though Kodak launched its "portable" camera in time for the Fair, photography in 1893 was still a cumbersome and very expensive enterprise. In addition, photography at the fair was highly regulated by costly permissions.

39. Image caption as printed in the booklet. Ferris Jr., *Souvenir of a Ride on the Ferris Wheel at the World's Fair, Chicago.*

40. "Origins of Motion Pictures," Library of Congress, https://www.loc.gov/collections/edison-company-motion-pictures-and-sound-recordings/articles-and-essays/history-of-edison-motion-pictures/origins-of-motion-pictures/, accessed January 13, 2024.

41. Charles Musser, "Kinetoscope" in *Encyclopedia of Early Cinema*, ed. Richard Abel (London: Routledge, 2005), 516. Virgilio Tosi, *Cinema Before Cinema: The Origins*

of Scientific Cinematography (London: British Universities Film & Video Council, 2005), 212.

42. Tosi, *Cinema Before Cinema*, 76.

43. Zoöpraxographical Hall can be clearly identified on the two photographs in the *Souvenir of a Ride on the Ferris Wheel at the World's Fair, Chicago*.

44. Mark Hudson, "Eadweard Muybridge: the Moving Story of a Mysterious Pioneer," *The Telegraph* (September, 2010), https://www.telegraph.co.uk/culture/art/art-features/7980477/Eadweard-Muybridge-the-moving-story-of-a-mysterious-pioneer.html, accessed January 13, 2024.

45. John J. Flinn, *Official Guide to Midway Plaisance* (Chicago: The Columbian Guide Company, 1893), 20, https://archive.org/details/officialguidetomooflin/page/20, accessed January 13, 2024.

46. Among many others, Hubert Howe Bancroft, *The Book of the Fair: An Historical and Descriptive Presentation of the World's Science, Art and Industry, as Viewed through the Columbian Exposition at Chicago in 1893*, vol. 9 (Chicago, San Francisco: The Bancroft Company, 1893), 863, https://archive.org/details/bookfair9banc/page/863, accessed January 13, 2024; and Eadweard Muybridge, *Descriptive Zoopraxography, or, The science of animal locomotion made popular* (Chicago: The Lakeside Press, 1893), 1, https://wellcomecollection.org/works/v6weam2e/items?canvas=19, accessed January 13, 2024. In Stanley Appelbaum, *The Chicago World's Fair of 1893* (New York: Dover Publications, Inc., 1980), 101, captions of the photograph No. 126 read "Muybridge's Zoöpraxographical Hall, with a minaret from A Street in Cairo." The photograph shows only a part of the hall with capital letters "ZOOP" visible above the entrance.

47. Roland Hancock, "The World's First Films," *The Telegraph*, October 1, 2010; no longer accessible online.

48. Jonathan Crary situates the origins of the thaumatrope back to the early 1820s, when the interest in the phenomena of afterimages led to experimental designs of a variety of optical devices. Crary, *Techniques of the Observer*.

49. See entry on "movement perception" in *Encyclopædia Britannica*, https://www.britannica.com/science/movement-perception#ref488126, accessed January 13, 2024.

50. Gunning, "Hand and Eye," 5.

51. Gunning, "Hand and Eye," 3.

52. Gunning, "Hand and Eye," 3.

CHAPTER 2

1. Ebenezer Slimmens (A. J. Dockarty), *The Midway Pleasance: The Experience of an Innocent Boy from Vermont in the Famous Midway* (Chicago: Chicago World Book Co., 1894).

2. Iain Sinclair, *Sorry Meniscus: Excursions to the Millennium Dome* (London: Profile Books, 1999), 8. Cited in Mark Dorrian, "'The Way the World Sees London': Thoughts on a Millennial Urban Spectacle," in *Writing on the Image: Architecture, the City and the Politics of Representation* (London: Bloomsbury Publishing, 2015), 78.
3. This has been the ongoing topic of the research by the New Film History as referred to in our introduction.
4. We have studied this structure in an earlier work. Please see *Par Hasard*, Bull. Miletic, https://bull.miletic.info/works/par-hasard, accessed January 13, 2024.
5. *Scene from the elevator ascending Eiffel Tower*, Library of Congress, https://www.loc.gov/item/00694299/, accessed January 13, 2024.
6. Tom Gunning, "The Cinema of Attraction: Early Film, Its Spectator, and the Avant-Garde," in *Eary Cinema. Space, Frame, Narrative*, ed. Thomas Elsaesser (London: BFI Publishing, 1990), 56–62.
7. *Scene from the elevator ascending Eiffel Tower*, Library of Congress, https://www.loc.gov/item/00694299/, accessed January 13, 2024.
8. Paula Amad, "From God's-Eye to Camera-Eye: Aerial Photography's Post-Humanist and Neo-Humanist Visions of the World," *History of Photography* 36, no. 1 (February 2012): 66–86.
9. Denis Cosgrove, *Geography and Vision: Seeing, Imagining and Representing the World* (London: Bloomsbury Publishing, 2012), 3.
10. Teresa Castro, "Cinema's Mapping Impulse: Questioning Visual Culture," *The Cartographic Journal* 46, no. 1 (July 2013): 9–15.
11. Christian Jacob and Edward H. Dahl, *The Sovereign Map: Theoretical Approaches in Cartography Throughout History [L'empire Des Cartes Approche Théoretique De La Cartographie À Travers L'histoire]* (Chicago: University of Chicago Press, 2006), 104.
12. "Die letzte Schraube. Die Vollendung des Riesenrades in 'Venedig' [The Last Screw: The Completion of the Ferris Wheel in 'Venice']," front-page headlines in *Illustrirte Wiener Extrablatt*, June 25, 1897, no. 173, reproduced in Helmut Jahn and Peter Petritsch, *The Vienna Giant Ferris Wheel* (1989), 11.
13. We are indebted to Mark Dorrian's brilliant account of the Ferris wheel in Mark Dorrian, "Cityscape with Ferris Wheel: Chicago, 1893," in *Urban Space and Cityscapes*, ed. Christoph Lindner (London: Routledge, 2006), 17–37. Even though Dorrian's investigation does not point out reference to the moving image, his analysis provides an important backbone to our investigation.
14. Bruno, "Haptic Space: Film and the Geography of Modernity," 13.
15. Bruno, "Haptic Space: Film and the Geography of Modernity," 14.
16. Bruno, "Haptic Space: Film and the Geography of Modernity," 14.
17. For an excellent reading on the popularity of the panorama in nineteenth-century visual culture and its relation to the moving image, see Tom Gunning, "Landscape and the Fantasy of Moving Pictures: Early Cinema's Phantom

Rides," in *Cinema and Landscape*, eds. Graeme Harper and Jonathan Rayner (Bristol: Intellect, 2010), 31–70.

18. Markman Ellis, "'Spectacles within Doors': Panoramas of London in the 1790s," *Romanticism* 14, no. 2 (July 2008), https://doi.org/10.3366/E1354991X0800024X, accessed December 30, 2024.
19. Caren Kaplan, *Aerial Aftermaths: Wartime from Above* (Durham, NC: Duke University Press, 2018), 78.
20. Walter Benjamin, *Arcades Project* (1999), 532, cited in Ellis, "'Spectacles within Doors.'"
21. On the importance of the horizon for the sense of virtual mobility, see Oettermann, *The Panorama*.
22. Erkki Huhtamo, *Illusions in Motion: Media Archaeology of the Moving Panorama and Related Spectacles* (Cambridge, MA: MIT Press, 2013).
23. Nadar, *Quand j'étais photographe* (Paris: Flammarison, 1900), 77–78, cited in Michel Frizot, "Another Kind of Photography: New Points of View," *A New History of Photography* (Cologne: Könemann, 1998), 386–97.
24. Roland Barthes, "The Eiffel Tower," in *A Barthes Reader*, ed. Susan Sontag (New York: Hill and Wang, 1982), 242.
25. Barthes, "The Eiffel Tower," 242.
26. Walter Benjamin, *Charles Baudelaire: A Lyric Poet in the Era of High Capitalism*, 174., cited in Dorrian, *Writing on the Image*, 26.
27. Mark Dorrian, "The Aerial View: Notes for a Cultural History," *Strates. Materiaux pour la recherche en sciences sociales*, no. 13 (2007), http://strates.revues.org/5573, accessed December 30, 2024. Dorrian notes in this article that the view of the city from above provided a recuperative effect.
28. Oslo's *Sneak Peak*, "a 90-metre lookout tower at Tjuvholmen with a glass elevator" is an alternative to the observation wheel that operates on the same principles. See "The Sneak Peak," Tripadvisor, https://www.tripadvisor.com/Attraction_Review-g190479-d4222488-Reviews-The_Sneak_Peak-Oslo_Eastern_Norway.html, accessed January 13, 2024.
29. Le Corbusier et al., *Aircraft*.
30. Haffner, *The View from Above: The Science of Social Space*.
31. Henri Lefebvre, *The Production of Space*, La Production De L'éspace (Oxford: Blackwell, 1991).
32. Cosgrove and Fox, *Photography and Flight*, 15.
33. Cosgrove and Fox, *Photography and Flight*, 15.
34. These ideas about the overview of the city were present in the discussion of early American urban development in the context of the construction of the Ferris wheel for the 1893 Columbian World's fair in Chicago.
35. Cosgrove and Fox, *Photography and Flight*, 21.
36. James A. Schmiechen, "The Victorians, the Historians, and the Idea of Modernism," *The American Historical Review* 93, no. 2 (1988): 315.

37. John R. Mullin and Kenneth Payne, "Thoughts on Edward Bellamy as City Planner: The Ordered Art of Geometry," *Landscape Architecture & Regional Planning* 34 (1997).
38. Gilbert, *Perfect Cities*, 19.
39. Gilbert, *Perfect Cities*, 19.
40. Cosgrove, *Geography and Vision: Seeing, Imagining and Representing the World*, 12, 173.
41. Gilbert, *Perfect Cities*, 19.
42. "Bird's Eye View of the World's Columbian Exposition, Chicago, 1893," Library of Congress, https://www.loc.gov/resource/g4104c.pm001522/, accessed January 13, 2024.
43. We return to 3D maps in the Airborne section of this book.
44. François Penz makes a good case for reading this collection of maps as an early form of cinema. François Penz, "The Cinema in the Map—the Case of Braun and Hogenberg's *Civitates Orbis Terrarum*," in *Cinematic Urban Geographies*, ed. François Penz and Richard Koeck (New York: Palgrave Macmillian, 2017).
45. Oxford English Dictionary, 2nd edition, cited in Dorrian, *Writing on the Image*, 25.
46. Alpers. (1983). The art of describing Dutch art in the seventeenth century (pp. xxvii, 273, pl.). John Murray.
47. Teresa Castro, "Cinematic Cartographies of Urban Space and the Descriptive Spectacle of Aerial Views (1898–1948)," in *Cinematic Urban Geographies*, ed. François Penz and Richard Koeck (New York: Palgrave Macmillan, 2017), 47.
48. Bruno, *Atlas of Emotion*.
49. The birthplace of this breed of progressive venues is generally held to be London, and the Great Exhibition of the Works of Industry of All Nations that took place in 1851.
50. Gilbert, *Perfect Cities*.
51. Gilbert, *Perfect Cities*.
52. Dean MacCannell, *The Tourist: A New Theory of the Leisure Class* (Berkeley: University of California Press, 1999), 13, 55.
53. Phrase from the millennium monument competition announcement in The Sunday Times, October 24, 1993. Cited in Marks Barfield Architects, ed. *Eye: The Story Behind the London Eye* (London: Black Dog, 2007).
54. Marks Barfield Architects, *Eye*.
55. Marks Barfield Architects, *Eye*.
56. Sir Richard Rogers, "Eye: The Story Behind the London Eye," in *Eye: The Story Behind the London Eye*, ed. Marks Barfield Architects (London: Black Dog Publishing, 2007), 8.
57. Guy Debord, *The Society of the Spectacle*, trans. Donald Nicholson-Smith (New York: Zone Books, 1994), 26. Emphasis original.

58. Dorrian, *Writing on the Image*, 86.

59. Dorrian, *Writing on the Image*, 86.

60. The entrance to London Eye experience is accompanied by a complimentary four-dimensional proxistant film abounding in masterful aerial cinematography.

61. As identified by the Columbia Film Language Glossary, "(a)n establishing shot is a long shot at the start of a scene (or sequence) that shows things from a distance. Often an aerial shot, it is intended to help identify and orient the location or time for the scene and action that follow." "Establishing Shot," *The Columbia Film Language Glossary*, https://filmglossary.ccnmtl.columbia.edu/term/establishing-shot/, accessed January 13, 2024. A compelling complication of cinematic establishing shots from well-known mainstream films can be seen at "Beautiful Establishing Shots Compilation in Movies [HD] by X2," YouTube video, 1:47, uploaded January 15, 2013, https://youtu.be/AxtonETgEXo, accessed January 13, 2024. A further discussion on the role of the establishing shot in narrative cinema is beyond the scope of this book.

62. "New York Wheel FlyOver," YouTube video, 1:43, uploaded May 7, 2017, https://youtu.be/erWRGCqVbBY, accessed January 13, 2024.

63. Dorrian, "The Aerial View," 15.

64. Dorrian, "The Aerial View," 15.

65. Cosgrove, *Geography and Vision*, 12, 178.

66. Latour, "Visualisation and Cognition."

67. Latour, "Visualisation and Cognition."

68. Gene Youngblood, *Expanded Cinema* (London: Studio Vista Limited, 1970), 84.

69. "Poetic Spaces of Human Experience—Art and Research | Jan Schacher & Daniel Bisig | TEDxZurich," YouTube video, 11:36, uploaded April 8, 2019, https://youtu.be/oFtoSVo9A_g, accessed January 13, 2024.

CHAPTER 3

1. In contrast to the English noun *readymade*, the French adjective *trouvé*, which translates as *found*, *invented*, or *imagined*, aptly describes the experience.

2. Gunning, "The Cinema of Attraction." Regarding Hale's Tours, it is interesting to note that this early cinematic experiment of rides and cinema has continued today in its most innovative fusion in dark-rides such as "Soarin' Around the World" (Disneyland) and "Harry Potter and the Forbidden Journey" (Universal Studios).

3. Genealogy here refers to the trace of early cinematic exploration of mechanical urban structures ref. argument developed in chapter 1.

4. Rosalind E. Krauss, *The Originality of the Avant-Garde and Other Modernist Myths* (Cambridge, MA: MIT Press, 1986), 272.

5. Tom Gunning, "An Unseen Energy Swallows Space: The Space in Early Film and Its Relation to American Avant-Garde Film," in *Film Before Griffith* (Berkeley: University of California Press, 1983).
6. Peter Gidal, "Theory and Definition of Structural/Materialist Film" in *Structural Film Anthology*, ed. Peter Gidal (London: British Film Institute, 1976, 1978), 1.
7. Gidal, "Theory and Definition of Structural/Materialist Film," 2.
8. Gidal, "Theory and Definition of Structural/Materialist Film."
9. Gidal, "Theory and Definition of Structural/Materialist Film," 14.
10. Malcolm Le Grice, *Abstract Film and Beyond* (Cambridge, MA: MIT Press, 1982) cited in Gidal, "Theory and Definition of Structural/Materialist Film," 27.
11. Gunning, "An Unseen Energy Swallows Space."
12. An excerpt of this title sequence can be seen in "La Notte. Antonioni. 1961. Opening Credits," YouTube video, 2:17, uploaded July 22, 2015, https://youtu.be/wM6j5AFv_hU, accessed January 13, 2024.
13. Steven Higgins, *Still Moving: The Film and Media Collections of the Museum of Modern Art* (New York: The Museum of Modern Art, 2006).
14. "Runa Islam: Time Lines," *White Cube*, https://whitecube.com/exhibitions/exhibition/runa_islam_hoxton_square_2005, accessed January 13, 2024.
15. "Runa Islam: Time Lines," *White Cube*.
16. Voiceover in *A Memorial to Failure* (2013) by Mahmod Khaled.
17. We began experimenting with this technique during our residency at the University of Chicago in spring 2012, in parallel with the initial research on the "original" Ferris wheel. In 2013, we publicly exhibited our first kinetic video installation *Heaven Can Wait* at KinoKino in Sandnes, Norway, by constructing twenty-four slowly revolving projectors that projected 360-degree video panoramas we filmed in revolving restaurants around the world since 2001. Notably, the exhibition was a culmination of artistic research project *Re:Place* (2012–2013)—the first of a kind funded by the Norwegian Artistic Research Program.
18. For an alternative way to put it, this is a study of how the moving image influences cognitive perception amidst conditions of perceptual ambiguity. However, there is a poetic dimension by which the moving image moves thought that we share with the scholarship of Gilles Deleuze in his legendary books *Cinema 1 and Cinema 2*.
19. Our research is particularly informed by the theories of Gilbert Simondon and Donna Haraway, and it is further contextualized by the contributions of Jennifer Gabrys, especially her work in her monograph Gabrys, *Program Earth*.
20. Henk Borgdorff, "The Debate on Research in the Arts," *Sensuous Knowledge* no. 02 (Bergen: Bergen Academy of Art and Design, 2006), 12. Here, Borgdorff builds on an earlier text by Christopher Frayling; Christopher Frayling, "Research in Art and Design," *Royal College of Art Research Papers* (London: Royal College of Art, 1993).

21. Scandinavian and many European institutions of higher art education, which now also offer PhD programs in artistic research, have collectively embraced this development since the early 2000s through organizations such as the Society for Artistic Research (SAR), the European League of Institutes of the Arts (ELIA), and the European Artistic Research Network (EARN).

22. Tom Holert, "Art in the Knowledge-based Polis," *e-flux Journal* 3 (2009), https://www.e-flux.com/journal/03/68537/art-in-the-knowledge-based-polis/, accessed January 13, 2024; see also his recent book Tom Holert, *Knowledge Beside Itself: Contemporary Art's Epistemic Politics* (Berlin: Sternberg Press, 2020).

23. Tim Ingold, "Search and Search Again: On the Meaning of Research in Art," Centre for Contemporary Arts Glasgow, https://www.cca-glasgow.com/journal/tim-ingold-search-and-search-again-on-the-meaning-of-research-in-art, accessed January 18, 2024. See also Tim Ingold's personal website, https://www.timingold.com, accessed January 13, 2024. Many previous publications are also relevant here, such as Tim Ingold, *Making: Anthropology, Archaeology, Art and Architecture* (Abingdon: Routledge, 2013).

24. Rahel Aima, "Firing Blanks: Hito Steyerl and the Voiding of Research Art," *Momus*, https://momus.ca/firing-blanks-hito-steyerl-and-the-voiding-of-research-art/, accessed January 13, 2024; and Laura Belik, "Mapping as Research with Trevor Paglen," Global Urban Humanities, University of California, Berkeley, https://globalurbanhumanities.berkeley.edu/blog/mapping-as-research-with-trevor-paglen, accessed January 13, 2024.

25. Six of these photographs are from the pamphlet produced to promote the wheel at the fair, also referenced in chapter 1.

26. The photographs were discovered at the University of Chicago Special Collections Research Center, Chicago Historical Society, Chicago Public Library, Douglas County Historical Society, Brooklyn Museum, and numerous private collections.

27. Artemis Willis, "Performing Pictures: The Magic Lantern c. 1900" (PhD diss., University of Chicago, 2020). Willis is currently working on a forthcoming monograph titled *Lanternology: The Magic Lantern and the Possibilities of the Projected Image*, to be published by MIT Press. "Lanternology: The Magic Lantern and the Possibilities of the Projected Image," *MIT Open Documentary Lab*, http://opendoclab.mit.edu/presents/lanternology/, accessed January 13, 2024.

28. This was made possible with the generous assistance of Jan C. Schacher at the Institute for Computer Music and Sound Technology, Zurich University of the Arts.

29. This rainbow effect pertains to single-chip DLP projectors, which feature color wheels. We will continue to refer to this type of projector throughout this text.

30. Evan Powell, "The Great Technology War: LCD vs. DLP," *Projector Central*, https://www.projectorcentral.com/lcd_dlp_update7.htm?page=Rainbow-Artifacts, accessed January 13, 2024.

31. More advanced projectors feature color wheels with more color filters.
32. More scientific literature on DMD can be found at "Digital Micromirror Device," *ScienceDirect*, https://www.sciencedirect.com/topics/engineering/digital-micro mirror-device, accessed January 14, 2024.
33. "The Great Wheel at Chicago," *Scientific American* 59, no. 1 (July 1893): 8–9. It is worth noting that a 1 kHz tone is the most common reference tone in audio engineering, used for calibration of audio/video equipment.
34. Edvine Larsen, Facebook message to authors, October 16, 2018.
35. Bruno Latour, "Visualisation and Cognition: Drawing Things Together," Avant: Trends in Interdisciplinary Studies 3, no. T (2012): 207–260.

PART II

1. The *Venetie 11111100110* (1500–2022) prototype was preliminarily exhibited as a single-channel video in the spring of 2017 in a group show You Gotta Say Yes to Another Access at the 2nd Research Pavilion in Venice. In the summer of 2017, the artwork was exhibited with the series of three ink-jet prints *Venetie MMXVII* (1500–2017) in a solo show *Venetie* at Anglim Gilbert Gallery in San Francisco. The kinetic version was completed in 2022 for Proxistant Vision, a solo exhibition at the Museum of Craft and Design in San Francisco. Another iteration of the kinetic version was publicly exhibited in a solo show at Regelbau 411 Center for Contemporary Art in Thyholm, Denmark, from September 2023 through January 2024. Video documentation of the work can be previewed online, https://bull.miletic.info/works/venetie-11111100110, accessed June 9, 2024.

CHAPTER 4

1. Jean Epstein and Stuart Liebman, "Magnification and Other Writings," *October* 3 (Spring 1977).
2. "Mmmm/Santa Monica Airlines—NYCFF 2015 FPV Proximity Technical Winner," *New York City Drone Film Festival*, accessed January 13, 2024, https://www.nycdronefilmfestival.com/winners.
3. "Mmmm/Santa Monica Airlines—NYCFF 2015 FPV Proximity Technical Winner," YouTube video, 3:54 uploaded July 6, 2015, https://youtu.be/KHuqJmiFpVg, accessed January 13, 2024.
4. YouTube and Vimeo channels as well as dedicated FPV piloting portals includes Filetest, Rotorriot, Dronestagram, and Travel by Drone.
5. Nikolai Smolyanskiy and Mar Gonzalez-Franco, "Stereoscopic First Person View System for Drone Navigation," *Frontiers in Robotics and AI* 4 (March, 2017), https://doi.org/10.3389/frobt.2017.00011, accessed January 13, 2024. An attempt of an overview of the scholarly field of drones and characteristics of their usages

in the field of entertainment and AVR (Augmented and Virtual Reality) is provided by Si Jung Kim, Yunhwan Jeong, Sujin Park, Kihyun Ryu, and Gyuhwan Oh. The study shows a significant peek in the use of drones in the field of entertainment and AVR and suggests this to be related to the 2012 TED talk titled "Robots that can fly . . . and cooperate," for which a variety of different uses of quadcopter drones were sketched out. Si Jung Kim, Yunhwan Jeong, Sujin Park, Kihyun Ryu, and Gyuhwan Oh, "A Survey of Drone Use for Entertainment and Avr (Augmented and Virtual Reality)," eds. Timothy Jung and M. Claudia tom Dieck, *Augmented Reality and Virtual Reality: Empowering Human, Place and Business* (Manchester: Springer International Publishing, 2018), 339–352.

6. Steve Brown and Leo Chiu, "Military Drones in Ukraine—a Beginners' Guide," *Kyiv Post*, October 25, 2023, https://www.kyivpost.com/post/23241, accessed January 13, 2024.

7. Anna Munster, "Transmateriality: Toward an Energetics of Signal in Contemporary Mediatic Assemblages," *Cultural Studies Review* 20, no. 1 (2014): 1.

8. According to geographers Francisco Klauser and Silvana Pedrozo, the term "drone," in cultural usage, can be said to cover "any type of vehicle, including aircraft, characterized by the absence of an on-board pilot and [is] either autonomous or piloted from the ground." Francisco Klauser and Silvana Pedrozo, "Power and Space in the Drone Age: A Literature Review and Politico-Geographical Research Agenda," *Geographica Helvetica* 70, no. 4 (2015). "Drone" is a commonly adopted term for what the military refers to as Unmanned Aerial Vehicle (UAV), Remotely Piloted Aircraft (RPA), or even Unmanned Aerial Systems (UAS). Grégoire Chamayou, *Drone Theory* (London: Penguin Books, 2015); Rob Coley and Dean Lockwood, "As Above, So Below: Triangulating Drone Culture," *Culture Machine* 16 (2015).

9. Clay Dillow, "A Brief History of Drones," *Fortune*, http://fortune.com/2014/10/09/a-brief-history-of-drones/, accessed January 13, 2024.

10. Adam Rothstein, *Drone* (London: Bloomsbury Publishing, 2015), 27. As Rothstein notes, the distinction between a drone and a guided missile in the early history of unmanned aviation was not always well defined. The World War I–era Kettering Bug, designed to deliver an explosive charge by crashing into its targets, is among many examples regarded as one of the first drones. "Special Military Operation" in Ukraine blurred the distinction further.

11. The Center for the Study of the Drone at Bard College, https://dronecenter.bard.edu/, accessed January 13, 2024. As the topic of drones grew out of proportions to serve as a single field of study, this center ceased active operations in the spring of 2020. According to market data, the leading player in this industry is Chinese company DJI, founded in 2006 in Shenzhen. By March 2020, DJI had an impressive seventy-seven percent share of the US consumer drone market, with no other company holding more than four percent. In 2021, its reported revenue reached a remarkable $3.83 billion. We personally utilized the DJI Mavic Pro in the productions of *Zoom Blue Dot* and *Venetie 11111100110*.

12. Chamayou, *Drone Theory*; Coley and Lockwood, "As Above, So Below."

13. For a thorough reflection on 9/11 and the drone war, see Kaplan, *Aerial Aftermaths*, and Caren Kaplan, "Mobility and War: The Cosmic View of Us 'Air Power,'" *Environment and Planning A* 38, no. 2 (2006).

14. Benjamin Noys, "Drone Metaphysics," *Culture Machine* 16 (2015), http://culture machine.net/drone-culture/drone-methaphysics/, accessed January 13, 2024.

15. Parks and Kaplan, *Life in the Age of Drone Warfare*.

16. Crampton, "Assemblage of the Vertical"; Shaw, *Predator Empire*.

17. Although some argue for a more militarized connection. See David Albert, "FPV History," RC Groups, accessed January 13, 2024, https://www.rcgroups.com /forums/showthread.php?1585073-FPV-History.

18. Joanne McNeil and Ingrid Burrington, "Droneism," *Dissent* 61, no. 2 (2014), https://www.dissentmagazine.org/article/droneism, accessed January 13, 2024.

19. Jay Williams and Raymond Abrashkin, *Danny Dunn, Invisible Boy* (New York: Pocket Books; Markham, Ont.: Distributed in Canada by PaperJacks, 1975).

20. Michel Foucault, *Discipline & Punish: The Birth of the Prison* (New York: Vintage Books, 1977).

21. Gilles Deleuze, "Postscript on the Societies of Control," in *Cultural Theory: An Anthology* (1992), 139–142.

22. This is also the claims of Klauser and Silvana Pedrozo's introduction to their theme issue of "Power and space in the drone age."

23. Williams Grimes, "Drones Kill, Yes, but They Also Rescue, Research and Entertain," *The New York Times* (2017), https://www.nytimes.com/2017/05/11/arts /design/drones-kill-yes-but-they-also-rescue-research-and-entertain.html, accessed January 13, 2024.

24. Naief Yehya, "The Drone: God's Eye, Death Machine, Cultural Puzzle," *Culture Machine* 16 (2015), http://culturemachine.net/drone-culture/the-drone-gods-eye/, accessed January 13, 2024.

25. Maximilian Jablonowski, "Drone It Yourself! On the Decentring of 'Drone Stories,'" *Culture Machine* 16 (2015), https://culturemachine.net/vol-16-drone -cultures/drone-it-yourself/, accessed January 13, 2024.

26. Brad Bolman, "Provocation: A Prairie Drone Companion," *Culture Machine* 16 (2015), http://culturemachine.net/drone-culture/a-prairie-drone-companion/, accessed January 13, 2024.

27. Carols "Charpu" Puertolas, "Left Behind -FPV," YouTube video, 2:48, uploaded March 14, 2015, https://youtu.be/1MBW8zoZUR4, accessed January 21, 2024.

28. Ellen Gammermann, "Drone Film Festival Prize Winner Talks About Getting the Shot," *The Wall Street Journal*, March 30, 2015, https://www.wsj.com/articles /BL-SEB-87677, accessed January 13, 2024. The speed appears incredibly fast, yet the sound of the propellers indicates that there was no manipulation of speed in post-production.

29. Carols "Charpu" Puertolas, "Abandonado -FPV," YouTube video, 2:43, uploaded December 18, 2015, https://youtu.be/PIXCpQPa6OA, accessed January 21, 2024.

30. Gammermann, "Drone Film Festival Prize Winner Talks About Getting the Shot." Robert McIntosh studied at the Savannah College of Art and Design before he became a film animator. After winning the Drone film festival, McIntosh "discovered drones while working in New Zealand on the 2009 movie 'Avatar.' On location, he spent his free time practicing flying in a forest on a jerry-rigged drone cushioned with a car-wash sponge."

    Andrew Zaleski, "Meet Charpu, the Drone-Racing Megastar Who Doesn't Feel Like Racing," *Wired*, September 6, 2016, https://www.wired.com/2016/09/meet-charpu-drone-racing-megastar-doesnt-feel-like-racing/, accessed January 13, 2024. Charpu, by contrast, "has a day job as a top animator at DreamWorks." Originally from Madrid, Spain he recalls how "as a child . . . , he was always taking apart the radio-controlled cars his dad bought him for Christmas. The interest for RC planes and helicopters continued and in 2014, [. . .] he moved on to FPV after seeing a video posted online by Boris B."

    See also Erik Olsen, "Gentlemen, Start Your Drones," *The New York Times*, November 12, 2015, https://www.nytimes.com/2015/11/12/sports/drone-racing-competition.html, accessed January 13, 2024.

31. Kike Calvo, "So You Want to Fly an FPV Racing Mini Quadcopter?," Kike Calvo, May 26, 2015, https://kikecalvoblog.com/so-you-want-to-fly-an-fpv-racing-mini-quadcopter/, accessed December 30, 2024.

32. Robert McIntosh, "Rise & Shine," Vimeo video, 1:58, uploaded December 23, 2015, https://vimeo.com/149850024#t=0m04s, accessed January 13, 2024. See description under the film.

33. Anthony McCosker, "Drone Media: Unruly Systems, Radical Empiricism and Camera Consciousness," *Culture Machine* 16, http://culturemachine.net/drone-culture/drone-media/, accessed January 13, 2024.

34. László Moholy-Nagy, The New Vision, from Material to Architecture, trans. Daphne M. Hoffmann (New York: W.W. Norton & Company, 1938); László Moholy-Nagy, Abstract of an Artist (New York: Viking Press, 1947).; Dziga Vertov, Kino-Eye: The Writings of Dziga Vertov, ed. and trans. Annette Michelson (Berkeley: University of California Press, 1984).

35. Samuel Weber, *Mass Mediauras: Form, Technics, Media* (Redwood City, CA: Stanford University Press, 1996), 115, 18.

36. For extreme droning and drone racing, it is advisable to use a dedicated FPV camera because of latency issues with the high-definition action cameras. The quadcopter body frames are typically a carbon fiber 250 mm class (motor to motor dimensions) airframe.

37. Examples of extensive parameters are distance and GPS while intensive parameters are air pressure and airflow.

38. Wolfgang Ernst, *Chronopoetics: The Temporal Being and Operativity of Technological Media*, trans. Anthony Enns (London: Rowman & Littlefield International, 2016), loc. 849.

39. Ernst, *Chronopoetics*, loc. 2313. "The switch from zero to one is actually micro-temporal. A switching organ 'spends only very little time transiently in the intermediate states that form the connecting continuum.'" Ralph W. Gerard, in Ernst, *Chronopoetics*, loc. 891.

40. Oscar Liang, "Flight Controller Explained: Understanding FPV Drone Control Systems," OscarLiang.com, https://oscarliang.com/best-flight-controller-quad-hex-copter/, accessed January 13, 2024.

41. John Aldred, "This Filmmaker Dismantled His Gopro to Make It Light Enough for His Tiny Drone," *DIY Photography*, http://www.diyphotography.net/filmmaker-dismantled-gopro-make-light-enough-tiny-drone/, accessed January 13, 2024.

42. "QAV-X Charpu," *Lumenier*, https://www.lumenier.com/consumer/qav-x, accessed January 13, 2024.

43. Aldred, "This Filmmaker Dismantled His Gopro to Make It Light Enough for His Tiny Drone."

44. Michael Zhang, "This Is What You Can Capture with the World's Smallest Gopro Drone," *PetaPixel*, https://petapixel.com/2017/05/26/can-capture-worlds-smallest-gopro-drone/, accessed January 13, 2024.

45. This distortion occurs because the wide-angle lens optically condenses the incident light in order to include more of the scene within the fixed frame determined by the lens's focal length.

46. Mark Gibbs, "Top 10 Problems in Turning Your Action Cam Videos into Masterpieces," *Red Shark News*, https://www.redsharknews.com/production/item/3120-sponsored-article-the-top-10-problems-in-turning-your-action-cam-videos-into-masterpieces, accessed January 13, 2024.

47. "Exactly how it will be distorted depends on the directions in which the camera and objects in the scene are moving as well as in which direction and speed the sensor data is read." Gibbs, "Top 10 Problems in Turning Your Action Cam Videos into Masterpieces."

48. As is pointed out by Wolfgang Ernst and others, the technology of presumed real-time playback is one achieved through micro temporal storage capacities embedded into our reality. Hence, one can say that the archive permeates the present. Ernst, *Chronopoetics*, loc. 1326.

49. Calvo, "So You Want to Fly an FPV Racing Mini Quadcopter?"

50. Olsen, "Gentlemen, Start Your Drones."

51. Juan Buis, "This Impressive Drone Video Makes Real Life Look Like a Video Game," *The Next Web*, https://thenextweb.com/news/drone-video-game, accessed January 13, 2024.

52. Omar Fast noted exactly those phrases in his film about the military staff who fly drones from Nevada. See Mark Brown, "Life as a US Drone Operator: 'It's Like Playing a Video Game for Four Years,'" *The Guardian*, July 28, 2013, https://www.theguardian.com/world/2013/jul/28/life-us-drone-operator-artist, accessed January 13, 2024.

53. Zaleski, "Meet Charpu, the Drone-Racing Megastar Who Doesn't Feel Like Racing."
54. "Best FPV Pilots | Drone Freestyle and Racing," *Ampow*, https://blog.ampow.com/best-fpv-pilots-drone-freestyle-and-racing/, accessed January 13, 2024.
55. "Why Should you fly Freestyle at 800mW? | FPV," YouTube video, 5:41, uploaded July 2, 2018, https://youtu.be/bBb_kSO3vTo, accessed January 13, 2024.
56. Nick Schrunk, "Drive2Extremes," YouTube video, 3:02, uploaded June 10, 2021, https://youtu.be/1U2aVQDbJ30, accessed January 13, 2024. FPV dronematography by Johnny "JohnnyFPV" Schaer.
57. Barry Salt, *Film Style and Technology: History and Analysis* (London: Starword, 1992).
58. Proxcinema is Robert McIntosh and Eric Maloney.
59. "Kohl's 2018 Spring Commercial," Instagram, https://www.instagram.com/p/BhIPsACH_Ik, accessed January 13, 2024.
60. "Shooting More Cinematic FPV Videos with Robert McIntosh," YouTube video, 11:15, uploaded January 18, 2018, https://youtu.be/e-IwH2mElLE, accessed January 13, 2024.
61. Ani Acopian (dir.), "AWAL Presents: 'A World Artists Love,'" YouTube video, 1:01, May 20, 2020, https://youtu.be/p8RP3eRoVGs, accessed January 22, 2024. FPV dronematography by Proxcinema (Robert McIntosh and Eric Maloney).
62. Gilbert Simondon conveyed this evolutionary perspective as an alternative to the regulatory and control-oriented cybernetic model in his book *On the Mode of Existence of Technical Objects*, trans. Cecile Malaspina and John Rogove (Minneapolis: Univocal Publishing, 2016). As a final FPV video, we recommend @nurkfpv, who also maintains a very informative YouTube channel; see "NURK's Flight of the Year 2018," YouTube video, 4:29, uploaded December 28, 2018, https://youtu.be/-DHd3BpJKTM, accessed January 13, 2024; and @blastrfpv "MOABLASTR 2—The Storm," YouTube video, 3:46, uploaded March 3, 2019, https://youtu.be/RHRiMQL7ZRE, accessed January 13, 2024.
63. Regina Duncan, "From Mach-20 Glider to Hummingbird Drone," *TED*, https://www.ted.com/talks/regina_dugan_from_mach_20_glider_to_hummingbird_drone, accessed January 13, 2024.
64. Duncan, "From Mach-20 Glider to Hummingbird Drone."
65. Duncan, "From Mach-20 Glider to Hummingbird Drone."
66. Sterling, *The Caryatids*.
67. Graham, *Vertical*; Elden, "Secure the Volume"; Crampton, "Cartographic Calculations of Territory"; Eyal Weizman, "Introduction to The Politics of Verticality," *Open Democracy*, https://www.opendemocracy.net/ecology-politicsverticality/article_801.jsp, accessed January 13, 2024.
68. Elden, "Secure the Volume."
69. Peter Adey, "Securing the Volume/Volumen: Comments on Stuart Elden's Plenary Paper 'Secure the Volume,'" *Political Geography*, 34.

70. Stuart Elden, *The Birth of Territory* (Chicago: University of Chicago Press, 2013), 323.

71. Newhall, *Airborne Camera*, 52.

72. Newhall, *Airborne Camera*, 53.

73. Crary, *Techniques of the Observer.*

74. Jens Schröter, "Volumetric Imaging as Technology to Control Space," *Acta Univ. Sapientiae, Film and Media Studies* 2.

75. Schröter, "Volumetric Imaging as Technology to Control Space."

76. Schröter, "Volumetric Imaging as Technology to Control Space."

77. Conversation with prize-winning visual effects professor Morten Moen at Kristiania University College, https://www.kristiania.no/en/about-kristiania/employees/school-of-arts-design-and-media/westerdals-department-of-film-and-media/morten-moen/.

78. "VFX Artist Rob Legato Discusses the Opening Scene of "Hugo," YouTube video, 2:43, uploaded October 11, 2015, https://youtu.be/DsNQdtwWRIU, accessed January 13, 2024.

79. See, for instance, accounts in this volume: 3D text by Elsasser, 2009; Hito Styerl, 2012; and Julia Leyda and Shane Denson, eds. *Post-Cinema: Theorizing 21st-Century Film* (Falmer, UK: Reframe Books, 2016).

80. "Mixed Use Master Plan Development 3D CGI Tower Flythrough," YouTube video, 6:21, uploaded February 19, 2013, https://youtu.be/cXoh_Xnlncc, accessed January 13, 2024.

81. "Mr Steele Best of FPV Drone Compilation," YouTube video, 4:07, uploaded October 28, 2017, https://youtu.be/i5ioSKQwOns, accessed January 13, 2024; Robert McIntosh, "Muscle-Up," Vimeo video, 1:40, uploaded May 24, 2017, https://vimeo.com/218839072/, accessed January 13, 2024.

82. November, Camacho-Hübner, and Latour, "Entering a Risky Territory," 582.

83. It might be quite clear that data visualization is a map of data executed as a digital flythrough model. Thinking further along the cine-cartographic path drawn up in previous chapters, spatial information drawn up and recorded by FPV drones and hummingbird drones in places not accessible to humans, these practices and recordings equally operate as forms of cartographic information and description of space.

84. November, Camacho-Hübner, and Latour, "Entering a Risky Territory," 586.

85. November, Camacho-Hübner, and Latour, "Entering a Risky Territory," 592.

86. November, Camacho-Hübner, and Latour, "Entering a Risky Territory," 589.

87. Alpers, *The Art of Describing*, 122.

88. Alpers, *The Art of Describing*, 164–68.

89. Alpers, *The Art of Describing*, 51.

90. Bruno Latour, "Drawing Things Together," *The map reader: Theories of mapping practice and cartographic representation* (2011), 9.

91. Alpers, *The Art of Describing.*

92. November, Camacho-Hübner, and Latour, "Entering a Risky Territory." That the painting only has one reference point is of course a simplification on the part of November et. al. but it makes sense when compared to how the map was used as a navigational aid on a mobile line of sight correspondence, that is, not meant to be understood from one fixed viewpoint. We address this aspect of maps and navigation in the section on the bird's-eye view as well.

93. November, Camacho-Hübner, and Latour, "Entering a Risky Territory," 589.

94. November, Camacho-Hübner, and Latour, "Entering a Risky Territory," 590.

95. November, Camacho-Hübner, and Latour, "Entering a Risky Territory," 585.

96. November, Camacho-Hübner, and Latour, "Entering a Risky Territory," 589.

97. Edwin Hutchins, *Cognition in the Wild* (Cambridge, MA: MIT Press, 1995); Kitchin and Dodge, "Rethinking Maps."

98. William James, *A Pluralistic Universe* (Cambridge, MA: Harvard University Press, 1977).

99. Mark Dorrian, "On Google Earth," in *Seeing from Above: The Aerial View in Visual Culture*, eds. Mark Dorrian and Frédéric Pousin (London: I. B. Tauris, 2013); Johnson, "The Long Zoom"; Vittoria Di Palma, "Zoom: Google Earth and Global Intimacy," in *Intimate Metropolis: Urban Subjects in the Modern City*, eds. Vittoria Di Palma, Diana Periton, and Marina Lathouri (London: Routledge, 2009).

100. Paul Virilio, *The Vision Machine* (Bloomington: Indiana University Press, 1994), 21. See also Tom Gunning, "Rounding Out the Moving Image: Camera Movement and Volumetric Space," paper presented at the Society for Cinema and Media Studies (SCMS) Conference, Montreal, March 2015.

101. Tom Gunning, "'Nothing Will Have Taken Place—Except Place': The Unsettling Nature of Camera Movement," in *Screen Space Reconfigured*, eds. Susanne Ø. Sæther and Synne T. Bull (Amsterdam: Amsterdam University Press, 2020).

102. Former intro text at *Google Earth*, https://earth.google.com/web/, accessed January 13, 2019.

103. The sample destination or the point of interest (POI) in our experiment was London Eye.

104. Johnson, "The Long Zoom"; Dorrian, "On Google Earth"; Di Palma, "Zoom." As will be apparent when we turn to the technical details of the production of such flythrough maps, this is in fact a combination of zoom and 3D-animated virtual camera movement. The most important aspect of our argument here therefore, is that when CGI flythrough models sometimes utilize a zoom, it is mixed with other methods, such as 3D modeling and animation, for which the ultimate goal is to simulate a spectacular and entertaining flight.

105. Bruno, "Haptic Space."

106. "CCS: A 2 Degree Solution," YouTube video, 4:28, uploaded September 22, 2014, https://youtu.be/RejAjfRkVuc, accessed January 13, 2024.

107. Original emphasis, Carbonvisuals.com, https://www.carbonvisuals.com/, accessed October 11, 2017.

108. Heather Houser, "Climate Visualizations: Making Data Experiential," in *The Routledge Companion to the Environmental Humanities*, eds. Ursula K. Heise, Jon Christensen, and Michelle Niemann (London: Taylor & Francis, 2017), 364.

109. Deleuze, "Cinema 1," 109. A description by Amy Herzog explains our use of the term here: "Deleuze develops his concept of the sensory-motor schema to describe structures and transitions that are governed by a linear, cause-and-effect logic. It emerges from Bergson's discussion of the faculties of perception and the actualization of images into action. In order to act upon its environment, a body must isolate from the undifferentiated flow that it perceives only those images that interest it in particular, upon which it can choose to act. The complex correlations between objects and images are thus reduced to causal (and spatial) links. Deleuze finds that the associations made between elements in the movement-image progress along a similar trajectory." Amy Herzog, "Images of Thought and Acts of Creation: Deleuze, Bergson, and the Question of Cinema," *In [Threshold of the Visible] Visible Culture* 3, https://www.rochester.edu/in_visible_culture/issue3/herzog.htm, accessed January 13, 2024.

110. Orit Halpern, *Beautiful Data: A History of Vision and Reason since 1945* (Durham, NC: Duke University Press, 2015), 22.

111. Deleuze, "Cinema 1"; André Bazin and Hugh Gray, *What Is Cinema?: Vol. 1* (Berkeley: University of California Press, 2005); *What Is Cinema?: Vol. 2* (Berkeley: University of California Press, 2005). Deleuze takes many of his points from Bazin.

112. Ezcurra Mara Polgovsky, "On 'Shock': The Artistic Imagination of Benjamin and Brecht," *Contemporary Aesthetics* 10 (2012).

113. That data visualization has power to unleash actions of catastrophic proportions was proven during the historic Briefing of the UN Security Council on February 5, 2003, when the US Secretary of State Colin Powell presented "evidence" of Iraq's failure to disarm. Arguably, in this case, data didn't even exist. Instead, Powell's PowerPoint presentation was constituted on fabricated and well-orchestrated visualizations. Although not in the smooth form, the presentation was delivered in a proxistant logic by verbally connecting the overview with the close-up of a point or object of interest. The transcript of Mr. Powell's presentation together with the slides can be reviewed at "Remarks to the United Nations Security Council," US Department of State, https://2001-2009.state.gov/secretary/former/powell/remarks/2003/17300.htm, accessed January 13, 2024. For an in-depth analysis of this case, see: David Zarefsky, "Making the Case for War: Colin Powell at the United Nations," *Rhetoric and Public Affairs* 10, no. 2 (Summer 2007): 275–302.

114. According to Tom Gunning, "phantom rides were early films that displayed camera movement as their chief attraction." For more on the phantom ride, see Gunning, "An Unseen Energy Swallows Space"; Farocki, "Phantom Images."

CHAPTER 5

1. Juraj Kittler and Deryck W. Holdsworth, "Digitizing a Complex Urban Panorama in the Renaissance: The 1500 Bird's-Eye View of Venice by Jacopo de' Barbari," *new media & society* 16, no. 5 (2014): 776. Media scholar Bernhard Siegert refers to city choreographies in his lecture, "The Chorein of the Pirate: A Kittlerian View on the Origin of the Dutch Seascape," The Sirens Go Silent: A Commemorative Colloquium for Friedrich Kittler, NYU, March 14–16, 2013, YouTube video, 55:26, uploaded July 18, 2013, https://youtu.be/-Teee1ZW-Kg, accessed January 13, 2024.
2. Newhall, *Airborne Camera*, 11.
3. Newhall, *Airborne Camera*, 11.
4. Juergen Schulz, "Jacopo de' Barbari's View of Venice: Map Making, City Views, and Moralized Geography before the Year 1500," *The Art Bulletin* 60, no. 3 (1978): 425–474; Paul D. A. Harvey, "Local and Regional Cartography in Medieval Europe," *The history of cartography* 1 (1987); Cosgrove and Fox, *Photography and Flight*.
5. Siegert refers to cultural historian Thomas Macho, who remarked how "cultural techniques are conceived as operative chains that precede the media concepts they generate." Siegert, *Cultural Techniques: Grids, Filters, Doors and Other Articulations of the Real, Trans*, 11.
6. "Ice Age Star Map Discovered," *BBC News*, August 9, 2000, http://news.bbc.co.uk/2/hi/science/nature/871930.stm, accessed January 13, 2024.
7. Cosgrove and Fox, *Photography and Flight*, 8.
8. "Press Release," The Nobel Prize, https://www.nobelprize.org/prizes/medicine/2014/press-release/, accessed January 13, 2024.
9. Cosgrove and Fox, *Photography and Flight*, 10.
10. For more on ontic knowledge and the philosophy of cartography today, see Jeremy W. Crampton, "Thinking Philosophically in Cartography: Toward a Critical Politics of Mapping," *Cartographic Perspectives*, no. 41 (2002): https://doi.org/10.14714/CP41.561.
11. Cosgrove and Fox, *Photography and Flight*, 10.
12. Stephanie Meece, "A Bird's Eye View—of a Leopard's Spots: The Çatalhöyük 'Map' and the Development of Cartographic Representation in Prehistory," *Anatolian studies* 56 (2006).
13. Recognized by UNESCO as a World Heritage Site, the rock drawings in Valcamonica constitute one of the largest collections of prehistoric petroglyphs in the world.
14. Cristina Turconi, "The Map of Bedolina, Valcamonica Rock Art," *Tracce Rock Art Bulletin* 9 (1997): http://www.rupestre.net/tracce/?p=2422, accessed January 13, 2024. See also Craig Alexander, "The Bedolina Map: An Exploratory Network Analysis," in *Layers of Perception: Proceedings of the 35th International Conference on Computer Applications and Quantitative Methods in Archaeology* (CAA, Berlin,

April 2–6, 2007), eds. A. Posluschny, K. Lambers, and I. Herzog (Bonn: CAA, 2008): 366–371, http://archiv.ub.uni-heidelberg.de/propylaeumdok/512/, accessed January 13, 2024; as well as Emanuela Casti, *Reflexive Cartography: A New Perspective in Mapping*, vol. 6 (Amsterdam: Elsevier, 2015).

15. Crampton, "Thinking Philosophically in Cartography"; Massey, "Imagining Globalization."
16. Harvey, "Local and Regional Cartography in Medieval Europe"; Schulz, "Jacopo de' Barbari's View of Venice."
17. Filippo Brunelleschi is mentioned in Leon Battista Alberti's theoretical descriptions in *Della Pittura*. Ambrogio Lorenzetti employed central perspective in his *Presentation at the Temple* in 1342. Denis Cosgrove and William L. Fox, *Photography and Flight* (London: Reaktion Books, 2010), 15. See also William Ravenhill, "Bird's-Eye View & Bird's-Flight View," *The Map Collector*, no. 35 (1986): 36–37.
18. Cosgrove and Fox, *Photography and Flight*, 15.
19. Cosgrove and Fox, *Photography and Flight*, 15.
20. Teresa Stoppani, "Representing Venice."
21. "Civitates Orbis Terrarum," *Stanford Libraries*, https://exhibits.stanford.edu/leonardo/catalog/db076zm5895, accessed January 13, 2024.
22. "Civitates Orbis Terrarum," *Stanford Libraries*.
23. Cosgrove and Fox, *Photography and Flight*, 17.
24. Bruno, *Atlas of Emotion*, 174. Leonardo da Vinci's late fifteenth-century aerial inventions which include both an airscrew prefiguring a helicopter design and a fixed-wing flyer but also several aerial views and maps.
25. We discuss Ptolemy's concept of *Geographia* and *Chorographia* in more detail in chapter 3.1.
26. Schulz, "Jacopo de' Barbari's View of Venice."
27. Kittler and Holdsworth, "Digitizing a Complex Urban Panorama in the Renaissance" 16; Schulz, "Jacopo de' Barbari's View of Venice."
28. Kittler and Holdsworth, "Digitizing a Complex Urban Panorama in the Renaissance."
29. Kittler and Holdsworth, "Digitizing a Complex Urban Panorama in the Renaissance."
30. Schulz, "Jacopo de' Barbari's View of Venice," 427.
31. Deborah Howard, "Venice as a Dolphin: Further Investigations into Jacopo de' Barbari's View," *Artibus et historiae* 18, no. 35 (1997): 101–111.
32. Schulz, "Jacopo de' Barbari's View of Venice."
33. The high number of surviving originals indicates the *Venetie MD*'s status as a work of art rather than a mere cartographic representation, according to Schulz. He compares it to other bird's-eye views of the same period, such as Francesco Roselli's lost views of Rome and Venice, and his view of Florence from circa 1470, which likely served as inspiration for de' Barbari. Only a replica from circa

1510 of Roselli's work has survived. See also Jessica Maier, "Francesco Rosselli's Lost View of Rome: An Urban Icon and Its Progeny," *The Art Bulletin* 94, no. 3 (September 2012): 395–411.

34. "Venetie MD," *Venice Project Center*, http://cartography.veniceprojectcenter.org, accessed January 13, 2024.

35. Musei Civici Venezia, "Venezia a volo d'uccello," YouTube video, 3:00, uploaded October 20, 2009, https://youtu.be/o3xPvV3ddEU, accessed January 13, 2024.

36. Schulz, "Jacopo de' Barbari's View of Venice," 439.

37. Bruno, *Atlas of Emotion*, 177.

38. Schulz, "Jacopo de' Barbari's View of Venice," 439.

39. Kittler and Holdsworth, "Digitizing a Complex Urban Panorama in the Renaissance," 779. See also Howard, "Venice as a Dolphin," 103.

40. Kittler and Holdsworth, "Digitizing a Complex Urban Panorama in the Renaissance"; Schulz, "Jacopo de' Barbari's View of Venice," 439. Schulz here has a more detailed list of available measuring and mapping techniques used at the time and makes many important reflections in this regard. He does not mention the perspective window but rather emphasizes the calculation based on triangulation calculation by way of bearings and line of sight, as well as Jacob's staff.

41. Balistieri-Tricanato, 2009, 167, cited in Kittler and Holdsworth, "Digitizing a Complex Urban Panorama in the Renaissance," 779.

42. Schulz, "Jacopo de' Barbari's View of Venice." The Venice project center however, has listed the Bird's-Eye by Vavassore, G. A. (1525), which is also very detailed and puts a question to this theory by Schulz and Kittler and Holdsworth. See http://cartography.veniceprojectcenter.org/, accessed February 22, 2019.

43. Kittler and Holdsworth, "Digitizing a Complex Urban Panorama in the Renaissance," 779.

44. "[T]he 320 gigapixel panorama was photographed by Jeffrey Martin, Holger Schulze, and Tom Mills (from expert panoramic photography firm 360Cities.net) and then subsequently created by Jeffrey Martin," "London 320 Gigapixel Panorama Photo," 360 Cities, https://360gigapixels.com/london-320-gigapixel-panorama/, accessed January 13, 2024.

45. Although they don't cover the tradition, we have provided some insights here. For a more detailed history of the bird's-eye view see Schulz, "Jacopo de' Barbari's View of Venice."

46. Kittler and Holdsworth, "Digitizing a Complex Urban Panorama in the Renaissance," 780.

47. Giorgio Bellavitis and Giandomenico Romanelli, *Venezia* (Rome: Editori Laterza, 1985), 247–48.

48. Schulz, "Jacopo de' Barbari's View of Venice," 439.

49. Schulz, "Jacopo de' Barbari's View of Venice," 468.

50. Schulz, "Jacopo de' Barbari's View of Venice," 468.
51. Schulz, "Jacopo de' Barbari's View of Venice," 468.
52. Siegert, "The Chorein of the Pirate."
53. Wikimedia, "The Battle with the Spanish Armada," https://upload.wikimedia.org/wikipedia/commons/4/43/Vroom_Hendrick_Cornelisz_Battle_between_England_and_Spain_1601.jpg, accessed January 13, 2024.
54. Venice Project Center, http://cartography.veniceprojectcenter.org/, accessed January 13, 2024. User must click the button with the globe icon to access the other maps of Venice. Bernardo and Gaetano Combatti's map is listed with 1856 as the date of creation.

CHAPTER 6

1. Dorrian discusses the different genealogies of the vertical and the oblique in Dorrian, "The Aerial View."
2. Edgar Morin, *The Cinema, or the Imaginary Man*, trans. Lorraine Mortimer (Minneapolis: University of Minnesota Press, 2005).
3. Cosgrove, *Apollo's Eye*, 243.
4. Amad, "From God's-Eye to Camera-Eye," 70. See also Karen Frome, "A Forced Perspective: Aerial Photography and Fascist Propaganda," *Aperture* 3, no. 3 (Summer 1993): 76–77.
5. Christina Lodder, "Transfiguring Reality: Suprematism and the Aerial View," in *Seeing from Above*, 96.
6. Gertrude Stein, *Picasso* (London: B. T. Batsford, 1938), cited in Paul K. Saint-Amour, "Modernist Reconnaissance," *Modernism/modernity* 10, no. 2 (2003): 350.
7. For example, Tato's (Guglielmo Sansoni), Flying over the Coliseum in a Spiral (Spiraling) (Sorvolando in spirale il Colosseo [Spiralata]), 1930.
8. "[I]l principio dell'Aeropittura, è un'incessante e graduata moltiplicazione di forme e colori con dei crescendo e diminuendo elasticissimi, che si intensificano o si spaziano partorendo nuove gradazioni di forme e colori." "Aeropittura Manifesto Futurista," *Futurismo* (1933), https://www.memofonte.it/files/Progetti/Futurismo/Manifesti/II/262.pdf, accessed January 13, 2024.
9. Mary Ann O'Farrell and Lynne Vallone, *Virtual Gender: Fantasies of Subjectivity and Embodiment* (Ann Arbor: University of Michigan Press, 1999), 22.
10. O'Farrell and Vallone, *Virtual Gender*.
11. Stan McClain, "A History of Aerial Cinematography," *Operating Cameraman* (Spring/Summer 1996), http://www.legendofpanchobarnes.com/index.php/screenings/21-main-content/static-pages/210-a-history-of-aerial-cinematography, accessed January 13, 2024.
12. McClain, "A History of Aerial Cinematography."

13. Stephen Budiansky, *Air Power* (London: Penguin Group, 2004), 128, cited in McClain, "A History of Aerial Cinematography."

14. Other pre-World War II American aviation films with daring aerials include *Test Pilot* (1937) by Victor Flemming, *Flight Command* (1940) by Frank Borzage, *I Wanted Wings* (1940), and *Air Force* (1942) by Howard Hawks.

15. "Helicopter," *Britannica*, https://www.britannica.com/technology/helicopter, accessed January 13, 2024.

16. In our previous chapter, we discussed how this film was influenced by the European city symphony genre, which showcases the evolution of aerial shots from early cinema to the establishing shot convention.

17. Press release, *Johnny Belinda*, cited in Leonard J. Leff, "What in the World Interests Women? Hollywood, Postwar America, and Johnny Belinda," *Journal of American Studies* 31, no. 3 (1997).

18. Nick Pinkerton, "Bombast: Everywhere with Helicopter," *Film Comment* (2015), https://www.filmcomment.com/blog/bombast-everywhere-with-helicopter/, accessed January 13, 2024.

19. Pinkerton, "Bombast."

20. Pinkerton, "Bombast." See "Opening of 'West Side Story,'" YouTube video, 1:42, January 31, 2013, https://youtu.be/-FlyNCwvyhw, accessed March 12, 2019. *West Side Story* also ends with a rather unrefined dissolve to a fixed elevated angle before it cuts to a close up of the characters, anticipating the later proxistant vision of the stabilized camera.

21. McClain, "A History of Aerial Cinematography."

22. Newhall, *Airborne Camera*, 11.

23. Cara Giaimo, "The 'Balloon Maps' That Aided Exploration, War, and Tourism," *Atlas Obscura* (2017), https://www.atlasobscura.com/articles/the-balloon-maps-that-aided-exploration-war-and-tourism, accessed January 13, 2024.

24. Castro, "Aerial Views and Cinematism 1898–1939."

25. See Rabinovitz, "From Hale's Tours to Star Tours," and Tom Gunning, "'The Whole World within Reach': Travel Images without Borders," in *Virtual Voyages: Cinema and Travel*, ed. Jeffrey Ruoff (Durham, NC: Duke University Press, 2006).

26. Kaplan, *Aerial Aftermaths*, Loc. 399.

27. Castro, "Cinema's Mapping Impulse."

28. Castro, "Cinema's Mapping Impulse."

29. "En dirigeable sur les champs de bataille [In airship on the battlefield] (1919)," Vimeo video, 1:02, uploaded July 12, 2016, https://vimeo.com/174367088, accessed January 13, 2024.

30. Euronews, "Shocking drone footage shows Aleppo destruction," YouTube video, 2:28, uploaded September 28, 2016, https://youtu.be/rkb3y6K3waU, accessed January 13, 2024.

31. "Triumph of the Will—Opening Scenes," YouTube video, 2:34, uploaded March 24, 2008, https://youtu.be/Yl2iIHRE1ng, accessed January 13, 2024.

32. Jay Griffiths, "Fire, Hatered and Speed!" *Aeon*, February 8, 2017, https://aeon.co/essays/the-macho-violent-culture-of-italian-fascism-was-prophetic, accessed January 13, 2024.

33. Noa Steimatsky, "From the Air: A Genealogy of Antonioni's Modernism," in *Camera Obscura, Camera Lucida: Essays in Honor of Annette Michelson*, ed. Richard Allen (Amsterdam: Amsterdam University Press, 2003), 183–214.

34. The 1960s and 1970s moving image avant-garde artists defined themselves as filmmakers and maintained the cinema theater as their main venue for exhibition, although deviations occurred. Notable figures such as Michael Snow, Paul Sharits, Gordon Matta-Clarke, Laura Mulvey, Peter Wollen, and Anthony McCall are representative of this era. Video art, utilizing the real-time transmission medium of video technology, found its home in galleries, often focusing on communications and social ontologies rather than cinematic narrative deconstruction. For further exploration of this topic, see: Tanya Leighton, *Art and the Moving Image: A Critical Reader* (London: Tate, 2008); Erika Balsom, *Exhibiting Cinema in Contemporary Art* (Amsterdam: Amsterdam University Press, 2013); Andrew V. Uroskie, *Between the Black Box and the White Cube: Expanded Cinema and Postwar Art* (Chicago: University of Chicago Press, 2014); Ina Blom, *The Autobiography of Video: The Life and Times of a Memory Technology* (Berlin: Sternberg Press, 2007); Ina Blom, *On the Style Site: Art, Sociality, and Media Culture* (Berlin: Sternberg Press, 2007).

35. Mark Lewis, "'Camera as a Sentient Being': Interview with Mark Lewis," in *Im/Possible Films*, ed. Hamid Taieb François Bovier (Geneva: Impressum, 2016), 116.

36. Lewis, "'Camera as a Sentient Being,'" 104; Daisy Stackpole, "Watch: Feminist Experimental Film "Riddles of the Sphinx" (1977) by Laura Mulvey and Peter Wollen," *Women & Film*, April 24, 2018, https://www.womenandfilm.net/home/2018/4/24/watch-feminist-experimental-film-riddles-of-the-sphinx-1977-by-laura-mulvey-and-peter-wollen.

37. Sanjoy Roy, "Step-by-step guide to dance: Yvonne Rainer," *The Guardian*, December 24, 2010, https://www.theguardian.com/stage/2010/dec/24/step-by-step-yvonne-rainer, accessed January 13, 2024; Douglas Crimp, "Dance Mom: Yvonne Rainer," *Interview*, December 18, 2012, https://www.interviewmagazine.com/culture/dance-mom-yvonne-rainer, accessed January 13, 2024; "Wavelength (Michael Snow, 1967)," YouTube video, 42:56, uploaded January 21, 2012, https://youtu.be/aBOzOVLxbCE, accessed January 13, 2024; and "Back and Forth (Michael Snow, 1969)," YouTube video, 51:38, uploaded October 20, 2019, https://youtu.be/ivryfBTpRxI, accessed January 13, 2024.

38. André Malraux, *Museum without Walls*, trans. Stuart Gilbert and Francis Price (London: Secker & Warburg 1967); Hal Foster, "Archives of Modern Art," *October* (2002).

39. Sarah Milroy, "The Louvre through a (Canadian-Born) Lens: Tour the Great Museum through This Artist's Short Films," *The Globe and Mail*, December

12, 2014, https://www.theglobeandmail.com/arts/art-and-architecture/the-louvre-through-a-canadian-born-lens-tour-the-great-museum-through-this-artists-short-films/article22067247/, accessed January 13, 2024.

40. Milroy, "The Louvre through a (Canadian-Born) Lens."

41. Milroy, "The Louvre through a (Canadian-Born) Lens."

42. Adriene Hurst, "Gramercy Park Studios Takes Flight through the Louvre Museum," *Digital Media World*, March 20, 2022, https://www.digitalmediaworld.tv/in-depth/gramercy-park-studios-takes-flight-through-the-louvre-museum, accessed January 13, 2024. "Recreating the famous Louvre Museum was a challenging and engaging project from both an artistic and technical point of view," said Francisco Lima, VFX Technology Supervisor. Gramercy Park Studios contributed unusual VFX and point cloud imagery to enhance the scenes with elegant, extreme camera work.

43. "The Mapping of Space: Perspective, Radar, and 3-D Computer Graphics," *Manovich*, http://manovich.net/index.php/projects/lev-manovich-all-articles-1991-2007, accessed January 13, 2024.

44. Except perhaps for Robert McIntosh's drone, which might not be allowed in the Museum. See chapter 4.

45. Refresh rate for modern screens vary between 60 Hz and 240 Hz. Screens with extreme refresh rates (e.g., 360 Hz or 480 Hz) are starting to emerge, but they are not yet widely available.

46. http://cartography.veniceprojectcenter.org/

47. Canada Council for the Arts, "Mark Lewis, media artist and 2016 Canada Council laureate—a film by Ross Turnbull," YouTube video, 3:38, uploaded March 7, 2016, https://youtu.be/CTL4TZyP4FI, accessed January 13, 2024.

48. "Venice Pick Mark Lewis in Conversation with Curator Barbara Fischer," Vimeo video, 31:50, uploaded December 14, 2008, https://vimeo.com/2526815, accessed January 13, 2024.

49. Drawing on Simondon's concept of "concretization," the camera can be seen as a system integrating components to function autonomously. Blom's work further supports this, suggesting that technology actively shapes experiences. This aligns with Manovich and Steyerl, who argue that digital tools act within complex systems, redefining cinematic composition through nonhuman agency. Gilbert Simondon, *On the Mode of Existence of Technical Objects* (Minneapolis: Univocal, 2017); Ina Blom, *The Autobiography of Video: The Life and Times of a Memory Technology* (Berlin: Sternberg Press, 2016); Lev Manovich, *The Language of New Media* (Cambridge, MA: MIT Press, 2001); Hito Steyerl, "In Defense of the Poor Image," e-flux journal 10 (2009), https://www.e-flux.com/journal/10/61362/in-defense-of-the-poor-image/, accessed January 13, 2024.

50. Ina Blom, et.al., ed. *Memory in Motion. Archives, Technology, and the Social* (Amsterdam: Amsterdam University Press, 2016), 12. Blom here refers to Wolfgang Ernst's chapter "Archives in Transition" in Wolfgang Ernst, *Digital Memory and the Archive* (Minneapolis: University of Minnesota, 2012), 95–101.

51. "Entrevista a Bernhard Siegert [Interview with Bernhard Siegert]," YouTube video, 4:18, uploaded July 21, 2014, https://youtu.be/4b_DmRbVXFI, accessed January 13, 2024.
52. Gregory Gondwe, "Exploring the Multifaceted Nature of Generative AI in Journalism Studies: A Typology of Scholarly Definitions," SSRN, May 31, 2023, https://ssrn.com/abstract=4465446, accessed January 13, 2024.
53. Gilles Deleuze and Félix Guattari, *A Thousand Plateaus: Capitalism and Schizophrenia*, trans. Brian Massumi (Minneapolis: University of Minnesota Press, 1987), chap. 3; James Corner, "The Agency of Mapping: Speculation, Critique, and Invention," in *Mappings*, ed. Denis Cosgrove (London: Reaktion Books, 1999), 213–252.
54. Stoppani, "Representing Venice."
55. Bruno Latour, "Visualization and Cognition: Drawing things Together," *Philosophical Literary Journal Logos* 27, no. 2 (January 2017): 95–156.
56. November, Camacho-Hübner, and Latour, "Entering a Risky Territory," 588.
57. Latour, Hermant, and Shannon, *Paris Ville Invisible*.

PART III

1. The *Zoom Blue Dot (1990–2020)* was exhibited as a prototype in a solo show in spring 2018 at Trøndelag Center for Contemporary Art under the auspices of Meta.Morf Biennial for Art & Technology. In the spring of 2019, a single-channel version of the artwork was screened in A Video Event at Experimental Intermedia in New York. From November 19, 2022, through March 19, 2023, Zoom Blue Dot was featured in Proxistant Vision, a solo exhibition at the Museum of Craft and Design in San Francisco. Video documentation of the work can be previewed online at https://bull.miletic.info/works/zoom-blue-dot, accessed June 9, 2024.

CHAPTER 7

1. Carl Sagan, *Pale Blue Dot: A Vision of the Human Future in Space* (New York: Random House, 1994), 8.
2. Jet Propulsion Lab NASA, California Institute of Technology, "Solar System Portrait—Earth as 'Pale Blue Dot,'" (1996), https://www.jpl.nasa.gov/spaceimages/details.php?id=PIA00452, accessed January 13, 2024.
3. Sagan, *Pale Blue Dot*, 8.
4. Jet Propulsion Lab NASA. Even though NASA calculated that the "pale blue dot" is actually a crescent only 0.12 pixels in size, the smallest unit in digital image display is nevertheless one pixel. Given that *Pale Blue Dot* is a mosaic of 640,000 individual picture elements (pixels), one pixel occupies 0.00015625 percent of the composition. "Solar System Portrait—Earth as 'Pale Blue Dot.'"

5. Sagan, *Pale Blue Dot*, 4.
6. Also known as the "Portrait of the Planets," this image shows our solar system as captured by *Voyager 1*, six billion kilometers (or 3.7 billion miles) from Earth. The image comprises sixty individual frames where six planets, Earth included, and a partial background, indicate their relative positions. The six planets were Jupiter, Earth, Venus, Saturn, Uranus and Neptune. The Sun is also indicated as a point of light in the image. Mercury and Mars did not appear due to the rays of the sun, while Pluto (then considered a planet) was too small to be detected. NASA, "First-Ever Solar System Family Portrait (1990)," https://science.nasa.gov/resource/first-ever-solar-system-family-portrait-1990/, accessed January 1, 2025.
7. *Voyager 1* attained the escape velocity with the help of Saturn's massive gravitational assistance—known as the gravitational slingshot technique, https://science.nasa.gov/mission/voyager/planetary-voyage/, accessed January 20, 2024.
8. On September 18, 1977, *Voyager 1* takes the first image of the Earth-Moon system in a single frame from a distance of 7.25 million miles and ultimately PBD in 1990, https://www.nasa.gov/image-article/voyager-1-takes-first-image-of-earth-moon-system-single-frame/, accessed January 20, 2024.
9. Jet Propulsion Lab NASA, California Institute of Technology, "Imaging Science Subsystem (ISS)," https://voyager.jpl.nasa.gov/mission/spacecraft/instruments/iss/, accessed April 28, 2019.
10. "Voyager 1 Narrow Angle Camera Description," https://pds-rings.seti.org/voyager/iss/inst_cat_na1.html, accessed January 20, 2024.
11. "The next big encounter for Voyager 1, in around 40,000 years, is expected to be a dwarf star dispassionately known as AC+793888 in the constellation of Camelopardalis." Quote from Brooks Barnes, "In a Breathtaking First, NASA's Voyager 1 Exits the Solar System," *New York Times*, September 12, 2013, https://www.nytimes.com/2013/09/13/science/in-a-breathtaking-first-nasa-craft-exits-the-solar-system.html, accessed January 20, 2024.
12. Sagan, *Pale Blue Dot: A Vision of the Human Future in Space*, 7.
13. NASA Jet Propulsion Lab, "Voyager Backgrounder," October 1, 1980, https://ntrs.nasa.gov/archive/nasa/casi.ntrs.nasa.gov/19810001583.pdf, accessed January 20, 2024.
14. Self-portrait of Earth is a poetic definition of this photograph. Generally speaking, the Voyager mission is conveyed as an "Earth project" and, so if we keep that in mind, we can see the Earth taking a selfie by way of *Voyager 1*. Detailed technical specifications of the instrument can be found at NASA, "Voyager 1 Narrow Angle Camera Description."
15. Sagan, *Pale Blue Dot*, 8.
16. Sagan, *Pale Blue Dot*, 9.
17. Howard E. McCurdy, "The Exploration Instinct," *Nature* 375 (1995): 287.
18. Sagan, *Pale Blue Dot*, 8.

19. Sagan, *Pale Blue Dot*, 8.
20. McCurdy, "The Exploration Instinct," 287.
21. McCurdy, "The Exploration Instinct," 287.

CHAPTER 8

1. Bruno Latour, "Spheres and Networks. Two Ways to Reinterpret Globalization," *Harvard Design Magazine*, no. 30 (2009).
2. The level of details pertains to resolution and is not equally distributed, as can be seen by comparing Paris and Dakhar.
3. For detailed information about orthophoto generation for digital models see Luigi Barazzetti, Maria Antonia Brovelli, and Luana Valentini, "Lidar Digital Building Models for True Orthophoto Generation," *Applied Geomatics* 2, no. 4 (2010): 187–196.
4. Di Palma, "Zoom," 240.
5. Cosgrove, *Apollo's Eye*; Amad, "From God's-Eye to Camera-Eye;" Kurgan, *Close up at a Distance*; to name but a few.
6. Denis Cosgrove, "Maps, Mapping, Modernity: Art and Cartography in the Twentieth Century," *Imago Mundi* 57, no. 1 (2005): 35–54.
7. Cosgrove, "Maps, Mapping, Modernity," 35–54.
8. Dorrian, "On Google Earth;" Kurgan, *Close up at a Distance*.
9. Donna J. Haraway, *Staying with the Trouble: Making Kin in the Chthulucene* (Durham, NC: Duke University Press, 2016).
10. Lisa Parks, *Cultures in Orbit: Satellites and the Televisual*, Console-Ing Passions (Durham, NC: Duke University Press, 2005), 1.
11. Deleuze, "Society of Control," and Friedrich A. Kittler, *Gramophone, Film, Typewriter* (Redwood City, CA: Stanford University Press, 1999).
12. *Game of Thrones*'s season 8 title sequence comes to mind to exemplify how this smooth proxistant modality currently figures across platforms. "Why *Game of Thrones* Season 8 Got a New Title Sequence," *Vulture*, April 14, 2019, https://www.vulture.com/2019/04/game-of-thrones-season-8-new-title-sequence.html, accessed January 13, 2024.
13. Zachary Horton, *The Cosmic Zoom: Scale, Knowledge, and Mediation* (Chicago: University of Chicago Press, 2021), 166. Horton here draws the concept of difference from Gilles Deleuze, *Difference and Repetition*, trans. Paul Patton (New York: Columbia University Press, 1994). We return to these primary scalar dynamics in chapter 8.
14. Zachary Horton, The Cosmic Zoom: Scale, Knowledge, and Mediation (Chicago: University of Chicago Press, 2021), 3.
15. Craig M. Dalton, "Sovereigns, Spooks, and Hackers: An Early History of Google Geo Services and Map Mashups," *Cartographica: The International Journal*

for Geographic Information and Geovisualization 48, no. 4 (2013): 265, https://doi.org/10.3138/carto.48.4.1621.

16. "Google Maps: A 15-Year-Old Adventure," Google Official Blog, February 8, 2020, https://blog.google/products/maps/15th-birthday-celebration, accessed June 2, 2024.

17. "Google Street View," Wikipedia, Wikimedia Foundation, May 27, 2024, https://en.wikipedia.org/wiki/Google_Street_View, accessed June 2, 2024.

18. Jack Dangermond and his wife Laura established Environmental Systems Research Institute (ESRI) in 1969 in Redlands, California, which has been referred to as the ancestor of digital maps and Earth models such as Google Earth. By viewing the source of Google Earth web version one can easily discover that it is based on ESRI's ArcGIS Explorer, making the connection between the two even more tangible. According to former leader of Google's mapping projects, John Hanke, Jack Dangermond laid the foundation for the online mapping industry. See Miguel Helft, "The Godfather of Digital Maps," *Forbes*, February 10, 2016, https://www.forbes.com/sites/miguelhelft/2016/02/10/the-godfather-of-digital-maps, accessed April 28, 2024.

19. Tibi Puiu, "Your Smartphone Is Millions of Times More Powerful Than All of Nasa's Combined Computing in 1969," *ZME Science*, October 13, 2015, https://www.zmescience.com/research/technology/smartphone-power-compared-to-apollo-432/, accessed January 13, 2024.

20. Viewing the source indicates that Google Earth is embedded into HTML as a portable module (pexe) via the following code:

```
<embed id="embed" window-height="739" window-width="1246"
rocktree-epoch="" rocktree-url="" recovery-mode="0"
origin="https://Earth.google.com" experiment-flags=""
client-version="9.2.76.4" browser-version="71.0.3578.98"
language="en" legal-country="NO" src="/static/9.2.76.4/
Earthnacl_pexe.nmf" type="application/x-pnacl">
```

.nmf is a map file created by ArcGIS Explorer, "a free mapping program developed by ESRI; may store terrain, coordinates, points of interest, drawn shapes, 3D environment effects, and other map objects; can also store directions, routes, and measurements; used for saving and loading custom maps as well as sharing maps online." ".NMF File Extension," FileInfo.com, https://fileinfo.com/extension/nmf, accessed January 13, 2024.

21. Jeremy W. Crampton, "Keyhole, Google Earth, and 3D Worlds: An Interview with Avi Bar-Zeev," *Cartographica: The International Journal for Geographic Information and Geovisualization* 43, no. 2 (2008): 85–93.

22. An online version of the book can be seen at "Cosmic View: The Universe in 40 Jumps," Vendian.org, http://www.vendian.org/mncharity/cosmicview/, accessed January 13, 2024.

23. “Powers of Ten™ (1977),” YouTube video, 9:00, uploaded August 26, 2010, https://youtu.be/ofKBhvDjuyo, accessed January 13, 2024.

24. Philip Morrison in “Powers of Ten™ (1977),” YouTube video, 9:00, uploaded August 26, 2010, https://youtu.be/ofKBhvDjuyo&t=45, accessed January 13, 2024.

25. 10^{24} meters or 100 million light-years was the size of the observable universe in 1977. Recent discoveries list discoveries at 10^{26} meters or 14 billion light years away. See “From Infinitely Large to Infinitely Small . . . ,” *Astronoo*, June 1, 2013, http://www.astronoo.com/en/articles/notion-distance.html, accessed January 13, 2024.

26. Morrison, *Powers of Ten*, circa 8:09.

27. Horton, 120. See also a similar argument about the film by Nobel Prize winner George Smoot in Latour, “How Better to Register the Agency of Things,” 28; Bruno Latour, Pablo Jensen, Tommaso Venturini, Sébastian Grauwin, and Dominique Boullier, “‘The Whole Is Always Smaller Than Its Parts’—A Digital Test of Gabriel Tarde’s Monads,” *The British Journal of Sociology* 63, no. 4 (2012).

28. Google Earth, https://Earth.google.com/web/, and the developers’ explanation on the touring feature at https://developers.google.com/kml/documentation/touring, accessed January 13, 2024. The existence of Google Earth as a web application entails the involvement of countless aspects of internet infrastructure, constituting a technological ecosystem of overwhelming proportions. The detailed process of fetching data from servers around the world and displaying them as images on personal computer screens alone is a subject worthy of lengthy study, requiring the expertise of many professionals.

29. Bitmaps are constantly updated by satellites, aircraft, and terrestrial cameras. Digital photographs are called bitmaps and each one of those is made up of millions of pixels. See “Bitmap,” *Britannica*, https://www.britannica.com/technology/bitmap, accessed January 13, 2024.

30. This is explored in our work *Venetie 11111100110*, and in addition, American visual artist Clement Valla explores this in his project *Postcards from Google Earth*, http://www.postcards-from-google-earth.com, accessed January 13, 2024.

31. For more information on how Google Earth collects images see “How images are collected,” *Google Earth Help*, https://support.google.com/Earth/answer/6327779, accessed January 13, 2024.

32. Planet.com, https://www.planet.com/, accessed January 13, 2024.

33. John Herrman, “How Google and Bing Maps Control What You Can See,” *BuzzFeed News*, March 1, 2013, https://www.buzzfeednews.com/article/jwherrman/how-google-and-bing-maps-control-the-world, accessed January 13, 2024.

34. Catherine Dignazio, “Art and Cartography,” in International Encyclopedia of Human Cartography, ed. Nigel Thrift Rob Kitchin (Oxford: Elsevier, 2009), 190–206.

35. “Google Data Center FAQ,” *Data Center Knowledge*, https://www.datacenterknowledge.com/data-center-faqs/google-data-center-faq, accessed January 13, 2024.

36. This job relies heavily on JS's close collaboration with two other core web technologies: Hypertext Markup Language (HTML) and Cascading Style Sheets (CSS), which work together seamlessly within modern web browsers like Google Chrome. As of January 2019, https://Earth.google.com/web/ is accessible on Google Chrome and Android, Google's mobile operating system.

37. Online interview with Data Scientist and Software Developer Eric S. Theise, PhD, January 21, 2019. "Smooth animation is highly sophisticated trickery. Contemporary JavaScript is fast, so camera motion and interface manipulation appear seamless. Prefetching tiles, caching, progressive enhancement, streaming data, all these combine to create that smooth illusion."

38. Zachary Horton, *The Cosmic Zoom: Scale, Knowledge, and Mediation* (Chicago: University of Chicago Press, 2021). Horton discusses the Eameses' films in detail in chapters 3 and 4.

39. Horton, *The Cosmic Zoom*, 23.

40. Latour, "From Aggregation to Navigation," 30:00. Gilles Deleuze, "The Brain Is the Screen: An Interview with Gilles Deleuze" in *The Brain Is the Screen: Deleuze and the Philosophy of Cinema* ed. Gregory Flaxman (Minneapolis: University of Minnesota Press, 2000), 365.

41. Latour, "Spheres and Networks," 141.

42. Haraway, "Situated Knowledges."

43. Latour indirectly suggested this by referring to a Hollywood version of a scientific worldview. Latour, "Spheres and Networks," 142.

44. Denis Cosgrove, *Mappings* (London: Reaktion Books, 1999).

45. Cosgrove, *Mappings*, 6.

46. Jorge Luis Borges, *A Universal History of Iniquity* (London: Penguin Classics, 2001). The story is fictionally credited to Suárez Miranda, Viajes de varones prudentes, Libro IV, Cap. XLV, Lérida, 1658 (Travels of prudent men, Book IV, Chapter XLV, Lérida, 1658).

47. Casey Cap claims that Borges actually used Carroll's story as an inspiration. Casey Cap, "The Allure of the Map," *New Yorker*, January 22, 2014, https://www.newyorker.com/books/page-turner/the-allure-of-the-map, accessed January 13, 2024.

48. Lewis Carroll and Harry Furniss, *Sylvie and Bruno* (London: MacMillan and Co., 1890).

49. Cosgrove, *Mappings*, 9.

50. El Hadi Jazairy, "Toward a Plastic Conception of Scale," *New Geographies* 4 (2011): 1–9.

51. We will return to this the second narrative on scale in this chapter. We also discuss Latour's concept of the immutable mobile in chapter 1.

52. Jazairy, "Toward a Plastic Conception of Scale."

53. Jazairy, "Toward a Plastic Conception of Scale." Benjamin Bratton, *The Stack: On Software and Sovereignty* (Cambridge, MA: MIT Press, 2016), e-book edition. Orit

Halpern, *Beautiful Data: A History of Vision and Reason since 1945*, 35 (Durham, NC: Duke University Press, 2015).

54. Cosgrove, *Mappings*, 9–18. See also: Rachel Quist, "Ptolemy's Geographia," *Geography Realm*, November 30, 2011, https://www.geolounge.com/ptolemys-geographia, accessed January 13, 2024.
55. J. Lennart Berggren and Alexander Jones, *Ptolemy's Geography: An Annotated Translation of the Theoretical Chapters* (Princeton, NJ: Princeton University Press, 2002).
56. Cosgrove, *Mappings*, 18.
57. Mary Ann Doane, "The Close-Up: Scale and Detail in the Cinema," *Differences: A Journal of Feminist Cultural Studies* 14, no. 3 (2003): 89–111.
58. Plan also means map in French, which is another trace of cine-cartography in linguistic terms.
59. Doane, "The Close-Up," 92.
60. Doane, "The Close-Up," 92.
61. Benjamin, "The Work of Art in the Age of Mechanical Reproduction."
62. Doane, "The Close-Up," 93.
63. Doane, "The Close-Up," 93.
64. Doane, "The Close-Up," 93.
65. Doane, "The Close-Up," 93.
66. Cosgrove, *Mappings*, 18.
67. Anthropocene Curriculum, "Anthropocene Lecture: Bruno Latour," YouTube video, 43:20, uploaded June 18, 2018, https://youtu.be/UtaEJo-jo8Q, accessed January 13, 2024.
68. Bruno Latour, "Some Advantages of the Notion of 'Critical Zone' for Geopolitics," *Procedia Earth and Planetary Science* 10 (2014): 3–6.

CHAPTER 9

1. Robert Smithson, "Four Conversations between Dennis Wheeler and Robert Smithson (1960–1970)," in *Robert Smithson: The Collected Writings*, ed. Jack Flam (Berkeley: University of California Press, 1996), 211.
2. John Uri, "20 Years Ago: First Image of Earth from Mars and Other Postcards of Home," NASA Johnson Space Center, March 7, 2024, https://www.nasa.gov/history/20-years-ago-first-image-of-earth-from-mars-and-other-postcards-of-home, accessed June 8, 2024.
3. Caitlin Dempsey, "The First Color Images of the Earth from Space," *Geography Realm*, last modified March 13, 2019, https://www.geographyrealm.com/the-first-color-images-of-the-earth-from-space/, accessed June 10, 2024.

4. NASA Goddard Space Flight Center, "ATS," https://science.nasa.gov/mission/ats/, accessed June 6, 2024. An earlier color image of Earth was obtained the same year by the U.S. Air Force's DODGE satellite but was little known.
5. The cover image was subsequently replaced by Apollo 8 pilot William Anders's *Earthrise* for the second and third editions of WEC, "Whole Earth Catalog," Wikimedia Foundation, last modified May 25, 2024, https://en.wikipedia.org/wiki/Whole_Earth_Catalog, accessed June 8, 2024.
6. Norbert Wiener, *Cybernetics: Or Control and Communication in the Animal and the Machine* (Cambridge, MA: MIT Press, 1948); Ludwig von Bertalanffy, *General System Theory: Foundations, Development, Applications* (New York: George Braziller, 1968).
7. James Nisbet, *Ecologies, Environments, and Energy Systems in Art of the 1960s and 1970s* (Cambridge, MA: MIT Press, 2014), 7.
8. The despair of the endless battles in Vietnam seemed to parallel the racial and gender wars at home. The situation spurred a growing distrust of politics and authority among the younger population, while exhibiting a divided nation to the general citizen. Commentators have claimed that the United States's situation today in part traces back to the major changes that happened during 1968. See "1968: The Year That Changed America Forever," *US News and World Report*, December 31, 2017, https://www.usnews.com/news/national-news/articles/2017-12-31/1968-the-year-that-changed-america-forever, accessed November 18, 2024.
9. Dorrian, "On Google Earth," 294.
10. Andrew Kirk, "Appropriating Technology: The Whole Earth Catalog and Counterculture Environmental Politics," *Environmental History* 6, no. 3 (2001): 375.
11. Fred Turner, *From Counterculture to Cyberculture: Stewart Brand, the Whole Earth Network, and the Rise of Digital Utopianism* (Chicago: University of Chicago Press, 2006).
12. Kirk, "Appropriating Technology," 375.
13. Dorrian, "On Google Earth." It is easy to see how this conglomeration and blend of illustrated text snippets sealed with the image of the whole Earth on its front cover can be seen as foreshadowing the introduction of Google. Steve Jobs noted in his commencement speech at Stanford University in June 2005, "[WEC] was sort of like Google in paperback form, 35 years before Google came along." Steve Jobs, "Stanford Commencement Address" Stanford News (2005), https://news.stanford.edu/2005/06/14/jobs-061505/, accessed April 28, 2019.
14. R. Buckminster Fuller, *Operating Manual for Spaceship Earth* (Carbondale: Southern Illinois University Press, 1969), 73.
15. Anselm Franke, "Earthrise and the Disappearance of the Outside," in *The Whole Earth: California and the Disappearance of the Outside*, ed. Anselm Franke and Diedrich Diederichsen (2013), 12.
16. Halpern, *Beautiful Data: A History of Vision and Reason since 1945*, 35.

17. Nisbet, *Ecologies, Environments, and Energy Systems in Art of the 1960s and 1970s*, 111.

18. Cosgrove, "Maps, Mapping, Modernity," 39.

19. Wystan Curnow, "Mapping and the Expanded Field of Contemporary Art," in *Mappings*, ed. Denis Cosgrove (London: Reaktion Books 1999), 253.

20. Ina Blom, "The Recording Machine: Art and Fact During the Cold War," *The Sixties* 11, no. 1 (2018): 126–128.

21. The unlikely comparison between the mapping practices of Situationists and Conceptualists has been addressed by Peter Wollen in his article "Mappings: Situationist and/or Conceptualists," in *Rewriting Conceptual Art*, eds. Jon Bird and Michael Newman (London: Reaktion Books, 1999). We will revisit this account shortly.

22. Denis Wood, John Fels, and John Krygier, *Rethinking the Power of Maps* (New York: Guilford Press, 2010). Geographers frequently express reservations when citing Wood, primarily due to his tendency to engage in uncritical discussions and his failure to reference other sources on the topic.

23. Wood, Fels, and Krygier, *Rethinking the Power of Maps*, 203, 313n66.

24. Wood, Fels, and Krygier, *Rethinking the Power of Maps*, 204.

25. Roberta Smith, *4 Artists and the Map: Image/Process/Data/Place: Jasper Johns, Nancy Graves, Roger Welch, Richard Long: April 5–May 24, 1981* (Lawrence: Spencer Museum of Art, University of Kansas, 1981).

26. Wood, Fels, and Krygier, *Rethinking the Power of Maps*, 214.

27. Peter Wollen, "Mappings: Situationists and/or Conceptualists," in *Rewriting Conceptual Art*, eds. Michael Newman and Jon Bird (London: Reaktion Books, 1999), 27–46.

28. Wollen discusses certain overlaps, but these are not the majority.

29. Alexander Alberro, *Conceptual Art and the Politics of Publicity* (Cambridge, MA: MIT Press, 2003); Benjamin H. D. Buchloh, "Conceptual Art 1962–1969: From the Aesthetic of Administration to the Critique of Institutions," *October* 55 (Winter, 1990): 105–143; Rosalind Krauss, "Notes on the Index: Seventies Art in America," *October* 3 (Spring, 1977): 68–81; Susan Sontag, "Against Interpretation," in *A Susan Sontag Reader*, ed. Elizabeth Hardwick (Harmondsworth, UK: Penguin Books, 1983); Sven Spieker, *The Big Archive: Art from Bureaucracy* (Cambridge, MA: MIT Press, 2008).

30. Gilles Deleuze and Felix Guattari, *A Thousand Plateaus* (London: Continuum International Publishing, 2000).

31. Ina Blom, *The Cut through Time: A Version of the Dada/Neodada Repetition* (Oslo: Unipub forl./Akademika, 1999).

32. Douglas Huebler's statement in the exhibition catalog that constituted the show *January 5–31, 1969*, ed. Seth Siegelaub (New York: Seth Siegelaub Contemporary Art, 1969), 13. "This publication, rather than accompanying an exhibition, functioned as the exhibition's primary manifestation, being the only physical object

on display during the show's run. In addition to presenting images of their work, each artist (apart from Robert Barry) also supplied a brief statement on the nature of their practice," cited in "January 5–31, 1969," *Primary Information*, http://www.primaryinformation.org/product/siegelaub-january-5-31-1969/, accessed January 13, 2024.

33. Huebler, *January 5–31, 1969*, 13.
34. Frédéric Paul, ed., *Douglas Huebler: Variable, Etc.* (Limoges, France: Fonds Regional D'Art Contemporain, 1992).
35. Huebler, *January 5–31, 1969*, 13.
36. "L'obsession De La Mesure Et De L'échelle [the Obsession with Measurement and Scale]," *Le Terrotoire dans L'Art des Années 60 [The Territory in the Art of the 60s]*, http://territoiresinoccupes.free.fr/art/partie212_2.html, accessed January 13, 2024.
37. De Landa, "Deleuze, Diagrams, and the Genesis of Form."
38. "Douglas Huebler: Gallery Presentation," Nova Scotia College of Art & Design, 1973, http://nscad.cairnrepo.org/islandora/object/nscad%3A4298/datastream/PROXY_MP3, accessed January 13, 2024.
39. De Landa, "Deleuze, Diagrams, and the Genesis of Form," 40.
40. Lucy R. Lippard, *Six Years: The Dematerialization of the Art Object from 1966 to 1972* (Berkeley: University of California Press, 1997), 61.
41. "The Copenhagen Interpretation of Quantum Theory" was the third of the Gifford Lectures given by Heisenberg in winter 1955–1956 at St. Andrews University, Scotland. The lecture has been published in the book Werner Heisenberg, *Physics and Philosophy: The Revolution in Modern Science* (New York: Harper & Brothers, 1962), 44.
42. "L'obsession De La Mesure Et De L'échelle [the Obsession with Measurement and Scale]."
43. Blom, "The Recording Machine," 127.
44. Smithson, "Four Conversations between Dennis Wheeler and Robert Smithson (1960–1970)," 211. Smithson presented together with Brian O'Doherty, John Hightower, and Paul Weiss.
45. In the end, TAMS did not win the proposal, but the engagement informed Smithson's subsequent work and his conception of scale.
46. Smithson, "Aerial Art (1969)," 116.
47. Smithson, "Aerial Art (1969)," 116.
48. Smithson, "Aerial Art (1969)," 116.
49. Smithson, "Aerial Art (1969)," 116.
50. Smithson, "Aerial Art (1969)," 211.
51. Smithson, "Aerial Art (1969)," 211.
52. Smithson, "The Spiral Jetty (1972)."

53. As understood in chemistry, an emergent property is one that transcends the sum of its individual components. For example, the salty taste of salt arises from the interaction between sodium and chlorine, a phenomenon that cannot be attributed solely to either component in isolation.

54. Horton, *The Cosmic Zoom*, 166.

55. Robert Smithson, "Consider an Aircraft in the Shape of an Enormous 'Slab' Hovering over Such an Expanse (1967)," in *Corr. General, W. Miscellaneous, Robert Smithson and Nancy Holt papers, 1905–1987, bulk 1952–1987, B2.35* (Washington, DC: Archives of American Art, Smithsonian Institution, 1968–1872).

56. Horton, *The Cosmic Zoom*, 191.

57. Jorge Luis Borges, Donald A. Yates, and James E. Irby, *Labyrinths: Selected Stories and Other Writings* (London: Penguin Books, 1970), 227.

58. Smithson, "Four Conversations between Dennis Wheeler and Robert Smithson (1960–1970)," 211.

59. Wheeler. From the two quotes on this page it is visible that Smithson himself used both nonsite and non-site, sometimes with capital N sometimes not. We here follow the convention presented in the original title of the first site-non-site work *A Non-Site, Pine Barrens, New Jersey* (1968).

60. Robert Smithson, "A Nonsite, Pine Barrens, New Jersey, 1967," National Gallery of Art, https://www.nga.gov/collection/art-object-page.161764.html, accessed January 13, 2024; Robert Smithson, "A Nonsite, Pine Barrens, New Jersey, 1967 (Photostat of map); 1968 (Nonsite)," National Gallery of Art, https://www.nga.gov/collection/art-object-page.161688.html, accessed January 13, 2024.

61. Gianni Pettena, "Conversation in Salt Lake City (1972)," in *Robert Smithson: The Collected Writings*, ed. Jack Flam (Berkeley: University of California Press, 1996), 299.

62. Smithson, "Art and Dialectics (1971)," in *Robert Smithson*, 370.

63. Ed. Eva Schmidt, "Four Conversations between Dennis Wheeler and Robert Smithson (1960–1970)," in *Robert Smithson*, 196.

64. Smithson, "A Provisional Theory of Non-Sites (1968)," in *Robert Smithson*, 364.

65. On the notion of political topology, see De Bruyn, "Topological Pathways of Post-Minimalism," 33–63.

66. The microscopy sequences for *Zoom Blue Dot* were produced using a Laser Scanning Confocal Microscope, with invaluable assistance from Holly Aaron at the Molecular Imaging Center, University of California Berkeley.

67. Walter Benjamin, *The Work of Art in the Age of Mechanical Reproduction*, trans. Harry Zohn (New York: Schocken Books, 1968).

68. Bernhard Siegert, *Cultural Techniques: Grids, Filters, Doors, and Other Articulations of the Real* (New York: Fordham University, 2015), 120.

69. NASA Jet Propulsion Lab, "Earth and Moon Seen by Passing Juno Spacecraft," https://www.jpl.nasa.gov/video/details.php?id=1260, accessed January 13, 2024.

70. The striking contrast between the post-apocalyptic connotations of a dry lake bed and the picturesque lakeside green in the *Powers* is intentional, further emphasized by a somewhat insider's philosophical tangent. Notably, one of the books lying on the picnic blanket in the *Powers of Ten* is *Voices of Time* (1966), ed. J. T. Fraser. This choice of literature brings to mind J. G. Ballard's *Voices of Time* (1962), a dystopian science fiction story in which the main character, curiously named Powers, works at a research clinic in a desert landscape strikingly reminiscent of this filming site.

71. Myer's extensive experience in the field of robotics also tremendously contributed to the design process.

72. Private conversation with Phill Niblock in his New York studio, March 19, 2019.

73. In his seminal book *Lines*, Tim Ingold recognizes how the guideline functions both as topographical sequence in the verbal maps of the indigenous cultures of the Southwestern United States and as an invisible or half-visible infrastructure of modernity to which any narrative can be inscribed. Our take on guideline here is situated in between these two notions, where the guideline scales with each venue in order for a *very specific* plotline can keep unfolding, transforming and provoking. Tim Ingold, *Lines: A Brief History* (New York: Routledge, 2016), 92, 160.

74. Tim Ingold, *Lines: A Brief History* (London: Routledge, 2007). Ingold has rearticulated this thought in several subsequent publications, for instance in this quote "[. . .]: the idea of life as lived along lines, or wayfaring; the primacy of movement; [. . .] the fluidity and friction of materials; the ex-periences of light, sound and feeling; what it means to make things; draw-ing and writing; and storytelling." Tim Ingold, *Being Alive: Essays on Movement, Knowledge, and Description*, 2nd ed. (New York: Routledge, 2022), xviii.

75. "Pierre Huyghe—2017 Nasher Prize Laureate," YouTube video, 11:18, uploaded April 4, 2017, https://youtu.be/xy3GFEaz-IY, accessed January 13, 2024.

76. Both the Fluxus movement and the post-minimalists, along with explorations in moving images such as *Suddenly Last Supper* (1964) by the Boyle Family, *Liquid Crystal Environment* (1965) by Gustav Metzger, *Ten Years Alive on the Infinite Plain* (1972) by Tony Conrad, and *Shutter Interface* (1975) by Paul Sharits, have shown a preoccupation with such concerns. These themes continue to be explored in contemporary artworks such as *Anywhen* (2016) by Philippe Parreno at Tate Modern's Turbine Hall and *UUmwelt* (2018) by Pierre Huyghe at Serpentine Galleries.

77. The artistic result was initially exhibited in a solo show *Zoom Blue Dot*, which took place in the spring of 2018 at Trøndelag Center for Contemporary Art under the auspices of Meta.Morf Biennial for Art & Technology. In the spring of 2019, a single-channel version of the artwork was screened in A Video Event at Experimental Intermedia in New York. *Zoom Blue Dot* featured in *Proxistant Vision*, a solo exhibition at the Museum of Craft and Design in San Francisco, November 19, 2022 through March 19, 2023. "Bull.Miletic: Proxistant Vision," Museum of Craft and Design, https://sfmcd.org/exhibitions/proxistant-vision/.

78. Bruno Latour, "Agency at the Time of the Anthropocene," *New Literary History* 45, no. 1 (2014): 1–18. Bruno Latour also curated the exhibition "Critical Zones: Observatories for Earthly Politics" at the ZKM | Center for Art and Media in Karlsruhe, Germany.
79. NASA, "ARES: Orbital Debris Program Office," https://orbitaldebris.jsc.nasa.gov, accessed January 13, 2024.
80. For this line of argument see for example: Jussi Parikka, "New Materialism as Media Theory: Medianatures and Dirty Matter" in *Communication and Critical/Cultural Studies* 9, no. 1 (October 18, 2011); Jussi Parikka, *A geology of Media* (Minneapolis: University of Minnesota Press, 2015); Jussi Parikka, *The Anthrobscene* (Minneapolis: University of Minnesota Press, 2015); and Seán Cubitt's *Finite Media: Environmental Implications of Digital Technologies* (Durham, NC: Duke University Press, 2017).
81. Cubitt, *Finite Media*, 65 in reference to Karl Marx, *Capital: A Critique of Political Economy*, trans. Rodney Livingstone (London: Penguin, 1976), 167.
82. Ina Blom, "Inhabiting the Technosphere: Art and Technology Beyond Technical Invention," in *Contemporary Art: 1989 to the Present*, eds. Alexander Dumbadze and Suzanne Hudson (Chichester, UK: John Wiley & Sons, Inc., 2013), 149.

CHAPTER 10

1. Smithson, "Discussion with Heizer, Oppenheim, Smithson, Liza Bear and Willoughby Sharp (1971)," 250.
2. "Dipesh Chakrabarty: History on an Expanded Canvas: The Anthropocene's Invitation," *Haus der Kulturen der Welt Mediathek*, https://mediathek.hkw.de/en/video/dipesh-chakrabarty--history-on-an-expanded-canvas--the-anthropocene-s-invitation--englisch-, accessed January 13, 2024.
3. T. J. Demos argues that although controversial, the term Anthropocene is here to stay: "[T]he term remains significant for one reason: it registers the geological impact of colonial and industrial activities on Earth's natural systems. As such, it offers an important wedge—one that unites climate science and environmental studies with the environmental arts and humanities—against climate change denial, funded generously by the destructive, profiteering fossil fuel industry." T. J. Demos, *Against the Anthropocene: Visual Culture and Environment Today* (Berlin: Sternberg Press, 2017), 85.
4. Gyorgy Kepes, "Art and Ecological Consciousness," in *Art of the Environment*, ed. Gyorgy Kepes (Oxford: Aidan Ellis, 1972), 7.
5. Kepes, "Art and Ecological Consciousness," 1.
6. Kepes, "Art and Ecological Consciousness." The "Spiral Jetty" essay by Smithson included here is the same one published in Art Forum in 1972.
7. Kepes, "Art and Ecological Consciousness," 10.

8. Dipesh Chakrabarty, "Anthropocene Time," *History and Theory* 57, no. 1 (2018): 5–32.

9. Bruce Kurtz and Robert Smithson, "Conversation with Robert Smithson (1972)," in *Robert Smithson: The Collected Writings*, ed. Jack Flam (Berkeley: University of California Pres, 1996), 267. The conversation between Smithson and Kurz on the issue of Moon Landing is very insightful. Kurtz has the following opinion: "The idea that we can completely control the environment, nature, is, I think, what creates the interest in the moon shot, and it's something like Disneyland. You can make your environment however you want to make it, but the way it's made is another kind of cultural control." This is not far off from certain ideas regarding climate science and the trust in geoengineering technology today. See also Leon Gurevitch's related article, where he asks if "public and scientific calls for a turn towards geoengineering can be viewed through a product design–engineered interface that reconstitutes the social machine as an engineer of the earth object itself." Leon Gurevitch, "Google Warming: Google Earth as Eco-Machinima," *Convergence* 20, no. 1 (2014): 86.

10. Smithson, "Letter to Gyorgy Kepes (1968)," 369.

11. Reynolds, *Robert Smithson*, 182. Aurora Tang discusses such analysis by Reynolds with great critical insight. Tang, *Site, Nonsite, Website: Technologies for Perception*, 27.

12. Philip Leider, Letter to Robert Smithson, April 17, 1969, Archive 3833, 1237. Cited in *Site, Nonsite, Website: Technologies for Perception*, 27.

13. Robert Smithson recalls that "I described the moon shot once as a very expensive non-site. [. . .]The discovery of the moon was mascoted by snoopy and this is because they are so abstracted that their imagery has to come from Mickey Mouse or Porky Pig." Kurtz and Smithson, "Conversation with Robert Smithson (1972)," 268.

14. Patricia Norwell, "Robert Smithson: June 20, 1969" in *Recording Conceptual Art*, 132. Cited in Aurora Tang, *Site, Nonsite, Website: Technologies for Perception* (Los Angeles: University of Southern California ProQuest Dissertations Publishing, 2010), 28. This is also the fundamental point of Heisenberg's uncertainty principle from 1927. Knowing that Smithson was fond of scientific literature, this phrasing is not surprising.

15. Robert Smithson in Gianni Pettena, "Conversations in Salt Lake City," *Domus*, no. 516 (1972). Cited in Loe, *The Spiral Jetty Encyclo: Exploring Robert Smithson's Earthwork through Time and Place*, 117.

16. Smithson, "Talking with Rober Smithson," 160.

17. Alex Knapp, "With Virgin Galactic's Latest Flight, Has Space Tourism Finally Arrived?" *Forbes*, December 14, 2018, https://www.forbes.com/sites/alexknapp/2018/12/14/with-virgin-galactics-latest-flight-has-space-tourism-finally-arrived/, accessed January 13, 2024. Dana Hull, "Elon Musk Just Sent His Tesla to Space," *Time*, February 6, 2018, http://time.com/5136400/spacex-elon-musk-tesla-space/, accessed January 13, 2024.

18. Environmental historian Sverker Sörlin has similarly mourned how Smithson's work and writings has gained prophetic qualities on our time. See Sverker Sörlin, "Uncovering the Non-Site: Robert Smithson on Art, Layers, and Time," in *Textures of the Anthropocene: Grain Vapor Ray*, ed. Katrin Klingan, et al. (Berlin: Haus der Kulturen der Welt, 2014), 33.

19. Anna Lowenhaupt Tsing, *The Mushroom at the End of the World: On the Possibility of Life in Capitalist Ruins* (Princeton, NJ: Princeton University Press, 2015).

20. Anthropocene Curriculum, "Anthropocene Lecture: Bruno Latour," YouTube video, 43:20, uploaded June 18, 2018, https://youtu.be/UtaEJo-jo8Q, accessed January 13, 2024.

21. "Some Advantages of the Notion of 'Critical Zone' for Geopolitics," *Procedia Earth and Planetary Science* 10 (2014). In the abstract to this paper, Latour defines the critical zone as "a spot on the envelope of the biosphere (Gaia's skin in Lovelock's parlance) which extends vertically from the top of the lower atmosphere down to the so-called sterile rocks and horizontally wherever it is possible to obtain reliable data on the various fluxes of ingredients flowing through the chosen site (which in practice generally means water catchments)." "Ingredients" here does not mean only chemicals or physical elements since "EU legislation," "agricultural practices," or "land tenure" might be part of the data to recover from the study just as well as the amount of nitrates.

22. Lynn Margulis and Dorion Sagan, *Microcosmos: Four Billion Years of Microbial Evolution* (Berkeley: University of California Press, 1997).

23. Kimberly Yavorski, "The Definition of Abiotic and Biotic Factors," *Sciencing*, March 12, 2023, https://sciencing.com/definition-abiotic-biotic-factors-8259629.html, accessed January 13, 2024. Yavorski here states that "[t]ogether, abiotic and biotic factors make up an ecosystem. Abiotic factors are the non-living parts of an environment. These include things such as sunlight, temperature, wind, water, soil, and naturally occurring events such as storms, fires, and volcanic eruptions. Biotic factors are the living parts of an environment, such as plants, animals, and micro-organisms. Together, they are the biological factors that determine a species' success. Each of these factors impacts others, and a mix of both is necessary for an ecosystem to survive."

24. Scott F. Gilbert, Jan Sapp, and Alfred I. Tauber, "A Symbiotic View of Life: We Have Never Been Individuals," *The Quarterly Review of Biology* 87, no. 4 (2012): 325–341. Latour favors this article as it is a take on his previous book. Latour, *We Have Never Been Modern*.

25. Bruno Latour, "On a Possible Triangulation of Some Present Political Positions," *Critical Inquiry* 44, no. 2 (Winter 2018): 2013–226.

26. Latour, "On a Possible Triangulation of Some Present Political Positions," 218.

27. Latour, "On a Possible Triangulation of Some Present Political Positions," 218.

28. Latour, "On a Possible Triangulation of Some Present Political Positions," 219–24.

29. In the interest of space and the nature of our argument, we will consider only two shots from this film.

30. Both Smithson's and Snow's bewildering cameras are visually referenced. The shot comes close to the elaborated yet not computer animated FPV is the acrobatic camera movements in the film *I Am Cuba* (1964) dir. Mikhail Kalatozov, camera by Sergey Urusevsky.

31. We are reminded of another proxistant excellence of cinema history, the scene in *Gold Diggers* (1935) by Busby Berkeley, in which the luminous face of Winny (Wini Shaw) sings "Lullaby of Broadway" against a pitch-black background, eerily expanding in tandem with the song.

32. Latour and Lenton, "Extending the Domain of Freedom, or Why Gaia Is So Hard to Understand."

33. Bruno Latour, "On a Possible Triangulation of Some Present Political Positions," 226.

34. *Robert Smithson: The Collected Writings*, ed. Jack Flam (Berkeley: University of California Press, 1996).

INDEX

Publisher contact:
The MIT Press
Massachusetts Institute of Technology
77 Massachusetts Avenue, Cambridge, MA 02139
mitpress.mit.edu

EU Authorised Representative:
Easy Access System Europe, Mustamäe tee 50, 10621 Tallinn, Estonia
gpsr.requests@easproject.com

Printed by Integrated Books International, United States of America